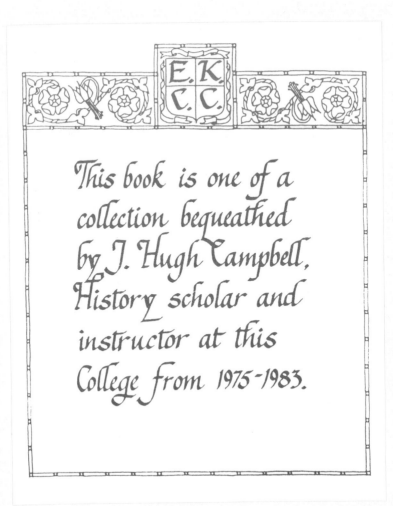

This book is one of a collection bequeathed by J. Hugh Campbell, History scholar and instructor at this College from 1975-1983.

HISTORIANS AT WORK

Other Books by Peter Gay

NEW YORK, EVANSTON, SAN FRANCISCO, LONDON

Historians at Work

VOLUME II

Edited by Peter Gay

and Victor G. Wexler

Harper & Row, Publishers

1817

HISTORIANS AT WORK, VOLUME II. Copyright © 1972 by Peter J. Gay and Victor G. Wexler. All rights reserved. Printed in the United States of America. No part of this book may be used or reproduced in any manner whatsoever without written permission except in the case of brief quotations embodied in critical articles and reviews. For information address Harper & Row, Publishers, Inc., 10 East 53rd Street, New York, N.Y. 10022.

FIRST EDITION

STANDARD BOOK NUMBER: 06–011472–X

LIBRARY OF CONGRESS CATALOG CARD NUMBER: 75–123930

Contents

Preface to Volume II

For the craft of history, the age beginning with the Renaissance and ending with the Enlightenment was a time of advance and return, and of advance *through* return. The Humanists of the fourteenth and fifteenth centuries joyously greeted the dawn of learning, spreading its dazzling light after centuries of barbaric night. The modern historian of history, though perhaps less melodramatic, may agree with the Humanists. In the first volume of this anthology, we defined history as critical thinking about the past. There can be no question that the historians anthologized in that volume retreated from critical thinking as classical paganism gave way to the centuries of Christianity. Now, as we can say in unison with the humanists, the time for recovery had come. Most Christian historians in these centuries—and most historians in these centuries *were* Christians—continued to write history in the manner suitable to their religious convictions and inherited from their precursors. They saw the record of the past filled with signs of special divine intervention, and dominated by events drawing their importance from their association with the One True Religion. The historical world of Bossuet, late in the seventeenth century, differs little from the world of pious chroniclers who had written four or five centuries before him. In a very real sense, the historical city of Bossuet was much like the city delineated by St. Augustine in his *City of God*. And when Bossuet wrote his discourse on universal history, Augustine's masterpiece of devout history was more than twelve hundred years old. Yet there were, in these centuries, changes as well, and they give this volume its character and direction. These changes amount, in a word, to the secularization of the historical world.

Since the writing of history is a cultural activity, this revolution in history-writing shares the qualities of most cultural revolutions. It was slow, gradual, often imperceptible, recognizable as a revolution only after the event, through hindsight. The first rebels against the traditional religious schema for historical thought were deeply pious Christians. They improved the craft of history not for the sake of unmasking religion, but for the sake of safeguarding and glorifying it. They wanted to approximate the truth about the past more closely than their predecessors had done, that they might celebrate the work of God and of their own sect. Nor was such devotion confined to the pioneers of the new historiography: the great Mabillon was the most unworldly of Benedictines. Yet it was Mabillon who, in 1681, revolutionized the writing of history practically singlehanded by placing diplomatics—the discipline of reading documents—on a scientific footing. Yet behind the rich organ tones of these Christian hymns to God's manifestations in the past, we hear, with growing volume, the sounds of pagan antiquity. When we spoke of these centuries as a time of advance and return, and advance *through* return, we were referring to this antique inspiration. The historians of ancient Rome, and to a lesser degree of ancient Greece, served these historians as models of style and spurs for thought. They liberated their readers.

This felicitous use of classical antiquity is a noticeable characteristic in the historians of the Renaissance. Beginning with Petrarch in the early fourteenth century, the Humanists came to think of antiquity *as* antiquity. They discovered that ancient Rome had not survived, was not eternal; it had fallen and been followed by a new age. And as the Humanists saw it, without as yet calling it the "Middle Ages," the centuries between glorious Rome and their own glorious dawn had been the enemies of good thinking and good writing. Hence they had been the enemies of good history too. By creating distance between themselves and Livy or Tacitus, they found it possible to use them. This kind of purposeful reading of the ancients marks not merely Valla in the fifteenth and Machiavelli in the sixteenth century, it marks as well that great quartet of Enlightenment historians of the eighteenth century, Hume, Robertson, Voltaire, and Gibbon. Much else went on in these centuries: the association of historical writing with law, with minute antiquarianism, with inventive scholarship, with stylistic innovation. But what characterizes these centuries best is the gradual emancipation of the historical world from its association with a theology in which the supernatural plays a central part. And this emancipation was achieved largely through this new, tendentious appreciation of pagan writers, long dead but intellectually more alive than ever. Classical antiquity was not to exhaust its capacity to inform and inspire until the nineteenth century, when professionalization placed history on a high platform of autonomy. But that will be the business of our third volume to explore.

Lorenzo Valla

1

It is appropriate to open our second volume, which contains selections from the first great works of modern historiography, with a passage from Lorenzo Valla's *Discourse on the Forgery of the Alleged Donation of Constantine*. Although this is not itself a historical work, without the methods of textual criticism employed by Valla in his treatise, the writing of critical history never would have been possible. The appearance of the *Discourse* in 1440 exposed the most famous forgery in the history of the Western World, and at the same time dispelled one of the most popular myths of the Middle Ages.

Valla loved controversy. Even before he undertook the studies leading to his venomous attack on the pope's temporal authority in the *Discourse,* he had engaged with other Humanist scholars in bitter literary disputes, and had offended the Church with his *Dialogue on Pleasure* in 1431, which suggested that perhaps the Epicurean pursuit of pleasure was as virtuous as the monastic vows of the Christian friars. He was fortunate to find a protector in Alphonso V, King of Aragon and Sicily, who took Valla into his service in 1435, and later made him his private secretary. Alphonso was an avowed enemy of Pope Eugenius IV. The two princes were still fighting over their rival claims to the kingdom of Naples when Valla wrote the *Discourse on the Donation of Constantine.*

According to the Donation, Constantine the Great, the first Christian emperor of Rome, gave to the bishop of Rome, Pope Sylvester I, in the fourth century, not only the imperial Lateran Palace in Rome and all the imperial insignia, including the diadem and tiara, but the rest of the Roman Empire in the West as well. At the same time, Constantine was supposed to have granted all the Christian clergy a privileged status in the Empire, and established forever the supremacy of the Roman See. From the ninth century to the fifteenth, it was popularly believed that Constantine made this extraordinary gift, which amounted to his total abdication as Emperor in the West, because of his newly found humility in converting to Christianity, and be-

1

cause of his miraculous cure from leprosy, which he attributed to the Christian god and the intervention of that god's officers in the Church. "Never," commented Edward Gibbon in his *Decline and Fall of the Roman Empire,* "was physician more gloriously recompensed." Just seven years before Valla exposed the unreliability of these legends, Nicolas Cusanus, scholar, theologian, and ecclesiastical statesman, had anticipated Valla's work; but it was Valla alone, through his biting polemic and brilliant linguistic analysis, who showed the Donation to be a confused collection of lies.

In the passage from the *Discourse* which we include, Valla is mainly concerned with internal criticism of the Donation. Here, he reveals the inconsistencies in usage, the anachronisms, and the barbarisms, which prove that the document could not have been written in the fourth century, but rather must have been written at a much later date; moreover, his listing of gross historical errors shows the Donation to have been the conglomeration of a hack forger. It is these critical techniques which later philological historians found indispensable, and which allowed Gibbon to credit Valla with "this fictitious deed." In the other sections of the *Discourse,* Valla demonstrates that on grounds external to the document itself—such as the absence of any record in the fourth century either of Constantine's enormous gift or of Sylvester's acceptance—there is no sound evidence for crediting the Donation. The entire *Discourse* is unified by Valla's contempt for the papal claim that temporal power and spiritual piety are compatible goals.

Only Alphonso's protection and a timely flight from Italy saved Valla from harassment by the inquisitors. Yet he persisted in unveiling sacred documents, such as Christ's letter to Abgarus, as spurious, cast doubt on the authenticity of the Apostle's Creed, and called St. Augustine's view of predestination heretical. However, after the death of Eugenius IV in 1447, he came to peace with the new pope, Nicholas V, and settled down to work steadily on some of the first Latin translations of Homer, Herodotus, and Thucydides. His text on the *Elegancies of the Latin Language* discredited the barbarous Latin of the Middle Ages while extolling the Latin of Cicero and Quintilian. His criticisms of the degenerate form of Latin in his own times extended to the Vulgate version of the New Testament, which he found defective when compared with the original Greek.

Valla's last official positions were as a papal secretary and as a professor of rhetoric. The Church of the Renaissance was gradually becoming a haven for Humanist scholars. Before his death, Valla congratulated the Church for having saved the Latin language from extinction during the Middle Ages. This did not deter Martin Luther and other reformers from hailing Valla as a precursor in their campaign of denouncing the institutions of the Church of Rome as historical fictions. For us, the most remarkable quality of Valla and his *Discourse* is the challenge offered by a critical mind to the myths of a previous age of belief.

Selected Bibliography

There is no up-to-date, critical study in English of Valla's career as a philosopher, philologist, or historian; however, when Franco Gaeta's *Lorenzo Valla: Filologia e storia nell' umanesimo* (1955) finds its worthy translator, we shall have such a study in the finest scholarly tradition. The only complete biography of Valla, Girolamo Mancini's *Vita di Lorenzo Valla* (1891), was written with care but contains much misinformation. There is a good estimate of Valla's place in the history of Humanist scholarship in John E. Sandys, *The History of Classical Scholarship from the Sixth Century B.C. to the End of the Middle Ages* (1908), 66–70. Donald R. Kelley has evaluated Valla's contribution to historiography with precision and fine judgment in *Foundations of Modern Historical Scholarship; Language, Law, and History in the French Renaissance* (1970). Some of Valla's philosophical ideas have attracted admirers ever since the Reformation; Luther, in particular, was fascinated by Valla's low estimate of man's free will. On the other hand, Ernst Cassirer, in our own time, cites Valla as an example of the bold critical-modern spirit awakening in the Renaissance. His pages on Valla in *The Individual and the Cosmos in Renaissance Philosophy* (1927), translated and edited by Mario Domandi in a 1963 Harper Torchbook edition, are typical of Cassirer's intellectual excitement in describing sympathetic historical figures. Valla's problematic *Dialogue on Free Will* is available in translation in *The Renaissance Philosophy of Man,* eds. Cassirer et al. (1948). Christopher B. Coleman's study, *Constantine the Great and Christianity* (1914), contrasts what is actually known about the emperor's relation to the Church with the legends that evolved during the Middle Ages concerning the conversion and miraculous cure from leprosy; in addition, Valla's exposure of the forgery is studied in the context of fifteenth-century philological scholarship. An excellent collection of lectures delivered at the Warburg Institute and published as *The Conflict Between Paganism and Christianity in the Fourth Century,* edited by Arnaldo Momigliano (1963), demonstrates that the antithetical aims of pagan and Christian historiography were part of the larger conflict between these two worlds. Valla may be interpreted as being an heir to the pagan tradition.

THE TREATISE OF LORENZO VALLA ON THE DONATION OF CONSTANTINE

I will not speak here of the barbarisms in [the forger's] language when he says "chief over the priests" instead of chief of the priests; when he puts in the same sentence "extiterit" and "existat" [confusing meanings, moods and tenses]; when, having said "in the whole earth," he adds again "of the whole world," as though he wished to include something else, or the sky, which is part of the world, though a good part of the earth even was not under Rome; when he distinguishes between providing for "the faith" of Christians and providing for their "stability," as though they could not coexist,[1] When he confuses "ordain" and "decree," and when, as though Constantine had not already joined with the rest in making the decree, he has him now ordain it, and as though he imposes a punishment, decree [confirm] it, and confirm it together with the people. [That, I pass by.] But what Christian could endure this [other thing], and not, rather, critically and severely reprove a Pope who endures it, and listens to it willingly and retails it; namely, that the Roman See, though it received its primacy from Christ, as the Eighth Synod declared according to the testimony of Gratian and many of the Greeks, should be represented as having received it from Constantine, hardly yet a Christian, as though from Christ? Would that very modest ruler have chosen to make such a statement, and that most devout pontiff to listen to it? Far be such a grave wrong from both of them!

How in the world—this is much more absurd, and impossible in the nature of things—could one speak of Constantinople as one of the patriarchal sees, when it was not yet a patriarchate, nor a see, nor a Christian city, nor named Constantinople, nor founded, nor planned! For the "privilege" was granted, so it says, the third day after Constantine became a Christian; when as yet Byzantium, not Constantinople, occupied that site.

The Treatise of Lorenzo Valla on the Donation of Constantine translated by Christopher B. Coleman, New Haven: Yale University Press 1922, pp. 93–141. Copyright 1922 by Yale University Press. Reprinted by permission of publisher. The words in brackets and the footnotes are the translator's.

[1]Part of this criticism rests upon the peculiarities of the text of the Donation which Valla used.

I am a liar if this fool does not confess as much himself. For toward the end of the "privilege" he writes:

> Wherefore we have perceived it to be fitting that our empire and our royal power should be transferred in the regions of the East; and that in the province of Bizantia [sic], in the most fitting place, a city should be built in our name; and that our empire should there be established.

But if he was intending to transfer the empire, he had not yet transferred it; if he was intending to establish his empire there, he had not yet established it; if he was planning to build a city, he had not yet built it. Therefore he could not have spoken of it as a patriarchal see, as one of the four sees, as Christian, as having this name, nor as already built. According to the history [the Life of Sylvester] which Palea cites as evidence, he had not yet even thought of founding it. And this beast, whether Palea or some one else whom Palea follows, does not notice that he contradicts this history, in which it is said that Constantine issued the decree concerning the founding of the city, not on his own initiative, but at a command received in his sleep from God, not at Rome but at Byzantium, not within a few days [of his conversion] but several years after, and that he learned its name by revelation in a dream. Who then does not see that the man who wrote the "privilege" lived long after the time of Constantine, and in his effort to embellish his falsehood forgot that earlier he had said that these events took place at Rome on the third day after Constantine was baptized? So the trite old proverb applies nicely to him, "Liars need good memories."

And how is it that he speaks of a province of "Byzantia," when it was a town, Byzantium by name? The place was by no means large enough for the erection of so great a city; for the old city of Byzantium was included within the walls of Constantinople. And this man says the [new] city is to be built on the most fitting place in it! Why does he choose to put Thrace, in which Byzantium lies, in the East, when it lies to the north? I suppose Constantine did not know the place which he had chosen for the building of the city, in what latitude it was, whether it was a town or a province, nor how large it was!

> On the churches of the blessed apostles Peter and Paul, for the providing of the lights, we have conferred landed estates of possessions, and have enriched them with different objects; and through our sacred imperial mandate, we have granted them of our property in the east as well as in the west; and even in the north and in the southern quarter; namely, in Judea, Greece, Asia, Thrace, Africa and Italy and the various islands; under this condition indeed, that all shall be administered by the hand of our most blessed father the supreme pontiff, Sylvester, and his successors.

O you scoundrel! Were there in Rome churches, that is, temples, dedicated to Peter and Paul? Who had constructed them? Who would have dared to build them, when, as history tells us, the Christians had never had anything but secret and secluded meeting-places? And if there had been any temples at Rome dedicated to these apostles, they would not have called for such great lights as these to be set up in them; they were little chapels, not sanctuaries; little shrines, not temples; oratories in private houses, not public places of worship. So there was no need to care for the temple lights, before the temples themselves were provided.

And what is this that you say? You make Constantine call Peter and Paul blessed, but Sylvester, still living, "most blessed"; and call his own mandate, pagan as he had been but a little while before, "sacred"! Is so much to be donated "for the providing of the lights" that the whole world would be impoverished? And what are these "landed estates," particularly "landed estates of possessions"? The phrase "possessions of landed estates" is good usage; "landed estates of possessions" is not. You give landed estates, and you do not explain which landed estates. You have enriched "with different objects," and you do not show when nor with what objects. You want the corners of the earth to be administered by Sylvester, and you do not explain how they are to be administered. You say these were granted earlier? Then why do you say that you have now begun to honor the Roman church, and to grant it a "privilege"? Do you make the grant now; do you enrich it now? Then why do you say "we have granted" and "we have enriched"? What are you talking about; what is in your mind, you beast? (I am speaking to the man who made up the story, not to that most excellent ruler, Constantine.)

But why do I ask for any intelligence in you, any learning, you who are not endowed with any ability, with any knowledge of letters, who say "lights" for lamps, and "be transferred in the regions of the east" instead of "be transferred to the regions of the east," as it should be? And what next? Are these "quarters" of yours really the four quarters of the world? What do you count as eastern? Thrace? It lies to the north, as I have said. Judea? It looks rather toward the south, for it is next to Egypt. And what do you count as western? Italy? But these events occurred in Italy and no one living there calls it western; for we say the Spains are in the west; and Italy extends, on one hand to the south and on the other to the north, rather than to the west. What do you count as north? Thrace? You yourself choose to put it in the east. Asia? This alone includes the whole east, but it includes the north also, like Europe. What do you count as southern? Africa, of course. But why do you not specify some province? Perhaps you think even the Ethiopians were subject to the Roman Empire! And anyway Asia and Africa do not come into consideration when we divide the earth into four parts and enumerate the countries of each, but when we divide it into three, Asia, Africa, Europe; that is, unless you say Asia for the province of Asia, and Africa for that province which is next to the Gaetuli, and I do not see why they, especially, should be mentioned.

Would Constantine have spoken thus when he was describing the four quarters of the earth? Would he have mentioned these countries, and not others? Would he have begun with Judea, which is counted as a part of Syria and was no longer "Judea" after the destruction of Jerusalem (for the Jews were driven away and almost exterminated, so that, I suppose, scarcely one then remained in his own country, but they lived among other nations)? Where then was Judea? It was no longer called Judea, and we know that now that name has perished from the earth. Just as after the driving out of the Canaanites the region ceased to be called Canaan and was renamed Judea by its new inhabitants, so when the Jews were driven out and mixed tribes inhabited it, it ceased to be called Judea.

You mention Judea, Thrace, and the islands, but you do not think of mentioning the Spains, the Gauls, the Germans, and while you speak of peoples of other tongues, Hebrew, Greek, barbarian, you do not speak of any of the provinces where Latin is used. I see: you have omitted these for the purpose of including them afterwards in the Donation. And why were not these many great provinces of the East sufficient to bear the expense of providing the lights without the rest of the world contributing!

I pass over the fact that you say these are granted as a gift, and therefore not, as our friends say, in payment for the cure of the leprosy. Otherwise,—well, any one who classes a gift as a payment is ill-bred.

To the blessed Sylvester, his [Peter's] vicar, we by this present do give our imperial Lateran palace, then the diadem, that is, the crown of our head, and at the same time the tiara and also the shoulder-band,—that is, the strap that usually surrounds our imperial neck; and also the purple mantle and scarlet tunic, and all the imperial raiment; and the same rank as those presiding over the imperial cavalry; conferring also on him the imperial scepters, and at the same time all the standards and banners and the different imperial ornaments, and all the pomp of our imperial eminence, and the glory of our power.

And we decree also, as to these men of different rank, the most reverend clergy who serve the holy Roman church, that they have that same eminence of distinguished power and excellence, by the glory of which it seems proper for our most illustrious Senate to be adorned; that is, that they be made patricians, consuls,—and also we have proclaimed that they be decorated with the other imperial dignities. And even as the imperial militia stands decorated, so we have decreed that the clergy of the holy Roman church be adorned. And even as the imperial power is ordered with different offices, or chamberlains, indeed, and door-keepers and all the bed-watchers, so we wish the holy Roman church also to be decorated. And, in order that the pontifical glory may shine forth most fully, we decree also that the holy clergy of this same holy Roman church may mount mounts adorned with saddle-cloths and linens, that is, of the whitest color; and even as our Senate uses shoes with felt socks, that is, they [the clergy] may be distinguished by white linen, and that the celestial [orders] may be adorned to the glory of God, just as the terrestrial are adorned.

O holy Jesus! This fellow, tumbling phrases about in his ignorant talk, —will you not answer him from a whirlwind? Will you not send the thunder? Will you not hurl avenging lightnings at such great blasphemy? Will you endure such wickedness in your household? Can you hear this, see this, let it go on so long and overlook it? But you are long-suffering and full of compassion. Yet I fear lest this your long-suffering may rather be wrath and condemnation, such as it was against those of whom you said, "So I gave them up unto their own hearts' lust: and they walked in their own counsels," and elsewhere, "Even as they did not like to retain me in their knowledge, I gave them over to a reprobate mind, to do those things which are not convenient." Command me, I beseech thee, O Lord, that I may cry out against them, and perchance they may be converted.

O Roman pontiffs, the model of all crimes for other pontiffs! O wickedest of scribes and Pharisees, who sit in Moses' seat and do the deeds of Dathan and Abiram! Will the raiment, the habiliments, the pomp, the cavalry, indeed the whole manner of life of a Caesar thus befit the vicar of Christ? What fellowship has the priest with the Caesar? Did Sylvester put on this raiment; did he parade in this splendor; did he live and reign with such a throng of servants in his house? Depraved wretches! They did not know that Sylvester ought to have assumed the vestments of Aaron, who was the high priest of God, rather than those of a heathen ruler.

But this must be more strongly pressed elsewhere. For the present, however, let us talk to this sycophant about barbarisms of speech; for by the stupidity of his language his monstrous impudence is made clear, and his lie.

"We give," he says, "our imperial Lateran palace": as though it was awkward to place the gift of the palace here among the ornaments, he repeated it later where gifts are treated. "Then the diadem"; and as though those present would not know, he interprets, "that is, the crown." He did not, indeed, here add "of gold," but later, emphasizing the same statements, he says, "of purest gold and precious gems." The ignorant fellow did not know that a diadem was made of coarse cloth or perhaps of silk; whence that wise and oft-repeated remark of the king, who, they say, before he put upon his head the diadem given him, held it and considered it long and exclaimed, "O cloth more renowned than happy! If any one knew you through and through, with how many anxieties and dangers and miseries you are fraught, he would not care to pick you up; no, not even if you were lying on the ground!" This fellow does not imagine but that it is of gold, with a gold band and gems such as kings now usually add. But Constantine was not a king, nor would he have dared to call himself king, nor to adorn himself with royal ceremony. He was Emperor of the Romans, not king. Where there is a king, there is no republic. But in the republic there were many, even at the same time, who were "imperatores" [generals]; for Cicero frequently writes thus, "Marcus Cicero, imperator, to some other imperator, greeting": though, later on, the Roman ruler, as the highest of all, is called by way of distinctive title the Emperor.

"And at the same time the tiara and also the shoulder-band,—that is the strap that usually surrounds our imperial neck." Who ever heard "tiara" [phrygium] used in Latin? You talk like a barbarian and want it to seem to me to be a speech of Constantine's or of Lactantius'. Plantus, in the Menaechmi, applied "phrygionem" to a designer of garments; Pliny calls clothes embroidered with a needle "phrygiones" because the Phrygians invented them; but what does "phrygium" mean? You do not explain this, which is obscure; you explain what is quite clear. You say the "shoulder-band" is a "strap," and you do not perceive what the strap is, for you do not visualize a leather band, which we call a strap, encircling the Caesar's neck as an ornament. [It is of leather], hence we call harness and whips "straps": but if ever gold straps are mentioned, it can only be understood as applying to gilt harness such as is put around the neck of a horse or of some other animal. But this has escaped your notice, I think. So when you wish to put a strap around the Caesar's neck, or Sylvester's, you change a man, an Emperor, a supreme pontiff, into a horse or an ass.

"And also the purple mantle and scarlet tunic." Because Matthew says "a scarlet robe," and John "a purple robe,"[2] this fellow tries to join them together in the same passage. But if they are the same color, as the Evangelists imply, why are you not content, as they were, to name either one alone; unless, like ignorant folk today, you use "purple" for silk goods of a whitish color? The "purple" [pupura], however, is a fish in whose blood wool is dyed, and so from the dye the name has been given to the cloth, whose color can be called red, though it may rather be blackish and very nearly the color of clotted blood, a sort of violet. Hence by Homer and Virgil blood is called purple, as is porphyry, the color of which is similar to amethyst; for the Greeks call purple "porphyra." You know perhaps that scarlet is used for red; but I would swear that you do not know at all why he makes it "coccineum" when we say "coccum," or what sort of a garment a "mantle" [chlamys] is.

But that he might not betray himself as a liar by continuing longer on the separate garments, he embraced them all together in a single word, saying, "all the imperial raiment." What! even that which he is accustomed to wear in war, in the chase, at banquets, in games? What could

----

[2]Matt. xxvii, 28; John xix, 2.

be more stupid than to say that all the raiment of the Caesar befits a pontiff!

But how gracefully he adds, "and the same rank as those presiding over the imperial cavalry." He says "seu" ["or" for "and"].[3] He wishes to distinguish between these two in turn, as if they were very like each other, and slips along from the imperial raiment to the equestrian rank, saying—I know not what! He wants to say something wonderful, but fears to be caught lying, and so with puffed cheeks and swollen throat, he gives forth sound without sense.

"Conferring also on him the imperial sceptres." What a turn of speech! What splendor! What harmony! What are these imperial sceptres? There is one sceptre, not several; if indeed the Emperor carried a sceptre at all. Will now the pontiff carry a sceptre in his hand? Why not give him a sword also, and helmet and javelin?

"And at the same time all the standards and banners." What do you understand by "standards" [signa]? "Signa" are either statues (hence frequently we read "signa et tabulas" for pieces of sculpture and paintings; —for the ancients did not paint on walls, but on tablets) or military standards (hence that phrase "Standards, matched eagles"[4]). In the former sense small statues and sculptures are called "sigilla." Now then, did Constantine give Sylvester his statues or his eagles? What could be more absurd? But what "banners" [banna[5]] may signify, I do not discover. May God destroy you, most depraved of mortals who attribute barbarous language to a cultured age!

"And different imperial ornaments." When he said "banners," he thought he had been explicit long enough, and therefore he lumped the rest under a general term. And how frequently he drives home the word "imperial," as though there were certain ornaments peculiar to the Emperor over against the consul, the dictator, the Caesar!

"And all the pomp of our imperial eminence, and the glory of our power." "He discards bombast and cubit-long words,"[6] "This king of kings, Darius, the kinsman of the gods,"[7] never speaking save in the plural! What is this imperial "pomp"; that of the cucumber twisted in the grass, and growing at the belly? Do you think the Caesar celebrated a triumph whenever he left his house, as the Pope now does, preceded by

---

[3]Here, as was common in medieval Latin, "seu" is the equivalent of "et," and means "and." Valla's criticism is correct, but might go further in fixing the time of the forgery.

[4]Lucan, *Pharsalia,* i, 7.

[5]In our best texts of the Donation this word is "banda," used in the eighth century for "colors" or "flags."

[6]Horace, *Ars Poetica,* l. 97.

[7]Julius Valerius, *Res Gestae Alexandri,* i, 37.

white horses which servants lead saddled and adorned? To pass over
other follies, nothing is emptier, more unbecoming a Roman pontiff than
this. And what is this "glory"? Would a Latin have called pomp and
paraphernalia "glory," as is customary in the Hebrew language? And
instead of "soldiers" [milites] you say soldiery [militia[8]] which we have
borrowed from the Hebrews, whose books neither Constantine nor his
secretaries had ever laid eyes on!

But how great is your munificence, O Emperor, who deem it not sufficient to have adorned the pontiff, unless you adorn all the clergy also! As
an "eminence of distinguished power and excellence," you say, they are
"made patricians and consuls." Who has ever heard of senators or other
men being made patricians? Consuls are "made," but not patricians. The
senators, the conscript fathers, are from patrician (also called
senatorial), equestrian, or plebeian families as the case may be. It is
greater, also, to be a senator than to be a patrician; for a senator is one
of the chosen counsellors of the Republic, while a patrician is merely one
who derives his origin from a senatorial family. So one who is a senator,
or of the conscript fathers, is not necessarily forthwith also a patrician.
So my friends the Romans are now making themselves ridiculous when
they call their praetor "senator," since a senate cannot consist of one man
and a senator must have colleagues, and he who is now called "senator"
performs the function of praetor. But, you say, the title of patrician is
found in many books.[9] Yes; but in those which speak of times later than
Constantine; therefore the "privilege" was executed after Constantine.

But how can the clergy become consuls?[10] The Latin clergy have denied
themselves matrimony; and will they become consuls, make a levy of
troops, and betake themselves to the provinces allotted them with legions
and auxiliaries? Are servants and slaves made consuls? And are there to
be not two, as was customary; but the hundreds and thousands of attendants who serve the Roman church, are they to be honored with the rank
of general? And I was stupid enough to wonder at what was said about
the Pope's transformation! The attendants will be generals; but the clergy
soldiers. Will the clergy become soldiers or wear military insignia, unless
you share the imperial insignia with all the clergy? [I may well ask,] for
I do not know what you are saying. And who does not see that this fabulous tale was concocted by those who wished to have every possible

---

[8]At Rome in the eighth century, the time of the forgery, "militia" indicated a
civil rank, rather than soldiers.

[9]The allusion is to the title of Patrician given to Pippin and to his sons as
defenders of the Roman See.

[10]The office of consul as it existed in the Republic and the Empire disappeared
in the time of the German invasions. The word was later applied quite differently,
to a group, practically a social class, at Rome.

license in the attire they were to wear? If there are games of any kind played among the demons which inhabit the air I should think that they would consist in copying the apparel, the pride and the luxury of the clergy, and that the demons would be delighted most by this kind of masquerading.

Which shall I censure the more, the stupidity of the ideas, or of the words? You have heard about the ideas; here are illustrations of his words. He says, "It seems proper for our Senate to be adorned" (as though it were not assuredly adorned), and to be adorned forsooth with "glory." And what is being done he wishes understood as already done; as, "we have proclaimed" for "we proclaim": for the speech sounds better that way. And he puts the same act in the present and in the past tense; as, "we decree," and "we have decreed." And everything is stuffed with these words, "we decree," "we decorate," "imperial," "imperial rank," "power," "glory." He uses "extat" for "est," though "extare" means to stand out or to be above; and "nempe" for "scilicet" [that is, "indeed" for "to wit"]; and "concubitores" [translated above, bed-watchers] for "contubernales" [companions or attendants]. "Concubitores" are literally those who sleep together and have intercourse; they must certainly be understood to be harlots. He adds those with whom he may sleep, I suppose, that he may not fear nocturnal phantoms.[11] He adds "chamberlains"; he adds "door-keepers."

It is not an idle question to ask why he mentions these details. He is setting up, not an old man, but a ward or a young son, and like a doting father, himself arranges for him everything of which his tender age has need, as David did for Solomon! And that the story may be filled in in every respect, horses are given the clergy,—lest they sit on asses' colts in that asinine way of Christ's! And they are given horses, not covered nor saddled with coverings of white, but decorated with white color. And what coverings! Not horse-cloths, either Babylonian or any other kind, but "mappulae" [translated above, saddle-cloths] and "linteamina" [linen cloths or sheets, translated above, linen]. "Mappae" [serviettes] go with the table, "linteamina" with the couch. And as though there were doubt as to their color, he explains, "that is to say, of the whitest color." Talk worthy of Constantine; fluency worthy of Lactantius; not only in the other phrases, but also in that one, "may mount mounts"!

And when he had said nothing about the garb of senators, the broad stripe, the purple, and the rest, he thought he had to talk about their shoes; nor does he specify the crescents [which were on their shoes], but "socks," or rather he says "with felt socks," and then as usual he explains,

---

[11]Where Valla's text of the Donation reads "concubitorum," Zeumer's reads "excubiorum" [guards].

"that is, with white linen," as though socks were of linen! I cannot at the moment think where I have found the word "udones" [socks], except in Valerius Martial, whose distich inscribed "Cilician Socks" runs:

> Wool did not produce these, but the beard of an ill-smelling goat.
> Would that the sole in the gulf of the Cinyps might lie.[12]

So the "socks" are not linen, nor white, with which this two-legged ass says, not that the feet of senators are clad, but that senators are distinguished.

And in the phrase "that the terrestrial orders may be adorned to the glory of God, just as the celestial," what do you call celestial, what terrestrial? How are the celestial orders adorned?[13] You may have seen what glory to God this is. But I, if I believe anything, deem nothing more hateful to God and to the rest of humanity than such presumption of clergy in the secular sphere. But why do I attack individual items? Time would fail me if I should try, I do not say to dwell upon, but to touch upon them all.

> Above all things, moreover, we give permission to the blessed Sylvester and his successors, from our edict, that he may make priest whomever he wishes, according to his own pleasure and counsel, and enroll him in the pious number of the religious clergy [i.e., regular clergy; or perhaps cardinals]: let no one whomsoever presume to act in a domineering way in this.[14]

Who is this Melchizedek that blesses the patriarch Abraham? Does Constantine, scarcely yet a Christian, give to the man by whom he was baptized and whom he calls blessed, authority to make priests? As though Sylvester had not and could not have done it before! And with what a threat he forbids any one to stand in the way! "Let no one, whomsoever, presume to act in a domineering way in this matter." What elegant diction, too! "Enroll in the pious number of the religious"; and "clericare," "clericorum," "indictu," and "placatus"!

And again he comes back to the diadem:

> We also therefore decreed this, that he himself and his successors might use, for the honor of the blessed Peter, the diadem, that is the crown, which we have granted him from our own head, of purest gold and precious gems.

[12]Martial, XIV, 141 (140).

[13]Valla for this part of his criticism uses the rather unintelligible order of words found in most texts of the Donation, instead of the more intelligible order which he used in his earlier quotations.

[14]Valla's text of the Donation in this paragraph differs greatly from Zeumer's, Hinschius', and Friedberg's. It is not very clear in any of the texts whether the intent is to give the Pope power to take any one whomsoever into the clergy and thus relieve him from civil and military duties, or to prevent the Roman nobility from forcing their way into ecclesiastical offices against the will of the Pope.

Again he explains the meaning of diadem, for he was speaking to barbarians, forgetful ones at that. And he adds "of purest gold," lest perchance you should think brass or dross was mixed in. And when he has said "gems," he adds "precious," again fearing lest you should suspect them of being cheap. Yet why did he not say most precious, just as he said "purest gold"? For there is more difference between gem and gem, than between gold and gold. And when he should have said "distinctum gemmis," he said "ex gemmis." Who does not see that this was taken from the passage, which the gentile ruler had not read, "Thou settest a crown of precious stone on his head"?[15] Did the Caesar speak thus, with a certain vanity in bragging of his crown, if indeed the Caesars were crowned, but cheapening himself by fearing lest people would think that he did not wear a crown "of purest gold and precious gems," unless he said so?

Find the reason why he speaks thus: "for the honor of the blessed Peter." As though, not Christ, but Peter, were the chief corner-stone on which the temple of the church is built; an inference he later repeats! But if he wanted to honor him so much, why did he not dedicate the episcopal temple at Rome to him, rather than to John the Baptist?

What? Does not that barbarous way of talking show that the rigmarole was composed, not in the age of Constantine, but later; "decernimus quod uti debeant"[16] for the correct form "decernimus ut utantur"? Boors commonly speak and write that way now; "Iussi quod deberes venire" for "Iussi ut venires." And "we decreed," and "we granted," as though it were not being done now, but had been done some other time!

> But he himself, the blessed Pope, did not allow that crown of gold to be used over the clerical crown which he wears to the glory of the most blessed Peter.

Alas for your singular stupidity, Constantine! Just now you were saying that you put the crown on the Pope's head for the honor of the blessed Peter; now you say that you do not do it, because Sylvester refuses it. And while you approve his refusal, you nevertheless order him to use the gold crown; and what he thinks he ought not to do, that you say his own successors ought to do![17] I pass over the fact that you call the tonsure

---

[15]Ps. xxi, 3, with variation.

[16]Valla does not, here, quote his own text of the Donation correctly.

[17]This singular confusion about the crown in the Donation is explained by Brunner, *Festgabe für Rudolf von Gneist,* pp. 25 et seq., as giving the Pope the possession, but not the use, of the imperial crown, thus paving the way for his prerogative of conferring the crown upon Louis the Pious in 816. Scheffer-Boichorst takes the whole episode as an attempt of the forger to glorify Sylvester by having the emperor honor him with the imperial crown, and having the Pope display the clerical humility (and pride) of rejecting it.

a crown, and the Roman pontiff "Pope," although that word had not yet begun to be applied to him as a distinctive title.

> But we placed upon his most holy head, with our own hands, a glittering tiara of the most dazzling white, representing the Lord's resurrection. And holding the bridle of his horse, out of reverence for the blessed Peter, we performed for him the duty of squire; decreeing that all his successors, and they alone, use this same tiara in processions in imitation of our power.

Does not this fable-fabricator seem to blunder, not through imprudence, but deliberately and of set purpose, and so as to offer handles for catching him? In the same passage he says both that the Lord's resurrection is represented by the tiara, and that it is an imitation of Caesar's power; two things which differ most widely from each other. God is my witness, I find no words, no words merciless enough with which to stab this most abandoned scoundrel; so full of insanity are all the words he vomits forth. He makes Constantine not only similar in office to Moses, who at the command of God honored the chief priest, but also an expounder of secret mysteries, a most difficult thing even for those long versed in the sacred books. Why did you not make Constantine supreme pontiff while you were about it, as many emperors have been, that he might more conveniently transfer his attire to the other high priest? But you did not know history. And I give thanks to God on this very score, that he did not permit this utterly vicious scheme to be suggested save to an exceedingly stupid man. Subsequent considerations also show this. For he suggests the fact that Moses performed for Aaron, seated on a horse, the duty of squire [dextratoris], and that in the midst not of Israel, but of the Canaanites and the Egyptians, that is, of an heathen state, where there was not so much a secular government as one of demons and demon-worshipping peoples.

> Wherefore, in order that the supreme pontificate may not deteriorate, but may rather be adorned with glory and power even more than is the dignity of an earthly rule; behold, we give over and relinquish to the most blessed pontiff and universal Pope, Sylvester, as well our palace as also the city of Rome and all the provinces, places and cities of Italy or of the western regions; and by our pragmatic sanction we have decreed that they are to be controlled by him and by his successors, and that they remain under the law of the holy Roman church.

We have already, in the oration of the Romans and that of Sylvester, said a good deal about this. Here it is in place to say that no one would have thought of including all the nations in a single word of a grant; and that a man who had earlier followed out the minutest details of straps, the shoes, the linen horse-cloths, would not have thought of omitting to cite by name provinces which now have separate kings or rulers equal to kings, and more than one to each. But this forger, of course, did not know which provinces were under Constantine, and which were not. For certainly not all were under him. When Alexander died, we see all the countries enumerated one by one in the division among the generals. We see the lands and rulers which were under the government of Cyrus, whether voluntarily or by conquest, named by Xenophon. We see the names of the Greek and barbarian kings, their lineage, their country, their bravery, their strength, their excellence, the number of their ships and the approximate number of their men, included by Homer in his catalog. And not only did many Greeks follow his example, but our Latin authors also, Ennius, Virgil, Lucan, Statius, and others. By Joshua and Moses, in the division of the promised land, even all the little villages were described. And you refuse to enumerate even provinces! You name only the "western provinces."[18] What are the boundaries of the west; where do they begin; where do they end? Are the frontiers of the west and east, south and north, as definite and fixed as those of Asia, Africa and Europe? Necessary words you omit, you heap on superfluous ones. You say, "provinces, places and cities." Are not provinces and cities, "places"? And when you have said provinces you add cities, as though the latter would not be understood with the former. But it is not strange that a man who gives away so large a part of the earth should pass over the names of cities and of provinces, and as though overcome with lethargy not know what he says. "Of Italy or of the western regions," as though he meant "either . . . or" when he means "both," speaking of "provinces . . . of the . . . regions," when it should rather be the regions of the provinces; and using the gerundive, "permanendas," for the future infinitive (permansuras).

> Wherefore we have perceived it to be fitting that our empire and our royal power should be transferred in the regions of the East; and that in the province of Byzantia [sic], in the most fitting place, a city should be built in our name; and that our empire should there be established.

I pass over the fact that in saying "a city should be built" [he uses the word for "the state" instead of "the city"], and cities, not states, are built; and the fact that he says "the province of Byzantia." If you are Constantine, give the reason why you should choose that as the best place for founding your city. For that you should "transfer" yourself elsewhere after giving up Rome, was not so much "fitting" as necessary. You should neither call yourself Emperor when you have lost Rome and deserved least from the Roman name whose meaning you destroy; nor call your-

---

[18]This phrase as used in the Donation probably meant Lombardy, Venetia and Istria; i.e., practically, northern, as distinct from peninsular, Italy. In classical Latin it would have been, as Valla insists, a vague term.

self "royal," for no one before you has done so,—unless you call yourself a king because you have ceased to be a Roman.[19] But you allege a reason sound and honorable:

> For where the chief of [all] priests and the head of the Christian religion has been established by the heavenly Emperor, it is not right that there an earthly Emperor should have jurisdiction.

O stupid David, stupid Solomon, stupid Hezekiah, Josiah, and all the other kings, stupid all and irreligious, who persisted in dwelling in the city of Jerusalem with the chief priests, and did not yield them the whole city! Constantine in three days is wiser than they could be in their whole life. And you call [the Pope] a "heavenly Emperor" because he accepts an earthly empire; unless by that term you mean God (for you speak ambiguously) and mean that an earthly sovereignty of priests was by him established over the city of Rome and other places, in which case you lie.

> We decreed, moreover, that all these things which through this sacred imperial [charter] and through other godlike decrees we establish and confirm, remain inviolate and unshaken unto the end of the world.

A moment ago, Constantine, you called yourself earthly; now you call yourself divine and sacred. You relapse into paganism and worse than paganism. You make yourself God, your words sacred, and your decrees immortal; for you order the world to keep your commands "inviolate and unshaken." Do you consider who you are: just cleansed from the filthiest mire of wickedness, and scarcely fully cleansed? Why did you not add, "Till heaven and earth pass, one jot or one title shall in no wise pass from this 'privilege' "?[20] The kingdom of Saul, chosen by God, did not pass on to his sons; the kingdom of David was divided under his grandson, and afterward destroyed. And by your own authority you decree that the kingdom which you give over without God, shall remain even until the end of the world! Whoever taught you that the world is to pass away so soon? For I do not think that at this time you had faith in the poets, who alone bear witness to this. So you could not have said this, but some one else passed it off as yours.

However, he who spoke so grandly and loftily, begins to fear, and to distrust himself, and so takes to entreating:

> Wherefore, before the living God, who commanded us to reign, and in the face of his terrible judgment, we entreat all the emperors our successors, and all the nobles, the satraps also and the most glorious Senate, and all the people in the

---

[19]King [rex] was a forbidden title at Rome after the time of the Tarquins.
[20]A parody on Matt. v, 18.

whole world, likewise also for the future, that no one of them, in any way, be allowed either to break this, or in any way overthrow it.

What a fair, what a devout adjuration! It is just as if a wolf should entreat by his innocence and good faith the other wolves and the shepherds not to try to take away from him, or demand back, the sheep which he has taken and divided among his offspring and his friends. Why are you so afraid, Constantine? if your work is not of God it will be destroyed; but if it is of God it cannot be destroyed. But I see! You wished to imitate the Apocalypse, where it says: "For I testify unto every man that heareth all the words of the prophecy of this book, If any man shall add unto these things, God shall add unto him the plagues that are written in this book: And if any man shall take away from the words of the book of this prophecy, God shall take away his part out of the book of life, and out of the holy city."[21] But you had never read the Apocalypse; therefore these are not your words.

> If any one, moreover—which we do not believe—prove a scorner in this matter, he shall be condemned and shall be subject to eternal damnation; and shall feel the holy apostles of God, Peter and Paul, opposed to him in the present and in the future life. And he shall be burned in the lower hell and shall perish with the devil and all the impious.

This terrible threat is the usual one, not of a secular ruler, but of the early priests and flamens, and nowadays, of ecclesiastics. And so this is not the utterance of Constantine, but of some fool of a priest who, stuffed and pudgy, knew neither what to say nor how to say it, and, gorged with eating and heated with wine, belched out these wordy sentences which convey nothing to another, but turn against the author himself. First he says, "shall be subject to eternal damnation," then as though more could be added, he wishes to add something else, and to eternal penalties he joins penalties in the present life; and after he frightens us with God's condemnation, he frightens us with the hatred of Peter, as though it were something still greater. Why he should add Paul, and why Paul alone, I do not know. And with his usual drowsiness he returns again to eternal penalties, as though he had not said that before. Now if these threats and curses were Constantine's, I in turn would curse him as a tyrant and destroyer of my country, and would threaten that I, as a Roman, would take vengeance on him. But who would be afraid of the curse of an overly avaricious man, and one saying a counterfeit speech after the manner of actors, and terrifying people in the role of Constantine? This is being a hypocrite in the true sense, if we press the Greek word closely; that is, hiding your own personality under another's.

---

[21]Rev. xxii, 18–19.

The page,[22] moreover, of this imperial decree, we, confirming it with our own hands, did place above the venerable body of the blessed Peter.[23]

Was it paper or parchment, the "page" on which this was written? Though, in fact, we call one side of a leaf, as they say, a page; for instance, a pamphlet[?] has ten leaves, twenty pages.

But oh! the unheard of and incredible thing [that Constantine did]! I remember asking some one, when I was a youth, who wrote the book of Job; and when he answered, "Job himself," I rejoined, "How then would he mention his own death?" And this can be said of many other books, discussion of which is not appropriate here. For how, indeed, can that be narrated which has not yet been done; and how can that which [the speaker] himself admits was done after the burial, so to say, of the records, be contained in the records? This is nothing else than saying that "the page of the privilege" was dead and buried before it was born, and yet never returned from death and burial; and saying expressly that it was confirmed before it had been written, and not with one hand alone at that, but with both of the Caesar's hands! And what is this "confirming"? Was it done with the signature of the Caesar, or with his signet ring? Surely, hard and fast that,—more so by far than if he had entrusted it to bronze tablets! But there is no need of bronze inscription, when the charter is laid away above the body of the blessed Peter. But why do you here suppress Paul, though he lies with Peter, and the two could guard it better than if the body of one alone were present?

You see the malicious artfulness of the cunning Sinon! Because the Donation of Constantine cannot be produced, therefore he said that the "privilege" is not on bronze but on paper records; therefore he said that it lies with the body of the most holy apostle, so that either we should not dare to seek it in the venerable tomb, or if we should seek it, we would think it rotted away. But where then was the body of the blessed Peter? Certainly it was not yet in the temple where it now is, not in a place reasonably protected and safe. Therefore the Caesar would not have put the "page" there. Or did he not trust the "page" to the most blessed Sylvester, as not holy enough, not careful nor diligent enough? O Peter! O Sylvester! O holy pontiffs of the Roman church! to whom the sheep of the Lord were entrusted, why did you not keep the "page" entrusted to you? Why have you suffered it to be eaten by worms, to rot away with mold? I presume that it was because your bodies also have wasted away. Constantine therefore acted foolishly. Behold the "page" reduced to dust;

---

[22]"Pagina" in medieval Latin often meant "document."

[23]In the Liber Pontificalis (ed. Duchesne, i, 454) the keys of Ravenna and other cities included in the so-called Donation of Pippin are said to have been placed in "the confession of St. Peter" (i.e., before his tomb). This association seems to have been common in the eighth century.

the right conferred by the "privilege" at the same time passes away into dust.

And yet, as we see, a copy of the "page" is shown. Who then was so bold as to take it from the bosom of the most holy apostle? No one did it, I think. Whence then the copy? By all means some ancient writer ought to be adduced, one not later than the time of Constantine. However, none such is adduced, but as it happens some recent writer or other. Whence did he get it? For whoever composes a narrative about an earlier age, either writes at the dictation of the Holy Spirit, or follows the authority of former writers, and of those, of course, who wrote concerning their own age. So whoever does not follow earlier writers will be one of those to whom the remoteness of the event affords the boldness to lie. But if this story is to be read anywhere, it is not consistent with antiquity any more than that stupid narrative of the glossator Accursius about Roman ambassadors being sent to Greece to get laws agrees with Titus Livius and the other best writers.

> Given at Rome, on the third day before the Kalends of April, Constantine Augustus consul for the fourth time, and Gallicanus consul for the fourth time.[24]

He took the next to the last day of March so that we might feel that this was done in the season of holy days, which, for the most part, come at that time. And "Constantine consul for the fourth time, and Gallicanus consul for the fourth time." Strange if each had been consul thrice, and they were colleagues in a fourth consulship! But stranger still that the Augustus, a leper, with elephantiasis (which disease is as remarkable among diseases, as elephants are among animals), should want to even accept a consulship, when king Azariah, as soon as he was affected with leprosy, kept himself secluded, while the management of the kingdom was given over to Jotham his son;[25] and almost all lepers have acted similarly. And by this argument alone the whole "privilege" is confuted outright, destroyed, and overturned. And if any one disputes the fact that Constantine must have been leprous before he was consul, he should know that according to physicians this disease develops gradually, that according to the known facts of antiquity the consulate is an annual office and begins in the month of January; and these events are said to have taken place the following March.

Nor will I here pass over the fact that "given" is usually written on letters, but not on other documents, except among ignorant people. For

---

[24]In the best text of the Donation this is not called the fourth consulship of Gallicanus. In any case, however, the date is impossible; no such consulship as this is known.

[25]II Kings xv, 5.

letters are said either to be given one (illi) or to be given to one (ad illum); in the former case [they are given to] one who carries them, a courier for instance, and puts them in the hand of the man to whom they are sent; in the latter case [they are given] to one in the sense that they are to be delivered to him by the bearer, that is [they are given to] the one to whom they are sent. But the "privilege," as they call it , of Constantine, as it was not to be delivered to any one, so also it ought not to be said to be "given." And so it should be apparent that he who spoke thus lied, and did not know how to imitate what Constantine would probably have said and done. And those who think that he has told the truth, and defend him, whoever they are, make themselves abetters and accessories in his stupidity and madness. However, they have nothing now with which to honorably excuse their opinion, not to speak of defending it.

Or is it an honorable excuse for an error, to be unwilling to acquiesce in the truth when you see it disclosed, because certain great men have thought otherwise? Great men, I call them, on account of their position, not on account of their wisdom or their goodness. How do you even know whether those whom you follow, had they heard what you hear, would have continued in their belief, or would have given it up? And moreover it is most contemptible to be willing to pay more regard to man than to Truth, that is, to God. [I say this] for some men beaten at every argument are wont to answer thus: "Why have so many supreme pontiffs believed this Donation to be genuine?" I call you to witness, that you urge me where I would not, and force me against my will to rail at the supreme pontiffs whose faults I would prefer to veil. But let us proceed to speak frankly, inasmuch as this case cannot be conducted in any other way.

Admitting that they did thus believe and were not dishonest; why wonder that they believed these stories where so much profit allured them, seeing that they are led to believe a great many things, in which no profit is apparent, through their extraordinary ignorance? Do you not, at Ara Coeli, in that most notable temple and in the most impressive place see the fable of the Sibyl and Octavian[26] depicted by the authority, they say, of Innocent III, who wrote it and who also left an account of the destruction of the Temple of Peace on the day of the Savior's birth, that is, at the delivery of the Virgin?[27] These stories tend rather to the destruction of faith, by their falsity, than to the establishment of faith, by their wonders. Does the vicar of Truth dare to tell a lie under the guise of piety, and consciously entangle himself in this sin? Or does he not lie? Verily,

---

[26]This apocryphal story ran that the Sibyl prophesied of Christ, and that Augustus erected an altar to him.

[27]The Temple of Peace was built by Vespasian and was not destroyed until it was burned down in the time of Commodus.

does he not see that in perpetrating this he contradicts the most holy men? Omitting others; Jerome cites the testimony of Varro that there were ten Sibyls, and Varro wrote his work before the time of Augustus. Jerome also writes thus of the Temple of Peace: "Vespasian and Titus, after the Temple of Peace was built at Rome, dedicated the vessels of the temple [of the Jews] and all manner of gifts in her shrine, as the Greek and Roman historians tell." And this ignorant man, alone, wants us to believe his libel, barbarously written at that, rather than the most accurate histories of ancient and most painstaking authors!

Niccolò Machiavelli

2

Machiavelli once wrote that politics was the passion of his life, and that he could think of nothing else. If the republican regime of Florence, which he supported and served, had endured for his lifetime, he probably would not have become a political pamphleteer or a historian. For fourteen years, from 1498 to 1512, Machiavelli devoted himself to the Florentine Republic, both as a chancellor and as the secretary to the council in charge of warfare, called the Ten of Liberty and Peace. He was sent on diplomatic missions within Italy and beyond the Alps to Germany and France, was entrusted with the correspondence of the Republic, and sought to create a strong and loyal indigenous militia. Coming from an uninfluential family, he became one of the most valuable and highly esteemed citizens of Florence, until, under the threat of destruction by the Spanish infantry, the Republic toppled and the rule of the Medici family was restored.

For Machiavelli, the fall of the Republic meant more than the end of a career. When the Medici discovered that the former chancellor was a party to a conspiracy against their government, they imprisoned and tortured him, and finally exiled him to the mountains outside of Florence, from where he could only glimpse his native city. A less active man might have been contented with a comfortable life on a country estate, but Machiavelli hated it.

Deprived of any role in Florentine politics, he resorted to political commentary and consoled himself with the wisdom of the ancient historians. His first literary production, *The Prince*, is his most famous; he may have written in some haste during his first months in exile, in the fall of 1513. Machiavelli's intentions in writing the amoral handbook on the ways of despotic government have given rise to never-ending controversy. It is enough to recall that the author loved the Florentine Republic, and that he wrote this explosive pamphlet in the bitterness of defeat and rejection. *The Prince* is perhaps as much an exposé and a satire of an exaggerated form of ruthless autocracy, as it is a straightforward set of maxims on how to achieve and retain power.

We can be sure that what Machiavelli wanted in dedicating the work to the young Giuliano de'Medici was to show the depth of his insight into the workings of practical politics and how helpful his advice could be, if he were taken back into the service of the state. Similiar motives inspired the creation of an elaborate, detailed treatise on classical military theory and practice, aptly entitled the *Art of War,* as well as the *Discourses on Livy.*

Where *The Prince* is short and incisive, the *Discourses* are long and discursive. Machiavelli took his time pondering Livy's history and gradually pieced together the many lessons he learned in comparing the greatness of the Roman Republic with the degenerate condition of his own Florence. The Roman Republic was a relatively durable institution, able to unite Italy and carry its civilization across Europe; Machiavelli's own career is testimony to the instability of the Florentine government. If the new leaders of Florence would read him, they might discover the secrets of Roman greatness (mainly the necessity for military discipline and a healthy tension between the Senate and the people, resulting in a patriotic spirit among the whole population) and would see how to achieve similar goals in their own state. Eventually, a few of the less vengeful aristocrats began to see the wisdom of Machiavelli's words. In November, 1520, Cardinal Giulio de'Medici, who was head of the Florentine University, agreed to engage Machiavelli to write a history of Florence. By the time the *History of Florence* was completed, its patron had become Pope Clement VII, and its author was back in politics, though in rather more humble capacities.

It is important to bear in mind that Machiavelli's *History* was a commissioned work, that he was meant to glorify and immortalize fifteenth-century Florence, and that he did so; but he also filled his work with the fruit of his own experience and with his peculiar brand of idealism. Like other Humanist historians before him, he modeled his work on that of the Roman historians, beginning with general observations and proceeding to particular instances; in addition, he used stylized literary devices such as the set speeches presenting both sides in political debates and minute descriptions of battle scenes. It was also quite natural that a Humanist historian would follow Cicero's dictum and use history to teach morality by practical example. Yet much of what Machiavelli taught was born of his own experience and vision.

Other Florentine chancellors had written official histories of their city in the same spirit as that of Machiavelli, but none had the purpose or power to preach reform as clearly or with as much passion. In the first of our two selections from the *History of Florence,* Machiavelli's scorn for the Duke of Athens' subjugation of Florence in 1342 implies a condemnation of contemporary tyranny; just as his praise for those who resisted this tyranny is meant to inspire emulation in his readers. The comparison of ancient Rome with fourteenth-century Florence in the second selection reveals what Machiavelli believed to be one of the many causes of Florentine weakness: the wasteful conflicts between the nobility and the people, and the internecine strife among the nobles themselves. If the energy required for these self-defeating pursuits had been directed toward the welfare of the Republic, Florence might have approached Roman greatness.

Medicean revenge forced the study of history on Machiavelli. Even though he resigned himself to his second-best vocation, he lent to his historical writing the same ideals and passion that infused his political career. It is precisely these qualities which distinguish the *History of Florence* from the more ordinary works of Humanist historiography. Machiavelli's *History* contains, as David Hume said it did, "the true sentiment of virtue."

Selected Bibliography

Over the centuries Machiavelli's writings have invited many critics; none is more learned or judicious than Felix Gilbert. His *Machiavelli and Guicciardini: Politics and History in Sixteenth-Century Florence* (1965) is indispensable to the understanding of Machiavelli as a Humanist historian and the relation of his works to Florentine politics. Two essays collected by William H. Werkmeister in *Facets of the Renaissance* (1959) illuminate some aspects of Machiavelli's thought without the polemics that were once typical of the literature on the Florentine historian. One of these, "The Renaissance Conception of the Lessons of History," 73–86, by Myron P. Gilmore, compares Machiavelli's historical didacticism with that of his contemporaries; while E. Harris Harbison's "Machiavelli's *Prince* and More's *Utopia,*" 41–71, offers some perceptive comments on the origin and purposes of the *Discourses* and *The Prince.* Although Federico Chabod does not quite succeed in achieving his aim of presenting the author of *The Prince* as the expression "of Italian life throughout the fourteenth and fifteenth centuries," he does go a long way toward correcting some unfair and simplistic interpretations of Machiavelli, which predated his *Machiavelli and the Renaissance* (1958). An accurate, full-length, modern biography is Roberto Ridolphi's *The Life of Niccolò Machiavelli* (1954; translated by Cecil Grayson, 1963), but readers may find more wisdom in Garrett Mattingly's economical essay, "Machiavelli," in *Renaissance Profiles* (1961), 19–35, a Harper Torchbook.

It should be noted that Machiavelli made remarkable contributions to Renaissance literature in the form of letters, two entertaining comedies, and a compact philological discourse, *A Dialogue on Language.* These have been edited and translated by J. R. Hale in *The Literary Works of Machiavelli* (1961).

HISTORY OF FLORENCE

The duke, having acquired the sovereignty of the city, in order to strip those of all authority who had been defenders of her liberty, forbade the Signory to assemble in the palace, and appointed a private dwelling for their use. He took their colors from the Gonfaloniers of the companies of the people; abolished the ordinances made for the restraint of the great; set at liberty those who were imprisoned; recalled the Bardi and the Frescobaldi from exile, and forbade everyone from carrying arms about his person. In order the better to defend himself against those within the city, he made friends of all he could around it, and therefore conferred great benefits upon the Aretini and other subjects of the Florentines. He made peace with the Pisans, although raised to power in order that he might carry on war against them; ceased paying interest to those merchants who, during the war against Lucca, had lent money to the republic; increased the old taxes, levied new ones, and took from the Signory all authority. His rectors were Baglione da Perugia and Guglielmo da Scesi, who, with Cerrettieri Bisdomini, were the persons with whom he consulted on public affairs. He imposed burdensome taxes upon the citizens; his decisions between contending parties were unjust; and that precision and humanity which he had at first assumed, became cruelty and pride; so that many of the greatest citizens and noblest people were, either by fines, death, or some new invention, grievously oppressed. And in completing the same bad system, both without the city and within, he appointed six rectors for the country, who beat and plundered the inhabitants. He suspected the great, although he had been benefited by them, and had restored many to their country; for he felt assured that the generous minds of the nobility would not allow them, from any motives, to submit contentedly to his authority. He also began to confer benefits and advantages upon the lowest orders, thinking that with their assistance, and the arms of foreigners, he would be able to preserve the tyranny. The month of May, during which feasts are held, being come, he caused many companies to be formed of the plebeians and very lowest of the people, and to these, dignified with splendid titles, he gave colors

History of Florence, pp. 94–101, 108–118. Harper Torchbook.

and money; and while one party went in bacchanalian procession through the city, others were stationed in different parts of it, to receive them as guests. As the report of the duke's authority spread abroad, many of the French origin came to him, for all of whom he found offices and emoluments, as if they had been the most trustworthy of men; so that in a short time Florence became not only subject to French dominion, but adopted their dresses and manners; for men and women, without regard to propriety or sense of shame, imitated them. But that which disgusted the people most completely was the violence which, without any distinction of quality or rank, he and his followers committed upon the women.

The people were filled with indignation, seeing the majesty of the state overturned, its ordinances annihilated, its laws annulled, and every decent regulation set at naught; for men unaccustomed to royal pomp could not endure to see this man surrounded with his armed satellites on foot and on horseback; and having now a closer view of their disgrace, they were compelled to honor him whom they in the highest degree hated. To this hatred, was added the terror occasioned by the continual imposition of new taxes and frequent shedding of blood, with which he impoverished and consumed the city.

The duke was not unaware of these impressions existing strongly in the people's minds, nor was he without fear of the consequences; but still pretended to think himself beloved; and when Matteo di Morozzo, either to acquire his favor or to free himself from danger, gave information that the family of the Medici and some others had entered into a conspiracy against him he not only did not inquire into the matter, but caused the informer to be put to a cruel death. This mode of proceeding restrained those who were disposed to acquaint him of his danger and gave additional courage to such as sought his ruin. Bertone Cini, having ventured to speak against the taxes with which the people were loaded, had his tongue cut out with such barbarous cruelty as to cause his death. This shocking act increased the people's rage, and their hatred of the duke; for those who were accustomed to discourse and to act upon every occasion with the greatest boldness, could not endure to live with their hands tied and forbidden to speak.

This oppression increased to such a degree, that not merely the Florentines, who though unable to preserve their liberty cannot endure slavery, but the most servile people on earth would have been roused to attempt the recovery of freedom; and consequently many citizens of all ranks resolved either to deliver themselves from this odious tyranny or die in the attempt. Three distinct conspiracies were formed; one of the great, another of the people, and the third of the working classes; each of which, besides the general causes which operated upon the whole, were excited by some other particular grievance. The great found themselves deprived of all participation in the government; the people had lost the power they possessed, and the artificers saw themselves deficient in the usual remuneration of their labor.

Agnolo Acciajuoli was at this time archbishop of Florence, and by his discourses had formerly greatly favored the duke, and procured him many followers among the higher class of the people. But when he found him lord of the city, and became acquainted with his tyrannical mode of proceeding, it appeared to him that he had misled his countrymen; and to correct the evil he had done, he saw no other course, but to attempt the cure by the means which had caused it. He therefore became the leader of the first and most powerful conspiracy, and was joined by the Bardi, Rossi, Frescobaldi, Scali Altoviti, Magalotti, Strozzi, and Mancini. Of the second, the principals were Manno and Corso Donati, and with them the Pazzi, Cavicciulli, Cerchi, and Albizzi. Of the third, the first was Antonio Adimari, and with him the Medici, Bordini, Rucellai, and Aldobrandini. It was the intention of these last, to slay him in the house of the Albizzi, whither he was expected to go on St. John's day, to see the horses run, but he not having gone, their design did not succeed. They then resolved to attack him as he rode through the city; but they found this would be very difficult; for he was always accompanied with a considerable armed force, and never took the same road twice together, so that they had no certainty of where to find him. They had a design of slaying him in the council, although they knew that if he were dead, they would be at the mercy of his followers.

While these matters were being considered by the conspirators, Antonio Adimari, in expectation of getting assistance from them, disclosed the affair to some Siennese, his friends, naming certain of the conspirators, and assuring them that the whole city was ready to rise at once. One of them communicated the matter to Francesco Brunelleschi, not with a design to injure the plot, but in the hope that he would join them. Francesco, either from personal fear, or private hatred of some one, revealed the whole to the duke; whereupon, Pagolo del Mazecha and Simon da Monterappoli were taken, who acquainted him with the number and quality of the conspirators. This terrified him, and he was advised to request their presence rather than to take them prisoners, for if they fled, he might without disgrace, secure himself by banishment of the rest. He therefore sent for Antonio Adimari, who, confiding in his companions, appeared immediately, and was detained. Francesco Brunelleschi and Uguccione Buondelmonti advised the duke to take as many of the conspirators prisoners as he could, and put them to death; but he, thinking his strength unequal to his foes, did not adopt this course, but took another, which, had it succeeded, would have freed him from his enemies and increased his power. It was the custom of the duke to call the citizens together upon some occasions and advise with them. He therefore having first sent to collect forces from without, made a list of three hundred citizens, and gave it to his messengers, with orders to assemble them under the pretense of public business; and having drawn them together, it was his intention either to put them to death or imprison them.

The capture of Antonio Adimari and the sending for forces, which could not be kept secret, alarmed the citizens, and more particularly those who were in the plot, so that the boldest of them refused to attend, and as each had read the list, they sought each other, and resolved to rise at once and die like men, with arms in their hands, rather than be led like calves to the slaughter. In a very short time the chief conspirators became known to each other, and resolved that the next day, which was the 26th July, 1343, they would raise a disturbance in the Old Market place, then arm themselves and call the people to freedom.

The next morning being come, at nine o'clock, according to agreement, they took arms, and at the call of liberty assembled, each party in its own district, under the ensigns and with the arms of the people, which had been secretly provided by the conspirators. All the heads of families, as well of the nobility as of the people, met together, and swore to stand in each other's defense, and effect the death of the duke; except some of the Buondelmonti and of the Cavalcanti, with those four families of the people which had taken so conspicuous a part in making him sovereign, and the butchers, with others, the lowest of the plebeians, who met armed in the piazza in his favor.

The duke immediately fortified the palace, and ordered those of his people who were lodged in different parts of the city to mount upon horseback and join those in the court; but, in their way thither, many were attacked and slain. However, about three hundred horse assembled, and the duke was in doubt whether he should come forth and meet the enemy, or defend himself within. On the other hand, the Medici, Cavicci-ulli, Rucellai, and other families who had been most injured by him, fearful that if he came forth, many of those who had taken arms against him would discover themselves his partisans, in order to deprive him of the occasion of attacking them and increasing the number of his friends, took the lead and assailed the palace. Upon this, those families of the people who had declared for the duke, seeing themselves boldly attacked, changed their minds, and all took part with the citizens, except Ugucc-ione Buondelmonti, who retired into the palace, and Giannozzo Caval-canti, who having withdrawn with some of his followers to the new market, mounted upon a bench, and begged that those who were going in arms to the piazza, would take the part of the duke. In order to terrify them, he exaggerated the number of his people and threatened all with death who should obstinately persevere in their undertaking against their sovereign. But not finding any one either to follow him, or to chastise his insolence, and seeing his labor fruitless, he withdrew to his own house.

In the meantime, the contest in the piazza between the people and the forces of the duke was very great; but although the place served them for defense, they were overcome, some yielding to the enemy, and others, quitting their horses, fled within the walls. While this was going on, Corso and Amerigo Donati, with a part of the people, broke open the stinche, or prisons; burnt the papers of the provost and of the public chamber; pillaged the houses of the rectors, and slew all who had held offices under the duke whom they could find. The duke, finding the piazza in possession of his enemies, the city opposed to him, and without any hope of assistance, endeavored by an act of clemency to recover the favor of the people. Having caused those whom he had made prisoners to be brought before him, with amiable and kindly expressions he set them at liberty, and made Antonio Adimari a knight, although quite against his will. He caused his own arms to be taken down, and those of the people to be replaced over the palace; but these things coming out of season, and forced by his necessities, did him little good. He remained, notwithstanding all he did, besieged in the palace, and saw that having aimed at too much he had lost all, and would most likely, after a few days, die either of hunger, or by the weapons of his enemies. The citizens assembled in the church of Santa Reparata, to form the new government, and appointed fourteen citizens, half from the nobility and half from the people, who, with the archbishop, were invested with full authority to remodel the state of Florence. They also elected six others to take upon them the duties of provost, till he who should be finally chosen took office, the duties of which were usually performed by a subject of some neighboring state.

Many had come to Florence in defense of the people; among whom were a party from Sienna, with six ambassadors, men of high consideration in their own country. These endeavored to bring the people and the duke to terms; but the former refused to listen to any whatever, unless Guglielmo da Scesi and his son, with Cerrettieri Bisdomini, were first given up to them. The duke would not consent to this; but being threatened by those who were shut up with him, he was forced to comply. The rage of men is certainly always found greater, and their revenge more furious upon the recovery of liberty, than when it has only been defended. Guglielmo and his son were placed among the thousands of their enemies, and the latter was not yet eighteen years old; neither his beauty, his innocence, nor his youth, could save him from the fury of the multitude; but both were instantly slain. Those who could not wound them while alive, wounded them after they were dead; and not satisfied with tearing them to pieces, they hewed their bodies with swords, tore them with their hands, and even with their teeth. And that every sense might be satiated with vengeance, having first heard their moans, seen their wounds, and touched their lacerated bodies, they wished even the stomach to be satisfied, that having glutted the external senses, the one within might also have its share. This rabid fury, however hurtful to the father and son, was favorable to Cerrettieri; for the multitude, wearied with their cruelty toward the former, quite forgot him, so that he, not being asked for, remained in the palace, and during night was conveyed safely away by his friends.

The rage of the multitude being appeased by their blood, an agreement was made that the duke and his people, with whatever belonged to him, should quit the city in safety; that he should renounce all claim, of whatever kind, upon Florence, and that upon his arrival in the Casentino he should ratify his renunciation. On the sixth of August he set out, accompanied by many citizens, and having arrived at the Casentino he ratified the agreement, although unwillingly, and would not have kept his word if Count Simon had not threatened to take him back to Florence. This duke, as his proceedings testified, was cruel and avaricious, difficult to speak with, and haughty in reply. He desired the service of men, not the cultivation of their better feelings, and strove rather to inspire them with fear than love. Nor was his person less despicable than his manners; he was short, his complexion was black, and he had a long, thin beard. He was thus in every respect contemptible; and at the end of ten months, his misconduct deprived him of the sovereignty which the evil counsel of others had given him.

Book III: Chapter I

Those serious, though natural enmities, which occur between the popular classes and the nobility, arising from the desire of the latter to command, and the disinclination of the former to obey, are the causes of most of the troubles which take place in cities; and from this diversity of purpose, all the other evils which disturb republics derive their origin. This kept Rome disunited; and this, if it be allowable to compare small things with great, held Florence in disunion; although in each city it produced a different result; for animosities were only beginning when the people and nobility of Rome contended, while ours were brought to a conclusion by the contentions of our citizens. A new law settled the disputes of Rome; those of Florence were only terminated by the death and banishment of many of her best people. Those of Rome increased her military virtue, while that of Florence was quite extinguished by her divisions. The quarrels of Rome established different ranks of society, those of Florence abolished the distinctions which had previously existed. This diversity of effects must have been occasioned by the different purposes which the two people had in view. While the people of Rome endeavored to associate with the nobility in the supreme honors, those of Florence strove to exclude the nobility from all participation in them: as the desire of the Roman people was more reasonable, no particular offense was given to the nobility; they therefore consented to it without having recourse to arms; so that, after some disputes concerning particular points, both parties agreed to the enactment of a law which, while it satisfied the people, preserved the nobility in the enjoyment of their dignity.

On the other hand, the demands of the people of Florence being insolent and unjust, the nobility, became desperate, prepared for this defense with their utmost energy, and thus bloodshed and the exile of citizens followed. The laws which were afterward made, did not provide for the common good, but were framed wholly in favor of the conquerors. This too, must be observed, that from the acquisition of power, made by the people of Rome, their minds were very much improved; for all the offices of state being attainable as well by the people as the nobility, the peculiar excellencies of the latter exercised a most beneficial influence upon the former; and as the city increased in virtue she attained a more exalted greatness.

But in Florence, the people being conquerors, the nobility were deprived of all participation in the government; and in order to regain a portion of it, it became necessary for them not only to seem like the people, but to be like them in behavior, mind, and mode of living. Hence arose those changes in armorial bearings, and in the titles of families, which the nobility adopted, in order that they might seem to be of the people; military virtue and generosity of feeling became extinguished in them; the people not possessing these qualities, they could not appreciate them, and Florence became by degrees more and more depressed and humiliated. The virtue of the Roman nobility degenerating into pride, the citizens soon found that the business of the state could not be carried on without a prince. Florence had now come to such a point, that with a comprehensive mind at the head of affairs she would easily have been made to take any form that he might have been disposed to give her; as may be partly observed by a perusal of the preceding book.

Having given an account of the origin of Florence, the commencement of her liberty, with the causes of her divisions, and shown how the factions of the nobility and the people ceased with the tyranny of the duke of Athens, and the ruin of the former, we have now to speak of the animosities between the citizens and the plebeians and the various circumstances which they produced.

The nobility being overcome, and the war with the archbishop of Milan concluded, there did not appear any cause of dissension in Florence. But the evil fortune of the city, and the defective nature of her laws, gave rise to enmities between the family of the Albizzi and that of the Ricci, which divided her citizens as completely as those of the Buondelmonti and the Uberti, or the Donati and the Cerchi had formerly done. The pontiffs, who at this time resided in France, and the emperors, who abode in Germany, in order to maintain their influence in Italy, sent among us multitudes of soldiers of many countries, as English, Dutch, and Bretons. As these, upon the conclusion of a war, were thrown out of pay, though still in the country, they, under the standard of some soldier of fortune, plundered such people as were least prepared to defend themselves. In the year 1353 one of these companies came into Tuscany under the command of Monsignor Reale, of Provence, and his approach terrified all the cities of Italy. The Florentines not only provided themselves forces, but many citizens, among whom were the Albizzi and the Ricci, armed themselves in their own defense. These families were at the time full of hatred against each other, and each thought to obtain the sovereignty of the republic by overcoming his enemy. They had not yet proceeded to open violence, but only contended in the magistracies and councils. The city being all in arms, a quarrel arose in the Old Market place, and, as it frequently happens in similar cases, a great number of people were drawn together. The disturbance spreading, it was told the Ricci that the Albizzi had assailed their partisans, and to the Albizzi that the Ricci were in quest of them. Upon this the whole city arose, and it was all the magistrates could do to restrain these families, and prevent the actual occurrence of a disaster which, without being the fault of either of them, had been wilfully though falsely reported as having already taken place. This apparently trifling circumstance served to inflame the minds of the parties, and make each the more resolved to increase the number of their followers. And as the citizens, since the ruin of the nobility, were on such an equality that the magistrates were more respected now than they had previously been, they designed to proceed toward the suppression of this disorder with civil authority alone.

We have before related, that after the victory of Charles I the government was formed of the Guelphic party, and that it thus acquired great authority over the Ghibellines. But time, a variety of circumstances, and new divisions had so contributed to sink this party feeling into oblivion, that many of Ghibelline descent now filled the highest offices. Observing this, Uguccione, the head of the family of the Ricci, contrived that the law against the Ghibellines should be again brought into operation; many imagining the Albizzi to be of that faction, they having arisen in Arezzo, and come long ago to Florence. Uguccione by this means hoped

to deprive the Albizzi of participation in the government, for all of Ghibelline blood who were found to hold offices, would be condemned in
the penalties which this law provided. The design of Uguccione was
discovered to Piero son of Filippo degli Albizzi, and he resolved to favor it: for he saw that to oppose it would at once declare him a Ghibelline; and thus the law which was renewed by the ambition of the
Ricci for his destruction, instead of robbing Piero degli Albizzi of
reputation, contributed to increase his influence, although it laid the
foundation of many evils. Nor is it possible for a republic to enact a
law more pernicious than one relating to matters which have long
transpired. Piero having favored this law, which had been contrived
by his enemies for his stumbling-block, it became the stepping-stone
to his greatness; for, making himself the leader of this new order of
things, his authority went on increasing, and he was in greater favor
with the Guelphs than any other man.

As there could not be found a magistrate willing to search out who were
Ghibellines, and as this renewed enactment against them was therefore
of small value, it was provided that authority should be given to the
Capitani to find who were of this faction; and, having discovered, to
signify and ADMONISH them that they were not to take upon themselves
any office of government; to which ADMONITIONS, if they were disobedient,
they became condemned in the penalties. Hence, all those who in Florence are deprived of the power to hold offices are called *ammoniti,* or
ADMONISHED.

The Capitani in time to acquiring greater audacity, admonished not
only those to whom the admonition was applicable, but any others at the
suggestion of their own avarice or ambition; and from 1356, when this
law was made, to 1366, there had been admonished above 200 citizens.
The Captains of the Parts and the sect of the Guelphs were thus become
powerful; for every one honored them for fear of being admonished; and
most particularly the leaders, who were Piero degli Albizzi, Lapo da
Castiglionchio, and Carlo Strozzi. This insolent mode of proceeding was
offensive to many; but none felt so particularly injured with it as the
Ricci; for they knew themselves to have occasioned it, they saw it involved the ruin of the republic, and their enemies, the Albizzi, contrary
to their intention, become great in consequence.

On this account Uguccione de' Ricci, being one of the Signory, resolved
to put an end to the evil which he and his friends had originated, and
with a new law provided that to the six Captains of Parts an additional
three should be appointed, of whom two should be chosen from the companies of minor artificers, and that before any party could be considered
Ghibelline, the declaration of the Capitani must be confirmed by twenty-
four Guelphic citizens, appointed for the purpose. This provision tem-

pered for the time the power of the Capitani, so that the admonitions were greatly diminished, if not wholly laid aside. Still the parties of the Albizzi and the Ricci were continually on the alert to oppose each other's laws, deliberations, and enterprises, not from a conviction of their inexpediency, but from hatred of their promoters.

Francesco Guicciardini 1483—1540

3

While Machiavelli was composing his *History of Florence* in the 1520's, he wrote to Francesco Guicciardini, who had already written a Florentine history (which was never completed), for advice on how to interpret the fifteenth-century Medicean rule in Florence. Even though the two Florentine historians were members of opposing political camps during the period of Machiavelli's chancellorship to the Republic, Machiavelli knew that his former political opponent would give him shrewd and well-informed advice. By the time Machiavelli had become a historian, Guicciardini, a member of one of the great patrician families of Florence, had been the Republic's ambassador to King Ferdinand of Aragon, had practiced law, had remained influential in Florentine politics after the fall of the Republic, and was now an able, powerful administrator in the government of the Medici Pope, Clement VII. Machiavelli admired his rival both for his ability as a politician who could survive in a variety of political environments, and for his historical aspirations.

The contrast offered by Guicciardini's political success to Machiavelli's exile is as striking as the divergence of their historical perspectives and methods. Machiavelli's *History of Florence* was a traditional piece of Humanist historical writing; it was a stylized, classical history of the city-state. For his sources, Machiavelli drew from well-known local annals and previous histories; he accepted and perfected set notions about his city's past. On the other hand, Guicciardini, as Florentine ambassador to Spain, as the governor of three distant papal states, and as lieutenant-general of the papal army, came to view the history of Florence as only a part of the evolution of the Italian peninsula as a whole. He also learned as a professional diplomat to distrust accepted stories, and saw the necessity of consulting original documents and of comparing and criticizing famous legends with what he discovered in the archives, in order to determine what really happened. It was from this vantage point that Guicciardini was able to see the importance of the year 1494, the year French troops marched into Italy, as a turning point not only in the history of Florence, but in the history of Italy, and indeed, of all Europe.

The invasion by the army of Charles VIII made the Humanist formula of historical interpretation obsolete. His troops brought devastation and changes in government that affected all Italy; moreover, Italians could no longer see their civilization as isolated from the rest of Europe. Italy was now thrust into European war and the confusion of dynastic conflicts between the great French and Spanish powers. It is not surprising, then, that Guicciardini abandoned his efforts at writing his second *History of Florence* and began, in 1536, his *History of Italy*. In this formidable work, Guicciardini became the first historian to understand that Italian history could no longer be meaningfully interpreted in terms of the city-state. He showed the history of the Italian states to be bound up in the web of foreign alliances, which attended the invasion of 1494 and which later issued from it.

In our selection, from the first of his twenty books, we can follow Guicciardini from Florence, Rome, Milan and Naples, to Spain and France, describing the tensions which culminated in the final invasion.

The cosmopolitanism of Guicciardini's *History of Italy* is not its only auspicious quality. In the same manner in which he departed from the Humanist form of historiography, he greatly improved the criticism of sources, a practice which has often earned him the praise of being the first historian to allow the records of past events to speak for themselves, instead of arranging historical events into suitable story-like reconstructions of the past. We know from his notebooks that he was indefatigable in the search for historical truth. He made prodigious use of his family archives for his Florentine histories, and of the papal archives for the *History of Italy*. The latter work underwent continuing revision during the last six years of his life, all in the effort to obtain factual accuracy.

Guicciardini subscribed, in part, to the popular notion that history taught lessons that could guide statesmen in the conduct of present-day affairs, but he censured Machiavelli for continually advocating the example of the Romans. Both in his *Ricordi,* or collection of maxims, which he wrote in several drafts over his long, active career, and in his *Considerations on the Discourses of Machiavelli* (1530), he was respectfully critical of Machiavelli's faith in the wisdom of the ancient historians, and of his belief that their teachings were closely relevant to contemporary politics. Guicciardini saw the role of chance or fate as an omnipotent historical force, which might disprove any precept based on the assumption that, in given circumstances, men will act according to predictable patterns. He was too acute an observer of politics not to believe that, in the end, the whims of princes and popes might be governed by anything save the lust for power.

Historians are, with good reason, reluctant to proclaim any historical period or any historical work completely different from its predecessors. It is impossible to establish a complete break with the past, or to be oblivious to previous modes of thought. So it is that we find in Guicciardini's *History of Italy* the conscious effort to follow the Humanist requirements that a history should be divided into an even number of books, and told, year by year, in the expected annalistic form. The superstitious omens, announcing the French invasion, at the end of our selection, reveal that however sophisticated Guicciardini's historical ambitions and achievements might have been, he was still a man of his times.

Selected Bibliography

Compared to the author of *The Prince*, Guicciardini, a better historian than Machiavelli, has received little attention from modern scholars. Fortunately, the high praise we give to Felix Gilbert's *Machiavelli and Guicciardini* in the preceding selection can be repeated here. Gilbert offers a critical comparison of the method of the two historians, as does Herbert Butterfield in *The Statecraft of Machiavelli* (1940). The nineteenth-century German historian Leopold von Ranke took great pleasure in the discovery that Guicciardini was not as accurate in detail as he was. The story of Ranke's condemnation of Guicciardini's *History of Italy* and of the rehabilitation of his reputation is ably traced in Vincent Luciani, *Francesco Guicciardini and His European Reputation* (1936). Although Roberto Ridolphi persists in his refusal to treat his Renaissance men as intellectuals, his *Life of Francesco Guicciardini* (1960; translated by Cecil Grayson, 1967) is superior to his biography of Machiavelli. It is a thorough and lively picture of Guicciardini's political career and personal life. Guicciardini's *Ricordi* are now available in an English translation by Mario Domandi as *Maxims and Reflections of a Renaissance Statesman* (1965), a Harper Torchbook. Selections from each of the twenty books of the *History of Italy* have been edited and translated by Sidney Alexander (1969).

HISTORY OF ITALY

BOOK I

Chapter 1

I have decided to write about the events which have taken place in Italy within living memory since the time when French armies called in by our own princes began to trouble her peace with great upheavals. A very rich theme for its variety and extent, and full of appalling disasters, for Italy has suffered for many years every kind of calamity that may vex wretched mortals either through the just wrath of God or through the impious and wicked actions of their fellow men. From the understanding of these events, so diverse and grave, all men will be able to draw many useful lessons both for themselves and for the public good. It will appear from countless examples how unstable are human affairs—like a sea driven by the winds; how pernicious, nearly always to themselves but invariably to the common people, are the ill-judged actions of rulers when they pursue only vain error or present greed. And forgetting how often fortunate changes, and converting to other peoples' harm the power vested in them for the public good, they become through lack of prudence or excess of ambition the authors of fresh upheavals.

The calamities of Italy began (and I say this so that I may make known what was her condition before, and the causes from which so many evils arose), to the greater sorrow and terror of all men, at a time when circumstances seemed universally most propitious and fortunate. It is indisputable that since the Roman Empire, weakened largely by the decay of her ancient customs, began to decline more than a thousand years ago from that greatness to which it had risen with marvelous virtue and good fortune, Italy had never known such prosperity or such a desirable condition as that which it enjoyed in all tranquillity in the year of Our Lord 1490 and the years immediately before and after. For, all at peace and quietness, cultivated no less in the mountainous and sterile places than in the fertile regions and plains, knowing no other rule than that of its

History of Italy translated by Cecil Grayson, New York: Washington Square Press, Inc. 1964, pp. 85–100, 113–123, 144–149. Copyright © 1964 by Washington Square Press, Inc. Reprinted by permission.

own people, Italy was not only rich in population, merchandise and wealth, but she was adorned to the highest degree by the magnificence of many princes, by the splendor of innumerable noble and beautiful cities, by the throne and majesty of religion; full of men most able in the administration of public affairs, and of noble minds learned in every branch of study and versed in every worthy art and skill. Nor did she lack military glory according to the standards of those times; and being so richly endowed, she deservedly enjoyed among all other nations a most brilliant reputation.

Italy was preserved in this happy state, which had been attained through a variety of causes, by a number of circumstances, but among these by common consent no little credit was due to the industry and virtue of Lorenzo de' Medici, a citizen so far above the rank of private citizen in Florence that all the affairs of the Republic were decided by his advice. Florence was at that time powerful by virtue of her geographical position, the intelligence of her people and the readiness of her wealth rather than for the extent of her dominion. Lorenzo had lately allied himself through marriage to Pope Innocent VIII (who listened readily to his counsels); his name was respected throughout Italy and his authority was great in all discussions on matters of common interest. Knowing that it would be very dangerous to himself and to the Florentine Republic if any of the large states increased their power, he diligently sought to maintain the affairs of Italy in such a balance that they might not favor one side more than another. This would not have been possible without the preservation of peace and without the most careful watch over any disturbance, however small. Ferdinand of Aragon, King of Naples, shared his desire for universal peace—undoubtedly a most prudent and respected prince; though in the past he had often shown ambitious designs contrary to the counsels of peace, and at this time was being egged on by Alfonso, Duke of Calabria, his eldest son, who resented seeing his son-in-law, Giovan Galeazzo Sforza, Duke of Milan—now over twenty years of age though quite lacking in ability—merely keeping the title of duke and being overborne and crushed by Lodovico Sforza, his uncle. The latter, more than ten years earlier, had taken over the guardianship of the young Duke because of the imprudence and lewd habits of his mother Madonna Bona, and thus little by little had taken into his own hands the fortresses, soldiers, treasury, and all the instruments of power; and he now continued to govern, no longer as guardian or regent, but in everything except the title of Duke of Milan, with all the outward shows and actions of a prince. Nevertheless Ferdinand did not desire any upheaval in Italy, having more regard for present benefits than past ambitions or for his son's indignation, however well-founded. Perhaps because a few years earlier he had experienced, with the gravest danger, the hatred of his barons and his common subjects, and knowing the affection which many of his people still held for the name of the royal house of France, he was afraid that discord in Italy might give the French an opportunity to attack the Kingdom of Naples. Or perhaps he realized that to balance the power of the Venetians, which was then a threat to the whole of Italy, he must remain allied with the other states —particularly Milan and Florence. Lodovico Sforza, though of a restless and ambitious nature, must have shared this view, because the danger from the Venetian senate threatened the rulers of Milan no less than the others and because it was easier for him to maintain the power he had usurped in the tranquillity of peace than in the vicissitudes of war. He always suspected the intentions of Ferdinand and Alfonso of Aragon, but knowing Lorenzo de' Medici's desire for peace and his fear of their power—and believing that because of the difference of attitude and ancient hatred between Ferdinand and the Venetians there was no fear that they might form an alliance—he felt fairly sure that the Aragonese would not find allies to attempt against him what they could not do alone.

Since there was the same will for peace in Ferdinand, Lodovico, and Lorenzo—partly for the same and partly for different reasons—it was easy to maintain an alliance in the name of Ferdinand, King of Naples, Giovan Galeazzo, Duke of Milan, and the Florentine Republic for the mutual defense of their states. This treaty, which was entered into many years before and subsequently interrupted for various reasons, had been renewed in 1480 for twenty-five years with the adherence of nearly all the small states of Italy. Its principal object was to prevent the Venetians from increasing their power, for they were undoubtedly greater than any one of the confederates, but much less so than all of them put together. They kept their own counsel, hoping to increase their power through friction and disunity among others, and stood ready to profit by any event which might open the way for them to the domination of the whole of Italy. It had been clear on more than one occasion that this was what they sought, especially when, on the death of Filippo Maria Visconti, Duke of Milan, they attempted to seize that state under color of defending the freedom of the Milanese; and more recently when in open war they tried to occupy the Duchy of Ferrara. It was easy for the confederation to curb the greed of the Venetian senate, but it did not unite the allies in sincere and faithful friendship, because—full of jealousy and rivalry—they constantly watched one another's movements, mutually thwarting every design whereby any one of them might increase its power or reputation. This did not make the peace any less stable, but rather inspired each with a greater promptness to put out any sparks which might be the origin of a new outbreak.

Chapter 2

Such was the state of things, such the foundation of the peace of Italy, so arranged and juxtaposed that not only was there no fear of any present disorder but it was difficult to imagine how, by what plots, incidents or forces, such tranquillity might be destroyed. Then, in the month of April 1492 there occurred the death of Lorenzo de' Medici. It was bitter for him, because he was not quite forty-four years of age, and bitter for his republic, which, because of his prudence, reputation and intellect in everything honorable and excellent, flourished marvelously with riches and all those ornaments and advantages with which a long peace is usually accompanied. But it was also a most untimely death for the rest of Italy, both because of the work he constantly did for the common safety and because he was the means by which the disagreements and suspicions that frequently arose between Ferdinand and Lodovico—two princes almost equal in power and ambition—were moderated and held in check.

The death of Lorenzo was followed a few months later by that of the Pope, as day by day things moved toward the coming disaster. The pontiff, though otherwise of no value to the common weal, was at least useful in that—having laid down the arms he had unsuccessfully taken up against Ferdinand at the instigation of many barons of the Kingdom of Naples at the beginning of his tenure—he turned his attention entirely to idle pleasures, and had no longer either any ambitions for himself or his family which might disturb the peace of Italy. Innocent was followed by Rodrigo Borgia of Valencia, one of the royal cities of Spain. A senior cardinal and a leading figure at the court of Rome, he was raised to the papacy, however, by the disagreements between the cardinals Ascanio Sforza and Giuliano di San Piero in Vincoli, and much more by the fact that, setting a new example in that age, he openly bought, partly with money and partly with promises of offices and favors he would bestow, many of the cardinals' votes. These cardinals, despising the teachings of the Gospels, were not ashamed to sell the power to traffic with sacred treasures in God's holy name, in the highest part of the temple. Cardinal Ascanio led many of them into this abominable contract, no less by his own example than by persuasion and pleading. Corrupted by an insatiable appetite for riches, he got for himself as the price of such wickedness the vice-chancellery, the principal office of the Roman court, churches, castles and his own palace in Rome, full of furniture of enormous value. But for all that he did not escape either divine judgment later or the just hatred and contempt of the men of his time, who were full of horror and alarm at an election conducted with such wicked devices, no less so because the character and habits of the man elected were in great part known to many. It is well known that the King of Naples, though in public he hid his grief, told his wife with tears—which he was unaccustomed to shed even at the death of his children—that a pope had been elected who would be fatal to Italy and the whole Christian world: truly a prophecy not unworthy of the wisdom of Ferdinand. For Alexander VI (as the new Pope wished to be called) possessed remarkable sagacity and acumen, excellent counsel, marvelous powers of persuasion and incredible ability and application in all difficult enterprises; but these virtues were far outweighed by his vices: utterly obscene habits, neither sincerity nor shame nor truth nor faith nor religion, insatiable avarice, immoderate ambition, more than barbarous cruelty and a burning desire to advance his many children in any possible way. Some of them—so that to execute his depraved designs a depraved instrument should not be lacking—were in no way less abominable than their father.

Such were the changes brought about in the state of the Church by the death of Innocent VIII. Yet the affairs of Florence had suffered no less a change by the death of Lorenzo de' Medici. Piero, the eldest of his three sons, had succeeded him without meeting any opposition. He was still very young and, both by age and other qualities, unfit to carry such a burden; and he was unable to proceed with that moderation by which his father—in internal and foreign affairs, while prudently temporizing with the allied princes—had in his lifetime extended his public and private estate, and at his death left among all men the firm opinion that, principally through his efforts, the peace of Italy had been preserved. For hardly had Piero entered the administration of the Republic than, in direct opposition to his father's advice and without informing the principal citizens whose advice was always sought in grave matters—induced by Virginio Orsino his kinsman (both Piero's mother and his wife were of the Orsini family)—he so closely allied himself with Ferdinand and Alfonso, on whom Virginio was dependent, that Lodovico Sforza had just cause to fear that, whenever the Aragonese wished to attack him, they would have the forces of the Florentine Republic with them by authority of Piero de' Medici. This alliance, the germ and origin of so many evils, though it was at first negotiated and concluded with great secrecy, was almost immediately by obscure conjecture suspected by Lodovico Sforza, a most vigilant prince and of very acute intelligence.

When, according to the age-old custom of all Christendom, ambassadors were to be sent to pay homage to the new Pope as the Vicar of Christ on earth, Lodovico Sforza suggested that all the ambassadors of the allies should enter Rome together, and together present themselves at the public consistory before the Pope, and that one of them should speak for all so that in this way, and with great increase of reputation to all, the whole of Italy should see that there existed between them not merely friendship and alliance, but rather such unity that they seemed as one prince and one state. It was typical of Lodovico to endeavor to appear superior to everyone else in prudence by putting forward ideas no one else had thought of. The value of this plan, he said, was evident, because it had been believed that the late Pope had been encouraged to attack the Kingdom of Naples by the appparent disunity of the allies in having sworn obedience to him at different times and with different orations. Ferdinand made no difficulties about accepting Lodovico's suggestion, and the Florentines approved it on the authority of both, while Piero de' Medici said nothing against it in public council. Privately, however, he disagreed strongly, because as he himself was one of the representatives elected by the Republic and he had planned to make his own train most brilliant with fine and almost regal trappings, he realized that entering Rome and presenting himself before the Pope with the other ambassadors of the allies, he would not be able in such a crowd to display the splendor of his magnificent preparations. He was supported in this youthful vanity by the ambitious counsels of Gentile, bishop of Arezzo, likewise one of the chosen ambassadors. As it was to be his duty, on account of his episcopal office and his having professed those studies which are called the Humanities, to speak in the name of the Florentines, he was disappointed beyond measure to lose in this unexpected and unusual way the opportunity to show off his eloquence on an occasion so honorable and solemn. Therefore Piero, inspired partly by his own frivolity and partly by the ambition of others, and yet unwilling that Lodovico Sforza should learn that he was against his plan, asked the King to suggest that each party should act separately as had been done in the past, and to explain that he had thought it over and now felt that these proceedings could not be carried out together without great confusion. The King was anxious to please him, but not so anxious that he would incur Lodovico's displeasure; and so he complied more in the result than in the manner, for he did not hide the fact that it was only at Piero de' Medici's request that he went back on what he had at first agreed to do. Lodovico was angrier at this sudden change than the importance of the occasion merited in itself, complaining bitterly that as the Pope and the entire Roman court already knew of the first plan and who had put it forward, it was now being withdrawn on purpose to damage his reputation. He was even more displeased when he began to realize, through this small and really unimportant incident, that Piero de' Medici had a secret understanding with Ferdinand. And this became more evident every day from the events which followed.

Chapter 3

Franceschetto Cibo, a Genoese and the natural son of Pope Innocent, owned Anguillara, Cervetri, and a few other small castles near Rome. After his father's death he went to live in Florence under the protection of Piero de' Medici, who was the brother of his wife Maddalena. Soon after his arrival in that city, at Piero's insistence, he sold those castles to Virginio Orsino for 40,000 ducats. This was negotiated primarily with Ferdinand, who secretly lent most of the money in the belief that it was to his advantage for Virginio, who was his own captain, supporter and kinsman, to extend his power in the neighborhood of Rome. The King thought that the papal power was an instrument very likely to disturb the Kingdom of Naples, an ancient fee of the Roman Church with an immensely long common frontier with the Church lands; and remembering the disputes he and his father had often had with the popes, and that there was always material at hand for fresh disagreements over frontier demarcation, levying of taxes, conferring of benefices, the petitions of the barons and many other differences which often arise between neighboring states and no less often between the feudal lord and his vassal, he always regarded as one of the bases of his own security that all or most of the most powerful barons of the Roman territory should be dependent on him. At this moment he pursued this aim the more readily, as it was thought that Lodovico Sforza's influence with the Pope would be very great through Cardinal Ascanio, his brother. Also perhaps, as many people thought, he was no less moved by fear that the hatred and greed of his uncle Pope Calixtus III might prove to be hereditary in Alexander. Calixtus, out of an overweening desire for the aggrandizement of his nephew Pietro Borgia, would have sent an army to occupy the Kingdom of Naples at the death of Ferdinand's father Alfonso, if his own death had not interrupted these plans. He claimed that Naples then reverted to the Church and forgot (so short is man's memory of the favors he has received) that it was through Alfonso himself, in whose dominions he was born and whose minister he had been for a long time, that he had obtained his other ecclesiastical preferments and considerable help in attaining the papacy. But it is all too true that wise men do not always discern or judge correctly: inevitably evidence of the weakness of the human mind must often appear. The King, though he was reputed to be a prince of great prudence, did not consider how much blame could be attached to that decision—which at best held hopes of small profit and at the worst could be the origin of serious trouble. For the sale of those insignificant castles aroused the desire for innovations in those very people who shared the common unity and harmony and in whose interests it would have been to ensure its preservation. The Pope asserted that, as they had been transferred without his knowledge, the lands had reverted to the Holy See according to the provisions of the law; feeling that a severe blow had been dealt to papal authority and considering moreover what Ferdinand's motives were, he filled the whole of Italy with complaints against him, against Piero de' Medici, and against Virginio. He swore that wherever his power reached, he would leave nothing undone to promote the dignity and interests of the Holy See.

Lodovico Sforza, who was always suspicious of Ferdinand's actions, was no less agitated; because having vainly deluded himself that the Pope would act according to the advice he and Ascanio gave, he felt that any diminution of Alexander's power would be his own loss. But above all he was worried by the fact that there was no longer room for doubt that the Aragonese and Piero de' Medici, since they worked together in matters of this kind, must have contracted a close alliance. He urged the pontiff as strongly as he could to preserve his own dignity in order to thwart their plans, which were a danger to his affairs, and to draw Alexander more closely to him. And he pointed out to him that he should bear in mind not so much the nature of the present incident, as the importance of the dignity of his high office having been thus openly insulted in the earliest days of his tenure of the Holy See by his own vassals. He should not believe that it was just Virginio's greed or the importance of the castles or any other motive which had inspired Ferdinand, but the desire to try his patience and his temper with insults which might at first seem small. After these, if the Pope put up with them, he would make bold from day to day to attempt something bigger. His ambitions were just the same as those of the other kings of Naples, who were perpetual enemies of the Roman Church; and they had repeatedly attacked the popes and several times occupied Rome. Had not this same King twice sent his armies against two popes under his son's command, right to the walls of Rome? Had he not always been in open enmity with his predecessors? Ferdinand was moved now not only by the example of former kings and by his natural desire for domination, but even more by his desire for revenge for the injury done him by the Pope's uncle Calixtus. The Pope should pay careful heed to these facts and consider that if he bore these early offenses with patience, honored only with outward shows and hollow deference, he would in fact be despised by everyone and give encouragement to more dangerous projects. But if he reacted strongly he would easily preserve the ancient majesty and greatness and the true veneration owed by all the world to the Roman pontiffs. To these powerful arguments he added even more efficacious deeds; for he promptly lent the Pope 40,000 ducats, and recruited 300 soldiers at their common expense, which should however be stationed wherever the Pope wished.

Nevertheless, wishing to avoid the need to enter into fresh difficulties, he urged Ferdinand to persuade Virginio to pacify the Pope with some respectful gesture, pointing out that otherwise serious disturbances might arise from these small beginnings. More freely and with greater insistence he several times advised Piero de' Medici that, considering how expedient for the preservation of the peace of Italy had been his father Lorenzo's policy of acting as mediator and common friend between Ferdinand and himself, he should follow this domestic example and imitate a great man rather than, believing new counsel, give others cause or need to make plans which in the end must be harmful to all. He should remember how the long friendship between the houses of Sforza and Medici had ensured the security and reputation of both, and how many offenses and injuries his father and forefathers and the Florentine Republic had suffered at the hands of the house of Aragon—how often Ferdinand and Alfonso his father before him had attempted, sometimes by force, sometimes by treachery, to occupy the state of Tuscany.

These persuasions and counsels did more harm than good, because Ferdinand, thinking it undignified to give way to Lodovico and Ascanio, whose incitements he considered responsible for the Pope's anger, and urged on by his son Alfonso, secretly advised Virginio not to delay taking possession of the castles in accordance with the contract, and promised to protect him from any attack that might be made on him. On the other hand, with his natural cunning he suggested various kinds of settlement with the Pope, though meanwhile secretly advising Virginio only to agree to terms which would leave him the castles and compensate the Pope with sums of money. Thus Virginio was emboldened to refuse repeatedly the settlements which Ferdinand, so as not to offend the Pope unduly, pressed him to accept. It was evident that in these negotiations Piero de' Medici followed the King's line and that it was useless to try to make him change his mind. Lodovico Sforza, therefore, realizing how serious it was that Florence should be influenced by his enemies, since its attitude had in the past constituted the principal basis of his security, and feeling that the future held many dangers for him, decided to make fresh provisions for his security. He knew how strongly the Aragonese desired his removal from the management of his nephew's affairs. Although Ferdinand, who brought to all his actions unbelievable guile and dissimulation, had tried to keep this feeling hidden, Alfonso, a man of a very open nature, had never refrained from lamenting openly the oppression of his son-in-law, uttering, with more freedom than prudence, threats and insults. Besides this Lodovico knew that Isabella, Giovan Galeazzo's wife, a vigorous young woman, constantly stirred up her grandfather and her father, saying that if they were not moved by the dishonor of seeing her and her husband in such a position, they should at least be moved by the danger to their lives in which they stood together with their children. But what most frightened Lodovico was the knowledge that his name was loathed by all the people of the Duchy of Milan, both because of the many unusual taxes he had levied on them and because of the sympathy everyone felt for Giovan Galeazzo, the legitimate prince. He tried to make people believe that the Aragonese wanted to take possession of the state of Milan and laid claim to it through the ancient provisions of the will of Filippo Maria Visconti who had made Alfonso, Ferdinand's father, his heir; and that to further this plan they wanted to deprive his nephew of his title. Nevertheless he did not succeed by these wiles in moderating the hatred they had conceived of him, nor did he prevent them from reflecting on the wickedness to which men are led by the pestilential greed for power.

Therefore, after he had considered at length the state of his affairs and the imminent dangers, setting aside all other concerns, he gave all his attention to seeking fresh alliances and support. Seeing a great opportunity in the Pope's anger against Ferdinand and the desire the Venetian senate was supposed to entertain that the former alliance should be broken up (which had for so long stood in the way of its ambitions), he proposed to the Pope and the Venetians a new alliance for their mutual advantage. However, the Pope's ruling passion, over and above anger or any other feeling, was a boundless greed for the advancement of his sons. He loved them excessively, and unlike the former popes who to cover up their sinfulness somewhat, used to call them nephews, he always called them sons and showed them to everyone as such. Finding as yet no other opportunity to begin his efforts in this direction, he was negotiating to obtain as a bride for one of his sons one of Alfonso's illegitimate daughters, with a dowry of some rich territory in the Kingdom of Naples. Until he finally lost all hope of this, he lent his ear rather than his mind to the alliance proposed by Lodovico. If he had achieved this ambition, the peace of Italy might not have been destroyed so soon. Although Ferdinand was not against it, Alfonso hated the ambition and pomp of the popes and always refused to agree; and therefore, not showing their distaste for the marriage but putting difficulties in the way of the dowry, they failed to satisfy Alexander. For this reason he was angry and decided to follow Lodovico's advice, driven to it by greed and indignation and in part by fear; for not only was Virginio Orsino in the pay of Ferdinand and at that time extremely powerful in all the Church territories through the excessive favors he enjoyed from the Florentines and from Ferdinand and through the following of the Guelph faction, but also Prospero and Fabrizio, the heads of the Colonna family. Furthermore the cardinal of San Piero in Vincoli, a cardinal of the highest reputation who had withdrawn to the fort of Ostia which he held as bishop of that place, out of fear that the Pope might have designs on his life, had become very friendly with Ferdinand after having been his dire enemy and incited against him in the past first his uncle Pope Sixtus and later Pope Innocent. The Venetian senate, however, was not as ready as had been supposed for this confederation; because although the disunity of others might please them well, they were given pause by the unreliability of the Pope, who grew daily more suspect to all, and by the memory of the leagues they had made with Sixtus and Innocent his immediate predecessors. From the former they had got much trouble without any advantage; and Sixtus, when the war against the Duke of Ferrara was at its height—which he at first had urged them to undertake—had then changed his mind and turned against them with spiritual arms, and also had taken up temporal arms against them together with the rest of Italy. But Lodovico's diligence and industry overcame all the difficulties with the senate and privately with many of the senators. Finally in April 1493 there was signed between the Pope, the Venetian senate and Giovan Galeazzo Duke of Milan (all the decisions of that state were taken in his name) a new league for mutual defense and specifically for the maintenance of Lodovico's rule, with the provision that the Venetians and the Duke of Milan each were to send at once to Rome two hundred men at arms for the safety of the ecclesiastical state and the Pope, and help him with these and if need be with larger forces to retake the castles occupied by Virginio.

These new deliberations had a notable effect throughout the whole of Italy because the Duke of Milan was now cut off from the alliance which for twelve years had maintained common security—although by it, it was expressly forbidden for any of the members to make new alliances without the consent of the others. Therefore, seeing that union on which the balance of power depended broken into unequal parts and the minds of the princes full of suspicion and anger, what else could one expect but that from such seeds like fruits must grow to the detriment of all Italy? The Duke of Calabria and Piero de' Medici, thinking it was safer to forestall than be forestalled, were inclined to listen to Prospero and Fabrizio Colonna. They, secretly encouraged by the Cardinal of San Piero in Vincoli, offered to occupy Rome by surprise with the men at arms of their companies and the men of the Ghibelline faction—provided the Orsini forces followed them, and the Duke took up a position whence, three days after they entered the city, he could come to their assistance. However, Ferdinand wished not to irritate the Pope further but to pacify him and to put right what had been done imprudently up to that time; and he absolutely rejected these counsels which he thought would engender not safety but greater trials and dangers. He made up his mind to do all he could, no longer merely in appearance but in fact, to make up the quarrel over the castles, believing that if that cause of so much discord were removed, Italy would easily and almost of herself return to her earlier condition. But one may not always remove the effects by removing their causes. For, as it often happens that decisions taken through fear seem unequal to the danger to those who fear, Lodovico was not sure he had found adequate support for his security. Doubting, because the purposes of the Venetian senate and the Pope were so different from his own, that he could rely for very long on the alliance with them, and that therefore his affairs might for various reasons meet with many difficulties, he applied his mind more to curing from the roots the first ill which appeared than to those which might in consequence arise later. He forgot how dangerous it may be to use medicine more powerful than the nature of the disease and the constitution of the patient warranted. As though embarking on greater risks was the sole remedy to present dangers, he decided, in order to ensure his own security with foreign arms—as he could not rely on his own forces and his Italian allies—to do everything he could to persuade Charles VIII King of France to attack the Kingdom of Naples, to which he laid claim through the ancient rights of the Angevins. . . .

Chapter 5

As rumors of what was being planned beyond the Alps were already beginning to spread in Italy—though at first from unreliable sources—people took up a wide variety of attitudes. Many thought it a matter of the greatest significance, because of the power of the Kingdom of France, the readiness of that nation for new enterprises and the divisions among the Italian peoples. Others regarded it more as a youthful impulse than a considered decision, and thought that when it had boiled up for a while, it would easily pass off. Their reasons for thinking so were the age and character of the King, the natural unreliability of the French and the difficulties which always beset great enterprises. Ferdinand, against whom all this was being contrived, did not show much fear, saying that it would be a very difficult campaign because if they intended to attack him from the sea they would find him provided with a fleet large enough to fight them in the open sea, and the ports well fortified and all in his hands: there was no baron in the country who could let them in as Jean d'Anjou had been by the Prince of Rossano and other great nobles. The expedition by land would be difficult, long and risky, since the whole length of Italy had to be traversed, so that every state would have cause to fear, and perhaps Lodovico Sforza most of all—although he pretended that the common danger applied only to others, because Milan was so near to France, and the King would find it easier and probably be more anxious to occupy it. As the Duke of Milan was so closely related to him, how could Lodovico be sure that the King did not intend to free him from Lodovico's oppression? Especially as just a few years before the King had openly stated that he would not allow his cousin Giovan Galeazzo to be so unjustly oppressed. The affairs of the Aragonese were not in such straits that the hope of their weakness should give the French courage to attack them, as he was well supplied with many fine troops, plenty of chargers, munitions, artillery, and all provisions needed for war, and so much money that he could easily obtain further supplies of anything he needed. Besides numerous able captains in his service, he had at the head of his armies his eldest son the Duke of Calabria, an officer of great renown and no less courage, with many years of experience in all the wars of Italy. To his own resources must be added the ready assistance of his relatives, since it was not likely that he would lack the help of the King of Spain, his cousin and his wife's brother, both on account of their close kinship and because he would not care to have the French so near to Sicily.

This was what Ferdinand was saying in public, exaggerating his own power and belittling as far as he could the strength and chances of his enemies. But as he was a king of remarkable prudence and very great experience, inwardly he was tormented by serious doubts, remembering the difficulties he had had with France at the beginning of his reign. He really believed that the war would involve him with an enemy who was extremely aggressive and powerful, far superior to himself in cavalry, foot soldiers, navies, artillery, money, and men full of ambition to expose themselves to any danger for the glory and greatness of their king. He on the other hand could rely on nothing, as his kingdom was full of hatred for the name of Aragon or strong sympathy for the rebels, and the majority of his people in any case always eager for a change. Fortune would weigh more than fidelity with them, and common opinion of his situation more than reality. The funds he had amassed would not cover the expenses of defense, and as rebellion and tumult would break out everywhere because of the war, in a flash all his revenues would vanish. He had many enemies in Italy, and not one reliable and constant friendship. Who had not been damaged at one time or another by his arms or intrigues? From Spain, as past experience and the conditions of that kingdom showed, he could hope for no other assistance in his peril than generous promises and great talk of preparations—but only small and tardy results. His fear was increased by many predictions of misfortune to his house, which had come to his notice at different times, partly through newly discovered ancient writings, partly through the words of men who, often unsure of the present, claim certain knowledge of the future: things which in prosperous times are little believed, but gain all too much credence when adversity comes. Anguished by these considerations, and fear seeming incomparably greater to him than hope, he realized that the only remedy to these dangers was either to dispel such thoughts from the mind of the King of France by making an agreement as soon as possible, or to remove some of the causes which incited him to war. He already had ambassadors in France, sent there to negotiate the betrothal of Ciarlotta, the daughter of his second son Don Federigo, to the King of Scotland. As this girl was the daughter of a sister of Charles' mother and had been brought up at the French court, the matter was being handled there. Ferdinand gave these ambassadors further instructions in these affairs, and sent out in addition Cammillo Pandone who had been to France before for him. He was secretly to offer the nobles great gifts and bribes, and if there were no other way of pacifying him, he was to do all he could to make peace with the King by offering him terms of tribute and other tokens of submission. Furthermore, not only did he intervene with all his energy and authority to settle the quarrel over the castles bought by Virginio Orsino, whose obstinacy he lamented as having been the cause of all the upheavals, but he also reopened with the Pope their former negotiations for a marriage alliance. But his main care and attention was directed toward mollifying and reassuring Lodovico Sforza, the origin and prime instigator of all the trouble, for he believed that it was fear more than anything else that had led him to so dangerous a step. So placing his own safety before the interests of his granddaughter and the safety of her child, he offered Lodovico through various channels to accept anything he liked to do in the affairs of Giovan Galeazzo and the Duchy of Milan. He ignored Alfonso's opinion, who, taking heart from Lodovico's natural timidity, and forgetting that the timid man is inclined to rash decisions through fear no less easily than the bold man through temerity, felt that the best way to make him withdraw from these plans of his was to frighten and threaten him.

In the end, after many difficulties arising more on Virginio's side than the Pope's, the dispute over the castles was settled. Don Federigo had a hand in the agreement, having been sent to Rome by his father for this purpose. It was agreed that Virginio should keep the castles, paying the Pope as much as he had paid Franceschetto Cibo for their purchase. The betrothal of Sancia Alfonso's natural daughter to Don Gioffredo the Pope's younger son was also concluded, though both were too young for the marriage to be consummated. The conditions were that Don Gioffredo should go to live in Naples in a few months time, and should receive in dowry the Principality of Squillace with an income of 10,000 ducats a year, and be given command of a hundred men at arms at Ferdinand's expense. This confirmed the belief held by many that what the Pope had negotiated in France had been done largely to frighten the

Aragonese into submitting to these conditions. Ferdinand also tried to ally himself with the Pope for their common defense, but the Pope raised many difficulties, and he obtained only a promise given by brief in strict secret, to help him defend the Kingdom of Naples if Ferdinand promised to do likewise for the papal state. When this was settled, the Pope dismissed from his territory the forces which the Venetians and the Duke of Milan had sent to help him. Ferdinand had equal hopes of success in the negotiations. He then began with Lodovico Sforza, who showed consummate art in soothing the other princes' fears and encouraging their hopes. Sometimes he expressed his disapproval of the French king's intentions as dangerous to all Italy; sometimes he put forward as his excuse that he had been obliged to listen to the demands made on him, as he said, by that king, because he held Genoa in fee and because of the ancient alliance with the house of France: sometimes he promised Ferdinand—and sometimes the Pope and Piero de' Medici separately—to do all in his power to discourage Charles, his object being to deter them from uniting against him before the French affair was decided and planned. He was believed the more easily because it was considered that bringing the King of France into Italy would be so unsafe for himself as well that it seemed impossible that he would not draw back in the end when he realized the danger.

The whole summer passed amid these discussions. Lodovico behaved in such a way that, while he avoided offending the King of France, neither Ferdinand nor the Pope nor the Florentines despaired of his promises nor entirely relied upon them. But all this time the preparations were being diligently made in France for the new expedition, for which the King's enthusiasm grew daily against the advice of nearly all the great nobles. To make his way easier, he made up his quarrel with Ferdinand and Isabella, King and Queen of Spain, who were rulers at that time very celebrated and renowned for their wisdom, for having brought their kingdoms out of great turbulence into the greatest peace and obedience, and because they had recently, in a war lasting ten years, regained for Christendom the Kingdom of Granada which had been held by the Moors of Africa for almost eight hundred years. Because of that victory they received from the Pope, with great approbation from all Christians, the title of Catholic Monarchs. In this treaty with Charles—which was confirmed with the greatest solemnity and with public oaths sworn by both parties in church—it was provided that Ferdinand and Isabella (Spain was ruled jointly in their names) would not help the Aragonese either directly or indirectly, would not form new ties of marriage with them or in any way oppose Charles by defending Naples. To obtain these pledges, Charles, beginning with certain loss in exchange for uncertain gain, returned without any payment whatever Perpignan and the whole

County of Roussillon, which had been pledged many years before to his
father Louis by King John of Aragon, Ferdinand's father. This was most
harmful to the whole Kingdom of France, because that county, situated
at the foot of the Pyrenees and therefore, according to the ancient frontiers, part of Gaul, prevented the Spaniards from invading on that side.
For the same reason Charles made peace with Maximilian King of the
Romans, and with Philip Archduke of Austria his son, who had serious
differences with him both old and new, their origin being that Louis his
father had, on the death of Charles, Duke of Burgundy and Count of
Flanders and of many other neighboring lands, occupied the Duchy of
Burgundy, the County of Artois and many other lands possessed by him.
As a result there had been a war between Louis and Marie, the Duke's
only child, who shortly after her father's death had married Maximilian.
Then Marie being dead and Philip her son by Maximilian having succeeded to his mother's inheritance, peace had been made with Louis of
France—more at the wish of the people of Flanders than that of Maximilian. To cement this peace Louis' son Charles was married to Marguerite,
Philip's sister, and although she was a minor she was brought to live in
France. After she had been there a number of years, Charles repudiated
her and took as his wife Anne, who held the Duchy of Brittany since her
father Francis had died without male issue. Thus Maximilian received
a double insult: being deprived at once of his daughter's marriage and of
his own bride, because earlier he had himself married Anne by proxy.
Nevertheless, as he was not powerful enough to carry on by himself the
war which had broken out again as a result of this offense; and as the
Flemish people, who were ruling themselves during Philip's minority,
refused to be at war with the French, and because the kings of Spain and
England had made peace with them, he agreed to do the same. By this
peace Charles restored to Philip his sister Marguerite, who had been kept
in France until then, together with the County of Artois, but retaining the
fortresses with the obligation to give them back at the end of four years
when Philip would attain his majority and so be able to ratify the agreement. These lands had been designated as Marguerite's dowry in the
earlier peace made with Louis.

When France had made peace with all her neighbors, the war against
Naples was fixed for the following year, and in the interval all the necessary preparations were to be made, which were constantly being urged
by Lodovico Sforza. He (as men's ambitions grow by degrees) no longer
thought only of making himself safe in power, but aiming at higher
things, had in mind to transfer the Duchy of Milan entirely into his own
hands through the opportunity offered by the difficulties of the Aragonese. To give some color of justice to so great an injustice and establish
his position more firmly against all eventualities, he married Bianca

Maria, his niece and Giovan Galeazzo's sister, to Maximilian who had lately succeeded to the Roman Empire through the death of his father Frederick. As a dowry he promised him in installments 400,000 ducats in cash, and 40,000 ducats in jewels and other goods. In return Maximilian, who was more eager for the money than for the family alliance, undertook to give Lodovico, at the expense of his new brother-in-law Giovan Galeazzo, the investiture of the Duchy of Milan for himself, his children and descendants, as though that duchy had always lacked a legitimate duke since the death of Filippo Maria Visconti. He promised to send him the privileges drawn up in complete form as soon as the last installment was paid.

The Visconti, who were noblemen of Milan, during the most bloody factions of the Guelphs and Ghibellines in Italy, when the Guelphs were finally driven out, became (for this is nearly always the outcome of civil war) from being leaders of one part of Milan, masters of it all. When they had been in this position of power for many years, they sought, according to the usual course of tyrannies (so that what was usurpation might seem theirs of right), to give their fortunes the color of legality and later to illustrate them with fine titles. So they obtained from the emperors—of whom Italy was beginning to know the name more than the power—first the title of Captains and then of Imperial Vicars; and finally Giovan Galeazzo, who, having received the County of Virtus from his father-in-law, King John of France, called himself Conte di Virtù, obtained from Wenceslas King of the Romans for himself and his male descendants the title of Duke of Milan—in which he was succeeded in turn by Giovan Maria and Filippo Maria his sons. The male line failed on the death of Filippo who, in his will named as his heir Alfonso King of Aragon and Naples on account of the great friendship the latter had formed for him after he had set him free, and even more in order to ensure that the Duchy of Milan, with so powerful a defender, would not be occupied by the Venetians, who were already visibly aspiring to do so. However, Francesco Sforza, a most distinguished captain of that time and no less gifted in the arts of peace than in those of war, helped by a combination of circumstances and no less by his own determination to rule rather than to keep faith, seized the Duchy by armed force and claimed it for his wife Bianca Maria, the natural daughter of Filippo Maria. It is said that afterward he could have had the investiture from the Emperor Frederick quite cheaply; but he scorned it, being sure that he could retain the Duchy with the same arts by which he had first acquired it. Galeazzo his son went on without investiture, and so did Giovan Galeazzo, his grandson. Hence Lodovico was not only criminal toward his living nephew, but insulted the memory of his dead father and brother by inferring that none of them had been legitimate Dukes of Milan, and he obtained the investiture from Maximilian as though the state had reverted to the Empire, taking the title of fourth Duke of Milan instead of seventh. However these actions were known only to very few while his nephew was alive. Besides he used to say—taking as his example Cyrus the younger brother of Ataxerxes King of Persia, and supporting it with the opinions of many legal authorities—that he had precedence over his brother, not in age, but in being their father's first son born after he had become Duke of Milan. These two arguments (leaving out the example of Cyrus) were stated in the Imperial Privilege. In order to cover up Lodovico's greed, though in a ridiculous manner, it was added in separate letters that it was not customary for the Holy Empire to give a state to anyone who had previously held it on the authority of others; and therefore Maximilian had turned down Lodovico's requests that Giovan Galeazzo should have the investiture, as the latter had already held the Duchy from the Milanese people. Lodovico's new family ties with Maximilian led Ferdinand to hope that he might be cooling off in his friendship for the King of France, supposing that his alliance with a rival—and an enemy for so many good reasons—together with his handing over so much money, would generate mistrust between them; and that Lodovico, taking courage from this new connection, would be bolder to separate himself from the French. Lodovico nourished these hopes with the greatest skill, and nonetheless (such was his sagacity and dexterity) at the same time he kept up relations with Ferdinand and the other rulers of Italy while remaining on good terms with the King of the Romans and the King of France. Ferdinand also hoped that the Venetian senate, to whom he had sent ambassadors, would object to a prince so much greater than themselves entering Italy where they held the highest position in power and authority. The Spanish monarchs too gave him hope and encouragement, promising him powerful assistance in case they were unable to prevent the expedition by their authority and persuasion.

On the other hand the King of France was making an effort to remove the obstacles and difficulties he might meet on this side of the mountains now that he had dealt with those on the other side. Therefore he sent Perron de Baschi, a man not unskilled in the affairs of Italy where he had been under Jean d'Anjou. He communicated to the Pope, to the Venetians and to the Florentines the King's decision to regain the Kingdom of Naples and urged them all to join him in an alliance. But all he took away were hopes and replies in general terms, because as the war was planned only for the following year, none was willing to reveal his intentions so early. The King also summoned the Florentine spokesmen who had been sent to him with Ferdinand's consent to reassure him that they were not supporting the Aragonese, and requested them to promise him free passage and victuals for his army through their territory against due payment, and to send with it a hundred soldiers which he demanded, he said, as a token of the Florentine Republic's continuing friendship. Although it was pointed out to him that they could not make such a declaration without grave danger before his army was actually in Italy, and that he could in any case rely on the city for anything that was in accord with their long friendship and fidelity to the crown of France, nevertheless they were forced by French impetuosity to promise—being threatened otherwise with the closing down of Florentine trade which was very considerable in that kingdom. As it was later evident, this was done on the advice of Lodovico Sforza, who was then the guide and director of all their negotiations with the Italians. Piero de' Medici endeavored to persuade Ferdinand that these demands would matter so little to the result of the war that it might be more useful to him for Piero and the Republic to remain friends with Charles and so perhaps be in a position to mediate in some settlement. Besides this he also pointed out the terrible blame and hatred which would fall on him in Florence if the Florentine merchants were expelled from France. It was, he said, a matter of good faith, the principal basis of alliances, that each of the allies should bear with patience a certain degree of inconvenience so that the other might not incur graver losses. But Ferdinand, considering how much his security and credit would be diminished if the Florentines abandoned him, did not accept these arguments and complained bitterly that Piero's constancy and faith should begin so soon to fall below what he had hoped of him. Therefore Piero, who was determined to keep the friendship of the Aragonese before all else, contrived to make the French wait for the answer they were urgently demanding, finally saying that the intentions of the Republic would be communicated through fresh ambassadors.

At the end of this year the alliance between the Pope and Ferdinand began to weaken, either because the Pope hoped by causing fresh difficulties to obtain from him greater concessions, or because he thought he could induce him in this way to force the Cardinal of San Piero in Vincoli to obey him. The Pope was extremely anxious for the cardinal to come to Rome, and offered as guarantors of his safety the College of Cardinals, Ferdinand and the Venetians. He was uneasy about his absence because of the importance of the fortress of Ostia (for around Rome he held Ronciglione and Grottaferrata), the considerable following and authority he enjoyed at the court, and finally because of his natural fondness for change and his obstinacy in affronting any danger rather than give way in the smallest degree over anything he had decided. Ferdinand argued effectively that he could not force Vincoli to return, as he was so full of mistrust that no surety seemed appropriate to the risk he ran. Ferdinand also complained of his ill luck with the Pope, who always blamed him for what was really the fault of others. The Pope had thought Virginio had bought the castles on Ferdinand's advice and with his money, and yet the purchase had been carried out without his participation; whereas it was he who had got Virginio to come to an agreement with the Pope and put up the money which was paid in compensation for the castles. The Pope did not accept these excuses, but went on complaining about Ferdinand with bitter and almost threatening words, so that it seemed that there could be no lasting basis to their reconciliation. . . .

Chapter 9

Now not only the preparations made by land and sea, but the heavens and mankind joined in proclaiming the future calamites of Italy. Those who profess to know the future either by science or by divine inspiration affirmed with one voice that greater and more frequent changes were at hand—events stranger and more horrible than had been seen in any part of the world for many centuries. Men were no less terrified by the wide-spread news that unnatural things in heaven and earth had appeared in various parts of Italy. One night in Puglia three suns stood in an overcast sky with horrible thunder and lightning. In the Arezzo district a vast number of armed men on enormous horses were seen passing through the air day after day with a hideous noise of drums and trumpets. In many places in Italy the sacred statues and images sweated visibly. Everywhere many monsters were born, both human and animal; and many other things outside the order of nature had happened in all kinds of places. All these filled the people of Italy with unspeakable fear, fright-ened as they were already by the rumors of the power of the French and the ferocity with which (as all the histories related) they had in the past overrun and despoiled the whole of Italy, sacked and put to fire and sword the city of Rome and conquered many provinces in Asia; indeed there was no part of the world that had not at some time felt the force of their arms. Men were only surprised that among so many portents there should not have been seen the comet which the ancients reputed a cer-tain harbinger of the downfall of rulers and states.

The approach of realities daily increased belief in heavenly signs, predictions, prognostications and portents. For Charles, firm in his re-solve, now came to Vienne in the Dauphiné. He could not be moved from his decision to invade Italy in person either by the entreaties of all his subjects or by lack of money, which was so scarce that he was only able to provide for his daily needs by pawning for a small sum certain jewels loaned to him by the Duke of Savoy, the Marchioness of Monferrat and other nobles of his court. The money he had earlier collected from the revenues of France, and that which had been given him by Lodovico Sforza, he had spent partly on the navy in which from the start great hopes of victory were placed, and part he had handed out thoughtlessly to a variety of persons before he left Lyons. As at that time princes were not so quick to extort money from their peoples as—riding roughshod over respect for God and men—they were later taught by avarice and excessive greed to do, it was not easy for him to accumulate any more. On so weak a basis was it proposed to mount so vast a war! For he was guided more by rashness and impetuousness than by prudence and good counsel.

Yet as often happens when one begins to carry out new, great and difficult enterprises, although the decision has been made, all the reasons that can be adduced against them come to mind; so when the King was about to leave and in fact his troops were already on their way toward the mountains, a grave murmur of complaint arose throughout the court, some pointing out the difficulties of so large an expedition, others the danger of the faithlessness of the Italians and especially of Lodovico Sforza—recalling the warning that had come from Florence of his treachery (and as it happened, certain moneys which were expected from him were slow in coming). So the expedition was not only boldly opposed by those who had always condemned it (as happens when events seem to confirm one's opinion), but some of those who had been its chief supporters—among them the bishop of St. Malo—began to waver considerably. Finally when this rumor reached the King's ears, it had such an effect throughout the court and in his own mind and created such a disinclination to go any further that he at once ordered his troops to stop. As a result many nobles who were already on their way, hearing the news that it had been decided not to invade Italy, returned to the court. And it is believed that this change of plan would have been easily put into effect if the Cardinal of San Piero in Vincoli—fatal instrument then and before and after of the ills of Italy—had not rekindled with all his authority and vehemence people's flagging enthusiasm and keyed the King up to his original decision. He not only reminded him of the reasons which had inspired him to undertake so glorious an expedition, but showed him with grave arguments what infamy would be his throughout the world from the frivolous changing of so worthy a decision. Why then had he weakened the frontiers of his kingdom by returning the County of Artois? Why to the deep displeasure of nobles and commoners alike had he opened one of the gates of France to the King of Spain by giving him the County of Roussillon? Other kings might give away such things either to free themselves from urgent danger or to achieve some great gain. But what need, what danger had moved him? What reward did he expect, what fruit could result from it if it were not to have bought most dearly a greater humiliation? What accidents had arisen, what difficulties supervened, what dangers appeared since he had made known his intentions to all the world? Had not rather the hope of victory visibly grown? For the foundations on which the enemy had based all their hopes for defense had proved vain. The Aragonese navy, which had shamefully fled into the harbor of Leghorn after its unsuccessful attack on Portovenere, could do nothing further against Genoa, defended by so many troops and by a fleet greater than theirs; and the land army which had been halted in Romagna by the resistance of a small number of French troops did not dare to advance any further. What would they do when the news spread throughout Italy that the King had crossed the mountains with so great an army? What tumults would arise everywhere? What would be the Pope's terror when from his own palace he saw the Colonna troops at the gates of Rome? How terrified Piero de' Medici would be, finding his own family against him and the city faithful to the French and longing to regain the liberty he had oppressed! There was nothing that could hold back the King's advance to the borders of Naples; and when he got there he would find the same tumults and fears and everywhere retreat and rebellion. Was he afraid their money might run out? When they heard the clash of his arms and the terrible roar of his artillery, all the Italians would vie with one another to bring him money. If any resisted, however, the spoils, plunder and wealth of the conquered would support his army. For in Italy, for many years used to the semblance of war rather than to its realities, there was no strength to restrain the fury of the French. What fears, therefore, what confusion, dreams, vain shadows had entered his mind? How had he lost his spirit so soon? Where was the ferocity with which four days earlier he boasted that he could conquer all Italy put together? He should consider that his plans were no longer in his own hands. Things had gone too far, with the handing over of territories, the ambassadors he had heard, sent and expelled, the expenses already laid out, the preparations made, the declarations published everywhere, and his own advance almost as far as the Alps. However dangerous the enterprise, he was obliged to go on with it; for there was now no compromise between glory and infamy, triumph and shame, between being either the greatest king in the world or the most despised. And as his victory and triumph were already prepared and manifest, what ought he to do?

These things, which are the substance of what the cardinal said— although conveyed according to his nature with direct statements and impetuous and fiery gestures rather than ornate words—so moved the King that without listening any longer except to those who urged him to war, he left Vienna the same day accompanied by all the nobles and captains of the Kingdom of France except the Duke of Bourbon in whose hands he left the administration of the realm in his absence, and the admiral and a few others delegated to govern and guard the most important provinces. He crossed into Italy over the pass of Montgenèvre which is much easier than Mont Cenis, and was the pass used by Hannibal the Carthaginian in ancient times though with incredible difficulty. The King entered Asti on September 9, 1494, bringing with him into Italy the seeds of innumerable disasters, terrible events and change in almost everything. His invasion was not only the origin of changes of government, subversion of kingdoms, devastation of the countryside, slaughter of cities, cruel murders, but also of new habits, new customs, new and bloody methods of warfare, diseases unknown until that day; and the instruments of peace and harmony in Italy were thrown into such confusion that they have never since been able to be reconstituted, so that other foreign nations and barbarian armies have been able to devastate and trample wretchedly upon her. To make her unhappy fate worse, so that our humiliation should not be tempered by the qualities of the victor, the man whose coming caused so many ills, though amply endowed with material blessings, lacked practically all virtues of mind and body.

For it is true that Charles from boyhood was physically weak and unhealthy, small in stature, and extremely ugly in appearance except for the brightness and dignity of his eyes. His limbs were so proportioned that he seemed more like a monster than a man. Not only did he lack all knowledge of the arts, but he barely knew how to read and write. He was greedy to rule but quite incapable of it, because allowing himself to be continually influenced by his favorites, he retained neither majesty nor authority with them. Averse from all duties and tasks, he showed little prudence and judgment even in those he did attend to. If anything in him seemed at all praiseworthy, when looked at closely, it appeared further removed from virtue than from vice. He aspired to glory but out of impulse rather than wisdom; he was generous but without discretion or discrimination, often firm in his decisons but more often out of ill-founded obstinacy than true constancy; and what many called kindness in him was more deserving of the name of indifference and weakmindedness.

Jean Bodin

4

Criticism of the traditional legal curricula of the French universities in the middle decades of the sixteenth century was of minor importance compared to the civil and religious warfare which was undermining the power of the French monarchy and the stability of the French nation. Yet it was Jean Bodin's concern for revising the study of jurisprudence that led him to seek a new method that could synthesize all human knowledge, and led him later on, as the anarchy of civil war worsened, to devote himself to the practical problems of achieving peace and religious toleration. The desire to bring order out of chaos, whether in learning, in politics, or in religion, was the one underlying motive of his life's work.

In 1551, after fourteen years of the monastic life near his native Angers, and at Paris, Bodin began the study of law at the University of Toulouse. He remained at the University for ten years, and had become a distinguished teacher of jurisprudence before he left the academy to practice law in the king's service. During these years he produced the *Method for the Easy Comprehension of History,* first published in 1566. Bodin's aim in the *Method* was to demonstrate how the study of law, hitherto mainly confined to the exegesis of Roman law and the revered *Code* of Justinian, might be expanded into the study of universal law, taking into account a comparison of the laws and customs of all nations. This was Bodin's way of responding to the criticism of other legal scholars, especially the Italian Humanists, that the law, as studied in the French universities, was too parochial in scope and too worshipful of the wisdom of the Roman lawyers. With an intimate knowledge of the great works of classical antiquity and a formal theological training behind him, Bodin wanted to combine all learning, encompassing the history of the various nations of the world, with special attention to the influence of geography and climate, into a well-ordered, organic whole.

These were ambitious goals and Bodin could achieve partial success at best. In his urge to find a method which could order, define, and limit the vast study of universal law, now called "history," he finds himself constantly caught up in a confusing mesh of endless deductive syllogisms. Even in our selection, which covers the relatively uncomplicated opening pages of the *Method,* Bodin goes back and forth in his discussion of divine, natural, and human history, which he had promised to keep separate.

The *Method* is significant, of course, not for the inevitable difficulties to be encountered in the study of all human activity, but for the progress Bodin makes toward expanding historical researches, and for the methods he employs in organizing historical investigation chronologically and geographically. He presents a catalogue of all the historians known to him, and provides criteria for judging the reliability of these historians, stressing the necessity for impartiality and his preference for primary over secondary material. Out of his zeal to encourage the profitable study of history comes Bodin's advice to students to take notes. One of the most attractive qualities of the *Method* is the sympathy it arouses in the reader for the author, who is obviously eager to learn yet is honestly frustrated by the enormous amount of historical literature, good and bad, which he must master.

The most modern aspect of the *Method* was the manner in which Bodin examined the connection between the laws and history of nations and their locations and climates. It looks ahead to Montesquieu. Bodin pursued this same type of analysis ten years later in the *Six Books on the Commonwealth,* but the change of subject from history to political theory reflected the events of the intervening ten years. From 1566 to 1576, the year that the *Six Books* were published, religious war had broken out with increasing ferocity four different times. Bodin himself was a witness in 1572 to the atrocious Massacre of Saint Bartholomew in Paris. He now turned his attention to finding the form of government that could suppress rebellion and prevent anarchy. The result was a famous work, more influential, and even more complex, than the *Method.*

The remedy Bodin found for the chaos of civil war was a strong monarchy based on the absolute sovereignty of the state. All nature bore testimony to the necessity of a patriarchal community where, in order to survive, the herd followed the leader. All history showed that the only governments able to endure were monarchies. It was the monarch's responsibility to establish laws that none but him could disobey. Such authoritarian rule was seen as the only remedy for a society plagued by ruinous and constant upheaval. There were ten editions of the *Six Books* in Bodin's lifetime, and numerous translations were subsequently made as civil war spread to the rest of Europe.

Bodin was entirely justified in maintaining that he was no advocate of unbridled absolutism. He insisted that the monarch be restrained by God's commandments, and that he institute laws that would benefit all the people. Bodin's own brief political career in the Estates of Blois in 1576 proved his interest in equitable government for the whole nation. As a representative of the third estate, he defended its right to dissent from the decrees of the two more highly privileged orders, the clergy and the nobility. He also opposed further persecution of the French Protestants, and objected to the confiscation of land by the nobility for their own profit. His outspoken opposition to these time-honored injustices of the old regime cost him the favor of the Court; and, despite his monarchist *Six Books*, Bodin retired to Laon as a minor administrative official, when his patron, the king's brother, died in 1583.

In the work of his retirement, the *Colloquium Heptaplomeres*, Bodin pleaded for an end to religious persecution in a dialogue which anticipates in form and in meaning some of the dialogues in Voltaire's *Philosophical Dictionary*. The discussion takes place among seven speakers: an authoritarian Roman Catholic, representatives of two forms of Protestantism, a Mohammedan, a Jew, a simple theist, and a skeptic who does not observe any form of religious worship. Bodin shows some sympathy for each of his interlocutors, and his lesson is tolerance of all religious views. If men could abandon dogma and idolatrous worship, and understand that a simple faith in the Decalogue is all that is necessary for practical morality, then they all might live in peace. Bodin's final work, although it had to wait for the nineteenth century for publication, contains the most eloquent expression of the purpose which informed all his works.

Any attempt to evaluate Bodin as a thinker, in any of the subjects he treated, is always complicated by his belief in witchcraft and astrology. The precursor of Montesquieu in sociology, and of Voltaire in the study of natural religion, he still believed that history was as much governed by the constellation of the stars and number mysticism as by climate and geography. It is best to accept Bodin as a pioneer in the study of history and social science, without expecting him to step outside his century.

Selected Bibliography

The excellence and scope of Roger Chauviré's *Jean Bodin, auteur de la République* (1914) have never been equaled. Apart from its comprehensive account of Bodin's life and writings, this splendid work has all the perspicuity that Chauviré finds lacking in Bodin. Julian H. Franklin's terse *Jean Bodin and the Sixteenth-Century Revolution in the Methodology of Law and History* (1963) manages to specify the ways in which Bodin modified and broadened the study of law and history. Beatrice Reynolds sympathetically examines Bodin's political thinking in the background of the sixteenth-century wars of religion in *Proponents of Limited Monarchy in Sixteenth Century France: Francis Hotman and Jean Bodin* (1931). George H. Sabine's essay "The *Colloquium Heptaplomeres* of Jean Bodin," in *Persecution and Liberty: Essays in Honor of George Lincoln Burr* (1931), 271–310, is a serious and helpful study of a complicated work.

Besides his illuminating observations in political theory and history, Bodin was the first to describe the course of inflation in sixteenth-century France. His little treatise on economics, which includes some of his suggestions for improvement, is available as the *Response of Jean Bodin to the Paradoxes of Malestroit* (translated by G. A. Moore, 1947).

METHOD FOR THE EASY
COMPREHENSION OF HISTORY

Preamble on the Ease, Delight, and Advantage of Historical Reading

Although history has many eulogists, who have adorned her with honest and fitting praises, yet among them no one has commended her more truthfully and appropriately than the man who called her the "master of life." This designation, which implies all the adornments of all virtues and disciplines, means that the whole life of man ought to be shaped according to the sacred laws of history, even as to the canon of Polycletus. Certainly philosophy, which itself is called the "guide of life," would remain silent among dead things, even though the extreme limits of good and evil had been set, unless all sayings, deeds, and plans are considered in relation to the account of days long past.[1] From these not only are present-day affairs readily interpreted but also future events are inferred, and we may acquire reliable maxims for what we should seek and avoid. So it seemed to me remarkable that, among so many writers and in so learned an age, until now there has been no one who has compared famous histories of our forbears with each other and with the account of deeds done by the ancients. Yet this could be accomplished easily if all kinds of human activities were brought together and if from them a variety of examples should be arranged, appropriately and each in its place, in order that those who had devoted themselves entirely to crime might be reviled by well-earned curses, but those who were known for any virtue might be extolled according to their deserts.

This, then, is the greatest benefit of historical books, that some men, at least, can be incited to virtue and others can be frightened away from vice. Although the good are praiseworthy in themselves, even if they are acclaimed by no one, nevertheless it is proper that both living and dead, in addition to other rewards offered to excellence, should attain due need of praise, which many people think is the only real reward. The wicked

Jean Bodin's Method for the Easy Comprehension of History translated by Beatrice Reynolds, New York: Columbia University Press, 1966, pp. 9–29. Reprinted by permission of the publisher. We reproduce the translator's footnotes.
[1]Philosophy would lack vitality without illustration from history.

may observe with annoyance that the good who have been oppressed by them are exalted even to the heavens, but that they themselves and the name of their race will suffer eternal disgrace. Even if they dissemble, yet they cannot bear this without the bitterest sense of grief. What Trogus Pompey[2] reported about Herostratus and Titus Livy[3] about Manlius Capitolinus is not true, not even probable, I think—that they were more eager for great fame than for good fame. I believe that despondency and madness impelled the former; the other was led by a hope of increased prestige through ruling his fellow citizens. Otherwise it must be confessed that men eager for glory bear insults with equanimity, which is a contradiction in itself. If the minds of the wicked were revealed, as we read in the pages of Plato, we should see there welts and lacerations from the scourge, bloody marks on the beaten body, or even impressions of a burning iron;[4] it is unbelievable to what extent the fear of infamy rends and consumes those among them who are more eager for glory. Even if they have no taste for true praise, yet they strive for empty fame. Although some are so stupid that they believe their souls die along with their bodies, yet as long as they live they think posterity's opinion is of the utmost importance, and they often pray that a conflagration of the world may follow their death. Nero, indeed, used to hope for this in his own lifetime. Tiberius Augustus is a case in point: although he did many things cruelly and lustfully, due to his weak character, yet he would have been worse if he had not cared for fame. So he sought a hiding place for his crimes in some remote isle, and since he judged himself unworthy to rule he obstinately refused the power and title of "father of his country" (as Suetonius said)[5] lest at a later day, as a greater disgrace, he should be found unequal to such high honors. There is extant a speech of his, delivered in the Senate, in which he says one thing must be won by a prince—a favorable reputation. Otherwise his virtues are ignored through his neglect of fame. Letters exist, written by him in mournful mood, in which he miserably laments his past life and complains that he already feels the grave scorn of posterity, yet cannot change his habits. This princely fear of infamy, this lesson of history, seemed to Cornelius Tacitus so significant that it alone ought to incite men to read and write on the subject.

But of what value is it that this branch of learning is the inventor and

---

[2]Trogus Pompey was a historian of the time of Augustus. In the *Historiae Philippicae* he covers the story of the Near East from Ninus to Philip of Macedon. This exists only in the epitome made by Justin.

[3]Titus Livy, *De urbe condita*, VI, 11.

[4]The idea is that the tyrant suffers within his own soul the tortures he has inflicted on others. See Plato, *Gorgias*, 525.

[5]Suetonius Tranquillus, *Lives of the Caesars*, III, 67.

preserver of all the arts and chiefly of those which depend upon action? Whatever our elders observe and acquire by long experience is committed to the treasure house of history; then men of a later age join to observations of the past reflections for the future and compare the causes of obscure things, studying the efficient causes and the ends of each as if they were placed beneath their eyes. Moreover, what can be for the greater glory of immortal God or more really advantageous than the fact that sacred history is the means of inculcating piety to God, reverence to parents, charity to individuals, and justice to all? Where, indeed, do we obtain the words of the prophets and the oracles, where the unending vitality and power of minds, unless we draw them from the fount of the Holy Scriptures?

But beyond that boundless advantage, the two things which are usually sought in every discipline, ease and pleasure, are so blended in the understanding of historical books that greater ease or equal pleasure does not seem to inhere in any other body of knowledge. The ease, indeed, is such that without help of any special skill the subject is understood by all. In other arts, because all are linked together and bound by the same chains, the one cannot be grasped without knowledge of the other. But history is placed above all branches of knowledge in the highest rank of importance and needs the assistance of no tool, not even of letters, since by hearing alone, passed on from one to another, it may be given to posterity. So Moses, in one chapter of the law, says you will tell these things to your sons, though it foretell the ruin of their state and their books.[6] Yet even if empires, states, and cities perish, this story nevertheless abides forever, as he says. Most accurately Cicero foresaw that Salamis would perish before the memory of the deeds done at Salamis,[7] for it was deeply engulfed by a whirlpool, as the waters have covered Aegira, Bura, and Helice, and a great part of Crete itself—which once on account of the multitude of towns was called "hundred-citied"[8] but now may be called "three-citied"—and in our century much of Holland also. But the story of the past, unless the ruin of the human race first comes about, will never die, but will linger forever, even in the minds of countryfolk and the unlearned.

To ease is added the pleasure that we take in following the narrative of virtue's triumphs. This, I suppose, is so great that he who once is captivated and won over by the delights of history can never suffer him-

---

[6]All four editions, 1566, 1572, 1583, 1595, agree on *librorum* rather than *liberorum*.

[7]Cicero *Tusculan Disputations*, I, 46.

[8]Pliny *Natural History*, IV, 20. The editions of the *Methodus* of 1583 and 1595 read *nubium*, whereas the edition of 1572 reads correctly *urbium*.

self to be torn from her sweet embrace. Moreover, if men are impelled by such eagerness for knowledge that they now take pleasure even in unreliable tales, how much greater will it be when events are recounted truthfully? Then, too, what is more delightful than to contemplate through history the deeds of our ancestors placed before our eyes as in a picture? What more enjoyable than to envisage their resources, their troops, and the very clash of their lines of battle? The pleasure, indeed, is such that sometimes it alone can cure all illnesses of the body and the mind. To omit other evidence, there are Alphonso and Ferdinand, kings of Spain and of Sicily; one recovered his lost health through Livy, the other through Quintus Curtius, although the skill of physicians could not help them. Another example is Lorenzo de' Medici (called "the father of letters"), who is said to have recovered from an illness without any medicine (although history is a tonic) through the narration of that tale told of the Emperor Conrad III. This ruler after he had in a long siege defeated Guelph, the duke of Bavaria, and would not be diverted on any terms from the proposed and attempted razing of the city, finally was won over by the prayers of noble ladies and permitted them to go away unharmed, on condition that they might take out nothing from the city which they could not transport on their backs. Then they, with greater faith, shall I say, or piety, started to carry off the duke himself, their husbands, their children, and their parents, borne on their shoulders. In this the emperor took such pleasure that, shedding tears of joy, he not only cast cruelty and wrath completely from his mind but also spared the city and formed a friendship with the bitterest of his enemies. Who, then, doubts that history may fill with the most exquisite delight the minds of even the most ferocious and boorish of men?

There is more danger that while we revel in too great appreciation, we may overlook the utility (although in delight, also, there is use). This happens to people who dwell on the details of trifling matters, as though they were feeding on condiments and spices, neglecting more solid food. Therefore, passing over the pleasure of this kind of reading, I go on to the utility. How great it is, not only in the most accurate narratives, but even in those where only a likeness to actual fact and some glimmer of truth shines, I shall make plain—not with countless proofs, since each one can draw these things from the same sources as I, but by bringing forward the example of Scipio Africanus alone. When he had grasped firmly in mind the *Cyropaedia* of Xenophon and had learned from it the vast treasure of all virtues and glories, he became such a great man that not only was a formidable war kindled in Spain for no other cause than awe of Scipio and contempt for other generals (thus Livy writes), but also he lived respected and unharmed by the robbers themselves. When brigands approached his country house and the serfs, gathered together, resolutely repulsed from the entrance men who apparently were hostile to Scipio, the latter, as suppliants, begged from the serfs permission to behold and to venerate that divine man; when he understood what was wanted, he consented, in order to transform to human kindness the barbarity of the robbers (although by his virtue he had already mitigated their barbarism). The benefit of real glory was produced by the story of the older Cyrus—a work not true to fact so much as expressive of the ideal of a very just and brave king.

But, not to concentrate on ancient times, there is no example more recent or more famous than that of Selim, prince of the Turks. Although his ancestors always avoided history on the ground that it is false, he himself first had the deeds of Caesar translated into the vernacular, and by imitating that general in a short time he joined a great part of Asia Minor and of Africa to the dominion of his ancestors. Moreover, what drove Caesar himself to such valor, if not emulation of Alexander? When he read of his victories, he wept copious tears because at an age when his hero had conquered all the world he himself had not yet done anything. Likewise, what was the cause of so many victories for Alexander, if not the valor of Achilles, depicted by Homer as the model of an excellent general? Without this work Alexander could not even sleep. What, lastly, to avoid foreign examples, brought Emperor Charles V to such glory, if not emulation of Louis XI, king of the French, from the book of Comines?

Now, indeed, since history has boundless advantages, is read with great ease, and gives even greater pleasure, it has not been open to anyone's reproach. Although many have misrepresented the other arts as dangerous or useless, no one has yet been found who has marked the record of the past with any stain of infamy—unless perchance the man who accused this art of mendacity when he had declared war on all the virtues and the disciplines. But such a reproach is for fables, not for history; if the account is not true, it ought not even to be called history, as Plato thought. He says that every product of thought is either true or false: he calls the latter poetry, the former knowledge.[9] But why argue? When so much of advantage may be extracted from the very fables of Homer, which take unto themselves the likeness of information and truth, then what sort of reward must we hope from history? Since this teaches us clearly not only the arts necessary for living but also those objectives which at all costs must be sought, what things to avoid, what is base, what is honorable, which laws are most desirable, which state is the best, and the happiest kind of life. Finally, since if we put history aside the cult of God, religion, and prophecies grow obsolete with the

---

[9]That is, fabrication, poesy (from ποιέω, to make) in contrast to information founded on investigation, history (from ἰστορέω, to inquire).

passing of centuries; therefore, on account of the inexpressible advantage of such knowledge, I have been led to write this book, for I noticed that while there was a great abundance and supply of historians, yet no one has explained the art and the method of the subject. Many recklessly and incoherently confuse the accounts, and none derives any lessons therefrom. Formerly men wrote books about the proper arrangement of historical treatises; how wisely, I do not discuss. They have, perhaps, a possible excuse for their project. Yet, if I may give an opinion, they seem to resemble some physicians, who are distrustful of all kinds of medicine: resolutely they once again examine their preparation and do not try to teach the strength and nature of the drugs which are proposed in such abundance or to fit them to the present illnesses. This applies also to those who write about the organization of historical material, when all books contain ample information about the past and the libraries contain the works of many historians whom they might more usefully have taken to study and imitate than to discuss oratorically the exordium, the narrative, and the ornaments of words and sentences.

Then, in order that what we are going to write about the historical method may have some outline, we shall at the beginning divide and delimit the subject, then indicate the order of reading. After this we shall arrange similar instances of human activities for history, so that this may be an aid to memory. Afterwards we shall consider the choice of individual writers. Then we shall discuss the correct evaluation of works in this field. Following this we shall speak about the governmental form of states, in which the discipline of all history is chiefly engaged. Then we shall refute those who have upheld the idea of the four monarchies and the golden age. Having explained these things, we shall try to make clear the obscure and intricate sequence of chronologies, so that one can understand whence to seek the beginning of history and from what point it ought to be traced. At length we shall refute the error of those who maintain the independent origin of races. Finally we move on to the arrangement and order of reading historians, so that it may be plainly understood what each man wrote about and in what period he lived.

Chapter 1. What History Is and of How Many Categories

Of history, that is, the true narration of things, there are three kinds: human, natural, and divine. The first concerns man; the second, nature; the third, the Father of nature. One depicts the acts of man while leading his life in the midst of society. The second reveals causes hidden in nature and explains their development from earliest beginnings. The last records the strength and power of Almighty God and of the immortal souls, set apart from all else. In accordance with these divisions arise history's three accepted manifestations[1]—it is probable, inevitable, and holy—and the same number of virtues are associated with it, that is to say, prudence, knowledge, and faith. The first virtue distinguishes base from honorable; the second, true from false; the third, piety from impiety. The first, from the guidance of reason and the experience of practical affairs, they call the "arbiter of human life." The second, from inquiry into abstruse causes, they call the "revealer of all things." The last, due to love of the one God toward us, is known as the "destroyer of vice." From these three virtues together is created true wisdom, man's supreme and final good. Men who in life share in this good are called blessed, and since we have come into the light of day to enjoy it, we should be ungrateful if we did not embrace the heaven-offered benefit, wretched if we abandon it. Moreover, in attaining it we derive great help from history in its three phases, but more especially from the divine form, which unaided can make mankind happy, even though they have no experience of practical affairs and no knowledge of secret physical causes. Yet if the two latter are added, I believe that they will bring about a great increase in human well-being.

Therefore it would follow that we should turn our first inquiries to the history of divine things. But since in man mother nature engenders first the desire for self-preservation, then little by little due to awe of Nature's workings drives him to investigate their causes, and since from these interests she draws him to an understanding of the very Arbiter of all things—for this reason it seems that we must begin with the subject of human affairs as soon as there shall have dawned in the minds of children perceptions of God, the All-Highest, not only probable but also inevitable for belief.[2] So it shall come about that from thinking first about ourselves, then about our family, then about our society we are led to examine nature and finally to the true history of Immortal God, that is, to contemplation. How difficult is the last to men who have not yet been admitted to the mysteries of revealed philosophy is understood well enough by those who have trained themselves somewhat in meditation on great matters. While they raise their minds little by little above their senses, as though over the waves in which the majority of mankind are submerged, they can, however, never liberate themselves far enough to avoid images created by their senses, like nebulae, placing themselves in opposition to the light of truth. On this account it happens that those who

---

[1]The word is *assensio*, which in philosophical parlance means the reality of sensible appearances. See Cicero, *Academica*, II, 12. These manifestations parallel the three divisions: human, which is not absolutely certain, but only probable, developing the use of foresight or prudence; natural history, exact, and therefore inescapable, giving us knowledge; and divine, which is beyond human appraisal and therefore requires faith.

[2]Compare the three manifestations of history mentioned in note 1.

start with divine history, without thinking about human affairs and natural science, and explain to boys or unlearned men difficult problems about divine matters, not only are mistaken in their expectations but also discourage many by the very magnitude of these problems. In the same way that we urge those who come from a thick blackish mist into the light to observe attentively the splendor of the sun first on earth, then in the clouds, then on the moon, in order that, having strengthened their vision, they may be able some time to gaze upon the sun itself, we must act for the benefit of the unlettered also. They should first notice the goodness of God and His pre-eminence in human affairs, then in manifest natural causes, then in the arrangement and splendor of the heavenly bodies; after that, in the admirable order, motion, immensity, harmony, and shape of the entire universe, so that by these steps we may sometime return to that intimate relationship which we have with God, to the original source of our kind, and again be united closely to Him. Those who interpret history differently seem to me to violate the eternal laws of nature.

Since eminent and learned men have expressed concisely in written works this threefold classification of the subject, I have proposed to myself just this—that I may establish an order and a manner of reading these and of judging carefully between them, especially in the history of human affairs. For, in general, divine and natural history differ greatly from human, particularly in this respect, that they not only deal with origins but also are comprised within definite limits. Natural history presents an inevitable and steadfast sequence of cause and effect unless it is checked by divine will or for a brief moment abandoned by it and, so to speak, yielded up to the prince of fluid matter and the father of all evils. From the abandonment are derived spectacles of distorted nature and huge monsters; from the interposition, outstanding miracles of God. From both are engendered in us the beginning of religion or superstition and awe of an inescapable divine will, so that the resplendent and manifest glory of God may become more visible to the race of men (even though it cannot be more shining or more clear).

But because human history mostly flows from the will of mankind, which ever vacillates and has no objective—nay, rather, each day new laws, new customs, new institutions, new manners confront us—so, in general, human actions are invariably involved in new errors unless they are directed by nature as leader. That is, they err if they are not directed by correct reasoning or if, when the latter has deteriorated, they are not guided without the help of secondary causes by that divine foresight which is closer to the principle of their origin. If we depart from this, we shall fall headlong into all sorts of infamy. Although the mind of man, plucked from the eternal divine mind, isolates itself as far as possible from earthly stain, still, because it is deeply immersed in unclean matter, it is so influenced by contact with it, and even distracted within itself by conflicting emotions, that without divine aid it can neither uplift itself nor achieve any degree of justice nor accomplish anything according to nature. Consequently it comes about that as long as we are handicapped by the weakness of our senses and by a false image of things, we are not able to discern useful from useless or true from false or base from honorable, but by a misuse of words we attribute our action to prudence in order not to trespass. Since for acquiring prudence nothing is more important or more essential than history, because episodes in human life sometimes recur as in a circle, repeating themselves, we judge that attention must be given to this subject, especially by those who do not lead a secluded life, but are in touch with assemblies and societies of human beings.

So of the three types of history let us for the moment abandon the divine to the theologians, the natural to the philosophers, while we concentrate long and intently upon human actions and the rules governing them. Investigation into human activity is either universal or particular: the latter includes the memorable words and deeds of a single man or, at the utmost, of a people. As the Academicians wisely did not assume any generalized concept of old women's affairs, so history should not concern itself with actions equally futile. Universal history narrates the deeds of many men or states, and in two ways: either of several peoples, for example, Persians, Greeks, Egyptians, or of all whose deeds have been handed down or, at least, of the most famous. This also can be done in many ways. That is to say, when events are listed according to time—for each day, or month, or year—then the accounts are called ephemerides, or diaries, and annals. Or writers may trace from the origin of each state, or as far as memory permits, or even from the creation of the world, the beginnings, growth, established type, decline, and fall of states. This also is done in two ways: briefly or fully, and the books are accordingly called chronicles or chronologies, respectively. Other writers achieve the same end in a slightly different way. Verrius Flaccus[3] called history a "tale spread abroad," in which the importance of affairs, persons, and places was weighed by whoever was present at these events. But Cicero gave the name "annals" to accounts reporting the deeds of each year without any ornament or troublesome inquiry into causes. History, said Cicero, is nothing but the making of annals. Diaries, or ephemerides, are the deeds of each day, as Asellio explained in the writings of Gellius.[4] But *fasti* are

---

[3]Verrius Flaccus was a lexicographer, probably of the first century B.C. His work is embodied in *De verborum significatione,* by Sextus Pompeius Festus.

[4]Aulus Gellius was a Latin grammarian who lived under Hadrian. The reference is to *Noctes Atticae,* v, xviii, 8.

annals in which all memorable things, the greatest magistrates, the most famous victories, defeats, triumphs, and secular games are briefly mentioned. Such are the works of Verrius Flaccus, Crator,[5] Ausonius,[6] Cassiodorus,[7] and Cuspinian,[8] yet they are generally called histories.

The above-mentioned division is equally appropriate for natural and divine histories. Either they tell the origin and development of one religion, that is, the Christian, or of several, or of all, especially the most famous—although there cannot be more than one religion which strikes a mean between superstition and impiety. In the same way the natural history of one thing can be collected—for example, of a plant or animal, or of all plants or animals. Such are the books of Theophrastus[9] and Aristotle, or we may even have an account of all the elements and of the bodies made from them, or finally, the description of all nature, such as Pliny encompassed.

If anyone does not wish to include mathematics with the natural sciences, then he will make four divisions of history: human, of course, uncertain and confused; natural, which is definite, but sometimes uncertain on account of contact with matter or an evil deity, and therefore inconsistent; mathematical, more certain, because it is free from the admixture of matter, for in this way the ancients made the division between the two; finally, divine, most certain and by its very nature changeless. And this is all about the delimitation of history.

Chapter 2. The Order of Reading Historical Treatises

The same system and method which is generally employed in treating the arts should, I think, be used in the discipline of history. It is not enough to have a quantity of historical works at home, unless one understands the use of each and in what order and manner each ought to be read. At a banquet, even if the seasonings themselves are most agreeable,

---

[5]Crator was a freedman of the time of M. Aurelius Verus. He wrote a history of Rome from the foundation to the death of Verus, in which the names of consuls and other magistrates were given.

[6]Ausonius lived in Gaul in the fourth century A.D. and wrote *Tetrasticha* on the Caesars from Julius to Elagabalus.

[7]Cassiodorus, c. 486–575, a Roman noble who influenced the intellectual development of medieval Europe through the library which he established at Vivarium. To teach those who were working there he wrote the *Institutiones,* covering the practices of the *scriptorium.* Under his supervision the ecclesiastical histories of Socrates, Sozomen, and Theodoret were translated into Latin under the title *Historia tripartita.*

[8]Cuspinian (Joannes Spiesshaymer), 1473–1529, German diplomat and scholar, was the author of *Commentarii de consulibus Romanorum.*

[9]Theophrastus, a pupil of Aristotle, and author of *History of Astronomy* and *History of Plants.*

yet the result is disagreeable if they are put together in haphazard fashion; so one must make provision that the order of the narratives be not confused, that is, that the more recent portion be not assigned to an earlier place for reading or the central portion to the end. People who make this error not only are unable to grasp the facts in any way but even seriously weaken the power of their memory. So in order that the understanding of history shall be complete and facile, at the start let us apply that pre-eminent guide to the teaching of the arts which is called analysis. This, in general, shows how to cut into parts and how to redivide each part into smaller sections and with marvelous ease explains the cohesion of the whole and the parts in mutual harmony. We must not attempt a synthesis, since the parts of all historical movements are nicely adjusted to each other and cemented into one body, as it were, by the great industry of scholars; but by some people they are unskillfully separated. There is, however, such great cohesion of the parts and of the whole that if they are torn asunder they cannot possibly stand alone. So Polybius reproached Fabius Maximus[1] and other writers on the Punic War because of this very thing—that they specialized on one or another phase of that struggle. He wrote that they were in a sense depicting the eye separated from the head, or some other member torn from the living being, so that one cannot properly understand of what it is a part. Dionysius of Halicarnassus[2] made the same charge against Polybius, Silenus,[3] Timaeus,[4] Antigonus,[5] and Jerome,[6] who had left mutilated and imperfect commentaries on Roman history. Somebody might make a like comment against Dionysius also. But they are not to be blamed, because not all subjects should be treated by every writer, nor can they be, since each with infinite labor and diligence collects only as much as he can gather. I believe that this reproach applies, not to the writing, but rather to the reading of histories, whose fragments, if they are torn apart, will not cohere to each other or to the whole. What they set down concerning Roman history let us in turn state about the universal history of all peoples. I call that history universal which embraces the affairs of all, or of the most

---

[1]Q. Fabius Pictor flourished 225 B.C. He was the most ancient writer of Roman history in prose and carried the story from Aeneas down to his own time. The reference is to Polybius, *The Histories*, I, i, 14. The rivalry between the house of Scipio and the Fabii is reflected in Polybius's unfavorable comments about Fabius.

[2]Dionysius of Halicarnassus flourished 30 B.C. He was the author of *Roman Archaeology,* a great work on Roman history in twenty books, coming up to 264 B.C. and preceding Polybius. He emphasized the Greek origins of Rome.

[3]Silenus was a Greek historian mentioned by Cicero (*De divinatione,* I, xxiv, 49). The reference is to Dionysius, I, vi.

[4]Timaeus flourished 260 B.C. He was a Sicilian who wrote a history of Sicily from the earliest times, using the Olympiads as a system of dating.

[5]Antigonus was a Greek historian of Italy of the third century B.C.

[6]Jerome of Cardia, a historian of the Hellenistic era.

famous peoples, or of those whose deeds in war and in peace have been handed down to us from an early stage of their national growth. Although many more things have been omitted than are included in any work, nevertheless so many remain that the life of a man, however prolonged, is hardly sufficient for reading them.

First, then, let us place before ourselves a general chart for all periods, not too detailed and therefore easy to study, in which are contained the origins of the world, the floods, the earliest beginnings of the states and of the religions which have been more famous, and their ends, if indeed they have come to an end. These things may be fixed in time by the creation and the founding of the City, then by the Olympiad, or even, if reason demands, by the year of Christ and the Hegira of the Arabs (which in popular chronicles is omitted). Conforming closely to this type are the works commonly called chronicles, characterized by spaces between the lines, brief indeed, but easy for beginners. Although their chronology is not exact, yet they approach fairly close to the truth of the matter. After this representation we shall use a somewhat fuller and more accurate book, which covers the origins, conditions, changes, and fall not only of illustrious peoples but also of all peoples, yet with a brevity such that one can see almost at a glance what was the established form of each state. Many have written works of this kind, but no one, it seems to me, more accurately than Johann Funck,[7] who collected in a definite scheme of chronology the things which have been recorded by Eusebius,[8] Bede,[9] Lucidus,[10] Sigismund,[11] Martin, and Phrygio.[12] He carefully corrected many errors in these writers. But since he sometimes lost himself in details, let us pass them over and touch upon only the most important. Having been somewhat informed by this writer about the condition of all states, we shall run through the history of Carion,[13] or rather, of Melanchthon, with a like care. He was sometimes too prolix on theological

[7]Johann Funck, 1518–1566, author of *Chronologia, hoc est omnium temporum et annorum ab initio mundi usque ad hunc praesentem . . . annum 1552.*

[8]Eusebius of Caesarea, historian and theologian of the fourth century, was author of *Chronographia* and the chronological canons as well as *Historia ecclesiastica* in Greek.

[9]Bede, 673–735, historian and theologian, was author of the *Ecclesiastical History of England* in Latin and *De temporum ratione,* which divided history into six ages from the creation, using the birth of Christ as the dividing point in dating.

[10]Johannes Lucidus Samotheus, a famous mathematician of the sixteenth century, was the author of *Emmendationes temporum.*

[11]Sigismund Meisterlin was the author of *Chronicon Augustanum ecclesiasticum.* He died c. 1488.

[12]Paul Constant Seidenstücker, 1483–1543, called himself Phrygio. He wrote *Chronicum . . . ab exordio mundi temporum seculorumque seriem complectens.*

[13]Johann Carion of Lübeck, 1499–1537, was author of *Chronicorum libri tres.* This was edited by Philip Melanchthon and Gaspar Peucer, and brought up to the time of Charles V.

disputes, as he was much given to religion and piety. If these accounts seem objectionable, it is very easy to skip them. The other things which can be said in general about famous states, it seems to me, he has covered briefly and accurately. If there is any other author (there are some) who has written universal history more fully than Melanchthon, I think that he ought to be read.

Then from the general we move on little by little to details, still in the order in which they are arranged in the tables of chronicles. Since the system of governing a state, knowledge, and lastly civilization itself have come from the Chaldeans, Assyrians, Phoenicians, and Egyptians, at first we shall study the antiquity of these races, not only in writers who have written of them especially, such as Berosus,[14] Megasthenes,[15] and Herodotus, but also from the Hebrew authors, whose affairs have much in common with the rest. Many more definite things about the neighboring peoples are commemorated in the *Antiquities* of Josephus[16] and in his *Books Against Apion* than in any other writers. Afterwards we shall investigate the history of the Hebrews, but in such a way that we shall study at first the system of establishing a state rather than a religion, which belongs to the third type of history and requires a more exalted state of mind. Then we shall come to the empires of the Medes, Persians, Indians, and Scythians. From these we turn to the Greeks, who propagated their kind from the Araxes, the Euphrates, and the gates of Syria even to the Hellespont, and from the Hellespont even to the Danube, the Acroceraunian, and the Aemian Mountains. They filled with a multitude of colonists the nearby isles of Asia and of Europe and then Italy itself. There is a threefold division of these: the first are called the Ionians; the second, the Aeolians; the last, the Dorians. From the Greeks we come to the Italians, who are surrounded by the Alps and both seas. Since they excelled all peoples in the majesty of their empire and the glory of their deeds and through their great reputation for justice became so pre-eminent that they appear to eclipse all other nations not only in laws and institutions but also in the superiority of their language until the present, the entire antiquity of this people must be diligently investigated. Moreover, since they waged long and costly wars with the Carthaginians, the history of both races is practically covered by the same writers.

I think that the Celts are nearest to the Romans, and they may be older

---

[14]Berosus was a priest of Bel in Babylon in the third century B.C. There are extracts from his *Chaldaica* in Josephus and in Eusebius.

[15]Megasthenes was a historian of about 300 B.C. who wrote *Annalium Persicorum liber I.*

[16]Flavius Josephus, c. 37–c. 95, was author of the *Wars of the Jews* and other works dealing with Jewish history. He won the favor of Vespasian, and lived during his later years in Rome, where a statue was erected to him, on the authority of Eusebius, *Ecclesiastical History,* III, 9.

than the Italians themselves. Certainly they were famous for military training before the Romans were, and they sent colonies not only into Italy but also into Spain, Germany, Greece, and Asia, as we shall recount in its proper place. Although Caesar confined them within the frontiers of the Garonne and the Seine, nevertheless they extended their rule from the Pyrenees and the ocean to the Rhine and the Alps. Next come the Germans, who are surrounded by the Alps, the Rhine, the Vistula, the Carpathian Mountains, and the Baltic Sea, and the people who are neighbors of the Germans—Danes, Norwegians, Swedes, and Scandinavians. Then come the peoples who trace their origin from these—Goths, Franks, Vandals, Huns, Heruli, Lombards, Burgundians, Angles, and Normans, who have done great deeds and established most flourishing empires in France, Britain, Spain, and Italy. Although the Spanish and the Britons are renowned on account of their past, yet their deeds have not been so famous as those mentioned earlier. In a similar category are the Arabs, who were noted for the antiquity of their race, but for a long time remained hidden away in slothfulness, until, bursting forth from the deserts, they drove the Persians and the Greeks from the control of Asia and Africa and won great victories in Europe. They spread not only their arms but also their religion, customs, institutions, and finally their own language throughout the whole world. The common man calls them Saracens; they are, however, a combination of various peoples, but the Arabs themselves hold the controlling position, as we shall make plain later.

From these we move on to the Turks, who, advancing from the shores of the Caspian Sea into Asia, little by little penetrated with their armies the regions of Asia Minor, all Greece, and Egypt. Nor shall we omit the empire of the Tartars, who rule far and wide beyond the Imaeus Mountains and the Caspian Sea, or of the Muscovites, who advanced their frontiers from the Volga River and the Don to the Dnieper and recently annexed Livonia. Last are the Americans and those who control the shores of southern Africa and India, whose history also it will be useful and pleasant to understand.

All these things ought to be run through lightly at first, then they must be examined more accurately, so that when we shall have grasped the most important heads of the narrative, as it were, we may come gradually to the details. We shall investigate not only the great states but also certain mediocre and unimportant ones, for example, the principalities of the Rhodians, Venetians, Sicilians, Cretans, Helvetians, Achaeans, Genoans, Florentines, and the like. Pausanias[17] has described with a fair degree of accuracy the separate states of the Greeks. When the history of

---

[17]Pausanias was a native of Lydia in the second century A.D. His main work was *Description of Greece.*

all countries has thus been learned, it remains for us to inquire into the deeds of the men who achieved fame through power, or by the splendor and riches of their race, or finally by their valor and conspicuous talent. Of these each reader will make selection according to his judgment and apply the words and deeds of each hero to his theories of life. After the history of human affairs, if anyone has leisure to scrutinize the natural sciences, he will find them much easier approaches to theology. If, on the other hand, the difficulty of the matter and the circumstances of life shall call him from this undertaking, he will enter upon his professional career. Or if for him no place is left in life's activities, let him be the spectator of others in order that with his own eyes he may survey those human affairs whose dead image he has seen in books. We can gather the most valuable fruits from history in no other way than by first taking a modest part in practical affairs or by diligently observing, as Pythagoras warned.

The last step will come when, having comprehended human and natural affairs, we approach the divine, as though with clean hands. First let us collect the chief teachings of each religion. Then let us see who was the author of each; what beginnings, what advances, finally what form and what end it had; what in each is accessory to virtue, what foreign. To these we shall add opinions of illustrious philosophers concerning religion and the highest good, so that from all their opinions, revealed to view, truth may shine forth the more clearly. From this material one may usefully garner many things from which to offer trophies to all-powerful God, as did the Hebrews from the loot of the Egyptians. But in this kind of learning we shall progress further by frequent prayers and the turning of a clean mind toward God than by any course of study.

The things which we have said about the arrangement of history are understood very easily on account of the analogy to cosmography. For such is the relationship and affinity of this subject to history that the one seems to be a part of the other. Indeed, we have plucked and wrested from the geographers alone the accounts of the Scythians, Indians, Ethiopians, and Americans. In addition to these things, historians use geographical data, and they always describe regions of the earth, so that if any art is essential to them I suppose geography must seem so in the highest degree. For this reason then, like a man who wishes to understand cosmography, the historian must devote some study to a representation of the whole universe included in a small map. Then he should note the relation of the celestial bodies with reference to elemental things and separate uranography from the elements: from the air, that is, the waters, and the lands. From these he must deduce anemography, hydrography, and geography, but must apportion the latter into ten circles and as many zones. Afterwards careful observation must be taken of the order of the winds, and the nature and the extent of both seas, and the distribution of the lands. Then the earth must be divided first into four or five parts approximately, that is to say, into Europe, Asia, Africa, America, and the southeastern land, and their situation must be compared with reference to each other and with the configuration of the heavens. Next, that part of the earth which is more temperate and better known, due to the fame of the inhabitants, that is to say, Europe, divide into Spain, France, Italy, Greece, Germany, Scythia, Scandinavia, Denmark, and the islands lying adjacent to each region. Likewise partition Asia into major and minor: the former can be divided into Assyria, Persia, Parthia, Media, Hyrcania [part of Persia], Ariana, Gedrosia, India, and Scythia, hither and farther Imaeus; the latter, into Phrygia, Lydia, Lycia, Cilicia, Caria, Pamphylia, Syria, Galatia, Cappadocia, Pontus, and Armenia. In the same way divide Africa into Mauritania, Libya, Cyrenaica, Egypt, Ethiopia, Numidia, and the regions of the Negritos. In this delimitation it will be sufficient to indicate noteworthy rivers, mountains, and seas as boundaries and to designate for each region suitable meridians and parallels of the heavens.

From geography finally to chorography, that is, to the description of the regions, the approach is easy. Unraveling our pattern more subtly, we shall describe each region. For example, Spain, which is the first part of Europe, we shall divide into Betica, Lusitania, and the Tarraconian province. This last, again, into Galicia, Castile, Navarre, and Aragon, having indicated the bounding rivers, the Ebro, Guadiana, Tagus, Guadalquivir, and Douro, and that mountain (popularly called Hadrian's) which separates hither from farther Spain. Then we shall define the central latitude of the region as forty[18] degrees, but the longitude as fifteen;[19] the size in length, fourteen degrees, in width, seven. A similar system must be used for other regions.

Finally we shall move from chorography to topography and geometry, that is, to the description and dimensions of separate places. First we shall cover the famous towns, ports, shores, straits, gulfs, isthmuses, promontories, fields, hills, slopes, rocks, peaks, open country, pastures, woods, groves, copses, prairies, thickets, hedgerows, parks, orchards, green spaces, willow plantations, and all fortified towns, colonies, prefectures, municipia, citadels, basilicas, villages, cantons, and manors (if the matter shall so demand). Not otherwise shall we define and delimit universal history. As they err who study the maps of regions before they have learned accurately the relation of the whole universe and the separate

---

[18]The edition of 1583 gives xi; the editions of 1566 and 1572 give xl.
[19]The prime meridian was reckoned at the Azores. See Jervis, *The World in Maps*, p. 31.

parts to each other and to the whole, so they are not less mistaken who think they can understand particular histories before they have judged the order and the sequence of universal history and of all times, set forth as it were in a table.

We shall use the same analysis in the detailed account of each race, so that if anyone wishes to understand clearly and to commit to memory the history of the Romans, let him read first Sextus Rufus,[20] who in four pages covered the entire story; from him to the epitome of Florus,[21] and then to Eutropius.[22] Afterwards let him undertake Livy and Polybius. I offer similar advice concerning the deeds of the Franks, which Jean du Tillet[23] covered briefly in one little book. I think that this should be read before Paul Aemilius,[24] and Xiphilinus[25] before Dio,[26] Justinus[27] before Diodorus[28] or Trogus, whose writings, however, have entirely disappeared. It is not enough, however, to understand universal history unless we understand also the details. But if the two kinds are joined together, Polybius said, they produce an unparalleled advantage. This view of the matter formerly escaped many who read the chief heads in Rufus or Florus, but overlooked Livy. On this account Livy's work has almost entirely perished. Likewise, Justin seems to have caused the disappearance of Trogus Pompey, and Xiphilinus of Dio.

Finally, it will happen that all sayings and deeds worthy of recall we shall consign to certain general repositories of memory as to a treasure chest. From these we shall appropriate whatever amount seems best to our judgment. Moreover, this cannot be done more conveniently than by putting before our eyes a classification of human activities.

---

[20]Sextus Rufus was the little-known author of *Breviarum de victoriis et provinciis populi Romani,* dedicated to the Emperor Valens.

[21]Lucius Annaeus Florus was the author of *Epitome rerum Romanarum* in the second century A.D.

[22]Eutropius was the secretary of the Emperor Constantine. He wrote *De inclytis totius Italiae provinciae ac Romanorum gestis* and *Historiae Romanae libri x,* which compresses into brief space 1,100 years of Roman history. It was enlarged by Paul the Deacon.

[23]Jean du Tillet, d. 1570, was bishop of Meaux and author of *Chronicon de regibus Francorum.* The edition of 1550 is bound with the *History of France* of Paul Aemilius, frequently quoted by Bodin.

[24]Paul Aemilius of Verona, d. 1529, was chancellor of Paris and historiographer of France. *De rebus gestis Francorum usque ad annos 1488 libri xx* is his chief work.

[25]Xiphilinus was a monk of Constantinople in the eleventh century. He made an abridgment of Dio.

[26]Dio Cassius flourished in the third century A.D. He wrote in Greek a history of Rome from Aeneas to A.D. 229.

[27]Justinus Frontinus composed an epitome of the work of Trogus Pompey on the Macedonian monarchy in the first century A.D.

[28]Diodorus of Sicily flourished in the first century B.C. He was author of *Bibliotheca historica,* an attempt at world history.

William Camden

5

Of British history here we have the father,
To look beyond were only useless bother.
> An inscription found in a 1674
> edition of Camden's *Remains*
> *Concerning Britain,* in the Special
> Collections Division of
> Columbia University library.

The historians of the Italian Renaissance turned to classical antiquity to explore the wisdom and morality of the ancient authors. Whether they wanted to imitate ancient examples or improve upon them, they were certain that the history of Rome was the parent of their own history. The task of the English historians during the Renaissance had to be different. Britain had been the most distant province of the Roman Empire in the West, and had never been incorporated into Roman civilization. Its ancient history was obscure and riddled with accounts of barbarous tribes and the victory of foreign troops. The aim of William Camden's epoch-making *Britannia,* as he proudly proclaimed in the Preface, was "to illustrate the ancient state of my native country of Britain, or, in other words, . . . restore antiquity to Britain and Britain to its antiquity."

The labors of Camden and his fellow antiquarians, as they began to call themselves about the time the *Britannia* was first printed in 1586, were impeded by the popularly credited legends invented by Geoffrey of Monmouth in the twelfth century. Perceiving no obvious respectable national pedigree, and lacking the means of investigating Britain's Roman heritage, Geoffrey produced a beautifully spun romantic yarn, a fabulous account of the founding of Britain in pre-Roman times by the Trojan Brutus, and the triumph of King Arthur's heroic knights over all Britain's enemies in the ancient world. In Geoffrey's *History of the British Kingdom,* it was the

Romans who became the slaves of the Britons. Before Camden, only an Italian, Polydore Virgil, and a Scotsman, John Major, had challenged the myth of Trojan-British history. Camden, later an English herald, wanted to be both patriotic and scientific. It was an enormous assignment, but he succeeded magnificently.

Camden was able to use the manuscript notes of an eccentric scholar, John Leland, who had planned a topographical survey similar to the *Britannia*. When Leland died the year after Camden's birth, his notes were still unorganized and his survey of the British Isles incomplete. A work of the scope and excellence of the *Britannia* would require years of organized research, and the cooperation of other antiquarians. Camden was well equipped to conduct such a project. From his boyhood on, he professed a love for the study of antiquity, and his years at Oxford, from 1566 to 1571, were years of preparation for the great work. After Oxford, he spent three years traveling in the country, observing the terrain, asking questions of the local inhabitants about the history of their counties. By 1575 he was a master at Westminster School, where he remained for twenty-three years. Despite his responsibilities there and his other literary interests, he never flagged in his zeal for the study of ancient Britain.

The *Britannia* became a formal undertaking in 1581 with the encouragement of a distinguished French jurist, Brisson, who had befriended Camden and recognized his genius. Camden knew what was required of him to achieve his ambitious goals. To elucidate the derivations of contemporary place names and to understand the inscriptions found in the ancient province, he mastered Welsh and Anglo-Saxon, at a time when Saxon studies were in inchoate form. Added to his philological studies were his six journeys throughout Britain, made over a period of fifteen years, during which the *Britannia* underwent six revised editions. As the work grew, he welcomed the contributions of other scholars, such as that of his friend, Sir Robert Cotton, whose collection of manuscripts and engravings significantly enhanced the value of the *Britannia,* the first book in English to contain archeological illustrations.

The cooperative effort behind the *Britannia* in no way detracts from the personal quality which we can detect immediately, and which draws us to this grand and joyous adventure in British history. In his exploration of Northumberland, included in our selection, Camden shows all the enthusiasm of a child on his first overnight hike, combined with the mature, questioning mind of a sophisticated topographer. Here he describes the western portions of the famous Roman Wall, whose discovery in Cumberland gave him so much delight that he returned to it with Robert Cotton. As he stops to ask an old woman what she knows of an ancient altar near her cottage, he gives us an irresistible invitation to join him in the discovery of his nation's history. His comments on the medieval chroniclers, his discussions of the history of the county during Saxon times, his manuscript studies in genealogy, and the history of the Percy family were all unprecedented results of antiquarian research, personal in tone, yet universally instructive.

Camden's career after the first publication of the *Britannia* was marred by the jealousies of contentious noblemen, who accused him of poor workmanship because he had ignored the genealogy of their families in his history. His elevation in 1589 to the office of Clarençaux, king of arms, provoked more jealousies and further charges of unscrupulousness—charges that have faded with the men who made them.

Camden's final historical production, the *History of the Events in England and Ireland During the Reign of Elizabeth,* became the subject of much controversy because of Camden's sympathies for Elizabeth and her Protestantism. In accordance with the author's wishes the *History* was not published in full until 1625, two years after his death. Although less impressive than the *Britannia,* this work, based on the manuscripts that Camden found in Cotton's marvelous library, became the basis of later histories of England written during the eighteenth and nineteenth centuries.

Camden gave token acknowledgment in his last work to the role of divine providence in history, but his account is presented in a secular setting, and is constructed on the basis of empirical evidence. Camden probably would have been at home in the scientific revolution about to take place in England, and it is not too much to say that the *Britannia* provided Camden's countrymen with a superb model of scientific investigation.

Selected Bibliography

The study of Camden should begin with T. D. Kendrick's *British Antiquity* (1950). This entertaining and learned little book provides the background for the *Britannia* as part of the struggle of the Elizabethan antiquarians against the mythical history of Geoffrey of Monmouth. Fred Jacob Levy's unpublished dissertation, *William Camden as Historian,* Harvard University (1959), is a fine piece of scholarship which compares Camden's historiographical achievements with those of the continental historians of his time. Levy also demonstrates intimate knowledge of the labor involved in the production of the various editions of the *Britannia* during Camden's lifetime. An article by Stuart Piggott, "William Camden and the *Britannia,"* in the *Proceedings of the British Academy,* 37 (1951), 199–217, is informative and very well written. The chapter on Camden in F. Smith Fussner, *The Historical Revolution* (1962), "William Camden and Territorial History," 230–252, is an examination of Camden's purposes and methods in writing history, but gives too little attention to the *Britannia,* which was Camden's most important work.

BRITANNIA

Preface

I shall address the candid reader in the same terms which I used in the first edition of this work twenty years ago, with a little addition. That excellent reviver of ancient geography, Abraham Ortelius, was extremely urgent with me thirty years ago to illustrate the ancient state of my native country of Britain, or, in other words, that I should restore antiquity to Britain and Britain to its antiquity, give ancient affairs a new air, throw light upon obscure points, and give credibility to doubtful facts, and reinstate truth in our histories, from which it had been banished either by the confidence of writers or the credulity of the vulgar. This, it must be confessed, was an arduous undertaking, and attended with more difficulty than can at first sight be conceived. For as no one can conceive the labour, so none but he who has made the experiment would credit it. But while the difficulty of the undertaking deterred me, the glory of my beloved country encouraged me. Thus, while on the one hand I dreaded the burden, and on the other could not bear the thoughts of not contributing to the glory of my country, I found united in my breast two opposite sensations, fear and courage; a circumstance which I could never have believed could have happened to any person. But when by the Divine assistance and my own attention I had once set about the work, I applied myself to it at my leisure hours with incessant thought, pains, and study.

My enquiries into the etymology and first inhabitants of Britain were conducted with hesitation; and in such uncertainty I have pronounced boldly on nothing, convinced that the origin of the nations of remote antiquity are necessarily obscure, like places rendered scarce visible by distance; and as the courses, windings, confluence, and mouths of great rivers are well known, while their sources are for the most part undiscovered, I have investigated the ancient divisions of Britain, and given a brief account of the orders and courts, and of the flourishing kingdoms of England, Scotland, and Ireland. In the same brief manner I have described as exactly as I could the bounds and qualities of the soil, the

---

Our selections from the *Britannia* are adapted from the eighteenth-century translation by Richard Gough (London, 1806), Vol. I, pp. xxv–xxxvii; Vol. III, pp. 489–502.

places memorable in antiquity, the dukes, earls, barons, and the most ancient and illustrious families; for it is impossible to mention them all. How I have performed my undertaking let those who are good judges determine, though it must be confessed they will find it no very easy task. Time, the most unbiassed witness, will determine it, when Envy, the attendant on living writers, is silent. Thus much, however, I may be allowed to say, that I have omitted nothing that tended to discover the truth in matters of antiquity; to which purpose I have called in the assistance of a smattering of the ancient British and the Saxon languages. I have travelled over almost all England, and consulted the most experienced and learned persons in each country. I have carefully read over our own writers, and those among the Greek and Roman authors who made the least mention of Britain. I have consulted the public records, ecclesiastical registers, many libraries, the archives of cities and churches, monuments, and old deeds, and have made use of them as of irrefragable evidence, and when necessary quoted their very words, however barbarous, that truth may have its full weight.

I hope, however, I shall not appear too presumptuous in thus venturing as an author from the lowest rank of antiquaries, where I might as well have remained concealed, on the theatre of this learned age, among the variety of tastes and opinions. But, to speak the truth ingenuously, the love of my country which includes all other affections, the glory of the British name, and the advice of my friends, have done violence to my modesty, and forced me against my will and judgment to undertake this task, to which I acknowledge myself unequal, and thrust me into public. I foresee I shall be beset on every side by judgments, prejudices, censures, calumnies, reproofs. There are some who despise and scout the whole pursuit of antiquity as an impertinent inquiry into past things. Their authority I neither totally reject, nor do I much regard their judgment. I want not arguments to recommend this undertaking to honest and worthy men who wish to see their native country illustrated, or to prove that these studies afford the most agreeable and liberal entertainment. If there are any who wish to remain strangers in their own country and city, and children in knowledge, let them enjoy their dream. I have neither written nor laboured for such men. Others may object to the lowness and inelegance of my style: I confess I have not, as Varro expresses it, weighed every word by the standard, nor affected all the flowers of speech. But where is the force of this objection, when, as Cicero himself, the father of eloquence, says, this subject will not admit flourishes, and, as Pomponius Mela observes, it is not a subject for oratory?

There may be many who may object that I have presumed to indulge conjectures on ancient names and etymologies. But if all conjectures are to be excluded, I fear a very considerable part of polite literature, and I may add of human knowledge, must of course follow. Our understandings are generally speaking so dull, that we are obliged to recur to conjecture in every science. In physic we have signs, symptoms, probabilities; which are nothing but conjectures. In rhetoric, civil law, and other sciences, conjectures maintain their ground. And as they are the means of discovering something concealed, and as Quintilian says, "serve to lead the reason to truth," I consider them among the helps which Time makes use of to draw truth out of Democritus' well. If, therefore, these objecters choose to give any weight to conjecture, I doubt not but my moderation in the application of it will plead my excuse with them. Plato in his Cratylus advises us to refer the etymologies of names to barbarous languages as the more ancient. Accordingly in etymology and conjecture I always recur to the British, or as it is now called the Welsh language, which was used by the original and most ancient inhabitants of this country. He recommends that names and things should correspond. Where they differ, I reject them. There is, says he, in things, a sound, a form, a colour; and where these are wanting, I scorn the word: such etymologies as are obscure, harsh, strained, or controvertible, I have not thought worthy a place among my observations; and I have been so cautious and sparing of conjectures, that if I am not very much mistaken the candid reader will think me neither venturous nor successfully bold. But though in this amusing exercise of the genius I may have offered more than one conjecture on the same subject, I have never forgotten the sacred unity of truth.

Others perhaps from motives of pride resent the omission of a particular family, not recollecting that my design was to mention only the more illustrious families, and not all those, for they would fill several volumes, but such as presented themselves to me in the course of my design. I hope, God willing, to have another opportunity to treat with due honour of the British nobility. But those who make the greatest stir about this matter are probably those who have deserved least of their country, and whose nobility is of late date.

The same may probably be said of those who charge me with praising some persons now living. This has been done both briefly and sparingly, and in the confidence of truth, with the concurrence of the best judges of merit, and without the least view to flattery. Let the sparing proportion of praise bestowed teach the objects of it to prove themselves not unworthy of it, and to support and increase the reputation they already enjoy. Whatever a writer says of his contemporaries, posterity will do justice to every character; and it is for posterity, and not for the present age, that I write. Meantime let it be remembered, that to praise worthy men is to hold up a light for them to follow; and it is a true observation of Symmachus, "The honours paid to merit are incitements to imitation, and virtuous emulation is kept alive by examples of respect paid to others." If it be objected that I have sought for opportunities of commending particular persons, I acknowledge it. Candid impartiality will not be blamed by the good, and something must be allowed to friendship. Virtue and glory will never want enemies, and men will reverence the past through envy of the present. Far be it from me to pass such an unjust judgment of men and things as to imagine our times under princes of such reputation incapable of producing praiseworthy characters. But those who envy the good their praise might as well suppose themselves included in the censure of the bad from a conformity of character.

Some will accuse me of omitting this or that little town or castle, forgetting that I meant to take notice of such places only as were of more than ordinary note, or had been mentioned by ancient writers. Nor would it have been worthwhile to name them when they had nothing remarkable but the name. My first and principal design was to trace out and rescue from obscurity those places which had been mentioned by Caesar, Tacitus, Ptolemy, Antoninus Augustus, the Notitia Provinciarum, and other ancient writers, and which Time had since involved in darkness by extinguishing, changing, or corrupting their names. In tracing these out, I have declined positive assertions on the one hand, and on the other have not concealed probabilities. It is not more my fault after all my pains and trouble I have not discovered every one, than it is in a miner if in searching for the principal veins of metal he passes by the lesser and concealed ones; and I may apply to myself the words of Columella: "In a great forest a good hunter will beat up and take as much game as he can, and none will be blamed for not catching all." Some things must be left to the industry of others; and a great writer has observed, "He is not a great teacher who teaches all at once, and leaves nothing for others to find out." Another age and other men will daily produce new discoveries. It is enough for me to have begun; and I shall be happy if I have stimulated others to the same pursuit, either to communicate their own discoveries, or to correct mine.

I am informed some are offended at my mention of religious houses and their foundations. I am sorry to hear this; but allow me to say, they would be as much offended, and perhaps would have it forgotten that our ancestors were Christians, and that we continue so: since there never were more certain and more illustrious monuments of their Christian piety and devotion, nor any nurseries whence Christianity and learning were transmitted to us; however in a corrupt age they have been too much overgrown by weeds which it was necessary to root out.

Mathematicians will charge me with egregious mistakes in stating the degrees of longitude and latitude. My answer to these is, I have carefully compared the several [manuscript] astronomical tables, new, old, at Oxford, Cambridge, and those of king Henry V, all which, though they differ greatly in the latitudes from Ptolemy, agree with each other. Yet I do not believe with Stadius that the earth is removed from its centre. These, therefore, I have followed. In the longitude there is no agreement or correspondence. What then could I do? As the modern mathematicians have found that there is no variation of the compass at the Azores, I have followed them in taking the longitude from thence as from the first meridian, though not with a critical exactness.

I hope no apology is necessary against a charge of obscurity, fable, or digressions. There is no danger on account of the first, except from such as have never looked into ancient literature and our history. To fable I have not paid the least regard; and that I might not be misled by digressions, I have frequently, as Pliny advises, read over my title, and asked myself what I had undertaken.

Maps have long been wished for by many in this work, as what would please the eye and be of great use in geography, especially when illustrated by descriptions. These it was not in my power to furnish: they are now added by the care of George Bishop and John Norton, from the descriptions of those excellent chorographers Christopher Saxton and John Norden.

But it is time to shorten this preface. I have applied my utmost diligence for several years to illustrate my native country with the strictest regard to truth and fidelity. I have reflected on no family, injured no man's reputation, trifled with no man's name, nor impeached the credibility of any writer, not even of Geoffrey of Monmouth, whose history (which I wish above all things to establish) is rather suspected by the learned; nor have I assumed to myself any persuasion of knowledge, except that I am always ready to learn. My ignorance and many errors I readily confess, nor would I indulge a single mistake. What marksman aims all day without one lucky hit? Many things in these pursuits are, as the poet says, *cineri supposta doloso*. Many errors may arise from memory; for who can treasure up every thing in his memory so as to be ready to produce it on occasion? More mistakes may be owing to unskillfulness. For who is so skillful as in this dark ocean of antiquity to struggle with time without splitting on the rocks? I may have erred on the authority of writers, and others whom I thought I might rely on; and, as Pliny observes, "nothing is so apt to mislead our belief as where an author of credibility vouches a falsehood." The peculiarities of places are better known to persons on the spot: their corrections shall be thankfully attended to, omissions inserted, points not sufficiently cleared up on better information illustrated, provided these hints are offered without spleen, and a love of controversy, which are absolutely unworthy candid minds who profess to have truth for their object.

Meantime, courteous reader, let me request this favour of your own good nature, my diligence, a common concern for our country, and the honour of the British name, that I may have leave to deliver freely my own opinion without offence to others, and to go on in the same way that others have taken in these studies, and that you will pardon my errors upon my acknowledging them. This I rather expect than ask from men of ingenuous minds. Those of the contrary cast, who take all opportunities of detracting, calumniating, and back-biting all persons, at all tables, and in all companies, I despise, having learned from the comic writer, that detraction is the treasure of fools which they carry in their tongues, and having found that envy (and I am not afraid to say it) resides only in degenerate little hungry minds. Candid and generous minds despise envy, and know not what it is. I therefore submit myself and my writings with all deference in every particular to the judgment of all religious and learned persons, who if they do not approve these professions of regard to my country, will at least, I trust, excuse them. Farewell, accept and enjoy it.

Northumberland

Northumberland is of a shape nearly resembling a triangle, but not equilateral. The south side next to Durham is bounded by the Derwent running into the Tyne, and by the Tyne itself. The east side is washed by the German ocean. But the west, which extends from the southwest to the northeast, has first a chain of mountains, and then the river Tweed, opposed to Scotland, and was the boundary of the two kingdoms, having in this county two wardens, one called warden of the middle border, the other of the western. The country is in great measure rough, unfit for cultivation, and seems to have communicated its hardness to its inhabitants, who are made more fierce by their Scottish neighbours either harassing them with war, or mixing with them in peace, making them most warlike, and excellent light horsemen. Being as it were devoted to war, there is no person of consequence among them who has not his fort or castle: and the county was divided into a number of baronies, whose lords formerly, before the time of Edward I, were commonly called barons, though some of them were very poor: but this was wisely done by our ancestors to encourage and keep up valour on the borders of the kingdom, at least as far as it could be done by honour and titles. But this title became extinct among them when under Edward I those only had the title of barons who had summons from the king to parliament. A little cultivation makes the country on the coast and Tyne agreeable to live in. In other places it is much more disagreeable and horrid. In many parts those minerals called Linthantraces, by us sea coal, are dug in great plenty to the great benefit of the inhabitants.

The hither part to the northwest is called Hexamshire, was long subject to the archbishop of York, and claimed the privileges of a county palatine, whether justly or not I cannot say. But being lately annexed to the crown by exchange with archbishop Robert it was united by act of parliament to the county of Northumberland to be subject to the same jurisdiction, and governed by the same sheriff.

South Tyne (so called, if we believe the Britans, from its banks narrowing in towards the north, which some will have to be the meaning of Tin in British), rising in Cumberland near Alstenmore, where is an ancient copper mine, running by Lambley, formerly a nunnery founded by the Lucies, now for the most part carried away by the stream, and Fetherston haugh, which was the seat of the ancient and well-descended family of Fetherston, when it comes to Bellister castle turns eastward, and continues its course straight with the wall, which is near three miles from it.

For the wall leaving Cumberland, and crossing the little river Irthing, crosses a rapid rivulet called Poltross over an arch, where I saw great mounts thrown up within the walls as for watchtowers. Near this is Thirlwale castle, not very large, but giving name and residence to the ancient and famous family before called Wade, where the Scots opened to themselves a way into the province between Irthing and Tyne, and very prudently too in the very place by which the heart of the kingdom was most accessible, without the intervention of any rivers. But this circumstance, and the name of the place, will be better understood from the Scottish historian John Fordun, whose words, as his book is not in every one's hand, I think proper to subjoin. "The Scots," says he, "being masters of the country on both sides of the wall, began to inhabit it as conquerors, and, calling together the peasantry with their hoes, quillets, or spades, rakes, forks, and mattocks, began to dig a number of cuts and pits all over it, by which they could easily pass and repass. From these holes the wall here takes its present name, the place being called in English Thirlewall, in Latin Murus Perforatus." From hence I saw Blenkensop, which gives name and residence to a famous family, and was formerly part of the barony of Nicholas de Bolthy, situated in a pleasant tract to the south.

From Thirlwall the wall opens for the rapid river Tippall, where, on the slope of a hill, a little within the wall, are to be seen the foundations of a square Roman camp, each side of which is 140 paces long. The foundations of buildings and track of streets still appear here very evident to view. The wardenmen say there was a military way composed of flints and stone over the high grounds to Maiden castle in Stanemore from hence; certain it is that it leads straight to Kirkby Thor already mentioned. An old woman who lived in a cottage just by showed us a small ancient votive altar inscribed to the local deity Vitirineus. The present name of the place is Caer Vorran; what its ancient one was is past my skill to say, none of the stations mentioned along the wall answering to it, and inscriptions throwing no light on it. Whatever it was, the wall is much the strongest and highest near it: for scarce a furlong or two from hence on a high hill it remains 15 feet high and 9 broad, faced with hewn stone on both sides, though Bede says it was only 12 feet high.

Hence the wall goes on more winding by Iverton, Forsten, and Chester in the Wall, near Busy gapp, infamous for robbers; where I was told were castles; for it was not safe to visit them for the moss troopers on the borders. They told us that Chester was a very great place, so that I should suppose it that second station of Dalmatians called Magna in the Notitia. . . .

After this we saw Willymoteswicke, the seat of the ancient family of the Ridleys, and near it the river Alon discharging a great body of water into the Tyne, the united stream of both the Alons. On East Alon is a village now called Oulde towne. But to return to the wall. The next station on it after Busy gap is called Seaven-shale, whose name, if my readers will agree with me to suppose derived from the Ala Saviniana, or rather Sabiniana, I should more boldly say it was Hunnun, where the Notitia mentions the Ala Sabiniana as stationed. Next after Carraw and Walton is Walwick, which some will have to be Gallana of Antoninus. In all these places are evident traces of ancient forts.

Here North Tyne runs through the wall. It rises among the mountains on the border between England and Scotland, and first running east, waters Tindale, to which it gives name, and then receives the river Rhead, which springing from Rheadsquire, a steep hill, where was frequently the True place, or place of conference for the East marches (the wardens of the east border of each kingdom here determining causes between the borders) gives name to a valley thinly inhabited on account of the marauders.

Both these valleys produce notable bog-trotters, and both have their hills so swampy on the top as to be inaccessible to cavalry: in which it is very extraordinary there should be many large heaps of stones called Lawes, supposed by the neighbours to have been piled up in memory of persons formerly slain there. In both valleys also are many ruins of ancient castles. In Tynedale are Whitchester, Delaley, Tarset, formerly belonging to the Commins. In Rheadesdale are Rochester, Greenchester, Rutchester, and several others whose ancient names are lost by length of time. But since at Rochester, which lies nearer the sources of the Read, on the top of a crag commanding an extensive view of the country below (whence it seems to have obtained this new name) an old altar was found among the ruins of an ancient castle. . . . For the limits of the empire were seas, great rivers, mountains, impervious wastes, such as here: also ditches, walls, timber mounds, and particularly castles erected in more suspicious places, of which here remain traces for a considerable length. After the barbarians broke through the wall of Antoninus Pius in Scotland, and carried their ravages a great way, and the wall of Hadrian lay neglected till the time of Severus, we may suppose the bound of the Roman empire to have been here, and hence the old Itinerary, which goes under the name of Antoninus, takes its beginning, as from the utmost bound. The additional words *a vallo* is a gloss of copyists, Bremenium being 14 miles north from the wall: unless it should be thought one of the field stations which were placed, as I before observed, in the enemy's country beyond the wall.

Scarce five miles south of old Bremenium is Otterburne, where was fought the famous battle between the English and Scots, victory inclining three or four times to each side, and at last declaring for the Scots. For Henry Percy (surnamed by the English Hotspur, from the heat of his youthful courage), who commanded the English, was taken prisoner, and 1500 of his men slain, and William Douglas, the Scottish general, killed with many of his troops, so that the bravery of each nation never appeared to greater advantage.

Another town of ancient date lower down is washed almost away by the Rhead. It is now called Risingham, i.e. in the old English and German language, the habitation of giants, as Risingberg in Germany means Giants' Mountain. Here are many and considerable remains of antiquity, and the inhabitants say that the god Mogon a long while defended this place against some Soldan or pagan prince. Nor do they speak at random. For that this god was worshipped here appears from two altars lately taken out of the river here.

From the first of these we may suppose that the place's name was Habitancum, and that the erector was a beneficiary of the Consul and chief preson or commander in the place. It is evident from the Theodosian code, that the chief magistrates of cities, villages, and castles, were called Primates. Whether this deity was the topical genius of the Gadeni, whom Ptolemy places next to the Ottadini, I am not yet clear, but leave to be discussed by others. Here were also found the following inscriptions, for which, as well as others, I own myself indebted to sir Robert Cotton, of Cottington, knt. who lately saw and copied them.

But to leave these subjects. The Rhead a little below discharges into the Tyne its own waters and those of several brooks which it had received, and so far reaches Rheadesdale, which, as I find in the book of the Exchequer, was "held by the Umsranvilles of the king in ancient fee by service to defend the vale from robbers."

All hereabouts in the wastes, as they call them, as also in Gillesland, one sees a set of people like the ancient Nomades, of a warlike disposition, who watch here with their flocks from April to August in scattered huts called Sheales and Shealings. The north Tyne runs next by Chipches, a little tower anciently belonging to the Umsranvilles, afterwards to the Herons; and not far from Swinborn, a small castle, which gave name to a famous family, and was formerly part of the barony of William Heron, afterwards the seat of the Woderingtons, approaches the wall, and crosses it below Cotterford, where it has a bridge of arches over it, and where are to be seen remains of a considerable castle at Wallwick. If this was not Cilurnum, where the second wing of the Astures was stationed, it was near it at Scilecester on the Wall, where after Sigga a nobleman had treacherously slain Elswald king of Northumberland, a church was erected by the faithful in honour of Cuthbert and Oswald, whose name so obscured the rest, that its original name is quite lost, and it is now called St. Oswald's. This Oswald, king of Northumberland, being about to march against Cedwall the Britan (for so Bede calls the person whom the Britans themselves call Caswallen) king of Cumberland, as it seems, set up a cross, and prostrating himself before it, humbly implored the aid of Christ to his worshippers, and immediately raising his voice, cried aloud to the army, "Let us all fall upon our knees and beseech the almighty, living, and true God, by his mercy to deliver us from this fierce and haughty foe. We do not find," says Bede, "that any sign of Christianity, any church, or any altar, had been set up in this whole nation before this banner of the holy cross was reared by this new commander of the army from the impulse of devout faith when he was upon the point of engaging with a most cruel enemy." Oswald experiencing in this battle the aid of Christ, which he had implored, immediately embraced Christianity, sent for Aidan the Scot to instruct his subjects in the Christian faith; and the field of victory had from succeeding ages the name the heavenly field, now to the same effect called Haledon. Of this transaction take the following lines, such as they are from the life of Oswald:

> Then first was found th' occasion of the name
> Heasenfield, the heavenly field; it founds its claim
> Thereto on old prescription to declare
> Certain presages of approaching war.
> Occasion to the name then soon was given,
> Divinely from the time the host from heaven
> Routed the host accurst. Lest age efface
> The glories of the victory and the place,
> From Hagulstad attend the chosen choir,
> And yearly to the Saviour's praise aspire;
> In further honour of the famous place,
> To Oswald's honour they a chapel raise.

Another poet has these lines, not absolutely indifferent considering the ignorance of the age:

> Who was Alcides? Alexander who?
> Or Julius Caesar? Let the first subdue
> Himself, the next the world, the last the foe;
> Oswald subdued himself, the world, the foe.

Below St. Oswald's both the Tynes unite after South Tyne, which for a mile or two runs parallel with the wall, has passed by Langley castle, where anciently under king John Adam de Tindale had his barony, which afterwards came to Nicholas de Boltby, and was lately held by the Percies; and at Aidon the river turns under a wooden bridge, now out of repair, and ready to fall. The Tyne now increased and presently after more so, makes its way to the sea in one channel, by Hexsham, which Bede calls Hagustald, which the name and high situation on a hill (the Britans calling a hill Dunum) would lead one to think was in the Roman times Axelodunum, where the first cohort of Spaniards was stationed. But of this hear Richard, prior of this place, who lived about 500 years ago.

> Not far from the river Tyne to the south stands a town, now indeed but small and thinly inhabited, but, as the remains of antiquity show, once large and magnificent. This is named Hextoldesham from the rivulet Hextold running by it, and sometimes swelling to a large stream called Hextold. Ethelreda, wife of king Egfrid, gave it to St. Wilfrid, A.D. 675, to dignify it with a bishop's see. He there built a church, which, for elegant workmanship and extraordinary beauty, stood foremost among all the monasteries in England.

Take also Malmesbury's account.

> This was part of the royal demesne when bishop Wilfrid got it in exchange for other estates of queen Etheldreda. Here were erected buildings with a towering height of walls, and various winding staircases finished in a surprising manner by the art of the masons, whom, by liberal promises, he had got from Rome, so that the buildings might have an air of Roman magnificence, and long resist the decays of time.

King Egfrid established an episcopal see in this little city at the same time. But this dignity entirely vanished with the 8th bishop in the fury of the Danish wars. From that time it was accounted only a manor of the archbishops of York, till the exchange with Henry VIII, by which they quitted their right to it, and it is famous for that fatal battle, in which John Nevill lord Montacute attacking the Lancastrians with great bravery, routed them with equal success, on which account Edward IV created him earl of Northumberland. At present all its glory consists in that ancient monastery, part of which is turned into a beautiful house of sir J. Foster. Except the west end, which is ruined, the church remains entire, and is certainly a noble pile, in whose choir one sees a handsome ancient tomb of that warlike family of the Umsranvilles, as appears by the shield, with a figure cross legged, in which posture were buried in that age (to remark it *en passant*) those who had taken the cross for a crusade to recover the Holy Land from the Mahometans. On the east side of the church, on the brown of a hill, stand two strong fortifications of hewn stone, which I was told belong to the archbishop of York.

From hence to the east we came to Dilston, the seat of the Ratcliffes, called in old books Divelston, from a small brook which empties itself into the river Tyne below it, and is by Bede called Devilesburn, where, as he writes, Oswald, armed with faith in Christ, slew in pitched battle Cedwall the Britan, an infamous tyrant, who had just cut off two kings of Northumberland, and ravaged the country far and wide. On the other side of the Tyne lies Curia Ottadinorum mentioned by Ptolemy, which, by the distance, seems to be Antoninus's Corstopitum, now called from the bridge Corbridge, in Hoveden Corobridge, in Huntingdon Cure. At present it has only a church, and near it a little turret built and inhabited by the vicars. No inconsiderable remains of antiquity, however, are to be found here, among which king John dug for treasure supposed to be buried by the ancients; but fortune mocked his vain pursuit, as she had formerly done Nero when searching for Dido's treasure at Carthage. He found nothing but stone with marks of brass, iron, and lead. Whoever views the adjoining heap of ruins called Colecester will pronounce it a station of Roman soldiers. On the same bank one next sees Biwell, a handsome castle, which in the reign of John was "the barony of Hugh Balliol, for which he was to find 30 soldiers to guard Newcastle upon Tyne." Below this is a very handsome weare for taking salmon, and two solid piles of hard stone formerly supporting a bridge stand up in the middle of the river. Next Prudhow castle, in the old writings spelled Prodhow, pleasantly situated on the ridge of a hill, commands the Tyne below. This, till I am better informed by time, I shall just suppose to have been Protolitia, or Procolitia, the station of the first Batavian cohort. It is remarkable for gallantly defending itself against William king of Scotland in Henry II, "after he had, as Neubrigensis expresses it, long beleaguered it to no effect, and with great loss of his men." It afterwards belonged to the Umsranvilles, persons of great renown, of whom sir Gilbert in the reign of Henry I distinguished himself in the field, and obtained the title of earl of Angus in Scotland in right of his wife. The lineal heiress, as our lawyers speak, was at length married into the family of Taleboys: and this castle afterwards by the royal favour came to the duke of Bedford.

But to return to the wall. Beyond St. Oswald's one sees in the wall foundations of two forts called Castle Steedes; then a place called Portgate, where the word in both languages shows there was a gate. Further in below this is Halton hall, where lives the family of Carnaby, eminent for antiquity and military renown, and near it stands Aidon castle, which was part of the barony of that Hugh Balliol beforementioned. But since more places on the wall are distinguished by this name of Aidon, which in the British language signifies a troop of horse, of whom many were formerly stationed along the wall, as appears from the Notitia, the reader will consider whether these places had not their names from that circumstance, as the towns where legions were quartered that of Leon. Near this place, however, was dug up a fragment of ancient stone, with a figure lying on a bed leaning on its left hand, the right hand touching the right knee. Without the wall rises the river Pont, and running by Fenwick hall, the seat of the ancient and military family of Fenwick, runs before the wall for several miles. It had on its banks in garrison the first cohort of the Cornavii at Pons Elii, built by Elius Hadrianus, now called Pont Eland, at which Henry III and the king of Scots concluded a peace, A.D. 1244, and near it lay the first cohort of Tungri at Borwick, called in the Notitia Borcovicus. From Portgate the wall runs on to Waltowne. Near this is an old fort called Winchester, which the Notitia informs us was formerly a frontier station of Gauls. And next to this Rouchester, where we saw plain foundations of a square fort contiguous to the wall. Near it is Headon, which was part of the barony of Hugh de Bolebec, who derived his descent by the mother from the most famous barons Montfichet, and left only daughters married to Ralph lord Greistocke, J. Lovell, Huntercomb, and Corbett.

Where the wall and the Tyne almost meet stands Newcastle, the chief town in these parts, famous for its harbour formed by the Tyne, which is deep enough to receive very large ships, and shelters them so well that they are not exposed to wind or shoals. The town stands on a very unequal declivity on the north side of the river, over which is a most beautiful bridge, on the left of which, as you enter, stands the castle. On a steep hill to the right are the market place, and the best-built part of the town, from whence you have a troublesome ascent to the higher part, which is much larger. It has four churches, is defended by stout walls, with sever gates, and a number of towers. Its ancient state is by no means clear. I should readily take it for Gabrosentum, its suburb Gateshead, a British name derived from Goats, expressing this as was before observed. The Notitia also places Gabrosentum and the second cohort of Thracians stationed there. That the rampart and wall run through this town is most certain, and at Pandon gate remains, as is supposed, one of the turrets of that wall; certain it is that it differs from the rest in shape and style, and bears the marks of great antiquity; and the name of Monk Chester convinces

me it was the station of a garrison. For it was so called from the monks
in the beginning of the Norman government; and soon after took the
name of Newcastle from the New Castle built there by Robert son of
William the Norman; and gradually increased very considerably by its
trade with the German ports, and by exporting all over the kingdom coals
wherewith the country abounds. In the reign of Edward I one of its
richest inhabitants being carried off by the Scots out of the heart of the
town, and ransoming himself with a great sum of money, took the earliest opportunity to fortify the town. The rest of the townspeople, animated
by his example, finished the work, and erected strong walls on all sides.
From this time the inhabitants lived in perfect security, in defiance of the
threats of the enemies and marauders that swarm in the neighbourhood,
and carried on such a trade, that, by its extensive commerce and wealth,
it has arrived at a flourishing state, on which account Henry VI made it
a county corporate by itself. It is situated in longitude 21° 30', and in
latitude 54° 57'. Of its suburb Gateshead joined to it by the bridge, and
belonging to the bishopric of Durham, we have spoken of above. This
town is celebrated by Johnston in his British cities in the following lines
for its situation and plenty of pit coal, of which there is great consumption, and to which the greatest part of England and Flanders is indebted
for their bright fires:

NEWCASTLE

Placed on a lofty rock, it thence surveys
Dame Nature's wonders, or with art conveys
Their use to others. Wherefore call we down
Etherial fire? She has it of her own,
Call'd from earth's inmost womb, not to be hurl'd
In dreadful blaze, the terror of the world,
But genial warmth invigorating earth,
And to the cheerful spirit giving birth.
This fuses iron and brass and liquid gold:
What raises not this shadow uncontroul'd?
And coarser metal into gold transform'd
The Chymist boasts it by the Gods inform'd.
If then such knowledge came from Heaven to men,
Or God-like powers these clods of earth contain,
How many Gods this ancient town must boast?
How many Gods still honour Scotland's coast?

Not to mention Gosseford, formerly the barony of Richard Sur-Teis,
who flourished in great repute under Henry I scarce three miles hence
is a little village called Walls end. The import of this name proves that
it was the station of the second cohort of Thracians called in the Notitia
Vindobala, in Antoninus Vindomora, the one implying *Finis Valli*, the

end of the Vallum, the other *Finis Muri,* the end of the Wall, in the provincial language of the Britans, who anciently called a wall Mur, and a rampart Gual.

Nor is it to be supposed the rampart or wall was continued further, there being no traces of it further, and the Tyne almost arrived at the ocean serving with its deep bed as the strongest wall. Some, however, will have the rampart, not the wall, reach to the very mouth of this river, now called the Tinmouth, and that it was called Pen-ball-crag, or the Head of the rampart on a rock, which I shall not dispute. But I shall presume to assert that this in the Roman times was Tunnocellum, that word meaning the Promontory of Tunna, or Tine, where the first cohort Elia Classica (by the name probably established by Elius Hadrianus) was quartered for the defence of the shipping. For the Romans had in the rivers on the borders of ships called *Lusoriae.* It is at present called Tinmouth castle, and boasts a noble and strong castle, which, as an ancient writer expresses it, "on the east and north side is inaccessible on a rock over the ocean, but on the other side is easily defended by favour of the higher ground." For this reason Robert Mowbray, earl of Northumberland, chose it for the seat of war when he rebelled against king William Rufus. But affairs, as is generally the case, took a turn unfavourable to this rebel, who being immediately closely besieged, retired to the adjoining monastery, which was a sanctuary, but being dragged from thence suffered though late the punishment due to his treason in the horror of a long imprisonment.

I am now to follow the course of the shore. Behind the promontory on which stands Tunnocelum next to Seton, which under Henry III was part of the barony of De-la-vall, one sees Seghill, anciently Segedunum, the station of the third cohort of the Lergi on the wall; and certain it is that Segedunum in British means the same as Seghill in English. Hence the shore after a few miles makes way for the river Blithe, which after washing Belsey, once a castle of the Midletons, and Ogle, of the barons Ogle, empties itself here, together with the Pont, into the sea. These families have had the title of baron ever since the beginning of Edward IV's reign, being enriched by intermarrying with the heiresses of Berthram de Bothall, Alan Heton and Alexander Kirkby. The male line of these barons failed lately in Cuthbert the seventh baron, who left two daughters; Joan married to Edward Talbot younger son of George earl of Shrewsbury, and Catharine to sir Charles Cavendish.

A little higher up the river Wentsbeck falls into the ocean, after passing by Mitford, which was burnt by king John and his Roitiers, when they grievously harassed these parts. Roitier was a name given in that age to those foreign marauding troops, brought over to the king's assistance by Fulcasius de Brent and Walter Buc. Brent was a savage fellow, afterwards driven out of the kingdom. But Buc being a soberer man, and faithfully serving the king, obtained of him in reward of his services lands in York and Northampton shires, and his posterity flourished there till John Buc attainted under Henry VII whose great grandson is sir George Buc, a very polite scholar and master of the king's revels, who (that I may acknowledge my obligation to my friends) made many curious historical observations and candidly communicated them to me. This was once the barony of William Berthram, whose posterity soon ended in Roger his grandson, and his three heiresses were married to Norman Darcy, T. Penbury, and William de Elmeley.

From hence the Wentsbecke glides through Morpit, a famous little town. The town stands on the north side of the river, on the south the church, and a castle on a shady hill, which together with the town came from Roger de Merlay, whose barony it was, to the lords of Greistock, and thence to the barons Dacre of Gillestand. I have no particulars from ancient history relative to this place, except that A.D. 1215 it was burnt by its own inhabitants out of hatred to king John. Fron hence Wentsbeck runs by Bothall castle, formerly the barony of Richard Berthram, from whose descendants it came to the barons Ogle. On the bank of this river I have long supposed, whether truly or by mere conjecture I know not, formerly stood Glanoventa, which had a Roman garrison of the first cohort of the Morini to defend the borders. The situation suggests this opinion, in which the name of the river and the place itself confirm me. For it stands *ad lineam valli,* on the line of the rampart or wall, where the Notitia puts it. The river is called Wentsbecke, and Glanoventa signifies in British the shore or bank of the Wenta, whence a town on the coast of France called Glanon, mentioned by Mela, seems to have had its name.

Not far from hence (to pass by small towers of less renown), near the shore one sees Witherington or Woderinton, an ancient castle, which gave name to the noble and knightly family of Witherington, whose valour often displayed itself in the Scottish wars. After this falls into the sea the river Coqued or Coquet, which rising among the rough hills of Cheviot, has not far from its source Billesdun, whence the famous family of the Selbies, and lower to the south Harbottle, whence came the family of Harbottle famous in the last age. It had formerly a castle destroyed by the Scots A.D. 1314. Contiguous to this is Halyston or the Holy stone, where Paulinus is reported to have baptized many thousand persons in the early state of the English church. At the mouth of the Coqued stands Warkworth, a handsome castle of the Percies, defending the coast, where is a chapel hewn in a surprising manner out of the rock without beams or timbers. King Edward III gave this castle to Henry Percy with the manor of Rochbury. It was before the barony of Roger Fitz Richmond, by gift of

Henry II king of England, who also gave Clavering in Essex to his son, on which account, by order of king Edward I they assumed the name of Clavering, quitting the ancient custom of taking names from the Christian name of the father: for before this they were called after their father's name Robert Fitz Roger, Roger Fitz John etc. Part of this estate fell by sine and covenant to the Nevilles, afterwards earls of Westmoreland, part by marriage with a daughter Eva to Thomas Ufford, from whose posterity it came by inheritance to the Fienes barons Dacres. From the younger sons descended the barons de Evers, the Evers of Axholme, the Claverings of Kalaly in this county, and others. Morwic also adjoins to this, which boasts lords of its own, whose male line became extinct about the year 1258. The estate came by daughters to the Lumleys, St. Maurs, Bulmers, and Roscells.

The shore afterwards opens for the river Alaun, which still retaining the name it had in Ptolemy's time is called by contraction Alne, on whose bank besides Twifford, where was held a synod under king Egfrid; and Effington the seat of the Collingwoods, distinguished for their military achievements, we see also Aln-wick, commonly called Anwick, a town renowned for the victory gained by the English, whereby the valour of our ancestors put William king of Scotland prisoner into the hands of Henry II. It is defended by a noble castle, which Malcolm III king of Scotland, having besieged, and so closely pressed, that it was upon the point of surrendering, was slain there by a soldier who coming out to deliver the keys to him rode at him with a lance in arrest, at the end of which they hung. At the same time his son Edward, eager to avenge his father's death, rushing unguardedly upon the enemy, received a mortal wound, of which he soon after died. This was once the barony of the Vescies, given by Henry II to Eustace son of John, father of William Vesci, by the service of twelve knights fees. John Vesey returning from the holy war first brought the Carmelite monks with him into England, and built them a convent here in the desart of Holne, not unlike mount Carmel in Syria. William, the last of the Vescies, leaving this castle to Anthony Bec, bishop of Durham, in trust for his bastard and only son, the bishop dishonestly retained the estate, and sold it for a sum of ready money to William Percy, from which time it has belonged to the Percies.

The shore hence wedging in in several angles proceeds by Dunstanburgh, a castle belonging to the dutchy of Lancaster, which some falsely suspected to be Bebba, which stands higher up, and is now called Bamborrow. Our countryman Bede, describing the besieging and burning of this castle by Penda the Mercian, says it had its name from queen Bebba. But Matthew of Westminster tells us, that Ida first king of Northumberland, built it, fortifying it first with wooden palisadoes, and afterwards with a wall. But take the following description of it from Roger Hoveden: "Bebba," says he, "is a strong city, not very large, but including about two or three acres, having one entrance hollowed out and raised with steps in a surprising manner, and on the top of the hill a beautiful church, and to the west at the top a fountain adorned with extraordinary workmanship, sweet to the taste and clear to the eye." At this time it is rather a castle than a city, though large enough to pass for a city. Nor was it accounted any other than a castle when king William Rufus erected over against it a tower called Malvoisin, to blockade Mowbray, who was in rebellion against him, and had concealed himself there, but afterwards privately withdrew himself. It lost the greatest part of its beauty long after in the civil war, when Bresse a Norman warrior, who sided with the house of Lancaster, cruelly defaced it. From that time it has suffered from time and winds, which throw up incredible quantities of sand from the sea upon its walls through the windows which are open. Contiguous to this is Emildon, formerly the barony of John Le Viscont, but Rametta, heiress of the family, sold their estates to Simon de Montfort earl of Leicester. In this place was born John Duns, surnamed Scotus, because of his Scottish descent, who was educated in Merton college, Oxford, and became uncommonly learned in logic and the abstruse divinity of that age, but by his doubts obscured the credibility of the scriptures, and, with his deep and admirable refinement, though in an obscure, uncultivated style, wrote so many things as to acquire the name of the Subtle Doctor, and formed a new sect called from him Scotish. But he came to a miserable end; for being seized with an apoplexy, and too hastily buried on a supposition that he was dead, recovering himself, and Nature too late overcoming the disorder, after many fruitless miserable cries for assistance, and beating himself a long while against the stone tomb, he at last dashed his brains out and expired. Whence an Italian poet made these lines on him:

> All human principles and all divine,
>   With all things else Duns Scotus call'd in doubt;
> What wonder then if death so drew the line,
>   That whether life was gone was not found out?
> Nor death the Doctor would of life deprive,
>   'Till he was clos'd up in the tomb alive.

That he was born in England I learn from some MS pieces of his in Merton college library, and on their authority I assert it. They end thus: "Here endeth the lecture of the Subtle Doctor in the university of Paris, John Duns, born in a little town in the parish of Emildon, called Dunston, in the county of Northumberland, belonging to the house of scholars of Merton hall in Oxford."

Nothing else remarkable occurs on this coast except Holy Island, of which in its place, till we come to the mouth of the river Twede, which, for a long way, divides England from Scotland, and is called the East march, whence our poet Necham wrote:

A certain bound'ry is the river fixt
Call'd Twede, between the English and the Picts.

This river rises with a copious stream out of the Scottish mountains, and, for a long time, meanders among the horsemen and marauders on the borders, to give no harsher name to a set of men, whose only property is, as one says, in their swords. When it approaches the village of Carr, increased by many streams, it begins to divide the two kingdoms; and after washing Werk, a castle formerly of the Rosses, but now of the Greys, who have long figured in the field, against which castle the Scots have frequently bent their fury, it receives an addition from the river Till. This last river has two names. At its source, which is in the heart of this county, it is called Bramish, and on it stands Bramton, a little obscure village, and of scarce any note, whence it proceeds north by Bengley, which with Brampton itself, Bromdun, Rodam, which gives name to a famous family in these parts, Edelingham, etc. was the barony of Patrick earl of Dunbar in Henry III who also was, as expressed in the book of Inquisitions among the royal records, Inborow and Outborow between England and Scotland; that is, if I understand it rightly, obliged to secure and protect the communication to and fro between the two kingdoms. For the old English call entrance and a porch in their language Inborou. Higher up on the right stands Chevelingham, then called Chilling-ham, which as well as Horton, not far distant, have both been castles of the Greys ever since the two families of that name were united by marriage.

Near these lies the barony of Wollover, which king Henry I gave to Robert de Muschamp. Robert was accounted in the reign of Henry III the most potent baron in these northern parts. But the estate was presently parcelled out among females, one of whom married the earl of Stra-therne in Scotland, another William de Huntercombe, a third Odonell de Ford. The river Glen next adds its waters from the west to those of the Till, and gives name to Glendal, a valley through which it runs. Of this rivulet Bede gives this account.

Paulinus coming with the king and queen to the royal manor called Ad-Gebrin (now Yeverin), stayed there thirty-six days with them employed in the duties of catechizing and baptizing. In all this time he did nothing from morn-ing to night but instruct the people who flocked to him from all the villages and places in the doctrine of Christ and Salvation; and, after they were instructed, baptizing them in the neighbouring river Glen. This palace was deserted by succeeding princes, and another built in its stead in a place called Melmin, but now Melfeld.

Here, near Brumridge, at Brumeford, king Athelstan in a pitched battle with Anlaf the Dane, Constatine king of Scotland, and Eugenius petty prince of Cumberland, came off so successful, that this battle was celebrated in all the pomp of language and poetry by the historians and poets of that age. Here Bramish takes the name of Till, and first visits Ford, once a castle of the warlike family of Heron, now of the Carrs; then Etall, where lived the Manours or de Maneriis, formerly renowned for their knightly rank, and whose posterity are now most noble earls of Rutland. Many castles in this tract I purposely omit: for it would be endless to enumerate them all, it being certain there were in Henry II's time 1115 castles in England.

Over against Ford to the west rises a very high hill called Floddon, remarkable for the death of James IV, King of Scotland, and the slaughter of his army, which while Henry VIII was besieging Tournay in France, invaded England with great courage and greater confidence, for they had parcelled out towns among them beforehand. But Thomas Howard earl of Surrey with his army gave them a warm reception here, and both sides fought furiously till night interposed, leaving it uncertain which had the victory. The next day discovered both the victor and the vanquished, and the king of Scotland himself was covered with wounds among the thickest heaps of slain. From this event the Howards gained an addition to their arms.

Twede, now increased by the Till, runs down with a fuller stream by Norham, or Northam, anciently a town of the bishops of Durham. It was built by bishop Egfrid, and his successor Ranulph erected a castle on the top of a steep rock, and fortified it with a ditch. On the outer wall, which is of great compass, were many little towers in the angle next the river; within is another circular wall much stronger, in the centre whereof rises a loftier tower: but the established peace of our age long suffered this castle, though on the border, to run to decay. Below it in a plain to the west lies the town, having a church in which is buried Ceolwulph, king of Northumberland, to whom venerable Bede addressed his books of the Ecclesiastical History of England. This prince afterwards "renouncing the world, became a monk in the church of Lindisfarn in the service of the kingdom of heaven, and his body was afterwards conveyed to the church of Northam." When the Danes ravaged Holy Island, where St. Cuthbert so much celebrated by Bede sat as bishop, and was buried, and certain persons, by a religious thievery, endeavoured to remove his body, the winds setting against them, obliged to leave the holy body, with due reverence, at Ubbanford, and we are not certain whether the see was not removed thither, near the river Twede, where it lay many years, till the accession of king Ethelred. . . .

A little lower we see the mouth of the Twede, on the further side of which stands the last and best fortified town in all Britain, Berwick. Some derive its name from an imaginary duke Berengarius. Leland derives it from Aber, which signifies in Britain a mouth, Aberwic, meaning the town at the mouth. But whoever knows the meaning of Berwic in the charters of our kings, wherein nothing is more common than "I give the towns of Cumberland and Durham with their berwics," will find the obvious etymology of this name. I cannot guess what it means, unless a village annexed as an appendage to some more considerable place. For, in the grants of Edward the Confessor, Totthill is called berwicus to Westminster and Wandlesworth to Patricsey, and innumerable other such instances. But to what purpose all this may some object. To little enough indeed if it should appear, as some will have it, that the Saxons anciently called it "Beonnica," a town of the Bernicians by which name it is sufficiently known and already observed these countries were distinguished. But from whencesoever it has its name, it runs a great way out to sea, so as to be almost surrounded by it and the Twede; and lying between two most potent kingdoms, as Pliny relates of Palmyra in Syria, it was always the first object of each on the breaking out of war, so that from the time that Edward I first wrested it from the Scots it was often retaken by them, and recovered by the English. With the reader's leave, we shall here give a brief history of it. I find no older account of this town of Berwick than that William king of Scotland being taken prisoner by the English in battle, surrendered it to our Henry II for his ransom, on condition that it should for ever belong to England, unless he paid the price of his release on a certain day, and Henry, as appears from the Polychronicon of Durham, immediately fortified it with a castle. But, on payment of the money, Richard I restored it to the Scots. Afterwards king John, as we read in the History of Mailros, "took both the town and castle of Berwick, when he burnt Werk, Roxburgh, Mitford, and Morpeth, and laid waste all Northumberland with his Rutars, because the Northumbrian barons had done homage to Alexander king of Scots at Feltun." Many years after, when Balliol king of Scotland broke his oath, Edward I reduced Berwick A.D. 1297, but soon after the fortune of war favouring the Scots, they finding it abandoned recovered it, and presently after our people retook it upon terms. Afterwards in that disordered reign of Edward II Peter Spalding surrendered it to Robert Brus, king of Scotland, who vigorously attacked us, and our people in vain besieged it till our Hector Edward III 1333, boldly assaulting it, happily made himself master of it. In the reign of Richard II some marauders surprised the castle, but Henry Percy, earl of Northumberland, retook it within nine days. Scarce seven years after the Scots again retook it, not by force but money, for which the said Henry Percy, who was governor of the place, was charged with high treason, but he again overcame the honour and courage of the Scots by money, and soon recovered it. A long while after, when England was miserably involved in a civil war, Henry VI taking shelter in Scotland, gave it up to the Scots to purchase their protection. But twenty-two years after, Thomas Stanley, with great loss of men, reduced it for Edward IV. From that time the kings of England have continually added works to it, particularly queen Elizabeth, who lately, to the terror of the enemy, and security of the townspeople, contracted the circuit of its walls, drawing within the old ones a very high wall, well built of strong stone, surrounded by a deep ditch, a regular rampart, redoubts, counterscarps, and covered ways, so that the form and strength of the fortifications is sufficient to discourage all hopes of carrying it by assault, not to mention the bravery of the garrison, and the stores in the place, which exceed belief. The governor of this town (to observe this *en passant*), was always one of the most able and tried of the English nobility, who is at the same time warden of the east border towards Scotland. It stands in longitude 21° 43', latitude 55° 48', whence, by this position, its longest day is 17 hours 22 minutes, and the night only six hours 38 minutes, so that Severus Honoratus rightly says, "Britain, rich in day-light, scarce allows any time for night," nor is it to be wondered at that the soldiers here play at dice all night without candles, if you consider the twilight, and that Juvenal should say, the Britans were content with very little night.

For a conclusion about Berwick take these lines of J. Johnston:

> The Saxon arms, by either nation rais'd,
> To varied ruin varied turns expos'd:
>   How stands she by such ruin uneffaced!
> She stands superior to her worst of woes,
>   And from her grave uprises stronger still;
> Equal to strongest towns her bulwark shows;
>   Her sons each talk of mighty Mars fulfil,
> By bondage and by hardest hazards tried:
>   She calm the banners of her joy displays,
> And happy now may boast her ancient pride;
>   While to her lord she due allegiance pays.
> Her lord, whose sway united Britain fears,
> While to the clouds her head she freely rears.

It may not be amiss to subjoin here the account formerly given of the borderers who live round about this place in his life, written by himself,

and published under another's name, by Aeneas Sylvius, afterwards pope
Pius II who lived in Scotland a private legate about 1448, as they are not
at all altered.

There is a river, which, spreading itself from a high mountain, parts the two
kingdoms. Aeneas having crossed this in a boat, and arriving about sunset at a
large village, went to the house of a peasant, and there supped with the priest
of the place and his host. The table was plentifully spread with large quantities
of pulse, poultry, and geese, but neither wine nor bread was to be found there,
and all the people of the town, both men and women, flocked about him as to
some new sight, and, as we gaze at negroes or Indians, so did they stare at
Aeneas, asking the priest where he came from, what he came about, and
whether he was a Christian. Aeneas, understanding the difficulties he must
expect on this journey, had taken care to provide himself at a certain monastery
with some loaves, and a measure of red wine, at sight of which they were seized
with greater astonishment, having never seen wine or white bread. Women
with child came up to the table with their husbands, and, after handling the
bread and smelling at the wine, begged some of each, so that it was impossible
to avoid distributing the whole among them. The supper lasting till the second
hour of the night, the priest and host, with all the men and children, made the
best of their way off, and left Aeneas. They said they were going to a tower a
great way off for fear of the Scots, who, when the tide was out, would come over
the river and plunder; nor could they, with all his intreaties, by any means be
prevailed on to take Aeneas with them, nor any of the women, though many of
them were young and handsome; for they think them in no danger from any
enemy, not considering violence offered to women as any harm. Aeneas, therefore remained alone for them with two servants, and a guide, and one hundred
women, who made a circle around the fire, and sat the rest of the night without
sleeping, dressing hemp and chatting with the interpreter. Night was now far
advanced when a great noise was heard by the barking of the dogs, and scream-
ing of the geese, all the women made the best of their way off, the guide getting
away with the rest, and there was as much confusion as if the enemy was at
hand. Aeneas thought it more prudent to wait the event in his bed room (which
happened to be a stable), apprehending if he went out he might mistake his way,
and be robbed by the first he met. And soon after the women came back with
the interpreter and reported there was no danger; for it was a party of friends
and not of enemies that were come.

In this country were certain clans called Seovenburghers and Fis-
burghings, of whom we have such obscure accounts that it is beyond my
skill to fix their situation. Nor can I determine whether they were Danes
or English. But Florence of Worcester published by lord William Howard, writes, that when a parliament was held at Oxford, "the more
worthy and powerful ministers of the Seovenburghers Sigeferth and
Morcar" were privately taken off by Edric Streon, that Edmund Clito
against his father's consent married Alfritha wife of Sigefrith, and going

to "the Fifburghings seized upon Sigefrith's land, and subdued that people." But let others discuss this point.

This province being reduced under the dominion of the Saxons by Ofca, brother of Hengist, and his son Jebusa, had at first its own dukes subject to the kings of Kent. Afterwards upon the establishment of the kingdom of the Bernicians, whom the Britans call Guir a Brinaich, or mountaineers, which reached from the Trees to the frith of Edinburgh, this was the best part of it, and subject to the king of Northumberland, upon the end of whose government all beyond the Twede became subject to the Scots. But Egbert, king of the East Saxons, added this country by a voluntary cession to his own dominions. Alfred afterwards yielded it to the Danes whom Athelstan, a few years after, drove out. The people, however, made Eilric the Dane king, who was presently driven out by king Ealdred. From that time the name of king ceased in this province, and those who governed were called earls. Of these our historians give the following names: Osulf, Ostac, Edulph, Waltheof the elder, Uchtred, Adulph, Alred, Siward, Tosti, Edwin, Morcar, Osculph, Siward that brave man, who, as he had lived in arms, would die in his armour. "But his earldom of York was given to Tosti brother of earl Harold, and those of Northampton and Huntingdon, with the rest of his lands, to the famous earl Waltheof, his son and heir." I have inserted these words of Ingulphus because some will not allow him to have been earl of Huntingdon. I shall now subjoin what I have read to this purpose in an ancient parchment MS in the library of John Stowe, that honest citizen and diligent antiquary of London. Copsi being made earl of Northumberland by grant of William the Conqueror drove out Osculph, by whom, however, he was slain a few days after. Osculph was afterwards stabbed by a robber with a spear, and died of the wound. Gospatric then bought the earldom of the Conqueror, who presently after turned him out, and appointed Waltheof, son of Siward, for his successor. He being beheaded was succeeded by Walcher bishop of Durham, who, as well as Robert Comin, his successor, was slain in an insurrection. Robert Mowbray afterwards obtained the same title, which he presently lost by his base treachery. Then king Stephen, as we read in the Ploychronicon of Durham, created Henry, son of David, king of Scots, earl of Northumberland, whose son William, after his accession to the crown of Scotland, wrote himself William de Warren earl of Northumberland, his mother being of the family of the earls Warren, as appears by the register of Brinkburn priory. A few years after this Richard I sold this earldom to Hugh Pudsey, bishop of Durham, for life. But when the king was imprisoned by the emperor at his return from the Holy Land, and Hugh contributed only 2000 lb. of silver towards his ransom, the king took this so unkindly, as thinking this very little in proportion to the immense sums which he understood he had collected under pretence of procuring his liberty, that he deprived him of the earldom.

At present this honour is enjoyed by the Percy family, which, descending from the earls of Brabant, took the name of Percy, with the estates of Percy, ever since Josceline, younger son of Godfrey duke of Brabant, the true issue of Charlemagne, by Gerberga, daughter of Charles, younger brother of Lothaire last king of France, of the Carlovingian race, married Agnes, daughter and sole heiress of William Percy, which Williams' great-grandfather William Percy, coming into England with William the Conqueror, received from him the lands in Tatcaster, Linton, Normanby, and other places. It was agreed between this Agnes and Josceline that he should take the name of Percy and retain his old arms of Brabant, a Lion Az. (which the Brabants afterwards changed) in a field Or. The first earl of Northumberland of this family was Henry Percy son of Mary, daughter of Henry earl of Lancaster, who, on account of his ancient nobility and achievements in war, was rewarded by Edward III with large estates in Scotland, and received such an increase of wealth with his second wife Maud Lucy, that though he had no children by her, yet she made him engage to bear the arms of Lucy, and Richard II created him earl of Northumberland. But he made him a base return for this favour, deserting him in his troubles, and opening the way to the crown for Henry IV who gave him the Isle of Man, and against whom, being secretly hurt in his conscience for the unjust deposition of Richard II through his means, and piqued at the neglect and imprisonment of his kinsman Edmund Mortimer, earl of March, the undoubted heir to the crown, he broke out into rebellion, first privately stirring up against him his brother Thomas, earl of Worcester, and his spirited son Henry, surnamed Hotspur, with an army: but both fell in the field at Shrewsbury. Being for this attainted, but soon after, by a certain connivance, taken into favour again by the king, who was afraid of him, he had all his goods restored, except the Isle of Man, which the king kept for himself. Shortly after, hurrying into new disturbances, and calling in the Scots to his assistance, he took up arms against the king as an usurper, and, being suddenly met and attacked at Braham moor by Thomas Rokesby, sheriff of Yorkshire, was routed and slain in a disorderly rencontre, A.D. 1408. Eleven years after Henry Percy, son of his son Henry Hotspur (whose mother Elizabeth was daughter to Edmund Mortimer the elder, earl of March by Philippa, daughter of Lionel duke of Clarence), was restored to his grandfather's honours by act of parliament under Henry V and, warmly espousing the interests of Henry VI against the Yorkists, fell in the battle of St. Albans. His son Henry, third earl of Northumberland, who married Eleanor, daughter of Richard baron Poynings, Brian, and Fitz Payn, lost his life in the same cause at the battle of Towton, A.D. 1461.

The house of Lancaster being in a manner ruined, and the name of Percy sunk with it, king Edward IV created John Nevill lord Montacute earl of Northumberland; but he shortly after surrendered up this title to the king, and received that of marquis Mont Acute. Afterwards Henry Percy, son of Henry just mentioned, by favour of Edward IV obtained his father's title, and in the reign of Henry VII was killed in an insurrection of the peasants against the collectors of a tax levied by act of parliament. He was succeeded by Henry Percy, fifth earl, who, by a daughter and coheiress of Robert Spenser, and Eleanor, daughter and coheiress of Edmund de Beaufort, lord of Somerset, had Henry, sixth earl, who, having no sons, and his brother Thomas being put to death for taking up arms against Henry VIII in the beginning of the Reformation, as if the family was almost reduced to nothing, lavished away the greatest part of that fine estate in presents to the king and others. A few years after John Dudley, earl of Warwick, took the title of duke of Northumberland when in the minority of Edward VI the leaders of the several parties disposed of honours among themselves to gratify their respective parties. This was that duke of Northumberland who some time disturbed the peace of his country like a blast, endeavouring to exclude Mary and Elizabeth, daughters of Henry VIII from the lawful succession, and contrived by the interest of the lawyers, ever ready to follow those in power, to settle the crown on Jane Grey, to whom he had married his son. For this being convicted of high treason, he lost his head, embracing the publicly professing at the block the Popish religion, which, to serve his turn, he had long before renounced, or pretended to renounce. On his death queen Mary restored in blood Thomas Percy, nephew to Henry, sixth earl and son of his brother Thomas, creating him first baron Percy, and soon after by a new patent earl of Northumberland "to him and the heirs male of his body, and in failure thereof, to his brother Henry and his heirs male." But this Thomas, seventh earl, disguising his treachery against his sovereign and country under the colour of a zeal for restoring Popery, lost his life and honour, A.D. 1572. However, by the special favour of queen Elizabeth, Henry his brother, eighth earl, succeeded according to the tenor of queen Mary's patent, and ended his days in prison, A.D. 1585, leaving his son Henry by Cathatine, eldest daughter and one of the heiresses of Nevill lord Latimer, who succeeds him, being ninth earl of Northumberland of this family.

William Bradford

1590—1657

6

Just one generation after William Camden had expanded the subject and advanced the methods of English historiography, William Bradford began to record the history of his own parish, the Plymouth Colony of Cape Cod. Camden delighted in his discovery of ancient Britain, and spared no effort to develop the means by which he could decipher the relics he uncovered. Bradford, governor of a separatist sect of Protestant Pilgrims, saw no need to find new ways of writing history. He wanted only to show what all pious Puritans already knew—that the hand of God directed all human history, and he hoped to vindicate that faith in divine providence by telling the story of how a brave, select, little colony of believers survived persecution in the old world and conquered the wilderness of a new one. He was to write the history he had lived; his only sources were his Bible, his memory, and notebooks; his only subject, a small band of saintly citizens.

In 1609, Bradford left what would have been the profitable life of a yeoman farmer to join a sect of Protestants who were emigrating to Holland to escape persecution in Scrooby, a small town in his native Nottinghamshire. Bradford was determined to remain with the devout flock in Holland, where he was obliged to learn cotton weaving to survive, and to sail with them first to England, and then, in a perilous voyage on the *Mayflower,* to a new land across the ocean. In America, the Pilgrims had to be victorious over adversity, not so much for their own prosperity as to prove once more that God had chosen them over all other Protestants to complete the work of the English Reformation, ridding the world of any remaining agents of the devil or, as Bradford put it, "popish and antichristian stuff."

The year after they arrived on the Cape, the Pilgrims elected Bradford their governor. To them, he was the natural choice, God's choice as it were, to lead them in their struggle against nature. In Europe, he had been a capable businessman on behalf of his brethren, conducting negotiations for the sea voyage; now he was to be the leader on land, heading the first expedition

112

to Plymouth, guiding the colony through the difficult times of settlement. From 1621 on, until the year before his death, Bradford was re-elected governor thirty times.

Bradford began *Of Plymouth Plantation* in 1630, after nine years as governor, and continued to work on it until 1650. He intended to write only a plain and worshipful story, one that all the faithful might understand. In fact, he gave us the most complete record we have of the settlement until 1646, the year he ended his narrative.

Of Plymouth Plantation is a beautifully written drama of destiny and doom. Bradford gives incessant thanks to God for leading the Pilgrims to Plymouth, for bringing rain when there was drought, for defeating the Indians when they threatened the peace of the colony. The story is skillfully developed, achieving at times a sublime climax, as in the description of the departure from Leyden, or of the landing on the Cape. The very simplicity of the prose takes us closer to the speech of the Pilgrims themselves. But the end of Bradford's moving story is sad and desolate—disgruntled pastors leave the fold; cattle die off; sin breaks forth; the old, virtuous colonists die, and the younger more selfish ones leave Plymouth "by reason of barrenness to find better accommodations." By 1644, in the last page of our selection, Bradford notes in his simple, moving way, that "thus was this poor church left . . . she that had made many rich became herself poor."

Selected Bibliography

Samuel Eliot Morison's sketch of Bradford's life in the *Dictionary of American Biography*, II (1946), 559–563, is a model for this type of reference work: precise, accurate, concerned with both the man and his literary productions. Not enough is known, at this point, about Bradford's life for a full-length biography; as a result, Bradford Smith in his *Bradford of Plymouth* (1951) resorts to some guesswork. *Literature and Theology in Colonial New England* (1949; Harper Torchbook edition, 1963), 80–84, by Kenneth B. Murdock, has an astute discussion of Bradford's style and intentions. The section on Bradford in Peter Gay, *A Loss of Mastery: Puritan Historians in Colonial America* (1966), 26–52, is an appreciative and critical analysis of Bradford as a gifted artist, shackled by his Augustinian understanding of history. Two surveys of American historiography give Bradford his due: Michael Kraus' *The Writing of American History* (1953), 20–24, is more superficial than the older *A History of American Literature, 1607–1795* (1878; reprinted, 1949), 101–109, by Moses Coit Tyler. All critics are given to relying on long quotations from Bradford, for no modern commentator can quite describe his lovely, old-world prose.

OF PLYMOUTH PLANTATION

And first of the occasion and inducements thereunto; the which, that I may truly unfold, I must begin at the very root and rise of the same. The which I shall endeavour to manifest in a plain style, with singular regard unto the simple truth in all things; at least as near as my slender judgment can attain the same.

Chapter 1 [The Separatist interpretation of the Reformation in England, 1550–1607]

It is well known unto the godly and judicious, how ever since the first breaking out of the light of the gospel in our honourable nation of England, (which was the first of nations whom the Lord adorned therewith after the gross darkness of popery which had covered and overspread the Christian world), what wars and oppositions ever since, Satan hath raised, maintained and continued against the Saints,[1] from time to time, in one sort or other. Sometimes by bloody death and cruel torments; other whiles imprisonments, banishments and other hard usages; as being loath his kingdom should go down, the truth prevail and the churches of God revert to their ancient purity and recover their primitive order, liberty and beauty.

But when he could not prevail by these means against the main truths of the gospel, but that they began to take rooting in many places, being watered with the blood of the martyrs and blessed from Heaven with a gracious increase; he then began to take him to his ancient stratagems, used of old against the first Christians. That when by the bloody and barbarous persecutions of the heathen emperors he could not stop and subvert the course of the gospel, but that it speedily overspread, with a wonderful celerity, the then best known parts of the world; he then began

---

Of Plymouth Plantation edited by Samuel Eliot Morison, New York: Alfred A. Knopf 1952, pp. 3–10, 47–51, 58–66, 68–72, 313–323, 324–330, 333–334. Copyright 1952 by Samuel Eliot Morison. Reprinted by permission of Alfred A. Knopf, Inc. We reproduce the editor's footnotes.

[1]Bradford uses the word *Saint* in the Biblical sense, as one of God's chosen people, or a church member, not one of those canonized by the Roman Catholic Chruch.

to sow errours, heresies and wonderful dissensions amongst the professors[2] themselves, working upon their pride and ambition, with other corrupt passions incident to all mortal men, yea to the saints themselves in some measure, by which woeful effects followed. As not only bitter contentions and heartburnings, schisms, with other horrible confusions; but Satan took occasion and advantage thereby to foist in a number of vile ceremonies, with many unprofitable canons and decrees, which have since been as snares to many poor and peaceable souls even to this day.

So as in the ancient times, the persecutions by the heathen and their emperors was not greater than of the Christians one against other:—the Arians and other their complices against the orthodox and true Christians. As witnesseth Socrates in his second book.[3] His words are these:

> The violence truly (saith he) was no less than that of old practiced towards the Christians when they were compelled and drawn to sacrifice to idols; for many endured sundry kinds of torment, often rackings and dismembering of their joints, confiscating of their goods; some bereaved of their native soil, others departed this life under the hands of the tormentor, and some died in banishment and never saw their country again, etc.

The like method Satan hath seemed to hold in these later times, since the truth began to spring and spread after the great defection made by Antichrist, that man of sin.[4]

For to let pass the infinite examples in sundry nations and several places of the world, and instance in our own, when as that old serpent could not prevail by those fiery flames and other his cruel tragedies, which he by his instruments put in ure[5] everywhere in the days of Queen Mary and before, he then began another kind of war and went more closely to work; not only to oppugn but even to ruinate and destroy the kingdom of Christ by more secret and subtle means, by kindling the flames of contention and sowing the seeds of discord and bitter enmity amongst the professors and, seeming reformed, themselves. For when he could not prevail by the former means against the principal doctrines of faith, he bent his force against the holy discipline and outward regiment of the kingdom of Christ, by which those holy doctrines should be conserved, and true piety maintained amongst the saints and people of God.

---

[2] *Professor,* as used by Bradford and by Puritans generally, had no educational connotation; it merely meant one who professed Christianity.

[3] Socrates Scholasticus, Greek historian of the 5th century A.D. His Ecclesiastical History translated by Meredith Hanmer was printed in London in 1577. Bradford's quotation is from lib. ii chap. 22.

[4] 2 Thessalonians ii.3.

[5] I.e., into practice.

Mr. Fox[6] recordeth how that besides those worthy martyrs and confessors which were burned in Queen Mary's days and otherwise tormented, "Many (both students and others) fled out of the land to the number of 800, and became several congregations, at Wesel, Frankfort, Basel, Emden, Markpurge, Strasburg and Geneva, etc." Amongst whom (but especially those at Frankfort) began that bitter war of contention and persecution about the ceremonies and service book, and other popish and antichristian stuff, the plague of England to this day, which are like the high places in Israel which the prophets cried out against, and were their ruin. Which the better part sought, according to the purity of the gospel, to root out and utterly to abandon. And the other part (under veiled pretences) for their own ends and advancements, sought as stiffly to continue, maintain and defend. As appeareth by the discourse thereof published in print, anno 1575; a book that deserves better to be known and considered.[7]

The one side laboured to have the right worship of God and discipline of Christ established in the church, according to the simplicity of the gospel, without the mixture of men's inventions; and to have and to be ruled by the laws of God's Word, dispensed in those offices, and by those officers of Pastors, Teachers and Elders, etc. according to the Scriptures. The other party, though under many colours and pretences, endeavoured to have the episcopal dignity (after the popish manner) with their large power and jurisdiction still retained; with all those courts, cannons and ceremonies, together with all such livings, revenues and subordinate officers, with other such means as formerly upheld their antichristian greatness and enabled them with lordly and tyrannous power to persecute the poor servants of God. This contention was so great, as neither the honour of God, the common persecution, nor the mediation of Mr. Calvin and other worthies of the Lord in those places, could prevail with those thus episcopally minded; but they proceeded by all means to disturb the peace of this poor persecuted church, even so far as to charge (very unjustly and ungodlily yet prelatelike) some of their chief opposers with rebellion and high treason against the Emperor, and other such crimes.

---

[6]Acts and Mon[uments]: pag. 1587 edition 2 (Bradford). His reference is to John Fox *Acts and Monuments* (familiarly known as the *Book of Martyrs*) p. 1587 of 2nd edition.

[7]William Whittingham *Brieff Discours of the Troubles begonne at Franckford,* printed at Zurich or Geneva in 1575. The row was between the Marian exiles who wished to abolish "service books" altogether (which Bradford and the entire left wing of English Protestantism believed should have been done), and those who adopted the typically English compromise of a Book of Common Prayer. The Marian exiles, or some of them, wished to reorganize the church on congregational principles which they believed alone to be sanctioned by the New Testament.

And this contention died not with Queen Mary, nor was left beyond the seas. But at her death these people returning into England under gracious Queen Elizabeth, many of them being preferred to bishoprics and other promotions according to their aims and desires, that inveterate hatred against the holy discipline of Christ in His church[8] hath continued to this day. Insomuch that for fear it should prevail, all plots and devices have been used to keep it out, incensing the Queen and State against it as dangerous for the commonwealth; and that it was most needful that the fundamental points of religion should be preached in those ignorant and superstitious times. And to win the weak and ignorant they might retain divers harmless ceremonies; and though it were to be wished that divers things were reformed, yet this was not a season for it. And many the like, to stop the mouths of the more godly, to bring them on to yield to one ceremony after another, and one corruption after another; by these wiles beguiling some and corrupting others till at length they began to persecute all the zealous professors in the land (though they knew little what this discipline meant) both by word and deed, if they would not submit to their ceremonies and become slaves to them and their popish trash, which have no ground in the Word of God, but are relics of that man of sin. And the more the light of the gospel grew, the more they urged their subscriptions to these corruptions. So as (notwithstanding all their former pretences and fair colours) they whose eyes God had not justly blinded might easily see whereto these things tended. And to cast contempt the more upon the sincere servants of God, they opprobriously and most injuriously gave unto and imposed upon them that name of Puritans, which is said the Novatians out of pride did assume and take unto themselves.[9] And lamentable it is to see the effects which have followed. Religion hath been disgraced, the godly grieved, afflicted, persecuted, and many exiled; sundry have lost their lives in prisons and other ways. On the other hand, sin hath been countenanced; ignorance, profaneness and atheism increased, and the papists encouraged to hope again for a day.

This made that holy man Mr. Perkins cry out in[1] his exhortation to repentance, upon Zephaniah ii:

---

[8]Bradford means the Congregational discipline. His account of church history during Elizabeth's reign is of course a partisan one, unfair to the acts and the motives of everyone not in the left wing of Protestantism.

[9]Eusebius lib. vi chap. 42 (Bradford). The Novatians were an obscure sect of the 3rd century. The term *Puritan,* like *Quaker,* was originally one of reproach, not accepted until nearly the close of the 17th century by the people to whom it was applied. The Puritans called themselves "God's people."

[1]William ("Painful") Perkins, a graduate of Emmanuel College, Cambridge, whose works were much esteemed by all branches of Puritans. The quotation is from his *Exposition of Christ's Sermon Upon the Mount* (1618) p. 421.

Religion (saith he) hath been amongst us this thirty-five years; but the more it is published, the more it is contemned and reproached of many, etc. Thus not profaneness nor wickedness but religion itself is a byword, a mockingstock, and a matter of reproach; so that in England at this day the man or woman that begins to profess religion and to serve God, must resolve with himself to sustain mocks and injuries even as though he lived amongst the enemies of religion.

And this, common experience hath confirmed and made too apparent. But that I may come more near my intendment.

When as by the travail and diligence of some godly and zealous preachers, and God's blessing on their labours, as in other places of the land, so in the North parts, many became enlightened by the Word of God and had their ignorance and sins discovered unto them, and began by His grace to reform their lives and make conscience of their ways; the work of God was no sooner manifest in them but presently they were both scoffed and scorned by the profane multitude; and the ministers urged with the yoke of subscription, or else must be silenced. And the poor people were so vexed with apparitors and pursuivants[2] and the commissary courts, as truly their affliction was not small. Which, notwithstanding, they bore sundry years with much patience, till they were occasioned by the continuance and increase of these troubles, and other means which the Lord raised up in those days, to see further into things by the light of the Word of God. How not only these base and beggarly ceremonies were unlawful, but also that the lordly and tyrannous power of the prelates ought not to be submitted unto; which thus, contrary to the freedom of the gospel, would load and burden men's consciences and by their compulsive power make a profane mixture of persons and things in the worship of God. And that their offices and callings, courts and canons, etc. were unlawful and antichristian; being such as have no warrant in the Word of God, but the same that were used in popery and still retained. Of which a famous author thus writeth in his Dutch commentaries,[3] at the coming of King James into England:

The new king (saith he) found there established the reformed religion according to the reformed religion of King Edward VI, retaining or keeping still the

---

[2]Officers of the Church of England whose duty was to enforce conformity.

[3]Emanuel van Meteren *General History of the Netherlands* (London 1608) xxv. 119. Bradford's reference, to which he adds this remark: "The reformed churches shapen much near[er] the primitive pattern than England, for they cashiered the Bishops with all their courts, canons, and ceremonies, at the first; and left them amongst the popish tr[ash] to which they per[tained]." Bradford passes over the fact that James I at the Hampton Court Conference in 1604 gave full opportunity of self-expression to the Puritans, who so exasperated him with their demands that he declared he would make them conform to the Church of England, "or . . . harry them out of the land, or else do worse."

spiritual state of the bishops, etc. after the old manner, much varying and differing from the reformed churches in Scotland, France and the Netherlands, Emden, Geneva, etc., whose reformation is cut, or shapen much nearer the first Christian churches, as it was used in the Apostles' times.

So many, therefore, of these professors as saw the evil of these things in these parts, and whose hearts the Lord had touched with heavenly zeal for His truth, they shook off this yoke of antichristian bondage, and as the Lord's free people joined themselves (by a covenant of the Lord) into a church estate, in the fellowship of the gospel, to walk in all His ways made known, or to be made known unto them, according to their best endeavours, whatsoever it should cost them, the Lord assisting them.[4] And that it cost them something this ensuing history will declare.

These people became two distinct bodies or churches, and in regard of distance of place did congregate severally; for they were of sundry towns and villages, some in Nottinghamshire, some of Lincolnshire, and some of Yorkshire where they border nearest together. In one of these churches (besides others of note) was Mr. John Smith,[5] a man of able gifts and a good preacher, who afterwards was chosen their pastor. But these afterwards falling into some errours in the Low Countries, there (for the most part) buried themselves and their names.

But in this other church (which must be the subject of our discourse) besides other worthy men, was Mr. Richard Clyfton, a grave and reverend preacher, who by his pains and diligence had done much good, and under God had been a means of the conversion of many. And also that famous and worthy man Mr. John Robinson, who afterwards was their pastor for many years, till the Lord took him away by death. Also Mr. William Brewster a reverend man, who afterwards was chosen an elder of the church and lived with them till old age.[6]

But after these things they could not long continue in any peaceable condition, but were hunted and persecuted on every side, so as their former afflictions were but as flea-bitings in comparison of these which now came upon them. For some were taken and clapped up in prison, others had their houses beset and watched night and day, and hardly

---

[4] A paraphrase of the words of the covenant that people made when they formed a Separatist (later called Congregational) church.

[5] An alumnus of Christ's College, Cambridge, who seceded from the Church of England in 1605 and preached to the Separatist church at Gainsborough. This congregation emigrated in 1608 to Amsterdam, where Smith embraced a number of strange opinions and his church broke up.

[6] Richard Clyfton and John Robinson also were Cambridge alumni in holy orders who separated. Clyfton and William Brewster organized the Separatist congregation at Scrooby, Nottinghamshire, which Bradford joined as a young man. The sentence on Brewster is written in a different ink from the rest of the chapter, having been inserted after the Elder's death in 1643.

escaped their hands; and the most were fain to flee and leave their houses and habitations, and the means of their livelihood.

Yet these and many other sharper things which afterward befell them, were no other than they looked for, and therefore were the better prepared to bear them by the assistance of God's grace and Spirit.

Yet seeing themselves thus molested, and that there was no hope of their continuance there, by a joint consent they resolved to go into the Low Countries, where they heard was freedom of religion for all men; as also how sundry from London and other parts of the land had been exiled and persecuted for the same cause, and were gone thither, and lived at Amsterdam and in other places of the land. So after they had continued together about a year, and kept their meetings every Sabbath in one place or other, exercising the worship of God amongst themselves, notwithstanding all the diligence and malice of their adversaries, they seeing they could no longer continue in that condition, they resolved to get over into Holland as they could. Which was in the year 1607 and 1608; of which more at large in the next chapter. . . .

Chapter 7 Of their departure from Leyden, and other things thereabout; with their arrival at Southampton, where they all met together and took in their provisions

At length, after much travel and these debates, all things were got ready and provided. A small ship[1] was bought and fitted in Holland, which was intended as to serve to help to transport them, so to stay in the country and attend upon fishing and such other affairs as might be for the good and benefit of the colony when they came there. Another was hired at London, of burthen about 9 score,[2] and all other things got in readiness. So being ready to depart, they had a day of solemn humiliation, their pastor taking his text from Ezra viii.21: "And there at the river, by Ahava, I proclaimed a fast, that we might humble ourselves before our God, and seek of him a right way for us, and for our children, and for all our substance." Upon which he spent a good part of the day very profitably and suitable to their present occasion; the rest of the time was spent in pouring[3] out prayers to the Lord with great fervency, mixed with abundance of tears. And the time being come that they must depart, they were accompanied with most of their brethren out of the city, unto a town

---

[1]Of some 60 tun (Bradford). This was the *Speedwell.*

[2]The *Mayflower,* 180 tons.

[3]Spelled *powering* by Bradford, which is the way *pour* was pronounced until the 19th century. "Mine eye powreth our tears unto God," says Job (xvi.20) in the Geneva Bible.

sundry miles off called Delftshaven, where the ship lay ready to receive them. So they left that goodly and pleasant city which had been their resting place near twelve years; but they knew they were pilgrims,[4] and looked not much on those things, but lift up their eyes to the heavens, their dearest country, and quieted their spirits.

When they came to the place they found the ship and all things ready, and such of their friends as could not come with them followed after them, and sundry also came from Amsterdam to see them shipped and to take their leave of them. That night was spent with little sleep by the most, but with friendly entertainment and Christian discourse and other real expressions of true Christian love. The next day (the wind being fair) they went aboard and their friends with them, where truly doleful was the sight of that sad and mournful parting, to see what sighs and sobs and prayers did sound amongst them, what tears did gush from every eye, and pithy speeches pierced each heart; that sundry of the Dutch strangers that stood on the quay as spectators could not refrain from tears. Yet comfortable and sweet it was to see such lively and true expressions of dear and unfeigned love. But the tide, which stays for no man, calling them away that were thus loath to depart, their reverend pastor falling down on his knees (and they all with him) with watery cheeks commended them with most fervent prayers to the Lord and His blessing. And then with mutual embraces and many tears they took their leaves one of another, which proved to be the last leave to many of them.

Thus hoisting sail,[5] with a prosperous wind they came in short time to Southampton, where they found the bigger ship come from London, lying ready, with all the rest of their company. After a joyful welcome and mutual congratulations, with other friendly entertainments, they fell to parley about their business, how to dispatch with the best expedition; as also with their agents about the alteration of the conditions. Mr. Carver pleaded he was employed here at Hampton, and knew not well what the other had done at London; Mr. Cushman answered he had done nothing but what he was urged to, partly by the grounds of equity and more especially by necessity, otherwise all had been dashed and many undone. And in the beginning he acquainted his fellow agents herewith, who consented unto him and left it to him to execute, and to receive the money at London and send it down to them at Hampton, where they made the provisions. The which he accordingly did, though it was against his mind

---

[4]Hebrews xi.13–16 (Bradford). It was owing to this passage, first printed in 1669, that the *Mayflower*'s company came eventually to be called the Pilgrim Fathers. Albert Matthew's exhaustive history of the use of that term is in Colonial Society of Massachusetts *Publications* XVII (1915) 300–92.

[5]This was about 22 of July (Bradford), 1620.

and some of the merchants, that they were there made. And for giving them notice at Leyden of this change, he could not well in regard of the shortness of the time; again, he knew it would trouble them and hinder the business, which was already delayed overlong in regard of the season of the year, which he feared they would find to their cost.

Mr. Weston, likewise, came up from London to see them dispatched and to have the conditions confirmed. But they refused and answered him that he knew right well that these were not according to the first agreement, neither could they yield to them without the consent of the rest that were behind. And indeed they had special charge when they came away, from the chief of those that were behind, not to do it. At which he was much offended and told them they must then look to stand on their own legs. So he returned in displeasure and this was the first ground of discontent between them. And whereas there wanted well near £ 100 to clear things at their going away, he would not take order to disburse a penny but let them shift as they could. So they were forced to sell off some of their provisions to stop this gap, which was some three or four-score firkins of butter,[6] which commodity they might best spare, having provided too large a quantity of that kind. Then they writ a letter to the merchants and Adventurers about the differences concerning the conditions, as followeth:

Southampton, Aug. 3, Anno 1620.

BELOVED FRIENDS,

Sorry we are that there should be occasion of writing at all unto you, partly because we ever expected to see the most of you here, but especially because there should any difference at all be conceived between us. But seeing it falleth out that we cannot confer together, we think it meet (though briefly) to show you the just cause and reason of our differing from those articles last made by Robert Cushman, without our commission or knowledge. And though he might propound good ends to himself, yet it no way justifies his doing it. Our main difference is in the fifth and ninth articles concerning the dividing or holding of house and lands; the enjoying whereof, some of yourselves well know, was one special motive amongst many other, to provoke us to go. This was thought so reasonable that when the greatest of you in adventure (whom we have much cause to respect) when he propounded conditions to us freely of his own accord, he set this down for one. A copy whereof we have sent unto you, with some additions then added by us; which being liked on both sides, and a day set for the payment of moneys, those of Holland paid in theirs. After that, Robert Cushman, Mr. Peirce, and Mr. Martin, brought them into a better form and writ them in a book now extant; and upon Robert's showing them and delivering Mr. Mullins a copy thereof under his hand (which we have) he paid in his money. And we of Holland had never seen other before our coming to Hampton, but only

---

[6]This would mean 3360 to 4720 lb. of butter.

as one got for himself a private copy of them. Upon sight whereof we manifested utter dislike but had put off our estates and were ready to come, and therefore was too late to reject the voyage.

Judge therefore, we beseech you, indifferently of things, and if a fault have been committed, lay it where it is, and not upon us who have more cause to stand for the one than you have for the other. We never gave Robert Cushman commission to make any one article for us, but only sent him to receive moneys upon articles before agreed on, and to further the provisions till John Carver came, and to assist him in it. Yet since you conceive yourselves wronged as well as we, we thought meet to add a branch to the end of our ninth article, as will almost heal that wound of itself, which you conceive to be in it. But that it may appear to all men that we are not lovers of ourselves only, but desire also the good and enriching of our friends who have adventured your moneys with our persons, we have added our last article to the rest, promising you again by letters in the behalf of the whole company, that if large profits should not arise within the seven years, that we will continue together longer with you, if the Lord give a blessing.[7] This we hope is sufficient to satisfy any in this case, especially friends; since we are assured that if the whole charge was divided into four parts, three of them will not stand upon it, neither do regard it, etc.

We are in such a strait at present, as we are forced to sell away £60 worth of our provisions to clear the haven, and withal to put ourselves upon great extremities, scarce having any butter, no oil, not a sole to mend a shoe, nor every man a sword to his side, wanting many muskets, much armour, etc. And yet we are willing to expose ourselves to such eminent dangers as are like to ensue, and trust to the good providence of God, rather than His name and truth should be evil spoken of, for us. Thus saluting all of you in love, and beseeching the Lord to give a blessing to our endeavour, and keep all our hearts in the bonds of peace and love, we take leave and rest,

Aug. 3, 1620   Yours, etc.

It was subscribed with many names of the chiefest of the company.

At their parting Mr. Robinson writ a letter to the whole company; which though it hath already been printed,[8] yet I thought good here likewise to insert it. As also a brief letter writ at the same time to Mr. Carver, in which the tender love and godly care of a true pastor appears.

All things being now ready, and every business dispatched, the company was called together and this letter read amongst them, which had good acceptation with all, and after fruit with many. Then they ordered and distributed their company for either ship, as they conceived for the best; and chose a Governor and two or three assistants for each ship, to

---

[7]It was well for them that this was not accepted (Bradford). Several members of the Leyden congregation who did not emigrate contributed to the "adventure" or investment; hence this lengthy explanation.

[8]In the extracts from Bradford's and Winslow's Journals, published in London 1622 and generally called *Mourt's Relation.*

order the people by the way, and see to the disposing of their provisions and such like affairs. All which was not only with the liking of the masters of the ships but according to their desires. Which being done, they set sail from thence about the 5th of August. But what befell them further upon the coast of England will appear in the next chapter. . . .

Chapter 9 Of their voyage, and how they passed the sea; and of their safe arrival at Cape Cod

September 6. These troubles being blown over, and now all being compact together in one ship, they put to sea again with a prosperous wind, which continued divers days together, which was some encouragement unto them; yet, according to the usual manner, many were afflicted with seasickness. And I may not omit here a special work of God's providence. There was a proud and very profane young man, one of the seamen, of a lusty, able body, which made him the more haughty; he would alway be contemning the poor people in their sickness and cursing them daily with grievous execrations; and did not let to tell them that he hoped to help to cast half of them overboard before they came to their journey's end, and to make merry with what they had; and if he were by any gently reproved, he would curse and swear most bitterly. But it pleased God before they came half seas over, to smite this young man with a grievous disease, of which he died in a desperate manner, and so was himself the first that was thrown overboard. Thus his curses light on his own head, and it was an astonishment to all his fellows for they noted it to be the just hand of God upon him.

After they had enjoyed fair winds and weather for a season, they were encountered many times with cross winds and met with many fierce storms with which the ship was shroudly[1] shaken, and her upper works made very leaky; and one of the main beams in the midships was bowed and cracked, which put them in some fear that the ship could not be able to perform the voyage. So some of the chief of the company, perceiving the mariners to fear the sufficiency of the ship as appeared by their mutterings, they entered into serious consultation with the master and other officers of the ship, to consider in time of the danger, and rather to return than to cast themselves into a desperate and inevitable peril. And truly there was great distraction and difference of opinion amongst the mariners themselves; fain would they do what could be done for their wages' sake (being now near half the seas over) and on the other hand they were loath to hazard their lives too desperately. But in examining

---

[1] An old form of *shrewdly* in its original meaning *wickedly.*

of all opinions, the master and others affirmed they knew the ship to be strong and firm under water; and for the buckling of the main beam, there was a great iron screw the passengers brought out of Holland, which would raise the beam into his place; the which being done, the carpenter and master affirmed that with a post put under it, set firm in the lower deck and otherways bound, he would make it sufficient. And as for the decks and upper works, they would caulk them as well as they could, and though with the working of the ship they would not long keep staunch, yet there would otherwise be no great danger, if they did not overpress her with sails. So they committed themselves to the will of God and resolved to proceed.

In sundry of these storms the winds were so fierce and the seas so high, as they could not bear a knot of sail, but were forced to hull[2] for divers days together. And in one of them, as they thus lay at hull in a mighty storm, a lusty[3] young man called John Howland, coming upon some occasion above the gratings was, with a seele[4] of the ship, thrown into sea; but it pleased God that he caught hold of the topsail halyards which hung overboard and ran out at length. Yet he held his hold (though he was sundry fathoms under water) till he was hauled up by the same rope to the brim of the water, and then with a boat hook and other means got into the ship again and his life saved. And though he was something ill with it, yet he lived many years after and became a profitable member both in church and commonwealth. In all this voyage there died but one of the passengers, which was William Butten, a youth, servant to Samuel Fuller, when they drew near the coast.

But to omit other things (that I may be brief) after long beating at sea they fell with that land which is called Cape Cod;[5] the which being made and certainly known to be it, they were not a little joyful. After some deliberation had amongst themselves and with the master of the ship, they tacked about and resolved to stand for the southward (the wind and weather being fair) to find some place about Hudson's River for their habitation.[6] But after they had sailed that course about half the day, they

---

[2]To heave or lay-to under very short sail and drift with the wind.

[3]Lively, merry; no sexual connotation. Howland, a servant of Governor Carver, rose to be one of the leading men of the Colony.

[4]Roll or pitch.

[5]At daybreak 9/19 Nov. 1620, they sighted the Highlands of Cape Cod. Full discussion in W. Sears Nickerson *Land Ho!—1620* chap. iv.

[6]This is the only direct statement in the *History* as to whither the *Mayflower* was bound. I see no reason to doubt its accuracy. It is borne out by Bradford's own journal in *Mourt's Relation* (see chap. 10 note 2, below): "We made our course south-southwest, purposing to go to a river ten leagues to the south of the Cape, but at night the wind being contrary, we put round again for the Bay of Cape Cod." Although the mouth of the Hudson is nearer 15 than 10 leagues south of the Cape

fell amongst dangerous shoals and roaring breakers, and they were so far entangled therewith as they conceived themselves in great danger; and the wind shrinking upon them withal, they resolved to bear up again for the Cape and thought themselves happy to get out of those dangers before night overtook them, as by God's good providence they did. And the next day[7] they got into the Cape Harbor[8] where they rid in safety.

A word or two by the way of this cape. It was thus first named by Captain Gosnold and his company,[9] Anno 1602, and after by Captain Smith was called Cape James; but it retains the former name amongst seamen. Also, that point which first showed those dangerous shoals unto them they called Point Care, and Tucker's Terrour; but the French and Dutch to this day call it Malabar by reason of those perilous shoals and the losses they have suffered there.[1]

Being thus arrived in a good harbor, and brought safe to land, they fell upon their knees and blessed the God of Heaven[2] who had brought them over the vast and furious ocean, and delivered them from all the perils

---

in latitude, the Pilgrims' knowledge of New England geography was far from exact, and the Hudson was doubtless meant. The Virginia Company, which had granted the Peirce Patent which the Pilgrims brought with them, had a right to colonize up to lat. 41° N, which included Manhattan Island. The Dutch did not settle Manhattan (the famous $24 purchase) until 1626, although they claimed the region by virtue of Hudson's voyage in 1609; the English never admitted their claim, and the Pilgrims, who certainly had heard of the Hudson River and Long Island Sound from the several Dutch voyages thither before 1620, doubtless hoped to be first at that natural center for fur trade and fishing, and were glad to rely on their Patent from the Virginia Company both for local self-government and for protection from Dutch encroachment. John Pory, the Secretary of Virginia who visited Plymouth Colony in 1622, reported that "their voyage was intended for Virginia." They carried letters, he says, from Sir Edwin Sandys and John Ferrar to Governor Sir George Yeardley recommending "that he should give them the best advice he could for trading in Hudson's River." Champlin Burrage *John Pory's Lost Description of Plymouth* (1918) p. 35. The theory that Master Jones of the *Mayflower* was bribed by the Dutch to set the Pilgrims ashore at a safe distance from Manhattan has a respectable antiquity but no basis in fact. No seaman who has weathered Cape Cod needs any better explanation than a head wind on unbuoyed Pollock Rip to explain why the *Mayflower* turned back.

[7]Nov. 11/21, 1620. Thus the *Mayflower's* passage from Plymouth took 65 days.
[8]Now Provincetown Harbor.
[9]Because they took much of that fish there (Bradford).
[1]The location of these places is discussed by W. Sears Nickerson chap. iii. He believes that the original Point Care and Tucker's Terror (so named by Gosnold) and Mallebarre (named by Champlain) were at Nauset Harbor. The name Mallebarre later became transferred to Monomoy, which is called Cape Malabar in the *Atlantic Neptune* (1774), Anthony Finley's *New General Atlas* (1832), U.S. Coast Survey Chart No. 11 (1860), *Black's General Atlas American Edition* (1879), and E. G. Perry *A Trip Around Cape Cod* (1898) p. 206. Thereafter it drops out, except as a name for John Alden's yachts.
[2]Daniel ii.19.

and miseries thereof, again to set their feet on the firm and stable earth, their proper element. And no marvel if they were thus joyful, seeing wise Seneca was so affected with sailing a few miles on the coast of his own Italy, as he affirmed, that he had rather remain twenty years on his way by land than pass by sea to any place in a short time, so tedious and dreadful was the same unto him.[3]

But here I cannot but stay and make a pause, and stand half amazed at this poor people's present condition; and so I think will the reader, too, when he well considers the same. Being thus passed the vast ocean, and a sea of troubles before in their preparation (as may be remembered by that which went before), they had now no friends to welcome them nor inns to entertain or refresh their weatherbeaten bodies; no houses or much less towns to repair to, to seek for succour. It is recorded in Scripture[4] as a mercy to the Apostle and his shipwrecked company, that the barbarians showed them no small kindness in refreshing them, but these savage barbarians, when they met with them (as after will appear) were readier to fill their sides full of arrows than otherwise. And for the season it was winter, and they that know the winters of that country know them to be sharp and violent, and subject to cruel and fierce storms, dangerous to travel to known places, much more to search an unknown coast. Besides, what could they see but a hideous and desolate wilderness, fall of wild beasts and wild men—and what multitudes there might be of them they knew not. Neither could they, as it were, go up to the top of Pisgah to view from this wilderness a more goodly country to feed their hopes; for which way soever they turned their eyes (save upward to the heavens) they could have little solace or content in respect of any outward objects. For summer being done, all things stand upon them with a weatherbeaten face, and the whole country, full of woods and thickets, represented a wild and savage hue. If they looked behind them, there was the mighty ocean which they had passed and was now as a main bar and gulf to separate them from all the civil parts of the world. If it be said they had a ship to succour them, it is true; but what heard they daily from the master and company? But that with speed they should look out a place (with their shallop) where they would be, at some near distance; for the season was such as he would not stir from thence till a safe harbor was discovered by them, where they would be, and he might go without danger; and that victuals consumed apace but he must and would keep

---

[3]Epistle 53 (Bradford). The sentence is in Seneca *ad Lucilium Epistulae Morales* liii §5: *Et ego quocumque navigare debuero, vicesimo anno perveniam.*
[4]Acts xxviii (Bradford); verse 2.

sufficient for themselves and their return. Yea, it was muttered by some that if they got not a place in time, they would turn them and their goods ashore and leave them. Let it also be considered what weak hopes of supply and succour they left behind them, that might bear up their minds in this sad condition and trials they were under; and they could not but be very small. It is true, indeed, the affections and love of their brethren at Leyden was cordial and entire towards them, but they had little power to help them or themselves; and how the case stood between them and the merchants at their coming away hath already been declared.

What could now sustain them but the Spirit of God and His grace? May not and ought not the children of these fathers rightly say: "Our fathers were Englishmen which came over this great ocean, and were ready to perish in this wilderness; but they cried unto the Lord, and He heard their voice and looked on their adversity,"[5] etc. "Let them therefore praise the Lord, because He is good: and His mercies endure forever." "Yea, let them which have been redeemed of the Lord, shew how He hath delivered them from the hand of the oppressor. When they wandered in the desert wilderness out of the way, and found no city to dwell in, both hungry and thirsty, their soul was overwhelmed in them. Let them confess before the Lord His lovingkindness and His wonderful works before the sons of men."[6]

Chapter 10 Showing how they sought out a place of habitation; and what befell them thereabout

Being thus arrived at Cape Cod the 11th of November, and necessity calling them to look out a place for habitation (as well as the master's and mariners' importunity); they having brought a large shallop with them out of England, stowed in quarters in the ship, they now got her out and set their carpenters to work to trim her up; but being much bruised and shattered in the ship with foul weather, they saw she would be long in mending. Whereupon a few of them tendered themselves to go by land and discover those nearest places, whilst the shallop was in mending; and the rather because as they went into that harbor there seemed to be an opening some two or three leagues off, which the master judged to be a river.[1] It was conceived there might be some danger in the attempt, yet

---

[5]Deuteronomy xxvi.5, 7 (Bradford).

[6]Psalm cvii.1–5, 8 (Bradford).

[1]Looking south from Provincetown Harbor where the Pilgrims then were, the high land near Plymouth looks like an island on clear days, suggesting that there is a river or arm of the sea between it and Cape Cod.

seeing them resolute, they were permitted to go, being sixteen of them well armed under the conduct of Captain Standish,[2] having such instructions given them as was thought meet.

They set forth the 15th of November; and when they had marched about the space of a mile by the seaside, they espied five or six persons with a dog coming towards them, who were savages; but they fled from them and ran up into the woods, and the English followed them, partly to see if they could speak with them, and partly to discover if there might not be more of them lying in ambush. But the Indians seeing themselves thus followed, they again forsook the woods and ran away on the sands as hard as they could, so as they could not come near them but followed them by the track of their feet sundry miles and saw that they had come the same way. So, night coming on, they made their rendezvous and set out their sentinels, and rested in quiet that night; and the next morning followed their track till they had headed a great creek and so left the sands, and turned another way into the woods. But they still followed them by guess, hoping to find their dwellings; but they soon lost both them and themselves, falling into such thickets as were ready to tear their clothes and armor in pieces; but were most distressed for want of drink. But at length they found water and refreshed themselves, being the first New England water they drunk of, and was now in great thirst as pleasant unto them as wine or beer had been in foretimes.

Afterwards they directed their course to come to the other shore, for they knew it was a neck of land they were to cross over, and so at length got to the seaside and marched to this supposed river, and by the way found a pond[3] of clear, fresh water, and shortly after a good quantity of clear ground where the Indians had formerly set corn, and some of their graves. And proceeding further they saw new stubble where corn had been set the same year; also they found where lately a house had been, where some planks and a great kettle was remaining, and heaps of sand

---

[2]Myles Standish, scion of an old Lancashire family, was now about 36 years old. A soldier of fortune in the wars of the Netherlands, he was engaged either by Weston or the Carver-Cushman committee to go with the colonists and handle their military affairs. Though a "stranger" to the Leyden Pilgrims, Standish, like John Alden the hired cooper, became one of their staunchest supporters. Bradford, Hopkins and Tilley accompanied Standish. More details on these exploring expeditions will be found in the extracts from Bradford's and Winslow's Journals which were published in London in 1622 as *A Relation or Iournall of the beginning and proceedings of the English Plantation setled at Plimoth in New England, by certain English Aduenturers both Merchants and others*. As the authors' names did not appear, and the preface was signed "G. Mourt," this is generally called *Mourt's Relation* (although who Mourt was, nobody knows). Several times reprinted, it is included in Alexander Young *Chronicles of the Pilgrim Fathers* (1841).

[3]The pond that gives its name to Pond Village, Truro.

newly paddled with their hands. Which, they digging up, found in them divers fair Indian baskets filled with corn, and some in ears, fair and good, of divers colours, which seemed to them a very goodly sight (having never seen any such before). This was near the place of that supposed river they came to seek, unto which they went and found it to open itself into two arms with a high cliff of sand in the entrance⁴ but more like to be creeks of salt water than any fresh, for aught they saw; and that there was good harborage for their shallop, leaving it further to be discovered by their shallop, when she was ready. So, their time limited them being expired, they returned to the ship lest they should be in fear of their safety; and took with them part of the corn and buried up the rest. And so, like the men from Eshcol, carried with them of the fruits of the land and showed their brethren;⁵ of which, and their return, they were marvelously glad and their hearts encouraged.

After this, the shallop being got ready, they set out again for the better discovery of this place, and the master of the ship desired to go himself. So there went some thirty men but found it to be no harbor for ships but only for boats.⁶ There was also found two of their houses covered with mats, and sundry of their implements in them, but the people were run away and could not be seen. Also there was found more of their corn and of their beans of various colours, the corn and beans they brought away, purposing to give them full satisfaction when they should meet with any of them as, about some six months afterward they did, to their good content.

And here is to be noted a special providence of God, and a great mercy to this poor people, that here they got seed to plant them corn the next year, or else they might have starved, for they had none nor any likelihood to get any till the season had been past, as the sequel did manifest. Neither is it likely they had had this, if the first voyage had not been made, for the ground was now all covered with snow and hard frozen; but

---

⁴Pamet River, a salt creek that almost bisects the Cape in Truro. The place where they found the corn is still called Corn Hill. It runs along the Bay side, just north of Little Pamet River.

⁵Numbers xiii.23–6.

⁶This second exploring expedition, which started by boat, 28 Nov., made for the mouth of the Pamet River (later called Cold Harbor), which still is good for boats only. Readers interested in further details may profitably consult *Mourt's Relation*, the 1865 edition of which, edited by Henry Martyn Dexter, has an excellent map with details of the routes. This second expedition ranged up and down the valleys of the Pamet and Little Pamet Rivers, and returned to Cape Cod Harbor on 30 Nov. by the shallop. The Indians who lived in this region were the Nauset; they built arborlike wigwams of boughs bent over and stuck in the ground at both ends, woven by smaller boughs into a stout frame and covered with woven mats or strips of bark. Descendants of the Nauset still survive in the village of Mashpee on Cape Cod.

the Lord is never wanting unto His in their greatest needs; let His holy name have all the praise.

The month of November being spent in these affairs, and much foul weather falling in, the 6th of December they sent out their shallop again with ten of their principal men[7] and some seamen, upon further discovery, intending to circulate that deep bay of Cape Cod. The weather was very cold and it froze so hard as the spray of the sea lighting on their coats, they were as if they had been glazed. Yet that night betimes they got down into the bottom of the bay, and as they drew near the shore they saw some ten or twelve Indians very busy about something. They landed about a league or two from them,[8] and had much ado to put ashore anywhere—it lay so full of flats. Being landed, it grew late and they made themselves a barricado with logs and boughs as well as they could in the time, and set out their sentinel and betook them to rest, and saw the smoke of the fire the savages made that night. When morning was come they divided their company, some to coast along the shore in the boat, and the rest marched through the woods to see the land, if any fit place might be for their dwelling. They came also to the place where they saw the Indians the night before, and found they had been cutting up a great fish like a grampus,[9] being some two inches thick of fat like a hog, some pieces whereof they had left by the way. And the shallop found two more of these fishes dead on the sands, a thing usual after storms in that place, by reason of the great flats of sand that lie off.

So they ranged up and down all that day, but found no people, nor any place they liked. When the sun grew low, they hasted out of the woods to meet with their shallop, to whom they made signs to come to them into a creek hard by,[1] the which they did at high water; of which they were

---

[7]The names of the ten (from *Mourt's Relation*) are Standish, Carver and his servant Howland, Bradford, Winslow, John and Edward Tilley, Richard Warren, Stephen Hopkins and his servant Doten; also the pilots, John Clarke and Robert Coppin, and the master gunner and three sailors, whose names are unknown. *Mourt's Relation* states that after the return of the second exploring expedition there was much debate on board the *Mayflower* whether they should settle at Pamet River, at Agawam (the later Ipswich), which looked good on Captain John Smith's map, at Cape Ann, or at Plymouth. On the strength of the recommendations of Coppin, who had been to Plymouth on a previous voyage and offered to pilot them thither, they decided to investigate that place before deciding.

[8]Somewhere in the present Eastham, at one of the several beaches (Kingsbury, Campground, Silver Spring), north of the Great Pond. The tide along this shore runs out very far. The barricade where they passed the night was (according to H. M. Dexter's researches) a few hundred yards northwest of the Great Pond.

[9]This was probably one of the blackfish *(Globicephala melaena)* that frequently get stranded on Cape Cod.

[1]The mouth of Herring River, in the present Eastham. The beach north of the river mouth, where the action about to be described took place, is still called First Encounter Beach.

very glad, for they had not seen each other all that day since the morning. So they made them a barricado as usually they did every night, with logs, stakes and thick pine boughs, the height of a man, leaving it open to leeward, partly to shelter them from the cold and wind (making their fire in the middle and lying round about it) and partly to defend them from any sudden assaults of the savages, if they should surround them; so being very weary, they betook them to rest. But about midnight they heard a hideous and great cry, and their sentinel called "Arm! arm!" So they bestirred them and stood to their arms and shot off a couple of muskets, and then the noise ceased. They concluded it was a company of wolves or such like wild beasts, for one of the seamen told them he had often heard such a noise in Newfoundland.

So they rested till about five of the clock in the morning; for the tide, and their purpose to go from thence, made them be stirring betimes. So after prayer they prepared for breakfast, and it being day dawning it was thought best to be carrying things down to the boat. But some said it was not best to carry the arms down, others said they would be the readier, for they had lapped them up in their coats from the dew; but some three or four would not carry theirs till they went themselves. Yet as it fell out, the water being not high enough, they laid them down on the bank side and came up to breakfast.

But presently, all on the sudden, they heard a great and strange cry, which they knew to be the same voices they heard in the night, though they varied their notes; and one of their company being abroad came running in and cried, "Men, Indians! Indians!" And withal, their arrows came flying amongst them. Their men ran with all speed to recover their arms, as by the good providence of God they did. In the meantime, of those that were there ready, two muskets were discharged at them, and two more stood ready in the entrance of their rendezvous but were commanded not to shoot till they could take full aim at them. And the other two charged again with all speed, for there were only four had arms there, and defended the barricado, which was first assaulted. The cry of the Indians was dreadful, especially when they saw their men run out of the rendezvous toward the shallop to recover their arms, the Indians wheeling about upon them. But some running out with coats of mail on, and cutlasses in their hands, they soon got their arms and let fly amongst them and quickly stopped their violence. Yet there was a lusty man, and no less valiant, stood behind a tree within half a musket shot, and let his arrows fly at them; he was seen [to] shoot three arrows, which were all avoided. He stood three shots of a musket, till one taking full aim at him and made the bark or splinters of the tree fly about his ears, after which he gave an extraordinary shriek and away they went, all of them. They[2] left some to keep the shallop and followed them about a quarter of a mile and shouted once or twice, and shot off two or three pieces, and so returned. This they did that they might conceive that they were not afraid of them or any way discouraged.

Thus it pleased God to vanquish their enemies and give them deliverance; and by His special providence so to dispose that not any one of them were either hurt or hit, though their arrows came close by them and on every side [of] them; and sundry of their coats, which hung up in the barricado, were shot through and through. Afterwards they gave God solemn thanks and praise for their deliverance, and gathered up a bundle of their arrows and sent them into England afterward by the master of the ship, and called that place the First Encounter.

From hence they departed and coasted all along but discerned no place likely for harbor; and therefore hasted to a place that their pilot (one Mr. Coppin who had been in the country before) did assure them was a good harbor, which he had been in, and they might fetch it before night; of which they were glad for it began to be foul weather.

After some hours' sailing it began to snow and rain, and about the middle of the afternoon the wind increased and the sea became very rough, and they broke their rudder, and it was as much as two men could do to steer her with a couple of oars. But their pilot bade them be of good cheer for he saw the harbor; but the storm increasing, and night drawing on, they bore what sail they could to get in, while they could see. But herewith they broke their mast in three pieces and their sail fell overboard in a very grown sea, so as they had like to have been cast away. Yet by God's mercy they recovered themselves, and having the flood[3] with them, struck into the harbor. But when it came to, the pilot was deceived in the place, and said the Lord be merciful unto them for his eyes never

---

[2]I.e., the English.

[3]I.e., the flood tide. The mean rise and fall of tide there is about 9 ft. Plymouth Bay, even today when well buoyed, is a bad place to enter in thick weather with a sea running and night coming on. For if you do not steer for the Gurnet, the high point that marks the northern entrance to Plymouth Bay, you run afoul of Browns Bank, which breaks all over in heavy weather or at low tide; in 1620 a part of this bank was dry at all tides. Coppin, I believe, mistook the Gurnet for Saquish Head; and Saquish for Goose Point; steering between them so as to enter the harbor, he was unnerved by seeing the breakers in Saquish Cove. Mr. Gershom Bradford, late of the U. S. Hydrographic Survey, has a different interpretation: that the storm blew from the NE, not the SE, that the shallop clung to the shoreline and worked through the boat channel between Browns Bank and Long Beach, and that the cove full of breakers was Warrens Cove east of Long Beach. In either case, it is clear that the rowers, encouraged by the "lusty seaman" at the steering oar, managed to weather Saquish Head, behind which they found shelter and good anchorage late in the night of Friday 8 Dec. 1620. They spent Saturday and Sunday 9 and 10 Dec. on Clarks Island, and made the famous "landing" on the 11th.

saw that place before; and he and the master's mate would have run her ashore in a cove full of breakers before the wind. But a lusty seaman which steered bade those which rowed, if they were men, about with her or else they were all cast away; the which they did with speed. So he bid them be of good cheer and row lustily, for there was a fair sound before them, and he doubted not but they should find one place or other where they might ride in safety. And though it was very dark and rained sore, yet in the end they got under the lee of a small island and remained there all that night in safety. But they knew not this to be an island till morning, but were divided in their minds; some would keep the boat for fear they might be amongst the Indians, others were so wet and cold they could not endure but got ashore, and with much ado got fire (all things being so wet); and the rest were glad to come to them, for after midnight the wind shifted to the northwest and it froze hard.

But though this had been a day and night of much trouble and danger unto them, yet God gave them a morning of comfort and refreshing (as usually He doth to His children) for the next day was a fair, sunshining day, and they found themselves to be on an island secure from the Indians, where they might dry their stuff, fix their pieces and rest themselves; and gave God thanks for His mercies in their manifold deliverances. And this being the last day of the week, they prepared there to keep the Sabbath.

On Monday they sounded the harbor and found it fit for shipping, and marched into the land and found divers cornfields and little running brooks, a place (as they supposed) fit for situation.[4] At least it was the best they could find, and the season and their present necessity made them glad to accept of it. So they returned to their ship again with this news to the rest of their people, which did much comfort their hearts.

On the 15th of December they weighed anchor to go to the place they had discovered, and came within two leagues of it, but were fain to bear up again; but the 16th day, the wind came fair, and they arrived safe in this harbor. And afterwards took better view of the place, and resolved

---

[4]Here is the only contemporary authority for the "Landing of the Pilgrims on Plymouth Rock" on Monday, 11/21 Dec. 1620. It is clear that the landing took place from the shallop, not the *Mayflower,* which was then moored in Provincetown Harbor; that no women were involved in it, and no Indians or anyone else were on the receiving end. Nor is it clear that they landed on the large boulder since called Plymouth Rock. That boulder was identified in 1741 by Elder John Faunce, aged 95, as the "place where the forefathers landed," and although he probably only meant to say that they used it as a landing place, for it would have been very convenient for that purpose at half tide, everyone seems to have assumed that they "first" landed there. The exploring party may have landed anywhere between Captain's Hill and the Rock.

where to pitch their dwelling; and the 25th day began to erect the first house for common use to receive them and their goods.[5]

THE SECOND BOOK

The rest of this history (if God give me life and opportunity) I shall, for brevity's sake, handle by way of annals, noting only the heads of principal things, and passages as they fell in order of time, and may seem to be profitable to know or to make use of. And this may be as the Second Book. . . .

[*Another troublesome minister*]

I had forgotten to insert in its place how the church here had invited and sent for Mr. Charles Chauncy,[1] a reverend, godly and very learned man, intending upon trial to choose him pastor of the church here, for the more comfortable performance of the ministry with Mr. John Rayner, the teacher of the same. Mr. Chauncy came to them in the year 1638 and stayed till the latter part of this year 1641. But there fell out some difference about baptizing, he holding it ought only to be by dipping, and putting the whole body under water, and that sprinkling was unlawful. The church yielded that immersion or dipping was lawful but in this cold country not so convenient. But they could not, nor durst not yield to him in this, that sprinkling (which all the churches of Christ do for the most part use at this day) was unlawful and an human invention, as the same was pressed. But they were willing to yield to him as far as they could, and to the utmost, and were contented to suffer him to practice as he was persuaded. And when he came to minister that ordinance he might so do it to any that did desire it in that way, provided he could peaceably suffer Mr. Rayner and such as desired to have theirs otherwise baptized by him by sprinkling or pouring on of water upon them, so as there might be no disturbance in the church hereabout. But he said he

---

[5] *Mourt's Relation* p. 23 says that after the *Mayflower's* arrival in Plymouth Bay on 16/26 Dec. the men explored the bay again and debated whether to settle at Plymouth, the mouth of Jones River (the present Kingston) or on Clark's Island. They decided on the first because much of the land was already cleared and a fort on the hill—now Burial Hill—could command the surrounding country; and because "a very sweet brook"—the Town Brook—"runs under the hillside."

[1] The Rev. Charles Chauncy B.D., sometime fellow and Greek lecturer at Trinity College, Cambridge, and subsequently a minister of the Church of England, was probably the most learned man of the Puritan migration; but he was handicapped by an overtender conscience and a tendency to adopt odd conceits. During his English career he was thrice brought up sharp by the University or by the Archbishop, thrice recanted and thrice retracted his recantation.

could not yield hereunto. Upon which the church procured some other ministers to dispute the point with him publicly, as Mr. Ralph Partridge of Duxbury, who did it sundry times, very ably and sufficiently; as also some other ministers within this government. But he was not satisfied. So the church sent to many other churches to crave their help and advice in this matter, and with his will and consent sent them his arguments written under his own hand. They sent them to the church at Boston in the Bay of Massachusetts, to be communicated with other churches there. Also they sent the same to the churches of Connecticut and New Haven, with sundry others. And received very able and sufficient answers, as they conceived, from them and their learned ministers who all concluded against him. But himself was not satisfied therewith. Their answers are too large here to relate.

They conceived the church had done what was meet in the thing, so Mr. Chauncy, having been the most part of three years here removed himself to Scituate, where he now remains a minister to the church there.[2]

Also about these times, now that cattle and other things began greatly to fall from their former rates and persons began to fall into more straits, and many being already gone from them, as is noted before, both to Duxbury, Marshfield and other places, and those of the chief sort, as Mr. Winslow, Captain Standish, Mr. Alden and many other, and still some dropping away daily, and some at this time and many more unsettled, it did greatly weaken the place. And by reason of the straitness and barrenness of the place, it set the thoughts of many upon removal, as will appear more hereafter.

Chapter 32 Anno Dom: 1642 [Wickedness breaks forth]

Marvelous it may be to see and consider how some kind of wickedness did grow and break forth here, in a land where the same was so much witnessed against and so narrowly looked unto, and severely punished when it was known, as in no place more, or so much, that I have known or heard of; insomuch that they have been somewhat censured even by moderate and good men for their severity in punishments. And yet all this could not suppress the breaking out of sundry notorious sins (as this year, besides other, gives us too many sad precedents and instances),

---

[2]Chauncy was not long getting in trouble there; Governor Winthrop in his *Journal* for 1642 tells of his baptizing his own twins by total immersion, which caused one of them to swoon, after which an irate mother whose child's turn came next, caught hold of the pastor and "near pulled him into the water." Chauncy also insisted on celebrating the Lord's Supper in the evening. In 1654 he was about to return to England when he was elected President of Harvard College, and accepted after promising to keep his views on baptism to himself.

especially drunkenness and uncleanness. Not only incontinency between persons unmarried, for which many both men and women have been punished sharply enough, but some married persons also. But that which is worse, even sodomy and buggery (things fearful to name) have broke forth in this land oftener than once.

1. I say it may justly be marveled at and cause us to fear and tremble at the consideration of our corrupt natures, which are so hardly bridled, subdued and mortified; nay, cannot by any other means but the powerful work and grace of God's Spirit. But (besides this) one reason may be that the Devil may carry a greater spite against the churches of Christ and the gospel here, by how much the more they endeavour to preserve holiness and purity amongst them and strictly punisheth the contrary when it ariseth either in church or commonwealth; that he might cast a blemish and stain upon them in the eyes of [the] world, who use to be rash in judgment. I would rather think thus, than that Satan hath more power in these heathen lands, as some have thought, than in more Christian nations, especially over God's servants in them.

2. Another reason may be, that it may be in this case as it is with waters when their streams are stopped or dammed up. When they get passage they flow with more violence and make more noise and disturbance than when they are suffered to run quietly in their own channels; so wickedness being here more stopped by strict laws, and the same more nearly looked unto so as it cannot run in a common road of liberty as it would and is inclined, it searches everywhere and at last breaks out where it gets vent.

3. A third reason may be, here (as I am verily persuaded) is not more evils in this kind, nor nothing near so many by proportion as in other places; but they are here more discovered and seen and made public by due search, inquisition and due punishment; for the churches look narrowly to their members, and the magistrates over all, more strictly than in other places. Besides, here the people are but few in comparison of other places which are full and populous and lie hid, as it were, in a wood or thicket and many horrible evils by that means are never seen nor known; whereas here they are, as it were, brought into the light and set in the plain field, or rather on a hill, made conspicuous to the view of all.

But to proceed. There came a letter from the Governor in the Bay to them here, touching matters of the forementioned nature which, because it may be useful, I shall here relate it and the passages thereabout.

SIR: Having an opportunity to signify the desires of our General Court in two things of special importance, I willingly take this occasion to impart them to you, that you may impart them to the rest of your magistrates and also to your Elders for counsel, and give us your advice in them. The first is concerning heinous offenses in point of uncleanness; the particular cases with the circumstances and the questions thereupon, you have here enclosed.

The second thing is concerning the Islanders at Aquidneck.[1] That seeing the chiefest of them are gone from us in offenses either to churches or commonwealth or both, others are dependents on them, and the best sort are such as close with them in all their rejections of us. Neither is it only in faction that they are divided from us, but in very deed they rend themselves from all the true churches of Christ and, many of them, from all the powers of magistracy. We have had some experience hereof by some of their underworkers or emissaries who have lately come amongst us and have made public defiance against magistracy, ministry, churches and church covenents, etc. as antichristian. Secretly, also, sowing the seeds of Familism and Anabaptistry, to the infection of some and danger of others; so that we are not willing to join with them in any league or confederacy at all, but rather that you would consider and advise with us how we may avoid them and keep ours from being infected by them.

Another thing I should mention to you, for the maintenance of the trade of beaver. If there be not a company to order it in every jurisdiction among the English, which companies should agree in general of their way in trade, I suppose that the trade will be overthrown and the Indians will abuse us. For this cause we have lately put it into order amongst us, hoping of encouragement from you (as we have had) that we may continue the same.

Thus not further to trouble you, I rest, with my loving remembrance to yourself, etc.

Your loving friend,

Boston, 28. 1. [March] 1642   RICHARD BELLINGHAM

The note enclosed follows on the other side.[2]

WORTHY AND BELOVED SIR: Your letter (with the questions enclosed) I have communicated with our Assistants, and we have referred the answer of them to such Reverend Elders as are amongst us, some of whose answers thereto we have here sent you enclosed under their own hands; from the rest we have not yet

---

[1] I.e., Rhode Island. Roger Williams was already settled at Providence, Anne Hutchinson at Portsmouth and William Coddington at Newport; Samuel Gorton was about to found a fourth settlement of sectaries at Warwick. The Bay authorities were in a great stew about the "Islanders," whom they viewed in much the same light as Catholics now regard Communists, and debated whether to annex their territory and try to suppress dissent by force, or to persuade Plymouth to do it, or to let them alone. Before they could reach a decision, Roger Williams obtained the Providence Plantations Patent from Parliament in 1644, which gave Rhode Island an unassailable legal standing.

[2] The verso of fol. 242, which Bradford usually means by "the other side," is not written on, and the next folio is numbered 244. Prince noted at the beginning of the ms. that there was no fol. 243 when the book came into his possession in 1728. There is, however, no evidence, such as a stub, of a leaf having been cut out at that place. I think that Bradford merely skipped a number inadvertently or that he intended to copy Governor Bellingham's "note enclosed" on 242 v. and number it 243, but either forgot to do so or decided that it was unnecessary. . . . The New England colonies had not yet got around to passing laws against unnatural vice, so they had to fall back on Biblical law; hence this reference to the theologians.

received any. Our far distance hath been the reason of this long delay, as also that they could not confer their counsels together.

For ourselves (you know our breedings and abilities), we rather desire light from yourselves and others, whom God hath better enabled, than to presume to give our judgments in cases so difficult and of so high a nature. Yet under correction, and submission to better judgments, we propose this one thing to your prudent considerations. As it seems to us, in the case even of wilful murder, that though a man did smite or wound another with a full purpose or desire to kill him (which is murder in a high degree before God), yet if he did not die, the magistrate was not to take away the other's life.[3] So by proportion in other gross and foul sins, though high attempts and near approaches to the same be made, and such as in the sight and account of God may be as ill as the accomplishment of the foulest acts of that sin, yet we doubt whether it may be safe for the magistrate to proceed to death; we think, upon the former grounds, rather he may not, As, for instance, in the case of adultery. If it be admitted that it is to be punished with death, which to some of us is not clear; if the body be not actually defiled, then death is not to be inflicted. So in sodomy and bestiality, if there be not penetration. Yet we confess foulness of circumstances, and frequency in the same, doth make us remain in the dark and desire further light from you, or any as God shall give.

As for the second thing, concerning the Islanders? We have no conversing with them, nor desire to have, further than necessity or humanity may require.

As for trade? We have as far as we could, ever therein held an orderly course, and have been sorry to see the spoil thereof by others, and fear it will hardly be recovered.[4] But in these, or any other things which may concern the common good, we shall be willing to advise and concur with you in what we may. Thus with my love remembered to yourself, and the rest of our worthy friends your Assistants, I take leave, and rest

Your loving friend,

Plymouth: 17, 3 month [May] 1642   WILLIAM BRADFORD

... Besides the occasion before mentioned in these writings concerning the abuse of those two children,[5] they had about the same time a case of

---

[3]Exodus xxi.22, Deuteronomy xix.11, Numbers xxxv.16–18 (Bradford).

[4]The local fur trade was evidently running out, since the General Court of Plymouth in 1640–1 offered to grant the monopoly to anyone for £ 20. *Plymouth Colony Records* II 4, 10.

[5]John Humfry, one of the Assistants of the Bay Colony, went back to England, leaving his 8- and 9-year-old daughters in charge of a former servant at Lynn, a married man "member of the church there, and in good esteem for piety and sobriety." This man and a hired man raped the girls. Despite the opinions of the reverend elders, both men got off with a fine and whipping, since the offense was not capital by any law of Massachusetts. Governor Winthrop gives the lurid details in his *Journal* for 1641.

buggery fell out amongst them, which occasioned these questions, to which these answers have been made.

[A horrible case of bestiality]

And after the time of the writing of these things befell a very sad accident of the like foul nature in this government, this very year, which I shall now relate. There was a youth whose name was Thomas Granger. He was servant to an honest man of Duxbury, being about 16 or 17 years of age. (His father and mother lived at the same time at Scituate.) He was this year detected of buggery, and indicted for the same, with a mare, a cow, two goats, five sheep, two calves and a turkey. Horrible it is to mention, but the truth of the history requires it. He was first discovered by one that accidentally saw his lewd practice towards the mare. (I forbear particulars.) Being upon it examined and committed, in the end he not only confessed the fact with that beast at that time, but sundry times before and at several times with all the rest of the forenamed in his indictment. And this his free confession was not only in private to the magistrates (though at first he strived to deny it) but to sundry, both ministers and others; and afterwards, upon his indictment, to the whole Court and jury; and confirmed it at his execution. And whereas some of the sheep could not so well be known by his description of them, others with them were brought before him and he declared which were they and which were not. And accordingly he was cast by the jury and condemned, and after executed about the 8th of September, 1642. A very sad spectacle it was. For first the mare and then the cow and the rest of the lesser cattle were killed before his face, according to the law, Leviticus xx.15; and then he himself was executed. The cattle were all cast into a great and large pit that was digged of purpose for them, and no use made of any part of them.

Upon the examination of this person and also of a former that had made some sodomitical attempts upon another, it being demanded of them how they came first to the knowledge and practice of such wickedness, the one confessed he had long used it in old England; and this youth last spoken of said he was taught it by another that had heard of such things from some in England when he was there, and they kept cattle together. By which it appears how one wicked person may infect many, and what care all ought to have what servants they bring into their families.

But it may be demanded how came it to pass that so many wicked persons and profane people should so quickly come over into this land and mix themselves amongst them? Seeing it was religious men that began the work and they came for religion's sake? I confess this may be marveled at, at least in time to come, when the reasons thereof should not be known; and the more because here was so many hardships and wants met withal. I shall therefore endeavour to give some answer hereunto.

1. And first, according to that in the gospel, it is ever to be remembered that where the Lord begins to sow good seed, there the envious man will endeavour to sow tares.

2. Men being to come over into a wilderness, in which much labour and service was to be done about building and planting, etc., such as wanted help in that respect, when they could not have such as they would, were glad to take such as they could; and so, many untoward servants, sundry of them proved, that were thus brought over, both men and womenkind who, when their times were expired, became families of themselves, which gave increase hereunto.

3. Another and a main reason hereof was that men, finding so many godly disposed persons willing to come into these parts, some began to make a trade of it, to transport passengers and their goods, and hired ships for that end. And then, to make up their freight and advance their profit, cared not who the persons were, so they had money to pay them. And by this means the country became pestered with many unworthy persons who, being come over, crept into one place or other.

4. Again, the Lord's blessing usually following His people as well in outward as spiritual things (though afflictions be mixed withal) do make many to adhere to the People of God, as many followed Christ for the loaves' sake (John vi.26) and a "mixed multitude" came into the wilderness with the People of God out of Egypt of old (Exodus xii.38). So also there were sent by their friends, some under hope that they would be made better; others that they might be eased of such burthens, and they kept from shame at home, that would necessarily follow their dissolute courses. And thus, by one means or other, in 20 years' time it is a question whether the greater part be not grown the worser?[6]

[Conclusion of a long and tedious business]

I am now come to the conclusion of that long and tedious business between the partners here and them in England, the which I shall manifest by their own letters as followeth, in such parts of them as are pertinent to the same.

Mr. Andrews his discharge was to the same effect.[7] He was by agree-

---

[6]Captain John Smith in his *Generall Histoire of Virginia, New England, and the Summer Isles* (1624) tells of a very similar outbreak of bestiality at Bermuda in 1622. "Such a multitude of wild people were sent to this Plantation," he says, that Governor Butler "thought himself happy his time was so near expired."

[7]As Sherley's release . . .; Sherley discharged the Undertakers for a payment of £ 1200, £ 900 of which was transferred to the Bay Colony to collect.

ment to have £ 500 of the money, the which he gave to them in the Bay, who brought his discharge and demanded the money. And they took in his release and paid the money according to agreement; viz. one third of the £ 500 they paid down in hand, and the rest in four equal payments, to be paid yearly, for which they gave their bonds. And whereas £ 44 was more demanded, they conceived they could take it off with Mr. Andrews, and therefore it was not in the bond. But Mr. Beauchamp would not part with any of his, but demanded £ 400 of the partners here, and sent a release to a friend to deliver it to them upon the receipt of the money. But his release was not perfect, for he had left out some of the partners' names, with some other defects, and besides the other gave them to understand he had not near so much due. So no end was made with him till four years after, of which in its place. And in that regard, that themselves did not agree, I shall insert some part of Mr. Andrews' letter, by which he conceives the partners here were wronged, as followeth. This letter of his was writ to Mr. Edmund Freeman, brother-in-law to Mr. Beauchamp.

This letter was writ the year after the agreement, as doth appear; and what his judgment was herein the contents doth manifest; and so I leave it to the equal judgment of any to consider as they see cause, only I shall add what Mr. Sherley further writ in a letter of his, about the same time, and so leave this business. His is as followeth on the other side.

Chapter 33 Anno Dom: 1643 [*The life and death of Elder Brewster*]

I am to begin this year with that which was a matter of great sadness and mourning unto them all. About the 18th of April died their Reverend Elder and my dear and loving friend Mr. William Brewster, a man that had done and suffered much for the Lord Jesus and the gospel's sake, and had borne his part in weal and woe with this poor persecuted church above 36 years in England, Holland and in this wilderness, and done the Lord and them faithful service in his place and calling. And notwithstanding the many troubles and sorrows he passed through, the Lord upheld him to a great age. He was near fourscore years of age (if not all out) when he died. He had this blessing added by the Lord to all the rest; to die in his bed, in peace, amongst the midst of his friends, who mourned and wept over him and ministered what help and comfort they could unto him, and he again recomforted them whilst he could. His sickness was not long, and till the last day thereof he did not wholly keep his bed. His speech continued till somewhat more than half a day, and then failed him, and about nine or ten a clock that evening he died without any pangs at all. A few hours before, he drew his breath short, and some few minutes before his last, he drew his breath long as a man fallen into a sound sleep without any pangs or gaspings, and so sweetly departed this life unto a better.

I would now demand of any, what he was the worse for any former sufferings? What do I say, worse? Nay, sure he was the better, and they now added to his honour. "It is a manifest token," saith the Apostle, 2 Thessalonians i.5, 6, 7, "of the righteous judgment of God that ye may be counted worthy of the kingdom of God, for which ye also suffer; seeing it is a righteous thing with God to recompense tribulation to them that trouble you; and to you who are troubled, rest with us, when the Lord Jesus shall be revealed from heaven, with his mighty angels." 1 Peter iv.14: "If you be reproached for the name of Christ, happy are ye, for the spirit of glory and a God resteth upon you."

What though he wanted[1] the riches and pleasure of the world in his life, and pompous monuments at his funeral? Yet "the memorial of the just shall be blessed, when the name of the wicked shall rot" (with their marble monuments). Proverbs x.7.[2]

I should say something of his life, if to say a little were not worse than to be silent. But I cannot wholly forbear, though happily more may be done hereafter. After he had attained some learning, viz. the knowledge of the Latin tongue and some insight in the Greek, and spent some small time at Cambridge, and then being first seasoned with the seeds of grace and virtue, he went to the Court and served that religious and godly gentleman Mr. Davison, divers years when he was Secretary of State. Who found him so discreet and faithful as he trusted him above all other that were about him, and only employed him in all matters of greatest trust and secrecy; he esteemed him rather as a son than a servant, and for his wisdom and godliness, in private he would converse with him more like a friend and familiar than a master. He attended his master when he was sent in ambassage by the Queen into the Low Countries, in the Earl of Leicester's time, as for other weighty affairs of state; so to receive possession of the cautionary towns, and in token and sign thereof the keys of Flushing being delivered to him in Her Majesty's name, he kept them some time and committed them to this his servant who kept them under his pillow, on which he slept the first night. And at his return the States honoured him with a gold chain and his master committed it to him and commanded him to wear it when they arrived in England, as they rid through the country, till they came to the Court. He afterwards remained with him till his troubles, that he was put from his place about the death of the Queen of Scots; and some good time after doing him many faithful offices of service in the time of his troubles. Afterwards he

---

[1]I.e., lacked.
[2]This quotation is from the Geneva Bible; the others from the King James.

went and lived in the country, in good esteem amongst his friends and the gentlemen of those parts, especially the godly and religious.

He did much good in the country where he lived in promoting and furthering religion, not only by his practice and example, and provoking and encouraging of others, but by procuring of good preachers to the places thereabout and drawing on of others to assist and help forward in such a work. He himself most commonly deepest in the charge, and sometimes above his ability. And in this state he continued many years, doing the best good he could and walking according to the light he saw, till the Lord revealed further unto him. And in the end, by the tyranny of the bishops against godly preachers and people in silencing the one and persecuting the other, he and many more of those times began to look further into things and to see into the unlawfulness of their callings, and the burthen of many antichristian corruptions, which both he and they endeavoured to cast off; as they also did as in the beginning of this treatise is to be seen.

After they were joined together in communion, he was a special stay and help unto them. They ordinarily met at his house on the Lord's Day (which was a manor of the bishop's) and with great love he entertained them when they came, making provision for them to his great charge, and continued so to do whilst they could stay in England. And when they were to remove out of the country he was one of the first in all adventures, and forwardest in any charge. He was the chief of those that were taken at Boston, and suffered the greatest loss, and of the seven that were kept longest in prison and after bound over to the assizes. After he came into Holland he suffered much hardship after he had spent the most of his means, having a great charge and many children; and in regard of his former breeding and course of life, not so fit for many employments as others were, especially such as were toilsome and laborious. But yet he ever bore his condition with much cheerfulness and contentation.

Towards the latter part of those twelve years spent in Holland, his outward condition was mended, and he lived well and plentifully; for he fell into a way (by reason he had the Latin tongue) to teach many students who had a desire to learn the English tongue, to teach them English; and by his method they quickly attained it with great facility, for he drew rules to learn it by after the Latin manner. And many gentlemen, both Danes and Germans, resorted to him as they had time from other studies, some of them being great men's sons. He also had means to set up printing by the help of some friends, and so had employment enough, and by reason of many books which would not be allowed to be printed in England, they might have had more than they could do.

But now removing into this country all these things were laid aside again, and a new course of living must be framed unto, in which he was no way unwilling to take his part, and to bear his burthen with the rest, living many times without bread or corn many months together, having many times nothing but fish and often wanting that also; and drunk nothing but water for many years together, yea till within five or six years of his death. And yet he lived by the blessing of God in health till very old age. And besides that, he would labour with his hands in the fields as long as he was able. Yet when the church had no other minister, he taught twice every Sabbath, and that both powerfully and profitably, to the great contentment of the hearers and their comfortable edification; yea, many were brought to God by his ministry. He did more in this behalf in a year than many that have their hundreds a year do in all their lives.

For his personal abilities, he was qualified above many. He was wise and discreete and well spoken, having a grave and deliberate utterance, of a very cheerful spirit, very sociable and pleasant amongst his friends, of an humble and modest mind, of a peaceable disposition, undervaluing himself and his own abilities and sometime overvaluing others. Inoffensive and innocent in his life and conversation, which gained him the love of those without as well as those within; yet he would tell them plainly of their faults and evils, both publicly and privately, but in such a manner as usually was well taken from him. He was tenderhearted and compassionate of such as were in misery, but especially of such as had been of good estate and rank and were fallen unto want and poverty either for goodness and religion's sake or by the injury and oppression of others; he would say of all men these deserved to be pitied most. And none did more offend and displease him than such as would haughtily and proudly carry and lift up themselves, being risen from nothing and having little else in them to commend them but a few fine clothes or a little riches more than others.

In teaching, he was very moving and stirring of affections, also very plain and distinct in what he taught; by which means he became the more profitable to the hearers. He had a singular good gift in a prayer, both public and private, in ripping up the heart and conscience before God in the humble confession of sin, and begging the mercies of God in Christ for the pardon of the same. He always thought it were better for ministers to pray oftener and divide their prayers, than be long and tedious in the same, except upon solemn and special occasions as in days of humiliation and the like. His reason was that the heart and spirits of all, especially the weak, could hardly continue and stand bent as it were so long towards God as they ought to do in that duty, without flagging and falling off.

For the government of the church, which was most proper to his office, he was careful to preserve good order in the same, and to preserve purity both in the doctrine and communion of the same, and to suppress any errour or contention that might begin to rise up amongst them. And accordingly God gave good success to his endeavours herein all his days, and he saw the fruit of his labours in that behalf. But I must break off, having only thus touched a few, as it were, heads of things.

[*Longevity of the Pilgrim Fathers*]

I cannot but here take occasion not only to mention but greatly to admire the marvelous providence of God! That notwithstanding the many changes and hardships that these people went through, and the many enemies they had and difficulties they met withal, that so many of them should live to very old age! It was not only this reverend man's condition (for one swallow makes no summer as they say) but many more of them did the like, some dying about and before this time and many still living, who attained to sixty years of age, and to sixty-five, divers to seventy and above, and some near eighty as he did. It must needs be more than ordinary and above natural reason, that so it should be. For it is found in experience that change of air, famine or unwholesome food, much drinking of water, sorrows and troubles, etc., all of them are enemies to health, causes of many diseases, consumers of natural vigour and the bodies of men, and shorteners of life. And yet of all these things they had a large part and suffered deeply in the same. They went from England to Holland, where they found both worse air and diet than that they came from; from thence, enduring a long imprisonment as it were in the ships at sea, into New England; and how it hath been with them here hath already been shown, and what crosses, troubles, fears, wants and sorrows they had been liable unto is easy to conjecture. So as in some sort they may say with the Apostle, 2 Corinthians xi.26, 27, they were "in journeyings often, in perils of waters, in perils of robbers, in perils of their own nation, in perils among the heathen, in perils in the wilderness, in perils in the sea, in perils among false brethren; in weariness and painfulness, in watching often, in hunger and thirst, in fasting often, in cold and nakedness."

What was it then that upheld them? It was God's visitation that preserved their spirits. Job x.12: "Thou hast given me life and grace, and thy visitation hath preserved my spirit." He that upheld the Apostle upheld them. "They were persecuted, but not forsaken, cast down, but perished not." "As unknown, and yet known; as dying, and behold we live; as chastened, and yet not killed"; 2 Corinthians vi.9.

God, it seems, would have all men to behold and observe such mercies and works of His providence as these are towards His people, that they in like cases might be encouraged to depend upon God in their trials, and also to bless His name when they see His goodness towards others. Man lives not by bread only, Deuteronomy viii.3. It is not by good and dainty fare, by peace and rest and heart's ease in enjoying the contentments and good things of this world only that preserves health and prolongs life; God in such examples would have the world see and behold that He can do it without them; and if the world will shut their eyes and take no notice thereof, yet He would have His people to see and consider it. Daniel could be better liking with pulse than others were with the king's dainties. Jacob, though he went from one nation to another people and passed through famine, fears and many afflictions, yet he lived till old age and died sweetly and rested in the Lord, as infinite others of God's servants have done and still shall do, through God's goodness, notwithstanding all the malice of their enemies, "when the branch of the wicked shall be cut off before his day" (Job xv.32) "and the bloody and deceitful men shall not live [out] half their days"; Psalm lv.23.

Chapter 34 Anno Dom: 1644 [Proposal to remove to Nauset]

Mr. Edward Winslow was chosen Governor this year.

Many having left this place (as is before noted) by reason of the straitness and barrenness of the same and their finding of better accommodations elsewhere more suitable to their ends and minds; and sundry others still upon every occasion desiring their dismissions, the church began seriously to think whether it were not better jointly to remove to some other place than to be thus weakened and as it were insensibly dissolved.[1] Many meetings and much consultation was held hereabout, and divers were men's minds and opinions. Some were still for staying together in this place, alleging men might here live if they would be content with their condition, and that it was not for want or necessity or much that they removed as for the enriching of themselves. Others were resolute upon removal and so signified that here they could not stay; but if the church did not remove, they must. Insomuch as many were swayed rather than there should be a dissolution, to condescend to a removal if a fit place could be found that might more conveniently and comfortably

---

[1]Bradford and likeminded Pilgrims welcomed the establishment of new towns and churches in the Colony by newcomers, as at Scituate and Taunton, but they wanted the original Plymouth church, including members of the second generation, to stick together. There was, however, a very narrow strip of arable land on Plymouth Bay; the back country was too rugged and rocky for profitable agriculture; and after the founding of Boston, ships from England found it more convenient to put in there. Boston gave them more business than Plymouth, which lay dead to windward of Cape Cod in the prevailing breezes, and where goods had to be lightered ashore instead of being landed on a wharf.

receive the whole, with such accession of others as might come to them for their better strength and subsistence; and some such-like cautions and limitations.

So as, with the aforesaid provisos, the greater part consented to a removal to a place called Nauset, which had been superficially viewed and the good will of the purchasers to whom it belonged obtained, with some addition thereto from the Court. But now they began to see their errour, that they had given away already the best and most commodious places to others, and now wanted themselves. For this place was about 50 miles from hence, and at an outside of the country remote from all society; also that it would prove so strait as it would not be competent to receive the whole body, much less be capable of any addition or increase; so as, at least in a short time, they should be worse there than they are now here. The which with sundry other like considerations and inconveniences made them change their resolutions. But such as were before resolved upon removal took advantage of this agreement and went on, notwithstanding; neither could the rest hinder them, they having made some beginning.

And thus was this poor church left, like an ancient mother grown old and forsaken of her children, though not in their affections yet in regard of their bodily presence and personal helpfulness; her ancient members being most of them worn away by death, and these of later time being like children translated into other families, and she like a widow left only to trust in God. Thus, she that had made many rich became herself poor.

Edward Hyde, First Earl of Clarendon

1609—1674

7

The economic and religious forces which motivated the parliamentarians of seventeenth-century England in their attack on the prerogatives of the monarchy have intrigued English historians more than any other subject in their nation's history. It is to be expected that the English, who constantly celebrate the stability of their political institutions, should so concern themselves with the interpretation of their seventeenth-century civil war. Every shade of historical interpretation of this period has been advocated by historians of the nineteenth and twentieth centuries, and debate continues.

Marxist historians and their opponents marshal statistics in their bitter and sometimes brilliant polemics over the rising prices and classes of the seventeenth century; but, in all this controversy we sometimes forget that the most striking thing about the civil war in England was its unpredictable and baffling course. The awful road from remonstrance to regicide and the abolition of the monarchy in 1649 horrified many Englishmen who witnessed these events and most Englishmen who lived in the century after the Restoration of the monarchy in 1660. To recapture the furious pace of the Revolution, and to glimpse the sentiments of the men who led and resisted the upheaval, we must return to the *History of the Rebellion and Civil Wars in England* by Edward Hyde, the first Earl of Clarendon, who played an important role both in the revolution and in the Restoration.

As a member of the Short Parliament of 1640 and of the Long Parliament, which was convened in the same year, Hyde opposed arbitrary and provocative measures on the part of both his fellow parliamentarians and on the part of the King, Charles I. He tried to mediate between the King, his hated ministers, and the group in parliament he later called in his *History* "the violent party." By 1642, however, as the leaders of this party made it clear that they would force the king to abandon his bishops and the Episcopal church system, Hyde could no longer consider himself a parliamentarian, and formally entered the king's service. For three years he wrote most of the king's

149

responses to parliamentary petitions and sought in vain to avert a violent confrontation. During the 1640's, parliament made its remonstrances more daring, and as war came the king heeded the advice of his more bellicose counselors and his supercilious queen, rather than that of the conciliatory Hyde. In 1645, Hyde was removed from the inner circle of the king's advisors and banished from London to join the entourage of the Prince of Wales in Bristol.

When violence broke out again in 1648, the Queen summoned Hyde to join her and the prince in exile, in France. From 1651 to 1660, Hyde was the chief advisor to the prince, who could be called King Charles II only by his exiled Court. Hyde persisted in offering sound guidance to his master and dissuaded him from a formal alliance with the French and an invasion of England. Hyde believed that the illegal, and in his view immoral, Commonwealth of England would come to its ruin from internal strife. The government of Oliver Cromwell did fall shortly after his death in 1658, although it was hardly for lack of moral pretension. In 1660, the restored monarch created Hyde Earl of Clarendon, and made him Lord Chancellor of England.

Clarendon is given most of the credit for negotiating the Restoration of 1660, and for the Declaration of Breda, the deft instrument of the Restoration, by which parliament was delegated all the thorny problems and responsibilities of the new government, such as granting compensation for noble and church lands confiscated during the revolution, and the establishment of a system of religious toleration. This faithful and wise servant of the Stuart kings soon became the victim of the jealousies of rival ministers because of his great influence with the king and the marriage of his daughter Anne to the Duke of York, the heir apparent. He was also resented by rival politicians for having sold the English installations at Dunkirk to the French, in his effort to finance the monarchy; and he was unreasonably held responsible for English losses in a war with the Dutch, a war which he had in fact opposed. An ungrateful king acquiesced in the impeachment of his Lord Chancellor and, in 1667, Clarendon once again faced exile, but this time he was never allowed to return to the country he had served so well.

The *History of the Rebellion and Civil Wars in England* was entirely a work written in exile. Clarendon began the *History* in 1646, when he was first removed from Charles I's confidence; by 1648, he had brought the narrative to 1644, when he left the Channel Islands to join the English court in France. He did not at first resume the *History* during the period of his second exile, but started his autobiography in 1668 and continued this long, personal vindication of his career until 1671, when his son was allowed to visit him in France, and brought him the manuscript of the early work. Clarendon then decided to incorporate his *Life* with the *History,* and produce a complete story of the revolution until the Restoration.

Clarendon's *History* is written with obvious bias, but unlike many other tendentious historians Clarendon made no pretense of impartiality. He wrote to condemn regicide, atheism, and tyranny. His scorn for "the sauciness and impudence of the parliamentary leaders" and for "the loss of reverence for the Church of England" during the Revolution makes his story powerful, stirring, and royalist. S. R. Gardiner, who wrote his extensive *History of the Civil War* late in the nineteenth century, was correct in his description of Clarendon's work as "instinct with party feeling." It must be stressed, however, that Clarendon was far more moderate and divided in his sympathies during his political career, especially before 1645, than he was in his *History,* which he wrote as a tale of woe seen through the king's eyes. He wanted to immortalize and denigrate the tragedy which had befallen the nation during the Civil War, and he succeeded.

Despite its royalist predilection and its sentimentality, nowhere more evident than in our selection, which includes the trial and execution of Charles I, Clarendon's *History* remains the most valuable contemporary record of the English Civil War period. Clarendon recounts the calamities as they happened; we come closer to the "Rebellion" and to the men who made it in his *History* than we ever can in the more detached studies of later times. His vivid character sketches, whether of the king's supporters or of his enemies, are unsurpassed contributions to English historiography, and the work as a whole was the most influential history written in the seventeenth century. Historians since Clarendon have relied on his *History* and his *Life* for their knowledge of men important to seventeenth-century English history: John Hampden, John Pym, and Oliver Cromwell.

Even Leopold von Ranke, who had little use for the *History of the Rebellion and the Civil Wars in England,* confessed that it was Clarendon who "fixed the circle of ideas for the English nation" about its era of upheaval. Before Ranke, David Hume wrote of Clarendon's *History* and of the historian himself that "an air of probity and goodness runs through the whole work; as these qualities did in reality embellish the whole life of the author."

Selected Bibliography

B. H. G. Wormald's *Clarendon: Politics, Historiography, and Religion* (1964) is a penetrating, indispensable study of Clarendon's political career and of his historical and religious thinking. Wormald's book repays the careful attention required in following him through Clarendon's political fortunes, as well as the contours of Clarendon's interpretation of the history of his time. After Wormald, Sir Charles Firth's well-known article on Clarendon in the *Dictionary of National Biography*, X (1891), 370–389, can be recommended as concise and dispassionate. Firth's three articles, "Clarendon's *History of the Rebellion*," in the *English Historical Review*, XIX (1904), 26–54, 246–262, 464–483, sort out the complex history of the writing of Clarendon's works.

Professor H. R. Trevor-Roper has offered some astute observations on Clarendon as a historian in a brief essay, "Clarendon and the Great Rebellion," in *Historical Essays* (1966), a Harper Torchbook publication. Professor J. G. A. Pocock, in his brilliant study, *The Ancient Constitution and the Feudal Law* (1957), examines the legalistic historiography of seventeenth-century England, of which Clarendon's *History* is an example.

HISTORY OF THE REBELLION

Trial of King Charles I

When he was first brought to Westminster Hall, which was upon the 20th of January, before their High Court of Justice, he looked upon them, and sat down, without any manifestation of trouble, never stirring his hat; all the impudent judges sitting covered, and fixing their eyes upon him, without the least show of respect. The odious libel, which they called a "charge and impeachment," was then read by the clerk, which contained, That he had been admitted King of England, and trusted with a limited power, to govern according to law; and by his oath and office was obliged to use the power committed to him for the good and benefit of the people: but that he had, out of a wicked design to erect to himself an unlimited and tyrannical power, and to overthrow the rights and liberties of the people, traitorously levied war against the present Parliament and the people therein represented. And then it mentioned his first appearing at York with a guard, then his being at Beverly, then his setting up his standard at Nottingham, the day of the month and the year in which the battle had been at Edgehill, and all the other several battles which had been fought in his presence; in which, it said, he had caused and procured many thousands of the freeborn people of the nation to be slain: that after all his forces had been defeated, and himself become a prisoner, he had in that very year caused many insurrections to be made in England, and given a commission to the Prince his son to raise a new war against the Parliament, whereby many who were in their service, and trusted by them, had revolted, broken their trust, and betook themselves to the service to the Prince against the Parliament and the people: that he had been the author and contriver of the unnatural, cruel, and bloody war, and was therein guilty of all the treasons, murders, rapines, burnings, spoils, desolations, damage, and mischieve to the nation, and which had been committed in the said war, or been occasioned thereby; and that he was therefore impeached for the said treasons and crimes,

History of the Rebellion and Civil Wars in England, Volume IV, pp. 484–495 Oxford: The Clarendon Press, 1888, pp. 11–28. Reprinted by permission of the publisher.

on the behalf of the people of England, as a tyrant, traitor, and murderer, and a public implacable enemy to the commonwealth of England; and prayed that he might be put to answer to all the particulars, to the end that such an examination, trial, and judgment might be had thereupon as should be agreeable to justice.

Which being read, their president Bradshaw, after he had insolently reprehended the King for not having stirred his hat, or shewed more respect to that high tribunal, told him, that the Parliament of England had appointed that court to try him for the several treasons and mis-demeanours which he had committed against the kingdom during the evil administration of his government, that upon the examination thereof justice might be done. And after a great sauciness and impudence of talk, he asked the King what answer he made to that impeachment.

The King, without any alteration in his countenance by all that inso-lent provocation, told them, he would first know of them by what author-ity they presumed by force to bring him before them, and who gave them power to judge of his actions, for which he was accountable to none but God; though they had been always such as he need not be ashamed to own them before all the world. He told them, that he was their King, and they his subjects, who owed him duty and obedience; that no Parliament had authority to call him before them; but that they were not the Parliament, nor had any authority from the Parliament to sit in that manner: that of all the persons who sat there, and took upon them to judge him, except those persons who being officers of the army he could not but know whilst he was forced to be amongst them, there were only two faces which he had ever seen before, or whose names were known to him. And after urging their duty that was due to him, and his superiority over them, by such lively reasons and arguments as were not capable of any answer, he concluded, that he would not so much betray himself and his royal dig-nity as to answer any thing they objected against him, which were to acknowledge their authority; though he believed that every one of them-selves, as well as the spectators, did in their own consciences absolve him from all the material things which were objected against him.

Bradshaw advised him in a very arrogant manner not to deceive him-self with an opinion that any thing he had said would do him any good; that the Parliament knew their own authority, and would not suffer it to be called in question and debated; therefore wished him to think better of it against he should be next brought thither, and that he would answer directly to his charge; otherwise he could not be so ignorant as not to know what judgment the law pronounced against those who stood mute, and obstinately refused to plead. And so the guard carried his majesty back to St. James's; where they treated him as before.

There was an accident happened that first day which may be fit to be remembered. When all those who were commissioners had taken their places, and the King was brought in, the first ceremony was to read their commission, which was the ordinance of Parliament for the trial; and then the judges were all called, every man answering to his name as he was called; and the president being first called and making answer, the next who was called, being the general, lord Fayrefax, and no answer being made, the officer called him the second time, when there was a voice heard that said, "he had more wit than to be there"; which put the court into some disorder, and somebody asking who it was, there was no other answer but a little murmuring. But presently, when the impeachment was read, and that expression used of "all the good people of England," the same voice in a louder tone answered, "No, nor the hundredth part of them!" upon which, one of the officers bade the soldiers give fire into that box whence those presumptuous words were uttered. But it was quickly discerned that it was the general's wife, the lady Fayrefax, who had uttered both those sharp sayings; who was presently persuaded or forced to leave the place, to prevent any new disorder. She was of a very noble extraction, one of the daughters and heirs of Horace lord Vere of Tilbury; who, having been bred in Holland, had not that reverence for the Church of England as she ought to have had, and so had unhappily concurred in her husband's entering into rebellion, never imagining what misery it would bring upon the kingdom; and now abhorred the work in hand as much as any body could do, and did all she could to hinder her husband from acting any part in it. Nor did he ever sit in that bloody court, though out of the stupidity of his soul he was throughout overwitted by Cromwell, and made a property to bring that to pass which could very hardly have been otherwise effected.

As there was in many persons present at that woeful spectacle a real duty and compassion for the King, so there was in others so barbarous and brutal a behaviour towards him that they called him *Tyrant* and *Murderer;* and one spit in his face, which his majesty without expressing any trouble wiped off with his handkerchief.

The two men who were only known to the King before the troubles were, sir Harry Mildmay, master of the King's jewel-house, who had been bred up in the Court, being a younger brother of a good family in Essex, and who had been prosecuted with so great favours and bounties by King James and by his majesty, that he was raised by them to a great estate, and preferred to that office in his house, which is the best under those which entitle the officers to be of the Privy Council. No man more obsequious to the Court than he whilst it flourished; a great flatterer of all persons in authority, and a spy in all places for them. From the beginning of the Parliament he concurred with those who were most violent against the Court, and most like to prevail against it; and being thereupon branded with ingratitude, as that brand commonly makes men most impudent, he continued his desperate pace with them till he became one of the murderers of his master. The other was sir John Danvers, the younger brother and heir of the earl of Danby, who was likewise a gentleman of the privy chamber to the King, who being neglected by his brother, and having by a vain expense in his way of living contracted a vast debt which he knew not how to pay, and being a proud, formal, weak man, between being seduced and a seducer, he became so far involved in their counsels that he suffered himself to be applied to their worst officers, taking it to be a high honour to sit upon the same bench with Cromwell, who employed and contemned him at once: nor did that party of miscreants look upon any two men in the kingdom with that scorn and detestation as they did upon Danvers and Mildmay.

The several unheard of insolences which this excellent prince was forced to submit to at the other times he was brought before that odious judicatory, his majestic behaviour under so much insolence, and resolute insisting upon his own dignity, and defending it by manifest authorities in the law as well as by the clearest deductions from reason, the pronouncing that horrible sentence upon the most innocent person in the world, the execution of that sentence by the most execrable murder that ever was committed since that of our blessed Saviour, and the circumstances thereof; the application and interposition that was used by some noble persons to prevent that woeful murder, and the hypocrisy with which that interposition was deluded; the saint-like behaviour of that blessed martyr, and his Christian courage and patience at his death; are all particulars so well known, and have been so much enlarged upon in a treatise peculiarly applied to that purpose, that the farther mentioning it in this place would but afflict and grieve the reader, and make the relation itself odious; and therefore no more shall be said here of that lamentable tragedy, so much to the dishonour of the nation and the religion professed by it.

But it will not be unnecessary to add the short character of his person, that posterity may know the inestimable loss which the nation then underwent, in being deprived of a prince whose example would have had a greater influence upon the manners and piety of the nation than the most strict laws can have. To speak first of his private qualifications as a man, before the mention of his princely and royal virtues; he was, if ever any, the most worthy of the title of an honest man; so great a lover of justice, that no temptation could dispose him to a wrongful action, except it were so disguised to him that he believed it to be just. He had a tenderness and compassion of nature, which restrained him from ever doing a hard-hearted thing; and therefore he was so apt to grant pardon to malefactors, that his judges represented to him the damage and insecurity to the public that flowed from such his indulgence; and then he restrained himself from pardoning either murders or highway robberies, and quickly discerned the fruits of his severity by a wonderful reformation of those enormities. He was very punctual and regular in his devotions; so that he was never known to enter upon his recreations or sports, though never so early in the morning, before he had been at public prayers; so that on hunting-days his chaplains were bound to a very early attendance. And he was likewise very strict in observing the hours of his private cabinet devotions; and was so severe an exactor of gravity and reverence in all mention of religion, that he could never endure any light or profane word in religion, with what sharpness of wit soever it was covered: and though he was well pleased and delighted with reading verses made upon any occasion, no man durst bring before him any thing that was profane or unclean; that kind of wit had never any countenance then. He was so great an example of conjugal affection, that they who did not imitate him in that particular did not brag of their liberty: and he did not only permit but direct his bishops to prosecute those scandalous vices in the ecclesiastical courts, against persons of eminence and near relation to his service.

His kingly virtues had some mixture and allay that hindered them from shining in full lustre, and from producing those fruits they should have been attended with. He was not in his nature bountiful, though he gave very much: which appeared more after the duke of Buckingham's death, after which those showers fell very rarely; and he paused too long in giving, which made those to whom he gave less sensible of the benefit. He kept state to the full, which made his Court very orderly; no man presuming to be seen in a place where he had no pretence to be. He saw and observed men long before he received any about his person, and did not love strangers, nor very confident men. He was a patient hearer of causes, which he frequently accustomed himself to, at the Council board; and judged very well, and was dexterous in the mediating part: so that he often put an end to causes by persuasion, which the stubbornness of men's humours made dilatory in courts of justice.

He was very fearless in his person, but not enterprising; and had an excellent understanding, but was not confident enough of it; which made him oftentimes change his own opinion for a worse, and follow the advice of a man that did not judge so well as himself. And this made him more irresolute than the conjuncture of his affairs would admit. If he had been of a rougher and more imperious nature, he would have found more respect and duty; and his not applying some severe cures to approaching evils proceeded from the lenity of his nature and the tenderness of his conscience, which in all cases of blood made him choose the softer way, and not hearken to severe counsels, how reasonably soever urged. This only restrained him from pursuing his advantage in the first Scots' expedition, when, humanly speaking, he might have reduced that nation to the most slavish obedience that could have been wished. But no man can say he had then many who advised him to it, but the contrary, by a wonderful indisposition all his Council had to fighting or any other fatigue. He was always an immoderate lover of the Scottish nation, having not only been born there, but educated by that people, and besieged by them always, having few English about him until he was king; and the major number of his servants being still of those, who he thought could never fail him; and then no man had such an ascendant over him, by the lowest and humblest insinuations, as duke Hambleton had.

As he excelled in all other virtues, so in temperance he was so strict, that he abhorred all deboshry to that degree, that, at a great festival solemnity, where he once was, when very many of the nobility of the English and Scots were entertained, being told by one who withdrew from thence, what vast draughts of wine they drank, and that there was one earl who had drank most of the rest down and was not himself moved or altered, the King said that he deserved to be hanged; and that earl coming shortly into the room where his majesty was, in some gaiety, to show how unhurt he was from that battle, the King sent one to bid him withdraw from his majesty's presence; nor did he in some days after appear before the King.

There were so many miraculous circumstances contributed to his ruin, that men might well think that heaven and earth conspired it, and that the stars designed it. Though he was, from the first declension of his power, so much betrayed by his own servants, that there were very few who remained faithful to him, yet that treachery proceeded not from any treasonable purpose to do him any harm, but from particular and personal animosities against other men. And afterwards, the terror all men were under of the Parliament, and the guilt they were conscious of themselves, made them watch all opportunities to make themselves gracious to those who could do them good; and so they became spies upon their master, and from one piece of knavery were hardened and confirmed to undertake another, till at last they had no hope of preservation but by the destruction of their master. And after all this, when a man might reasonably believe that less than a universal defection of three nations could not have reduced a great King to so ugly a fate, it is most certain that in that very hour when he was thus wickedly murdered in the sight of the sun, he had as great a share in the hearts and affections of his subjects in general, was as much beloved, esteemed, and longed for by the people in general of the three nations, as any of his predecessors had ever been. To conclude: he was the worthiest gentleman, the best master, the best friend, the best husband, the best father, and the best Christian, that the age in which he lived had produced. And if he was not the best King, if he was without some parts and qualities which have made some kings great and happy, no other prince was ever unhappy who was possessed of half his virtues and endowments, and so much without any kind of vice.

This unparalleled murder and parricide was committed upon the 30th of January, in the year, according to the account used in that country, 1648, in the forty and ninth year of his age, and when he had such excellent health, and so great vigour of body, that when his murderers caused him to be opened, (which they did, and were present at it with great curiosity,) they confessed and declared that no man had ever all his vital parts so perfect and unhurt, and that he seemed to be of so admirable a composition and constitution that he would probably have lived as long as nature could subsist. His body was immediately carried into a room at Whitehall; where he was exposed for many days to the public view, that all men might know that he was not alive. And he was then embalmed, and put into a coffin, and so carried to St. James's where he likewise remained several days. They who were qualified to look after that province declared that he should be buried at Windsor in a decent manner, provided that the whole expense should not exceed five hundred pounds. The duke of Richmond, the marquis of Hartford, the earls of Southampton and Lyndsy, who had been of his bedchamber, and always very faithful to him, desired those who governed that they might have leave to perform the last duty to their dead master, and to wait upon him to his grave; which, after some pauses, they were permitted to do, with this, that they should not attend the corpse out of the town, since they resolved it should be privately carried to Windsor without pomp or noise; and then they should have timely notice, that, if they pleased, they might be at his interment. And accordingly it was committed to four of those servants who had been by them appointed to wait upon him during his imprisonment, that they should convey the body to Windsor; which they did. And it was that night placed in that chamber which had usually been his bedchamber: and the next morning it was carried into the great hall, where it remained till the lords came; who arrived there in the afternoon, and immediately went to colonel Whitchcott, the governor of the castle, and shewed the order they had from the Parliament to be present at the burial; which he admitted. But when they desired that his majesty might be buried according to the form of the Common Prayer Book, the bishop of London being present with them to officiate, he expressly, positively, and roughly refused to consent to it, and said it was not lawful; that the Common Prayer Book was put down, and he would not suffer it to be used in that garrison where he commanded; not could all the reasons, persuasions, and entreaties prevail with him to suffer it. Then they went into

the church, to make choice of a place to bury it in. But when they entered
into it, which they had been so well acquainted with, they found it so
altered and transformed, all tombs, inscriptions, and those landmarks
pulled down, by which all men knew every particular place in that
church, and such a dismal mutation over the whole, that they knew not
where they were, nor was there one old officer that had belonged to it, or
knew where the princes had used to be interred. At last there was a fellow
of the town who undertook to tell them the place, where, he said, there
was a vault, in which King Harry the Eighth and Queen Jane Seymour
were interred. As near that place as could conveniently be, they caused
the grave to be made. And there the King's body was laid, without any
words, or other ceremony than the tears and sighs of the few beholders.
Upon the coffin was a plate of silver fixed with these words only, *"King
Charles.* 1648."

Jean Mabillon

1623—1707

8

Marc Bloch, one of the finest medieval historians of our century pronounced the year 1681, the year of Dom Jean Mabillon's two-volume work, *On Diplomatics*, "a truly great one in the history of the human mind, for the criticism of documents of archives was definitely established." Bloch, like Mabillon a superb historian and an exemplary human being, deeply appreciated the extraordinary fact that the first complete treatise on diplomatics, the science of deciphering ancient charters and manuscripts, and of determining their authenticity, should also be the definitive work on that subject. Nineteenth- and twentieth-century paleographers have broadened the scope of diplomatics, and have shown Mabillon to have been mistaken in certain details; but he remains the universally acclaimed master of a crucial aspect of historical science.

Born into a modest peasant family, Mabillon desired a monastic life at an early age. In 1653, he entered the Abbey of St. Remi near his native city, Rheims. He was soon shifted from St. Remi to several other small monasteries, including St. Denis, a royal abbey outside of Paris. His entry into the abbey of St.-Germain-des-Prés in Paris, the center of the Maurist congregation of Benedictine monks, in 1664, was a fortunate coincidence; for here Mabillon found an environment where he could cultivate his interest in the history of the Church in the early Middle Ages.

Since the fifteenth century, the Maurists had distinguished themselves as devout scholars of patristic history. The young brothers had to undergo rigorous intellectual training as well as the regular monastic indoctrination required of monks everywhere; the libraries of their abbeys were built and embellished with as much care as their chapels. By the time Mabillon arrived at St.-Germain-des-Prés it already contained one of the best libraries in France. The weekly meetings devoted to discussion of the monks' research and their correspondence with other historians in France, Italy, and southern Germany lent an atmosphere of intellectual excitement to the abbey. The

Maurists had also become famous for their literary expeditions throughout Europe, visiting monastic libraries and family archives in search of books and manuscripts. Mabillon was to flourish here, and become the greatest scholar, and one of the most beloved monks, in a brilliant little society.

Immediately after entering the abbey, Mabillon began his first project, an edition of the works of St. Bernard. His notes and prefaces have made this edition an irreplaceable contribution to monastic history. He soon became an assistant to the Abbot d'Archey in the production of a series of six volumes on the lives of the monastic saints, which appeared between 1668 and 1680; again Mabillon's work made this series outstanding: his appendixes and notes on liturgy and monastic customs and his general observations on the history of the early Church are still valuable sources of information. It was not until 1681, however, that Mabillon showed himself worthy of being named the founder of a new science.

On Diplomatics was intended as a reply to the excessive skepticism of the Bollandist scholar, Daniel Papebroch, who in 1675, in his *Propylaeum,* or introduction to the study of the lives of the saints, concluded that most of the charters of the Merovingian age, which had been preserved in the monasteries of France, were forgeries. Moreover, he impugned the authenticity of the charters on which the abbey of St. Denis had been founded. Mabillon, loyal to his former house, rose to the occasion heroically. He forced Papebroch to retract his criticism. But that was only the negative side of his achievement.

Mabillon, in *On Diplomatics,* provided all historians with the methods whereby they might determine the authenticity of any ancient document by comparing the style, form, seal, and signatures of various charters with others of the same period. Some charters Mabillon had to reject as forgeries, and others he accepted only in part for containing interpolations; but others, particularly the ones found in St. Denis, were proved to be genuine. Our selections from *On Diplomatics* are examples of Mabillon's application of his critical method in the effort to establish that the succession of abbots at St. Denis dates from the Merovingian age, and that the charters which verify the antiquity of that monastery are authentic.

It is exhilarating to watch Mabillon proceed—as he does in all three of our selections from the 1704 *Supplement* of *On Diplomatics* and from the text itself—as a modern scientist calling for a consensus of expert opinion based on empirical investigation, instead of insisting on absolute certainty and irrevocable conclusions, which are impossible in experimental science. Mabillon rejects the crippling skepticism, known in his day as the "Pyrrhonism of history," and anticipates the constructive skepticism of David Hume and other moderns, who could never justify a credulous acceptance of unexamined evidence, but who also regarded the refusal to reach at least tentative conclusions as an abjuration of the task of the inquiring mind.

Soon after the publication of *On Diplomatics,* the humble Mabillon was presented to the Sun King, Louis XIV, as the most learned man in his kingdom (which was enormously proud of its learning), while the haughty Bishop Bossuet looked on in envious silence. Mabillon obtained entry into the King's library and the libraries of his greatest ministers, and was sent to Italy to obtain books and documents for these libraries. He continued to make these journeys for the rest of his life, but without abandoning his career as the greatest historian of the Benedictines. In 1686, he wrote a study, *On the Gallican Liturgy,* yet another landmark in the field of pre-Carolingian monastic history; and in 1691, he defended the learning of the Maurists against the anti-intellectual attacks of the Trappist monks in his *Treatise on Monastic Studies.* His last great work was the *Annals of the Benedictine Order,* which he started in 1703, and worked on until six months before his death in 1707. This beautifully written, exhaustive four-volume history remains the most complete record of the early years of the Benedictine Order by its most learned disciple.

Mabillon was not without predecessors in the search for scientific methods to study historical documents. Valla, for one, showed similar insight into the ways of textual criticism, but Mabillon was not interested in unmasking forgeries in the polemical spirit of Valla. He preferred to invite all fair-minded scholars to expand our knowledge of the cryptic Middle Ages, and he proceeded to show them the way.

Selected Bibliography

A series of essays collected under the title of *Great Historical Enterprises* (1963), by David Knowles, provides a good introduction to the age of pious erudition, of which Mabillon is the finest example. Knowles has also written an article, "Jean Mabillon," in the *Journal of Ecclesiastical History,* X:1 (1959), 153–173, which, despite its occasional rhapsodic lapses, is comprehensive. Dom Henri Leclerq's biographical article on Mabillon in the *Dictionnaire d'Archéologie Chrétienne et de Liturgie,* X:1 (1931), 427–723, is thorough and vivid; it has since been expanded into two bulky volumes, *Mabillon* (1953, 1957). A detailed exposition of *De Re Diplomatica (On Diplomatics)* is offered by L. Levillain in *Mélanges et documents publiés à l'occasion du 2e centenaire de la mort de Mabillon* (1908), 195–252.

Mabillon's *On Diplomatics* is one of those works always adulated, but seldom consulted, and almost never read. Until now the classical, lucid Latin of the original has never been translated into any modern language, nor has there been a reprinting of the original since the eighteenth century.

ON DIPLOMATICS

SUPPLEMENT

Chapter 1

I. The usefulness of ancient documents and records.
II. The necessity of the science of diplomatics for distinguishing genuine documents from forgeries.
III. Documents are distinguished not on the basis of individual characteristics considered separately, but on the total interconnection of these characteristics. Experience is the greatest aid in making this distinction.
IV. In these matters hasty judgments must be avoided, especially by novices.

Those who attempt to diminish the authority and trustworthiness of ancient documents and records do harm to the study of literature and, in my opinion, attack and undermine constitutional law, not to mention legal privilege. For, in fact, from these sources each individual obtains his rights and without them there is no security in civil matters. Consider history: the knowledge we have of the Middle Ages and following periods will be uncertain and incomplete if it is not supported and supplemented by these documents. For, I ask, what will become of the *Gallia Christiana,* the *Italia Sacra,* the *Sicilia Sacra,* and other similar histories; what will become of the *Annales Historici Francorum,* not to mention the *Annales Baroniani,* if anyone should disparage and undermine these records? All these historical works will be no more than a badly confused catalogue of names and various events resembling a skeleton. The result would be the same with the *Historia Bearnensis,* and the *Marca Hispanica* by the distinguished Peter de Marca, who understood better than anyone the usefulness and necessity of documents of this kind. Not only do the histories of churches need support from these sources, but also the antiquity, the genealogy, and the dignity of noble families cannot be established without this means of proof. The work on the genealogies of noble families composed by André Duchesne, a man without equal in

---

On Diplomatics, Naples: 1789, Vol. I, 226–234, 646–651; Vol, II 1–5, 57–67. Richard Wertis of Oberlin College has translated the selections for this volume.

this field, demonstrates this clearly; and so do the works of others who drew almost all their means of proof from the archives of churches, monasteries, and the particular houses in question; that is, from ancient manuscripts and records. Therefore, one cannot help seeing how important the treatment of this subject is, for it concerns not only literature and antiquities, but also churches, monasteries, and noblemen as well; in short, the status of one and all is at stake. Consequently, those who strive to diminish either in whole or in large part the trustworthiness and authority of ancient documents of that kind on very slight grounds or because of minor difficulties do great harm and damage to the entire commonwealth.

II. But, you say, most manuscripts of this kind are spurious or, at least, interpolated; and they make the authenticity of all the others suspect. First of all, I utterly deny that there are as many false or interpolated documents in churches or monasteries as critics charge. On the contrary, Peter Francis Chissleti of the Society of Jesus, the Bollandist, states that he very rarely found interpolated documents when he investigated the archives of a large number of churches. I do not deny that in fact some documents are false and others are interpolated, but all of them should not be dismissed for that reason. Rather, it is necessary to devise and hand down rules for distinguishing genuine manuscripts from those that are false and interpolated. This, to be sure, was my purpose in my work *On Diplomatics*: let impartial, honest, and learned scholars who can judge these matters decide whether I accomplished my purpose or, at least, in what measure I succeeded. If I may estimate from the favorable judgment I have received from most scholars thus far, it seems that they not only approved of my work but were enthusiastic about it. Moreover, and this I can state without boasting, I spared no effort in investigating this difficult and little-discussed subject. For I did not undertake this task with only my own intelligence and judgment to guide me, nor did I rely upon the random inspection of a few documents or a hasty and cursory examination of them, nor did I spend only a few days reading them. Rather, I undertook this task after long familiarity and daily experience with these documents. For almost twenty years I had devoted my studies and energies to reading and examining ancient manuscripts and archives, and the published collections of ancient documents. Finally, I have carefully examined the ancient books, records, and authentic documents not of just one church, monastery, or province but of many churches and regions; and I compared and weighed them with one another that I might be able to compile a body of knowledge which was not merely scanty and meager, but as accurate and as well-tested as possible in a field which had not been previously investigated.

Furthermore, since the archive of the royal monastery of St. Denis, which I think is more famous and has more documents than any other archive, at least in France, was more accessible to me, I did not rely upon the evidence of my own eyes or upon my own judgment. Rather, I asked the most learned men in Paris to examine diligently and carefully the authentic documents of that sacred place and in particular the manuscripts which I wanted to use in this work, and to tell me frankly and openly their opinion about them. Their unanimous opinion was that they should be considered genuine and authentic documents, and that I could use them as such to examine and judge others. The most eminent of these scholars, the illustrious Étienne Baluze, who, as all know, is most experienced in this field, will support my statement. The other scholars whom I consulted are Charles du Fresne Du Cange, Anthony Herovalle, and Jean-Baptiste Cotélier. No one, unless he lacks all acquaintance with scholarship, does not know of the learning and authority of these men in this field. Relying upon the judgment of these men I undertook a task which was, to be sure, difficult but, I think, necessary; and with the help of God I completed it twenty-two years ago. At this time I would have revised it, had not circumstances compelled me to defer it to a more opportune time.

III. At this point perhaps someone may object and say that there is no certain method, no sure arguments by which genuine documents can be distinguished from spurious ones; and, therefore, that these documents cannot be used in historical matters with certainty and freedom from error. And although we cannot use them, the loss is not serious since it can be made up for more than satisfactorily from other records, namely from the works of ancient authors. And, you will say, what certain and proved marks of authenticity can be used for distinguishing these documents? No argument can be based upon the material on which the document is written, whether it be papyrus or paper or vellum, or upon the type of script, or the style, or the dates, or the subscriptions, seals, or any other characteristics, because any one of these could be duplicated by a skilled forger and imposter.

But, granted that each and any one of these characteristics can be duplicated, the genuineness and trustworthiness of ancient documents depends not upon these things considered separately, but upon the total interconnection of all of them. And all these characteristics cannot be duplicated by any forger, no matter how skilled, without there being some indication of spuriousness which can be detected by an experienced and accomplished antiquarian. Real and genuine ancient documents have a kind of appearance of genuineness stamped upon them which those who are experienced often detect at first glance. In the same way skilled goldsmiths often distinguish true gold from the false by touch alone; painters distinguish originals from copies at a glance;

and those who know coins always distinguish the genuine from the false simply at sight. But if any of these things has been so skillfully forged that they very closely resemble the genuine, a skilled man will in the end detect the forgery by a careful examination. He does this not so much by arguments and methods as by experience. This experience is, as it were, the touchstone by which goldsmiths detect real gold, and anyone who does not have it will easily fall into error. Look at the color: there is nothing more nearly resembling true gold; look at the image of the emperor: no material takes on his likeness so well; examine the inscription: it is the one which is stamped on genuine coins. Let the goldsmith use the touchstone, and then at last he will recognize the dross. So in distinguishing genuine documents from forgeries experience is necessary, and cleverness of mind and reason alone cannot be substituted for it. If you should ask why I regard some documents as genuine and reject others, I reply that I consider the former to be genuine because the type of script, the style, and everything else convinces me that they are genuine, and the fact that there is nothing in them contrary to historical fact; on the other hand, I judge the forgeries to be such because one of these conditions is not fulfilled. If you should further ask why I consider one type of script and one style as genuine as against another, I shall reply that I have learned this from experience and from comparing many such documents of different dates and from different places. He who has equipped himself with this experience will perceive at a single glance the individual aspects of anything presented to him, and so will be capable of giving a correct judgment immediately. But an unskilled and inexperienced novice will pause over particulars; and, if he is wise, he will suspend judgment; but if he is hasty and a bit rash, he will give an unconsidered opinion about something which he does not fully understand. So it is with the unskilled logician who, when the subject of his dispute is presented, pauses in uncertainty over the individual propositions; but the skilled logician perceives at once whether the proposition is true or false.

The same method of judgment should be applied to the art of distinguishing genuine documents from spurious or interpolated ones and of determining their dates. All who are experienced in this matter agree that this art cannot be learned except through constant comparison of manuscripts which give a certain indication of their date with others that do not. It is agreed that manuscripts written in capital letters are ancient. What is the reason? Even the great Sirmond, who especially liked that script, would give no other reason than that he knows this from experience.

The state of preservation of ancient works on any subject is no better. In fact, there is no class of authors in which false and spurious works are not found mixed with true and genuine ones. Neither historical works, nor the writings of the Fathers, nor decretal letters, nor the records of Councils, nor the lives of the Saints—out of reverence I will not mention Scripture—were immune from this type of corruption. In what way will you distinguish the spurious from the genuine? Only by the testimony of the ancient authors, by the comparison of suspect works with genuine ones; and, finally, by a certain taste which is acquired by constantly reading the genuine works of each author. For in this way the genuine works of the Fathers are separated from the supposititious; genuine epistolary decrees are distinguished from spurious ones; and the genuine acts of the martyrs and other Saints are separated from the forgeries.

But, you say, in order to establish the authenticity or spuriousness of documents by comparing them with documents accepted as genuine, first the authenticity of those documents upon which the comparison is based must be demonstrated and established so that a correct judgment can be made about the others from them. To be sure, it is not enough that they do not clearly betray themselves as spurious: it has to be demonstrated by a certain method that those documents which are considered genuine are completely beyond suspicion. But there are no certain arguments to prove that archetypes at least of the Merovingian and Carolingian ages are genuine. What grounds should be used for proof? The type of script, the style, the seals, the signatures? All these can be duplicated by skilled forgers, and so no archetype of those periods whose authenticity can be proved by sure arguments can be offered. At least you ought to have procured those archetypes which you use from places least likely to arouse suspicion, for example, from public archives, which have always been protected against the treachery of forgers.

However, if we allow this kind of argument, the question of the authenticity of all manuscripts and records, whether they go back to ancient times, or whether they belong to later and more recent times, is already settled. For in what way, by what argument, could the genuineness and authenticity of any archetype be established? By comparison, you will say, with an authentic manuscript which is genuine and free from suspicion. But, given any authentic manuscript, you will similarly require that its authenticity be proved by certain and irrefutable arguments. And the same with a third manuscript, a fourth, and so on. The matter will go on infinitely, if in fact no archetype which could not be made by a skilled forger can be produced. And so no authentic document either of the Merovingian and Carolingian ages, or the age of the Capets, or even of a later period, will be recognized as genuine and free from suspicion.

This negative method of reasoning will prevail not only in the science of diplomatics but also in distinguishing the genuine works of the ancients from the supposititious and spurious ones. For in order to make a sure judgment, you will have to compare one work with another, so that some of them can be considered the genuine products of the author rather than others. To clarify the matter by an example, I cite the letters of the Roman Pontiffs. All agree that many of them are spurious. By what arguments would you distinguish them? By comparing them? But first you must decide which are genuine, so that the rest may be judged by comparison with them.Now tell me how you distinguish them. You will surely, I think, say that the ones you regard as genuine exhibit in every detail the style and manner of that Pope whose name they bear, but that the others clearly do not. But what prevented some forger from being so skillful that he could imitate in every detail that style of that Pope? The same must be said about the letters of Ignatius and about most of the writings of the Fathers, for we cannot detect their genuine works in any other way. I am aware that besides these methods of proof, which can be called intrinsic, there are also extrinsic proofs, which are drawn from the testimony of other authors. But those subtle disputants will easily avoid accepting this evidence by claiming that these *testimonia* were drawn from unsatisfactory authors, or that they have been interpolated into the text of the author in question. They may even claim that the authors from whom the *testimonia* are drawn are spurious, and so everything will become a matter for skepticism.

But, you say, the archives from which my archetypes were taken are not free from suspicion. These archetypes would certainly be accepted as genuine if they had been taken from public archives, which have always been impervious to forgers.

I shall not answer that kind of objection, for it is improper and unworthy of a gentleman. Nor shall I point out that in the past there were hardly any other archives besides those of the churches and monasteries, from which my genuine documents were taken. Indeed, there was formerly in France the palace archive, and the archives of the Chambre des Comptes and of the Royal Treasury, as they call it, still exist; but the latter two were founded in recent times, and the former, the palace archive, ceased to exist long ago, and no archetype can be recovered from it. But, even if any could be recovered from it, what would prevent those capricious critics from saying that the documents in question had been brought there from somewhere else, or that they were planted there (for perhaps they could even prove that by other examples); and that they therefore regarded them as suspicious or even as forged? In fact, the document on the tax privilege, which was formerly in the royal library at Fontainebleau, is now preserved in the Royal Library in Paris; and yet some do not hesitate to assail its authenticity. Nothing is too sacred to escape their criticism. But I fear that there is no public archive in which some false and interpolated documents have not been mixed with authentic and genuine ones. But I am not going to pause over this lest I seem to be guilty of the same fault which I complain of in others.

Therefore, the only reason I should be required to give for considering genuine the documents and records which I used as examples is that the type of script, the style, and everything else about them clearly indicate that they belong to the ages whose dates they bear. This was not my opinion alone, but also the opinion of those who are most expert in this field. To put it briefly, for deciding a question of this kind one should not require a metaphysical reason or demonstration, but rather a moral one of the kind which can be applied in these matters, and which is no less certain in its own right than a metaphysical demonstration. For in these matters, just as in moral matters, we deal with falsehood and error as well as truth. Beyond a doubt moral certitude cannot be acquired without long and constant observation of all the coincidences and circumstances which can lead to attaining the truth. In exactly this way the authenticity or spuriousness of ancient documents can be demonstrated. It is specified by law, and all intelligent judges of these documents agree that a document which cannot be proved spurious by any certain and invincible arguments must be considered authentic and genuine. Many fines have been imposed upon those who for no good reason accused an ancient document of spuriousness. Let those who capriciously deny the authenticity of all ancient documents see what others receive as their punishment. No one ever attempted to do this unless he was a complete novice who had no experience at all in antiquities, and who did not understand how useful and necessary such documents are not only to the study of literature but also to the commonwealth.

IV. Therefore, those who wish to learn the art of criticizing ancient documents must consider themselves experts only after careful and thorough preparation. For if it is difficult for someone without experience in this field to give an authoritative judgment about one single document, how much more arduous and dangerous will it be for him to judge all kinds of documents if he does not have as his guide that experience which cannot be acquired without long familiarity with documents of this kind? The liberal arts, the study of finished oratory, and the constant reading of the classical authors are not enough to produce this ability to judge documents; rather, these studies are a great obstacle if the same elegance or purity or diction is expected in those ancient documents. For in rejecting and disputing those documents the student would be guided by his own fancy because he is so familiar with those polished authors. The stylistic niceties of these authors must in some way be unlearned so that the mind may become more accustomed to the vulgar Latin of these documents. And yet often those who are so familiar with the classical authors arrogantly claim expertise in judging ancient documents, and they ridicule those who disagree with their judgments.

Therefore, the same must be required of those who wish to call themselves experts in diplomatics as Quintilian demanded of children's tutors: "Either they should be completely educated or they should realize their deficiencies."

BOOK VI

Corollary 3. On the Abbots of St. Denis and Other Matters Pertaining to That Monastery

I have deliberately deferred to this place the treatment of certain topics which pertain to the monastery of St. Denis near Paris. The learned scholar Coint began the dispute over these matters, but when the publication of this work had already been well advanced, the fine old gentleman was struck down by death. I would rather offer prayers for his soul than carry on a dispute with him when he is dead, and I owe this consideration to him because of the intimate friendship which endured between us while he was alive. Indeed, our friendship was so strong that no difference of opinion could ever cause ill-feeling between us. Since I cannot discuss with him in writing the matters over which we disagreed, and since I do not want to forsake the subject completely, I shall treat it in such a way that I may seem not to be quarreling with him, but rather to be explaining a matter which is obscure.

I shall begin with the founding of St. Denis, whose origins are usually traced to Dagobert I. But before Dagobert I succeeded to the reign over Neustria, after the death of his father Chlotar, that monastery already existed, and the Abbot Dodo was head of it in the forty-third year of the reign of Chlotar. The king died in the next year. But in his forty-third year, Teodetrude or Theodila, a very powerful lady, gave many tracts of land "to the Abbot Dodo and his brothers, who zealously serve the church of St. Denis." The document I cite is found on page 653 of Doublet's collection. The land in question was located in the districts of Madrie, Beauvais, and Limoges. This lady had considerable possessions in the last district, as you can see from document IV, dated in the fourth year of King Dagobert, which I published earlier in this work. The same Abbot Dodo is mentioned in the genuine document of Chlotar II which I publish in the *Supplement*. Fredegarius, the scholastic, in his treatment of the church of St. Denis does not attribute the origin of that monastery to Dagobert, but he does mention four facts about it in chapter LXXIX. It is not surprising that Dagobert was buried in that church, for we read that he "adorned it in a worthy manner with gold, jewels, and many very precious statues, and he had buildings constructed in its precinct"; in addition, Dagobert "gave so much wealth and so many villas and possessions" in many areas "to that church that many marveled at his generosity." Lastly, "the singing of hymns in the manner in which it was done at the monastery of the Saints of Agaune was instituted there," which "the Abbot Aigulf heedlessly" abolished. By the words "he ordered buildings to be constructed in the precinct of that (church)," Fredegarius seems to mean the surrounding houses for the monks, which Dagobert added to the church he had so magnificently decorated. And so Dagobert must be considered the founder of the new church and the new monastery, and he was justly honored by posterity as the original founder because, as Fredegarius reports, he gave spacious villas and vast possessions to that church. I have fully discussed the institution of the annual singing of hymns in that church in the first preface of the *Annals of the Order of Saint Benedict* in the fourth century.

The location of the first monastery of St. Denis was clearly shown by the very painstaking Adrien de Valois to have been at the fifth milestone from the city of Paris. He demonstrated this in his treatise on churches and in his defense of that work against Jean de Launoy, a learned Doctor at Paris. Charles Coint also refuted de Launoy after de Valois in the third volume of the *Annales Francorum* under the year 630. The document numbered XXVIII above also confirms this fact. It is a document of Childebert III, which states that "in the past, in a time of calamity, the market had been moved from the area of St. Denis," where he said the body of the martyr was buried, "and had been transferred and brought to the city of Paris, between the churches of St. Lawrence and St. Martin." Whether the old monastery of St. Denis stood in the place where the church with the priory called "St. Denis by the Way" now stands, I cannot discuss at length here. I can only point out that the church is mentioned in chapter XXIV of Book I of the *Miracles of St. Denis*. Lastly, Coint also proves under the same year that the companions of St. Denis, Rusticus and Eleutherius, were known in the reign of Clovis the Younger. The document of Clovis which I have published above from the autograph as number VII demonstrates this, and the edict of Theoderic of Calais, number XXXVI, supports it.

I do not deny that of the seventeen documents, which Doublet gives as written by Dagobert for the monastery of St. Denis, some are suspicious or interpolated, but I cannot agree with the criticism of Coint, who rejects most of them for rather trivial reasons. I cannot conceal the fact that he sometimes indulged excessively in conjectures and trusted his own fancy far too much in refuting and mutilating ancient documents. The first document of Dagobert in Doublet is an example. It is about the *nundinae* or market, and it is dated "on the 30th of July, in the second year of the reign of Dagobert, at Compiègne." He argues that it is spurious "because," he says, "in the second year of his reign, Dagobert did not yet have possession of Neustria, nor can the second year of the reign over Neustria, which was added to his possessions partly in 629 and partly in 630, be explained in any way, for the years of King Dagobert, with which the documents in question are dated must of necessity be numbered not from the death of his father, Chlotar, but from the beginning of his rule over Austrasia. For Dagobert did not rule in Neustria and Burgundy for ten whole years; in fact, the tenth, eleventh, thirteenth, fourteenth, fifteenth, and sixteenth years of King Dagobert are mentioned as dates in the documents of St. Denis." He says this at number X under the year 630. But his entire argument is overthrown if we point out that in different documents of Dagobert the years of his reign were numbered differently, sometimes from beginning of his rule over Austrasia, and sometimes from that over Neustria. I grant that some documents in Doublet are dated from the reign over Austrasia. But why should others not be dated from the reign over Neustria, as is the case with the document in question? For different methods of dating occur frequently in other documents of the kings, namely on those of Charles the Bald, Henry I, Philip I, and others, as I have noted in the earlier books. Coint himself, moreover, allowed this system of reckoning the date in the case of a certain document of King Childeric for the monks of St. Denis. In this document the first year of Childeric's reign is given as the date. "That first year of King Childeric must be understood to refer to his reign over Neustria." This is what Coint says about the date in the third volume under the year 679, at number XIV. Certainly the edict of Dagobert concerning the market is beyond suspicion, and it is supported by number XXVII, which is one of the later edicts of Childebert III. But the pronoun "I" must be expunged from this document of Dagobert, for it seems to have been added at later date to the king's subscription. In the same way other documents of Dagobert in Doublet's collection could be defended, especially the third, the fourth, the eighth, and the thirteenth, by correcting certain trivial errors which easily find their way into copies. But this requires more time; here I must make certain observations about the Abbots.

The list of Abbots of St. Denis up to Hilduin is full of errors, and it is difficult to be certain about the number of Abbots before him or their order of succession. They are usually given in this order: Aigulf I, Chunald, Dodo, Leobefarius, Aigulf II, Aigulf III, Godobald, Chaino. That Dodo should be put before Aigulf is clear from what I have said above. The documents which are adduced from Doublet do not convince me that there were three Abbots named Aigulf. Godobald is wrongly dated in the reign of Theoderic, the son of Clovis the Younger. I shall prove that he was a contemporary of Theoderic of Calais. Considering all this I think that the catalogue of the earlier Abbots, until more certain evidence can be adduced, should read as follows: Dodo in the reign of Chlotar II; Chunald or Chunoald in the reign of Dagobert the son of Chlotar II; Aigulf in the reign of the same Dagobert and Clovis II, his son; Vandebert in the reign of Chlotar III; and then, as we note in the *Supplement,* Charderic and Chaino.

Charderic is mentioned in the year 678 in document X above, which is a decree of King Theoderic concerning the removal of Chramlinus, Bishop of Embrun. This Bishop Chramlinus is mentioned in the will of Abbo, the *Patricius,* for the monastery of Novalicium. The will is number LXII. After he was removed, Chramlinus petitioned the king that he might be allowed to "live out his life" in the monastery of St. Denis, "where Charderic was Abbot, in obedience to the rule of the monastery," and this request was granted. The same Abbot is mentioned in 688 in a decree of the same Theoderic which is number XII. That this Charderic later became a Bishop we know from number XXIV, in which "Charderic, sometime Bishop," is said to have founded the monastery of Tunsonis-Vallis in the district of Camliacensis. This district, about which I spoke in Book IV, belongs to the diocese of Beauvais, and I therefore conclude that Charderic was Bishop of Beauvais, certainly before Constantine, who is frequently mentioned in decrees XVIII, XIX, and XXIV.

Many documents which I have published mention Chaino. He is "the venerable Chaino, the Deacon," and he is mentioned in number IX, a decree of Theoderic about Sancy, which was written while Charderic was Abbot. Chaino succeeded him around 690. In that year, Theoderic issued a decree concerning the villa at Lagny, which is number XIII here, giving it to the monastery of St. Denis, where, he says, "the Abbot Chaino presides over groups of monks from many monasteries, whom he has united in his holy monastery for singing the praises of Christ." Chaino is likewise mentioned in the same year in the document of Vandemir, number XIV; then in the year 692 in the decree of Clovis III which is number XVI, and in numbers XVII and XVIII. Later, in 694, in the decree of Childebert III on the villa at Nassigny, which "the Bishop of Lyons, the apostolic lord Godinus" owned previously, Chaino is mentioned. This document is number XX. The following document also mentions the Abbot Chaino. He lived until 696 at least, as the famous document of Agerad, Bishop of Chartres, number XXIII, shows. In the time of Chaino Chrotchar the Deacon lived, and he is mentioned in numbers XV and XIX. He was afterwards made Abbot of the monastery of Mary, which the previously mentioned Agerad built at Blois. This is proven by number XXIII, in which Chrotchar is mentioned as Abbot of that monastery.

Dalfinus succeeded Chaino before 710, in which year Childebert III issued his decree, number XXVIII, concerning the market of St. Denis. In this decree the Abbot Dalfinus is mentioned, and also in the decree of the following year concerning the mill at the villa of Cadolaicus.

The Abbot Chillardus or Hellardus lived in the reigns of Dagobert III and Chilperic II, as several decrees of these kings prove. For in the document of Pepin, Mayor of the Palace, which is number XXXVIII, several matters are mentioned pertaining to St. Denis concerning which "the Abbot Chillardus had received a judgment during the reign of King Dagobert." He is also mentioned in three documents of King Chilperic which were issued in the first year of his reign in March, 716. These documents are numbers XXX, XXXI, and XXXIII. In addition to this, an excellent piece of evidence about the Abbot Chillardus, is furnished by a manuscript at Rheims, which I shall discuss presently. In this manuscript he is called Hellardus, and the beginning of his Abbotship is firmly dated to a few years after the death of St. Lambert the Bishop, in 709. From what has been said the document of Childebert III, number XXVI, on Solemius, issued in the twelfth year of his reign, when Chillardus is already mentioned as Abbot, must be corrected. In his place, Chaino, or rather Dalfinus, whom I have proved came before the Abbot Chillardus, must beyond a doubt be substituted. The rest of the document on Solemius is beyond suspicion, and it is supported by the decree of Pepin, Mayor of the Palace. I could not find the autograph of this document, but only a copy, and the mistake could easily have come about by scribal error. This is the case in Doublet, who first published that document, where the terrible error in the case of the fictitious name Corfintisca occurred. This gave rise to the fine story which I mentioned in Book IV.

Turnoald became a monk after being Bishop of Paris, and then he became Abbot of St. Denis. He is mentioned as Bishop in the reign of Clovis III in document XIX and again in the reign of Childebert III in documents XXIII and XXIV. As Abbot, he is mentioned in a document of Chilperic on page 689 of Doublet, which is dated February 28, at Compiègne, in the second year of his reign. Since Chilperic speaks of the monastery of St. Denis, "where," he says, "lord Turnoald the Bishop is in charge," we must conclude that Chillardus died in 716.

Hugo should be placed next during the reign of King Chilperic, as document XL shows. Perhaps he is the Hugo, Bishop of Rouen, who obtained "the famous monasteries of Fontanelle and Jumieges" through the favor of Prince Charles, as the *Chronicle of Fontanelle* reports.

Berthoald was Abbot in 723 according to number XXXVI, which is a document of Theoderic of Calais.

Godobald was Abbot during the reign of the same Theoderic, as can be inferred from the document bearing his name which is published on pages 686 and 687 of Doublet. This document is wrongly attributed to Theoderic the son of Clovis the Younger. It is dated March 3 in the sixth year of his reign, at Ponthion. But the testimony of the short treatise on the *Miracles of St. Denis* leads me to assign the document to Theoderic of Calais. This work gives the origin of Godobald, the events of his life, and also the length of his Abbotship. It is preserved in a vellum manuscript in the principal church at Rheims, and it was written at least eight hundred years ago. This is the opinion of the eminent Antonius Faurus, Doctor of Paris and Provost of the church at Rheims, to whom I showed that manuscript. The author of the three books on the *Miracles of St. Denis* who composed his work in the reign of Charles the Bald used this short treatise. His work is published in the second part of the *Annals of the Order of Saint Benedict* under the third century. Most of the earlier miracles are described in the same words as in the Rheims manuscript. Several are omitted, one of which is related at number 248 in the Rheims manuscript:

> During the reign of Charles, King of the Franks and Mayor of the Palace [this was a customary title of the king at that time], a certain Godobald, from the province of Hasbain and the town known as Arbrido, participated with a certain Count Dodo in the murder of the blessed Bishop Lambert, and God punished him by making him lame. This punishment made him realize what a horrible deed he had done, and for a long time he wandered about the places associated with the saints and prayed that he might be granted forgiveness and be healed. At last he came to the shrine of St. Peter in Rome. Through divine revelation he was made to understand that he could be healed in France at the graves of the holy martyrs Denis, Rusticus, and Eleutherius. He therefore returned from Rome and sought out the place which had been divinely designated, and there he received the cure which he had zealously sought. Helardus was at that time Abbot there, and he congratulated him over his divine cure and allowed him to live there and share the monastery's accommodation. And so he lived his life there, and since everyone considered him a virtuous man, he assumed the office of Abbot upon the command of Prince Charles, and he devoted himself completely to his duties as Abbot for twenty-five years.

No better evidence could be cited to illustrate the life and times of the Abbot Godobald. From this it is clear that he lived during the reign of Charles Martel, and that he was Abbot of St. Denis for twenty-five years, that is, from 723 when he succeeded Berthoald to 748. In that year Amalbert succeeded him. While Godobald was Abbot, Sigobert, a recluse at St. Denis, according to the *Annales Francorum,* was sent by Prince Charles along with Grimo, the Abbot of Corbie, to Pope Gregory III. The commonly known lists state that Sigobert was Abbot.

Amalbert is mentioned in a decree of Pepin, Mayor of the Palace, in the fourth year of the reign of King Childeric. This coincides with the year 748 mentioned above. This decree is number XXXVII.

Fulrad was already Abbot in 750. The documents published here and others in Doublet corroborate that fact. I cite four in particular, numbers

XXXVIII, XXXIX, XL, and XLIII, which are dated 750, 751, 752, and 754 respectively. All are addressed to the Abbot Fulrad. There are three in Doublet starting at page 692, of which the first is dated in the time when Pepin was Mayor of the Palace, the second in the second year of Pepin's reign as King, and the third in the fourth year of his reign. All of these are addressed to the Abbot Fulrad. Four of the archetypes of these letters, in which the name of Fulrad is clearly read, survive. In addition, there is the testimony of Anastasius, who, in his life of Pope Stephen III, calls Fulrad Abbot in the beginning of the seventh Indiction, that is, at the end of the year 753. Despite this evidence, Charles Coint, under the year 749, gives three reasons why he does not think that Fulrad was Abbot before the seventh year of Pepin's reign. The first reason is the testimony of St. Boniface, who addresses one letter CVI, "to my fellow priest Optatus, the Abbot of Monte Cassino," and another one, number XCII, "to my fellow priest, the Priest Fulredus." This letter was written at the time of Boniface's preparation for his last journey to Frisia, which was in 754. Coint argues he would have said "Abbot," if Fulrad were then an Abbot. The second reason is that Pepin issued a document in the sixth year of his reign "with all respect to Constramnus, the venerable Abbot of the monastery of St. Denis the Martyr, in which monastery the body of St. Denis rests." The third reason is that a letter of Pope Stephen III, dated in the tenth Indiction, that is, in 757, was addressed "to Fulrad, the Archpriest and Abbot pleasing to God, who presides over the holy monasteries founded under his auspices." From this evidence the scholar concludes that the Abbot Constramnus was then living and that Fulrad later became the Abbot of the monastery of St. Denis. According to Coint, St. Denis cannot be included under those holy monasteries, because he recognizes Dagobert and not Fulrad as its founder, and so he concludes: "Therefore, expunge the name of the Abbot Fulrad from those documents which Pepin either as Mayor of the Palace or as King issued for that monastery before the year 757." His judgment is certainly authoritative, but this is a rash conclusion based upon weak evidence which ought not outweigh the indubitable autographs and records in which Fulrad is clearly mentioned as Abbot from the ninth year of the reign of Childeric. To treat his first objection, it is common for the writers of that age when they refer to an Abbot Priest to mention only the title Priest, with the title Abbot omitted, as I have proven elsewhere many times. In regard to the name of the Abbot Constramnus which is found in a document of Pepin dated in the sixth year of his reign, that should not outweigh the testimony of the seven other documents which give Fulrad as Abbot, especially since Coint assigns the faulty Indiction of that document, issued to Constramnus, to the year 657. Rather, he should delete the Indiction. I could not find the archetype of that document although I searched diligently for it. However, the addition of the Indiction contrary to the custom of Pepin, and the error in that Indiction, where the fourth Indiction is made in the seventh year of Pepin's reign, which was the tenth Indiction, suffice to weaken its authority. Someone may suggest that the Indiction should be deleted: I would further argue that the name of Constramnus should be deleted and that of the Abbot Fulrad put in its place, as the completely trustworthy autographs of the other documents require. Lastly, what Coint says about the letter of Pope Stephen is foolish. They were addressed "to Priest Fulrad who is pleasing to God, the Abbot of the holy monasteries which he founded under God's auspices" with no mention of St. Denis in the title. But if Coint were to accept the other words of that document (as he would certainly be bound to do) he would come to another conclusion, for in the text of that document of privilege there are other passages which clearly designate Fulrad as the Abbot of St. Denis. For this is what Stephen says further on in the letter: "We grant through our apostolic authority to you and to all the succeeding Abbots of the monastery of the Martyrs and Saints Denis, Rusticus, and Eleutherius, the permission and the authority to construct monasteries. . . ." Nothing clearer can be quoted to prove my assertion, but the historian marks those words with an obelus for no other reason than that he wanted Constramnus and not Fulrad to be Abbot in that year. However, it is certain that Fulrad was Abbot of the monastery of St. Denis from 750 and that he ruled it until 784, as I have stated in my comment on his life in the second part of the *Annals of the Order of Saint Benedict* under the third century.

Magenarius succeeded Fulrad and lived only a few years. He is also mentioned in the life of Fulrad and in chapter XIX of Book I of the *Miracles of St. Denis.*

It is clear from the same life that Fardulf was not only a *Decanus,* but that he was also Abbot after Magenarius. The Abbot Fardulf is mentioned in the document of Count Theudold, number LX, which is dated 798, and in chapter XX and the four following chapters of Book I of the *Miracles of St. Denis.*

According to chapter XXV of the *Miracles,* Walto followed him as Abbot. He died in 814, as the achrostic poem on the *Vision of Wetinus* proves. I have restored the text of this poem in part one of the *Annals of the Order of Saint Benedict* under the fourth century.

Hilduin, whom I have mentioned frequently elsewhere, took charge of the monastery in the same year. This is all that need be said for the present about the early Abbots of St. Denis in order to correct the lists which are commonly used. I have not mentioned Cailedulf, who is dated in the time of Dagobert III, and Sigobert, who is dated to the time of Childeric, because their Abbotships are not supported by any evidence. I return to Fulrad.

Three events which are worth considering here occured when Fulrad was Abbot of the monastery of St. Denis. The first event concerns the Bishop Herbert, about whom we read, in connection with the healing of a certain peasant, in chapter VI of Book I of the *Miracles of St. Denis:* "On the next day he went to Bishop Herbert [it was the custom for that church to sometimes have Bishops residing in it], and he confessed his sins to him." I related and explained these words in the preface of the *Annals of the Order of Saint Benedict* under the fourth century. I did this not with the intention of claiming that the church of St. Denis was the seat of a Bishop, but I intended only to show what the words of themselves indicate, that it was not unusual at that time for extraordinary Bishops without dioceses, who had the dignity of a Bishop along with the duties of the office, but no title, to reside at that church. It is well established that there were in times past many such Bishops in the churches of France and Spain, and even in the East. Among them were the monks Barses, Eulogius, and Lazarus, as Sozomenus states in chapter XXXIV of Book VI of the edition of Valois: "They were consecrated Bishops in their own monasteries, not of any city but only as an honor, as if in reward for their outstanding works." In the *Journey to Mt. Libanus* two kinds of Bishops are mentioned, to one of which the Abbots of monasteries belong. See the notes on this matter in chapter XXII. I am not going to pause over this here, but I mention this to prove that the above parenthesis did not intrude itself into the text from the margin as Coint tires to prove at number XLIII under the entry for the year 768. For this parenthesis appears not only in the manuscript at St. Victor (which he thinks is not very old) and in that at St. Denis, which was written almost four hundred years ago, but also in the manuscript at Rheims which I mentioned earlier, and which I said was written in the ninth century.

Another observation must be made at this point. Among the various privileges granted to the monastery of St. Denis during that time (two of which I published as numbers XLI and XLII) there are two others of Pope Stephen III among the documents in Doublet on pages 447 and 449. Both of them conclude as follows: "Farewell. Issued on February 26th, during the reign of Constantine Augustus crowned by God as mighty Emperor, in the thirteenth year of his reign, and in the fourth year of the reign of his son the Emperor Leo the Elder, in the tenth Indiction." The first document has this ending in Sirmond's collection: "Issued on February 26th, in the eighteenth year of his reign and the thirty-eighth year after his consulship, and in the fourth year of the reign of his son Leo the Elder, in the tenth Indiction." These dates come to the same thing. The testimony of Hilduin in *Dionysius the Areopagite* allows no doubt about the privilege granted by Pope Stephen III to the monks of St. Denis. The following is said of Stephen: "He exalted this most sacred place with privileges of great authority, and above the altar which he consecrated he left the pallium of his apostolic dignity as a sign of the blessing of St. Peter, and the keys for the veneration of his prerogative, . . ." The manuscript of de Thou and Colbert, number 780, agrees with this. In this manuscript, written eight hundred years ago, the second privilege granted by Stephen is included, but it ends with "Farewell" with no indications of its date. Copyists often omit this, as you can observe everywhere in the archives, to history's loss. But this is not the place to treat these matters. In the closing quoted above there are two problems. The first is that the fourth year of Leo's reign is made identical to the tenth Indiction, which is the year 757. But this was the sixth year of Leo's reign, if in fact Constantine declared his son Leo as consort in his rule in the fourth Indiction, that is, in 751, as Theophanes states. The second problem is that Leo is called "the Elder," although he is called "the Younger" on certain coins, and by Ado of Vienne, as the learned Du Cange observes in treatise XLIII at the end of his *Glossarium* on coins of the middle ages, where he discusses this topic. Coint finds a third problem in the matter of the years of Constantine Copronymus. Since he began his reign in his eighteenth year, after the death of his father in June, in the ninth Indiction, that is, in 741, the eighteenth year of his reign could not fall in the tenth Indiction, that is, in 757. The closing of the document granting privilege in Sirmond, which reads: "in the thirty-eighth year of his reign" corresponds exactly with the beginning of his reign in 720 while his father was still living. But the same difficulty arises with the eighteenth year after his consulship, which should be counted from the death of his father. Perhaps an error has occurred in the Indiction. This frequently happens even in autographs, as I have shown elsewhere. In regard to the fact that Leo is called "the Elder," that term is also applied to him in Rubeus at the beginning of Book VI of the *History of Ravenna* in the closing of a document of Paul I which reads: "Issued on February 5, in the reign of the most pious Constantine Augustus, crowned by God as our mighty Emperor, in the fortieth year of his reign, and in the twentieth year of the peace he concluded; and in the seventh year of the reign of his son Leo the Elder, in the twelfth Indiction," that is, in 759. For "of the peace he concluded" the correct reading is "P.C.," that is, "after his consulship." There is an error in the years of Constantine whether you count the years of his reign from 720 or from 741. But the years of Leo agree with the reckoning of Stephen III in the St. Denis document. He is called Leo "the Elder" also in the document of Paul I in which he put the monastery of St. Hilary at Galiatensis under the church at Ravenna. Was this the style of the Roman Curia, that he be called "the Elder" by it although he is called "the Younger" elsewhere? Or is he called "the Elder" as being the oldest of the sons of Copronymus? In this way Honorius the son of Theodosius is called "the Elder" in comparison with Arcadius in chapter XI of Book I of Bede. This term can also be used of first-born even before the birth of later children, as Christ is called the first-born of the Blessed Virgin although he was her only child. But whatever the solution of this difficulty is, the manuscript of de Thou alone gives the second letter of Pope Stephen for the monks of St. Denis, and it was written eight hundred years ago (as I said) but with no indications of the date of the privilege.

The third miracle of St. Denis occurred when Fulrad was Abbot, and it is related in the manuscript at Rheims. I must retell the story here. After the miracle described above concerning Godobald there follows in that manuscript the story which I have related in chapter IV of Book I about a certain soldier of King Pepin; then comes another tale which I shall add here.

Moreover, we think that a story of what the Almighty wished to be accomplished for His praise through the same martyr should not be omitted. Now, in the time of the aforesaid King Pepin there was a certain Count Gerard of Paris, whose wife was named Rotrud. She lived at the estate at Riogilo not far from Paris, and on the feast day of St. Denis she saw that her servant girls were idle. When they had been summoned to her presence, she asked them why they were idle and reprimanded them severely. One of them who had a position higher than the others said, "It is the feast of St. Denis, and for that reason we thought the day should be solemnly observed." And their mistress said, "Go, and begin your work at once. We who are beyond the Saint's dominion have no cause to celebrate his feast." But when they were about to obey her command, through the favor of the Lord and the merits of Christ and of the martyrs, there was suddenly such a great flash of lightning and such a great storm arose that the whole house along with its furnishings was all at once carried off and submerged into the river Seine. And she who did not want to celebrate one feast day lost all that she had acquired during the year, but through God's providence the people were saved from that storm. We believe that this was done so that the day might always be observed as solemn.

So much from the manuscript at Rheims. Gerard Count of Paris is mentioned a few times in the preceding documents, namely in XLIV and LI. From this miracle we learn that his wife's name was Rotrud. From the same manuscript I add the variant readings of chapter X, which is about the Count, who died while pasturing his flocks on the meadow of the Saint. In the documents I published, the wording at the beginning is: "a certain Count Bertrandus," and in the Rheims manuscript: "Count Bertcaudus of old," and farther on: "into the meadow to the bridge," not "to the spring." Next, "Bertcaudus"; afterwards, "and so the keys of the church are administered by the Count's guard"; "all the monks requested that he leave the meadow"; then, " 'Give me the keys,' says the Count, 'that I may lose my fear of them.' " Lastly, "He orders them to take away his torturer, and to kill the man who inflicted such cruel lashes upon him." Perhaps these were the very keys which Pope Stephen III is said to have placed upon the altar of St. Denis, as I mentioned earlier.

Now I thought that I had completely disentangled myself from all these difficulties, but I am again confronted with Coint's criticism of the documents granting the two privileges to St. Denis which are published in Doublet. One of them belongs to Pepin, Mayor of the Palace, and it has no indications of its date. This document is on page 692 of Doublet. The second was granted by Pepin as King and is dated in the second year of his reign. This is on page 694. Both are addressed to Fulrad, the Abbot of St. Denis. I treated the first earlier, and I noted that it was placed under the year 650 by Charles Coint as number XLV, but that the name of the Abbot Fulrad was expunged. It should not be, for the name of Fulrad appears in the autograph which is preserved in the archive of St. Denis. A seal is affixed to it immediately after the final words of the text. Then these words follow: "The seal of the illustrious Pepin, Mayor of the Palace." The document has no indications of its date. A copy of it, made almost in the same time as the archetype, is preserved. All this is more than enough for proving its authenticity.

The criticism directed against the second document of King Pepin concerning the market is far more serious. Coint not only corrects this document, as he did the first, but he rejects it as if it were supposititious under the year 753, where it is number XXXIII. The most overwhelming (for so he calls it) reason for rejecting it is that in this document six kings are mentioned who are said to have shown their generosity towards the monastery of St. Denis by their various decrees. They are Dagobert the Great; his son Clovis II; his nephews Chlotar III, Childeric II, and Theoderic III; his great-grandson Childebert III. Added to them is Grimoaldus, Mayor of the Palace. But no document of those kings or of Grimoald, which mentions a market of that kind exists, with the exception, he says, of a document of Dagobert the Great, which he publishes in the second volume under the year 630. I have examined this document and proven it to be spurious, because it is dated "on July 30th," in the second year of the reign of Dagobert. Consider that "most overwhelming" reason: if the matter is weighed without prejudice, it will appear to be very unconvincing. Suppose that there are in Doublet's collection no decrees of these kings concerning the market. Is it for this reason that only some of them are preserved in the archive of St. Denis? Even if they no longer exist, must the document of privilege whose autograph is preserved whole and undamaged to this day be judged spurious? Would it not be more reasonable for our critic to say that they were lost and that he regretted their loss? The originals of similar documents, which are mentioned in decrees of later kings, and which have been preserved, are, in many cases, lost. But the case for the monastery of St. Denis does not depend upon this evidence alone, for besides the document of Dagobert the Great, which I defended earlier against the attacks of Coint, a decree of Childebert III is preserved complete and in the original. It concerns the market of St. Denis, and in it the decrees of the earlier kings, Clovis, Theoderic, and Chlothacarius, are mentioned. Even the agreement of Grimoald, Mayor of the Palace, concerning that market which he tried to claim for himself is mentioned. That decree is number XXVIII, and I published it from the autograph. Doublet had passed over it along with many other documents because they were difficult to read. Now then, we have the documents of Dagobert the Great and of Childebert III for that market which Pepin confirms, and we would certainly have the remaining documents of the other kings if they had not been lost due to the ravages of time. But the triple cord which I have established is too strong to be broken by the weak argument which seems "most overwhelming" to no one but its own author. The other argument concerning the name of the Abbot Fulrad in that document is of the same type. The scholar argues that Fulrad became head of the monastery of St. Denis much later; but, as I have shown above, he is wrong. Finally, he finds fault with the fact that Pepin complains that the privilege of this monastery was violated by Soanachild and Gairefred "when Carlus was removed." What is this removal of Carlus or Charles, he says. When was it done and by whom? I reply that not every event of that age was recorded in writing: the annals of that period are meager and scanty. Therefore, the learned historian ought rather to have been glad that he had this material to illustrate the history of Prince Charles, who, as we learn from that source, was removed "on account of the avarice of Soanachild, and the plot of Gairefred, Count of Paris," although we do not know the date and circumstances of that event. We discover only this piece of information concerning his misfortune, that Plectrudis put him in prison in 714. Perhaps the disturbance caused by Soanachild and Gairefred occurred when Theoderic of Calais died. After his death there was a dispute among the princes over who should rule, and this was that interregnum of five years which lasted until the accession of Childeric. I am glad that my conjecture is confirmed by the authority of the *Chronicle of the Monastery of Saint Wandrille* (or Fontenelle), in chapter X. This was published in the third volume of the *Spicelegium* of my friend Acherius. Here the Abbot Wido is said "to have been accused before Prince Charles, because he had planned a conspiracy against him along with others, and he was therefore condemned to be beheaded." This was after 738, in which year this Wido took charge of the monastery at Fontenelle. And so it is clear that a conspiracy was made against Charles at that time, and we know from the document at St. Denis that Soanachild and Gairefred participated in it. Does the historian claim that Soanachild and Gairefred are unknown? But if this passage is not enough evidence for him, the document of Carloman, number XLVIII, gives more. In it both these men are mentioned, and likewise the market of St. Denis. Furthermore, in the earlier part of that document Gairehard or Gerard the Count of Paris is also mentioned, whom I spoke about earlier. But enough about that document of Pepin, which is well protected even by the sole authority of the remaining autograph. And enough about the documents and the archive of the monastery of St. Denis, to which I am especially indebted for anything I was able to accomplish in this discussion. I add only one thing more, namely that in the document of Charlemagne published on pages 705 and 706 of Doublet, in the date, where only "in the first year of our reign" is read, the wording should be "in the seventh and first year." This is the wording of the two other documents on pages 709 and 710.

BOOK III

Chapter 1

I. After explaining what I thought were the essential principles for determining whether a document is genuine or spurious, I intended at this point to give my readers some relief from that involved subject matter, but new objections have been raised which require my attention and summon me back to my task. For although this systematic treatment is unpleasant for the reader, and although I neither enjoy assuming the role of a teacher, nor am suited for it; yet, because I did undertake this subject, I think that I must make every effort so that my treatment of it, even if it is not considered definitive, may at least not be judged careless. In accordance with my purpose this is what remains to be discussed: whether the documents which Papebroch presents as specimens of authentic documents are such. Then I must refute some objections of my critics; and, lastly, the question of the authority of private legal documents and the status of documents in private cases must be settled. I shall treat these matters in order.

II. If the question of the privilege granted by Dagobert to the monastery of St. Maximin rested upon the authenticity of one document only, I would willingly and even gladly have refrained from criticizing it, and I would have been satisfied with explaining the principles by which other scholars could judge it. But since Papebroch offers this document as an example of the others, I fear that if I do not reveal its defects, the trustworthiness of the genuine documents will be imperiled. Therefore, I have decided to give scholars the various reasons which cause me to regard that document with the greatest suspicion, but I leave the final judgment to them.

The first cause for my suspicion comes from the invocation, "In the name of the Father, and of the Son, and of the Holy Spirit." I find this kind of invocation in none of the genuine documents of the first dynasty of kings, not to mention those of Dagobert himself. It was their practice to begin simply with their names and without any such invocation.

The second cause for suspicion comes from the inscription: "In what manner I, Dagobert, the most powerful king . . ." Now the Merovingian kings always use this kind of beginning: "The illustrious Dagobert, King of the Franks . . ." Furthermore, nowhere so far as I know did they use the pronoun "I" at the beginning of a document, nor did they refer to themselves in the singular number. I think that these two facts are clear from chapter VI of Book II.

I find a third cause for suspicion in the words "When my Bishops and Counts assembled I sent envoys in my name to the Abbot Maemilianus." Those words, "my Bishops," and "in my name" do not at all belong to that age.

A fourth reason is found in the words which immediately follow: "I commanded him to inquire diligently and to tell me in person by whose order that monastery of St. Maximin had been built, or under whose authority it had been placed from its earliest days." This and all that follows seem entirely foreign to the form of a document, and it has the flavor of a narrative rather than a document.

The fifth reason is that this manner of expression, "with the advice and at the request of my princes," was not used before the tenth or eleventh century, when the Emperors sometimes referred to "their princes." And certainly these words, "unless it is increased by means of lands or treasures given through the generosity of Emperors or Princes of succeeding ages," belong to the usage of the Emperors of the tenth and eleventh centuries.

The sixth reason is that this kind of closing was unknown in the time of Dagobert: "And, so that the confirmation of that document may endure through the ages, I have had it copied, and I ratified it with our seal." For, apart from the fact that this formula is completely different from what the Merovingians used, as my examples and facsimiles prove, Dagobert would never have used the words "our seal," indeed very few of our kings use them before the tenth century. In fact, the Merovingians used the words "subscriptions in our hand"; the Carolingians used "with our ring," or "by the impression of our ring." I have illustrated this in chapter X of Book II.

The seventh cause for suspicion is that this formula, "Issued auspiciously on April 4th, in the eleventh year of our reign," not only is foreign to the usage of the Merovingians, but also it comes before the seal of Dagobert contrary to the practice of all the Merovingian and Carolingian kings. They always put their seal and name before the date, as I have shown in chapters X and XXVI of Book II.

The eighth reason is that no place is specified along with the date of the document. This rarely, if ever, happens in documents of the Merovingian and Carolingian kings.

The ninth reason is that Dagobert uses a monogram. Now during the period of the first dynasty this was rarely done, except in the documents of those kings who did not know how to write. I have shown this in chapter X of Book II. But Dagobert did know how to write, as can be seen from facsimile XVI in Book V.

The tenth reason is that the subscription of the Chancellor, "I, Heriveus the Chancellor, read the document in place of Ricolfus, *Archicapellanus,*" is similarly irregular. For, not to mention the names "Heriveus" and "Ricolfus," which seem to belong to men who lived at a later date, namely, Ricolfus of Mayence and Heriveus of Rheims, the name *"Archicapellanus"* for the high Chancellor does not seem to have been in use before the tenth century, and then by the Emperors of Germany. I noted this in chapter XI of Book II.

I shall neglect the unusual words in this document, and I would not wish to use them for my argument since such matters belong to a more detailed investigation. Certainly what I have just mentioned clearly shows that this document of Dagobert either is spurious, or that it is not so undoubtedly genuine that it can or should be presented as a genuine and legitimate example of the other documents. If, however, anyone could solve these difficulties to my satisfaction, I would have a more favorable opinion of this document.

III. In support of this document of Dagobert concerning the privilege of the monastery of St. Maximin critics offer another document which bears Dagobert's name. But it is generally agreed that this document is not genuine both for the reasons given by Zyllesius and on account of the year A.D. and the types of subscriptions, which are not at all in accordance with the usage of that period.

IV. At this point I intended to end these critical examinations lest I appear to be the same type of overzealous critic which I accuse others of being. But, since in the *Propylaeum* we are also presented with a facsimile of a document of Charlemagne as an example of his other documents, and likewise another facsimile of a document of King Lothar, the son of the Emperor Lothar, as an example of his other documents, I thought it my duty to warn the attentive reader that these facsimiles, at least, are of the type which is anomalous, and they cannot be regarded as typical examples. In the first place, several scholars have pointed out that the document of Charlemagne begins with the invocation "In the name of the Father, and of the Son, and of the Holy Spirit." This is an exception to the usage of the other documents of Charlemagne written before 800. Those written before that date begin simply with the inscription "Charles, King of the Franks by the grace of God . . ." But, because some documents of Charlemagne with the same invocation have been published, for example, the one numbered XIX in the appendix on the Capitularies in the work of Baluze (although that document is taken not from the autograph but from an archive only, and so this invocation seems to have been interpolated), I do not wish to say anything against it here. I only warn that this formula is not regular and was not used in any original document which I, at least, have examined. No one should use this formula as evidence for suspecting genuine documents.

The second objection to this document of Charlemagne is more serious, namely that it begins with this formula: "Let all who faithfully believe in Christ, kings, bishops, and dukes, know how I, Charles, King of the Franks, Lombards, by the grace of God, and *Patricius* of the Romans, for the welfare of my soul and the stability of my kingdom . . ." Who ever read words like this in the genuine documents of Charlemagne, "Let all who faithfully believe in Christ . . . know . . ."? And the following, "kings, bishops"? Does any one of the kings include the other kings with this formula? Then you may ask whether Charles when speaking of himself ever used the singular pronoun "I." Furthermore, would he have spelled "Lombards" with an "o" *(Longobardi)* instead of with an "a" *(Langobardi),* and would he have omitted the conjunction "and" between

"Franks" and "Lombards"? Would he have used semi-Saxon script in contrast to all his other documents? Finally, do these words, "for the welfare of my soul and the stability of my kingdom," belong to his style? Far more usual is the beginning formula of number XVIII in Baluze's appendix: "Charles, King of the Franks and Lombards by the grace of God, and *Patricius* of the Romans, to all our faithful now living and to come." Because this document was copied not from an autograph but from an archive, the name "Charles" is spelled with a "K" *(Karolus)* and not a "C" *(Carolus)* (as it is usually spelled in autograph manuscripts of Charlemagne with very few exceptions), and Lombards is spelled with an "o" instead of an "a." This is the usual practice of those who copied the archives, as I see in many cases when I compare the autographs with the later copies which were made in the archives. Another document which immediately follows the latter in Baluze's appendix is far more usual. It begins: "In the name of the Father, and of the Son, and of the Holy Spirit. Charles, the most serene King of the Franks and Lombards by the grace of God, and *Patricius* of the Romans. Let all the Bishops, Abbots, Dukes, Counts, and all the faithful who are now living, as well as those to come, know . . ." The next document which follows has a similar form; in it the invocation and the words "most serene" are omitted. The autographs of these documents surely spelled Lombards with an "a" instead of an "o," as is the case in the document I here publish: "Charles, King of the Franks and Lombards by the grace of God, and *Patricius* of the Romans, trusts that all our faithful know."

Thirdly, perhaps another feature of that document of Charlemagne which I am discussing will seem worth noting. The seal has no inscription, nor does it display the face of Charlemagne as it is portrayed on other seals; in fact, the seal was not affixed in the normal and proper place. Now in the examples given in Zyllesius' work some traces of a title remain, and sometimes the place where the seal is affixed varies, as I have said earlier. Fourthly, another feature may cause some scholars to suspect the document. In the indications of its date the document is said to have been issued "in the month of August" without any indication of the day, and the year of the King's reign in France is given without the year of the reign in Italy. This is always added in genuine autographs. But since in certain other documents neither the day of the month nor the year of the reign in Italy is given, I only note that this is abnormal. You have an example of the former omission in number XIX in Baluze's appendix, and of the latter in a document of St. Martin of Tours. In addition, the number XL should be read for XI, as Zyllesius does, and the shape of the number confirms this, as I have shown earlier. *Ata* should be read for *Actum,* and *super ipsa* for *super Lipsia.* This river flows past Paderborn, where the document was dated. All these facts show that the original (if such it can be called) was of a very mixed character, or that the example that Papebroch gives was carelessly copied from its original. This seems more likely.

V. The same criticism must be made of the example of a document of Lothar which begins with an invocation different from that which is regular in his genuine documents. This document begins: "In the name of the Father, and of the Son, and of the Holy Spirit." The genuine ones begin with the words "In the name of almighty God and of our Savior Jesus Christ," as the genuine example which I published proves. Secondly, Papebroch's document gives the year A.D., which mine does not, nor do the other documents both of Lothar himself and of other contemporary kings. In addition, the inscription of the seal, *Lotharius,* does not follow the ancient practice of the Carolingian kings. I say nothing about the image of Lothar, which looks very different from the usual portraits of the Carolingian kings. Certainly Lothar retained the inscription of his father whose name he bore in the seals of the genuine documents. An example is the document in the monastery of St. Arnulfus at Metz, which has this inscription: "O Christ, help King Lothar." Lastly, in the document of Lothar as well as in that of Charlemagne the writing is similar to Saxon script, but this is not the case in their other autographs. I thought it worthwhile to caution my readers about these irregularities so that no one may fall into error if he finds them in documents which are absolutely genuine.

VI. Finally, I must explain the three- or four-part rule about diplomatics which a certain scholar who is not known to me proposed. Part one is: "All documents in which the title of Duke or Count is conferred personally upon anyone before the age of Charles the Simple in France and Henry the Fowler in Germany are spurious; likewise, those which grant to churches or monasteries the right of coining money before that time are spurious." This rule, although it is correct as far as the titles of Duke and Count are concerned, seems in my opinion incorrect in its second part, in the matter of the date when the right of coining money was granted. For in the *Acts of the Transfer of the Relics of St. Sebastian,* which was composed by the monk Odilo during the reign of Charles the Simple, we read that Louis the Pious granted the monastery of St. Médard "the right of coining money, and he gave them dies and an official scale for their continual use to serve their sacred needs." Why could not Louis the Pious have issued a decree on this matter similar to the one of King Odo for the monastery at Tournos which is found in the *Historia Trenorchiensis?* What of the fact that Charles the Simple granted the same privilege to Walo, the Bishop of Autun, when he "re-established by his own act the privilege of coining money in that city which had *for a long time* been unjustly withheld from that church by certain evil men"? The document which is quoted in the *History of the Monastery of Vergy* supports this. But what especially confirms the matter is that Louis the Pious restored to Aldric the Bishop of le Mans the same privilege which had been granted by his father Charles, his grandfather Pepin, and others before them. A copy of this edict is found in the deeds of Aldric himself, which were recently published by the learned Baluze. Here are the words of Louis: "We wish all the faithful to know . . . that the venerable Bishop of le Mans, Aldric by name, is known to us because his predecessors, namely Merolus and Gauziolenus, and their predecessors in the aforesaid city, had the privilege of coining money granted by order of Charles, my master and father of happy memory, and by order of Pepin my grandfather, and King Theoderic and the earlier Kings, and this privilege was granted with their full authority." Corvaiserius gives a document of King Theoderic dealing with this matter, but I am not sure to what extent it is genuine. But the document of Louis dealing with this matter is beyond all cavil, and it proves that the practice of granting the privilege of coining money was older than Charles the Simple. Many scholars hold the opposite opinion, and perhaps they maintain this because of the authority of the Assessors of Charlemagne and Charles the Bald, who returned this right to the palace and to certain cities. But this does not prevent the churches from having had these privileges.

VII. In regard to the Counts, I here add the observation that at least from the time of the reign of Charles the Simple their titles and privileges were hereditary, and I do not remember having seen the word "Countess" before that time except in two places. The first is in a Bull of John VIII for the monastery of Aniensis; the second is in the letter of Countess Ava for Riopullo, and this is the passage: "I, Countess Ava, and my sons, namely, Count Juniofred, Count Wilfred, Count Oliba, and Miro the Deacon, who are donors along with me, give to the monastery of St. Mary, which is located in the County of Auson at the place called Riopullo, and which was founded in honor of St. Mary the Mother of God and the Perpetual Virgin, or to the Abbot Ennegone or to the monks who there serve God. . . . Written on June 20th, in the sixth year of the reign of King Louis, the son of Charles," that is, Louis the Pious. If this is the true interpretation, this passage must be dated to 787. The poet Chilienus or whoever it was who wrote the eighth century poem about St. Brigid the Irish virgin used the word "Countess."

VIII. The second rule is: "All documents of the Emperors before Otto I and of all our Kings in which we find the terms 'Our *Camera*' (Chamber) or 'Our *Curia*' (Court) are likewise spurious." I do not give this rule as certain, nor do I reject it as false, until the matter is proved to my satisfaction by more reliable evidence. But even if it is true, it does not invalidate the letters of our Kings which are dated "during the *curia* of the Epiphany," "during the *curia* of Pentecost," and so on. This means at the time of the solemn meeting held during that part of the Church year. The Emperor Louis II granted the fifth privilege of the monastery of Casauriensis "at the royal court at Olonna." A document of Balduinus the Count of Flanders "was issued at Berg during the solemn *curia* of Pentecost in the year of Our Lord 1067."

IX. The third rule is: "All documents of Emperors before Henry I the Fowler and of our Kings before Rotbertus which have the words 'Our Princes' are likewise spurious." This rule needs fuller investigation, but it does not invalidate many documents even of the Merovingian age in which Bishops are called "Fathers and Successors to the Apostles," and men of very great authority *"Optimates* [or "Aristocrats"] and Illustrious Men," and the other subjects are called "our faithful." But that word, "Prince" or "Princes," although its meaning is ambiguous, can be applied in a broad and in a narrow sense. When used in a broad sense it signifies the leading men or primates, and in this sense even during the time of the Merovingian kings the primates in the Assembly of the Orders of the kingdom are called "Princes." For this reason the following words are prefixed to the ancient laws of the Alamanni: "The law of the Alamanni begins, which was established by King Chlotar along with his Princes, that is, his twenty-three Bishops, thirty-four Dukes, thirty-two Counts, and with the rest of his subjects." Here you see that Bishops and also Abbots preceded even Dukes, and they kept this rank until the twelfth century. When used in a narrow sense the word "Princes" denotes some important person. It is used for secular as well as spiritual princes, especially in Germany. Its use in this sense actually came later, to be exact, in the time of the reign of Otto the Great; and not before the eleventh century was it used in this sense of Bishops, if we are to believe Coringius.

X. A scholar, whose name I do not know, adds a fourth rule to these three. It is the observation that there are many spurious documents whose indications of date are genuine; and likewise there are many genuine documents whose dates are faulty. They are to be detected by the difference of their style from that of the age in which they were supposedly written, or by some circumstance which is at odds with historical truth. This observation is of great importance and could be illustrated by many examples. I give one here from the *History of the Parthenon of St. Mary of Soissons.* It is a description of the possessions of the Parthenon given in the Synod of Bishops with Charles the Bald present. The substance of it and its sequence seem thoroughly ancient, and it fits a writer of the ninth century even though the indications of its date and certain subscriptions are faulty. This description is said to have been written "in the year 858 A.D., in the thirty-second year of the reign of our master the

Emperor Charles, in the sixth Indiction." Here the year of the reign of King, not Emperor, Charles the Bald does not agree with the year 858 A.D., but with the year 862 A.D. Some of the subscriptions are faulty, as my friend Michel Germain observed in that history. Among these the subscription "Adelard, the Abbot of Corbie" must be censured. Here the word "Corbie" has to be expunged, since long before that time Adelard the Abbot of Corbie had died. At that time Adelard the Abbot of St. Vedastus was alive, and others of that name, one of whom should be restored here. Otherwise, the context of the document itself is (as I have already said) perfectly acceptable, and even though it is faulty here and there, all scholars consider it genuine. Any learned and unprejudiced scholar can easily think of other cases similar to this one.

XI. Lastly, another rule must be added here from the second volume for March in the Bollandist series. It is stated as follows: "False documents sometimes contain true information, and genuine documents false information." It often happens that the authors of documents are completely wrong when they mention past events; on the other hand, forgers tend to be more accurate. Not only can errors creep into documents, even originals, when any event in the distant past is mentioned, but also copyists who are careless can deceive or be deceived in the case of fairly recent events. Examples of this are found in various documents, especially those which relate the early history of churches or monasteries, in which events whose dates are unknown are reported in order along with other events of the early history, especially when those histories were composed long after the founding of the church or monastery.

Chapter 2

I. Papebroch's opinion of ancient documents.
II. and III. The author refutes this opinion.
IV. Papebroch's criticism of the archive of St. Denis.
V. The author defends the archive.
VI. The opinions of a recent author are likewise refuted.

I. I thought that I had at last finished my task when I saw that the archive of St. Denis had been unjustly criticized. This disturbs me, for the monastery is spoken of as if it were a factory for spurious documents of popes and kings, and the criticism made against that archive reflects upon the reputation of every archive in the kingdom of France. Papebroch thought he would be doing a great service to scholarship if in the conclusion of the first *Propylaeum,* or *Introduction to the Distinction of the Genuine and Spurious in Ancient Manuscripts,* which he wrote on the subject of distinguishing genuine from spurious documents, he devoted the entire thrust of his discussion to the single archive of St. Denis.

It is the most important archive in France, and by attacking it he hoped to damage the reputation of all other archives. "Considering all my investigations up to this time," he says, "I find in all of France not one genuine and trustworthy document written before the reign of Dagobert I, and very few documents which were written during and after his reign up to the kings of the second dynasty can be called autographs or trustworthy copies of autographs. I completely agree with the warning expressed by John Maresham, a man who is certainly an unorthodox Christian, but who is very familiar with monks and matters pertaining to monasteries. In the *Propylaeum* on British Monasticism he said: 'Manuscripts of this kind must be examined carefully: the older they appear to be, the less trustworthy they are.' " Then he adds that it cannot be proven from Bede and Gregory of Tours that writing was used by the English and French for transferring property or for granting privileges.

II. I would gladly agree with the criticism of this scholar if it were based upon legitimate grounds. But since it is in every aspect based upon false, doubtful, or uncertain grounds, I must disagree with it. It is false that in all of France there is not one genuine document written before the reign of Dagobert I. The document of Clovis the Great for the monastery of Mitiacensis is genuine and authentic. Likewise, the document of Ansemund and Ansleubana for the Parthenon of St. Andrew at Vienne, which is dated in the ninth year of the reign of Chlotar I, is genuine and authentic. The wills of Perpetuus the Bishop of Tours, of Aredius the Abbot of Atanensis, and of St. Radegund are genuine and authentic. Lastly (let me omit some examples which I have already mentioned and others which are controversial), the ancient formulas of Marculfus and others, which were collected one thousand years ago from older documents, are genuine.

III. Even if no genuine document written before the age of Dagobert I had survived due to damage over such a long period of time, it would not therefore follow that donations in writing had not been made before Dagobert's time. Nor does the silence of Gregory of Tours contradict this, but rather his testimony and that of others proves the exact opposite by such clear evidence that it is surprising that a man who can think clearly should fall into such error when the truth is so obvious. A large number of genuine documents of Dagobert I and his successors survives. Indeed, in the archive of St. Denis alone there are at least thirty autograph documents of Dagobert I, Clovis II, Theoderic II, Clovis III, Childebert III, Chilperic II, Theoderic III, and Childeric the last of the Merovingian kings. I pass over many other documents of private individuals which were written during the time of these kings and in the reign of Chlotar I. Papebroch's conclusion that no such documents exist is therefore wrong, and this is no surprise, for his premises are wrong. For what is farther from the truth than his statement that from the time of Christ onwards paper was not used as a writing material? Or the statement that no privileges were granted by the Roman Pontiffs in the seventh century or earlier? Or that the year of the Incarnation of Our Lord was first used by Pope Eugene IV to date Bulls? Furthermore, is the privilege of Dagobert I for the monastery of St. Maximin, which all scholars ought to regard as very suspicious at the least, to be thrust upon us as an example of a genuine document which is beyond suspicion? How much opportunity for false conclusions is furnished by statements such as the following: Dagobert called himself "most powerful king" contrary to the practice of all the other members of his dynasty; he used a monogram and the word "seal"; he signed his documents after the date; his high Chancellor was called *"Archicapellanus."* Once these false statements are accepted, it is not surprising if this scholar concludes that all the documents of the first dynasty of kings which are preserved in St. Denis and the other archives in France are spurious. Had Papebroch examined these documents, no doubt he would have reversed his opinion; but he ought not to have expressed such a confident opinion about something which he had not examined.

IV. Who would express such a severe and harsh judgment as he does in document number 130? Here, after having examined the rescripts of Pope Zacharias and Pope Stephen III concerning the monastery of St. Denis, which he rashly pronounces spurious because they are written on paper or papyrus (I showed earlier that this does not prove them to be spurious), he continues: "So much for the Papal Briefs; I do not intend to discuss in detail the many things which follow, nor have I the time to do so. Seventeen privileges of King Dagobert, the founder of St. Denis, are subjoined, seven others of his sons and his successors, then eight of King Pepin and seventeen more of Charlemagne, and so on. All or a good many of them are untrustworthy, as anyone who carefully examines the records of St. Denis can easily see from what I have already said."

V. I would dare to say that I have carefully examined the records of St. Denis, and I would also dare to say without reservation that all or a good many of those documents are trustworthy, and that no objections can be made against them from the rules of Papebroch. Those rules are either false or doubtful, as any attentive reader can see from what I have already said. Furthermore, not only those documents in Doublet which I consider genuine but also many other documents of the Merovingian age which I publish in this work are completley trustworthy, for they were copied from genuine and authentic autographs. I have not come to this conclusion on my own, but I called upon the assistance of the learned and distinguished Antonius Faurus, Doctor at the Sorbonne; Charles du Fresne Du Cange, Antonius Wion Herovallius, Étienne Baluze, and Jean-

Baptiste Cotélier. All of those scholars examined these venerable relics of antiquity and in their own opinion pronounced them genuine. I could also summon outstanding legal scholars to testify in my behalf, but I fear that I may insult them if I call as witnesses these men whom we revere as judges. So then, you say, would you dare to pass off as indubitably genuine all the documents which were published by Doublet? No indeed, but I consider most of them genuine, and I hold the same opinion of many others which Doublet either could not copy from the autographs or which escaped his notice. Such are those which I publish in this work: I assert without hesitation that they are authentic, true, sincere, and genuine; and I am prepared to defend them. Nevertheless, I would not deny that certain documents in Doublet's collection are either completely spurious, or interpolated, or suspicious; and these include documents of both the first and second dynasties. I do not argue that they are genuine or spurious only from their physical appearance, which seems ancient enough, but also from other characteristics, and especially from their style. I am not deceived by the traces of the forger concealed beneath the surface, or by the imitation of an ancient script, if everything else about the document is not as it should be. Doublet was a good and simple man who published whatever came into his hands with no attempt to deceive. His collection contains at least six hundred manuscripts. Amidst such a large number of ancient documents it is difficult to avoid including some which are doubtful, spurious, or interpolated. And we could surely correct a good many errors in these documents if we could find all the autographs which Doublet mentions. Either accident or some individual destroyed many of them. Nevertheless, many whose exemplars cannot be found are certainly genuine, and probably not more than ten documents in such a large number are spurious or doubtful. Among the spurious documents are some of Dagobert and Clovis; a document of Pepin concerning the Abbot Constramnus is interpolated; three of the documents of Charlemagne are spurious, namely, those on pages 722, 725, and 727, that is, the three earlier ones with the exception of the next to the last, which is genuine. In certain others, and these are very few in number, some errors occur, but they can easily be corrected from the autographs. An example is the document on page 718, where instead of "in the twelfth and eighth year" the autograph has "in the fourteenth and eighth year." There are very many of this kind, and I was eager to compare them with their autographs and emend them. Some of the documents enhance the work of Doublet by their own importance, and no rational critic would deny that his work has shed much light upon the past. If Doublet sometimes erred, this bold corrector who thought he understood the system of dates used in Lothar's documents better than Lothar's own Chancellor deserves to be excused. (He was wrong about

Lothar's documents. Many of Lothar's autographs have had their dates wrongly emended in a later handwriting which is completely undisguised. The honest man who made these corrections did not realize that Lothar used different systems of dating under different circumstances.) Yet I wish that Papebroch's criticism of him had been more just. I would willingly have refrained from criticism out of my respect for Doublet if I could have done so without harm to truth.

VI. At this point I am confronted with a young scholar who, because he is eager to attack someone in his first onslaught, rashly slanders the Canons and monks as "schismatics" and "heretical Catholics," because they defend the privileges granted to them. Now this certainly needs correction. But I shall not attack the efforts of this well-born youth, whom I would like to help if I can, and I will not mention his name since there has long been a bond between us. Nevertheless, I cannot conceal several errors which he made in his criticism of a certain privilege of St. Denis. I shall explain the matter briefly.

Among the various documents of Dagobert which Doublet published there is one concerning the immunity of the monastery of St. Denis. The young scholar whom I mentioned published another document pertaining to the same matter and of the same substance from a manuscript which belonged to de Thou. He thought that the latter document was better than the former, and so he claimed that the document published in Doublet was spurious and the one which he published was genuine and authentic. He supports his claim with three arguments. "Certainly," he says, "my copy of the privilege has this to commend it, that it belongs to a very powerful gentleman who is completely honest in such matters, and he has much experience in separating genuine documents from forgeries. Secondly, it is established that this copy was made very accurately from the archive of the monastery of St. Denis. Last and most important, it contains nothing which is absurd or contrary to ecclesiastical rule." I willingly acknowledge and agree with the first argument, that the very distinguished Antonius Herovallius, from whom our author says that he received this copy of the privilege, is very honest and very accomplished in the study of literature and antiquity. But I do not understand how it follows that this copy of the privilege is genuine and authentic and the other in Doublet is not. For no testimony of the distinguished gentleman on this matter is quoted. I shall not at this point examine the matter itself, nor do I intend to pass judgment upon these two documents, but I inquire only into the manner of his criticism and its basis. Secondly, I agree that the copy of the privilege which is now in the collection of de Thou and Colbert was very accurately transcribed from the archive of St.Denis, but I utterly deny that it was faithfully published by the author. The manuscript of de Thou has at the end "in the second year of our reign." This is also the reading of the document at St. Denis, but the author prints "in the eleventh year." However, I do not wish to question the sincerity of the author on this point: he should simply be more careful. But suppose that there was no mistake in his edition, and that for "eleventh" he printed "second," which is what the documents read. What then would the author conclude? The document in Doublet is therefore spurious; the document of de Thou alone is genuine because it was "very accurately copied" from its exemplar. But the document in Doublet could have been copied accurately from the same manuscript of de Thou, which contains the text of the document in Doublet in the same number of words. The text of both of these documents is also contained in another document in St. Denis. And so the arguments for the authenticity of each of the documents are thus far equal.

It is no objection that the substance of each document is almost the same; for there are many other documents written in almost the same words, such as the documents of Clovis II and of Pepin concerning the continual chanting of the Office in the monastery of St. Denis. We have seen that these documents are autographs. Another example is the autographs in St. Denis of Charles and Carloman his brother which differ mainly in the names of the authors and the time and place of composition. Furthermore, the manuscript of de Thou is dated "at Compiègne, in the second year of the reign" of Dagobert. In the document in Doublet what was issued at Compiègne, namely, the document of de Thou, is confirmed "in the tenth year of the reign" of Dagobert "at Paris."

Why is it surprising if the two documents agree in almost the same words, since the document in Doublet is a ratification of the document in de Thou with some expansion? Also, the document of de Thou was addressed to several Counts and leading men who are designated by name; the document in Doublet is directed "to all the Bishops, Dukes, Counts . . ." The documents differ in these respects, do they not?

Let us proceed to what the author considers "the most important" argument, namely that the document of de Thou contains nothing "which is absurd or contrary to ecclesiastical rule." Such is not the case with the document in Doublet. Why? "Dagobert of his own free will divests himself and his successors of legal power over the monks. What," he says, "is more contrary to the dignity and character of a king?" These are the words of the privilege in Doublet: "We order and establish that neither we nor our successors nor any Bishop or Archbishop nor anyone who has judicial authority may ever have any power over the holy church itself or those dwelling in it, except by the consent of the Abbot and his monks, but let this holy mother church which is dedicated to our Lord and the great St. Denis be completely free from all invasion or disturbance by any man, of whatever order or rank he may be." This is the entire sentence in which the document in Doublet differs most seriously from that of de Thou, which it confirms. These are the words in which Dagobert "of his own free will divests himself and his successors of legal power over the monks." The author thinks that there is nothing more absurd than this. If he observes nothing else remarkable in those words, he could say the same about the third formula in Book I of Marculfus, which is "immunity from the power of the king," just as in the document in Doublet. For the king says the following in that formula: "And we granted this in the name of the Lord and for the welfare of our soul, with full devotion, and this is binding upon our offspring to come; and may neither the power of the king nor the avarice of any judge attempt to rescind this decree." Observe how the king removes from the power of the king, that is, from himself and his successors, not so much the authority over what has been granted, but rather the power of rescinding the grant. Will the author not say that this is absurd? Let him solve this difficulty if he can. What if the reading of the document in Doublet were "neither you nor your successors," as it is in the document of de Thou? But I shall inquire no further into this matter, but rather into the false principles by which the author separates the document in Doublet from that of de Thou, as if the one were spurious and the other authentic. Such principles can neither vindicate the document of de Thou nor refute the document in Doublet. If you want examples from another country, I give you a document of Edward, King of England, which grants immunity to Westminster, so that "neither we nor our successors nor any Bishop, nor anyone with judicial power may have authority over that holy church or those who dwell in it." No one should become disturbed at me, because my intention is only to illustrate formulas and not to limit the royal power, to which I willingly confess myself and all my possessions to be subject.

Many more things could be said here in defense of the archive of St. Denis and the various documents in that archive which have been rashly condemned as spurious by critics. But it will be easier to discuss this in Book VI, where I shall examine these and several other documents.

Jacques Bénigne Bossuet

1627—1704

9

On Palm Sunday of 1662, Jacques Bénigne Bossuet preached for the first time before King Louis XIV. "Sire," he announced to Louis, "you are God." It was a perfect sermon for both the king and his priest. Louis was well on his way to becoming the model absolute monarch, and the object of envy of princes throughout Europe. He was no doubt gratified to hear Bossuet officially confirm his divine-right status. Bossuet promoted his own advancement with his timely words: by 1671, he was tutor to the king's oldest son, the Dauphin; and by 1681, he was the Bishop of Meaux, who in his coronation ceremony prayed that the dignity and majesty of the Palace of Versailles, where the king and his courtiers were about to install themselves, would "blaze out for all to see the splendid grandeur of the royal power."

The king and his bishop were able to celebrate their extravagant theological and political philosophies at the magnificent palace, where threats of spiritual heresy and civil disorder could be kept far distant. None of the nobles who came to live at Versailles could afford to contradict the king's theory (corroborated by Bossuet) that he ruled by divine right; nor would they find any objection in Bossuet's teachings on the necessity of maintaining one orthodox version of Catholicism as the religion of France. Versailles and the French government were carefully controlled, well-ordered establishments—there was simply no room for dissent.

Bossuet's philosophy of history, as expressed in the *Discourse on Universal History,* which he wrote in 1681 for the Dauphin's instruction, is both providential and parochial. Every historical event, Bossuet wanted his pupil to learn, was directed and determined by God's will, so that the *élus,* or the chosen people, might flourish. Bossuet's chosen nation was the Roman Catholic Church and, despite the title of his work, he was interested only in writing the history of this small segment of the world's population. The history of the ancient world was significant only in so far as it bore testimony to the early history of the Jews, a history which culminated in the birth of Jesus Christ.

199

From that moment on, it was only the struggle between Christ's disciples and the adherents of "false religions" which was of any lasting importance; and this was the only subject that had to be studied by Christian princes in order that they might understand their mission of recalling into Catholic Christianity "whosoever has strayed from it." The Dauphin could not help but absorb Bossuet's eloquently expressed lesson, but he died before he could apply it in the role of king.

In 1685, Louis XIV revoked the Edict of Nantes, which had allowed tacit toleration of Protestantism in France, since the time of Henry IV. Huguenots were persecuted with renewed vigor, their temples were burned, while their pastors were forced to renounce their faith or flee the country. The effect of the Huguenots' exodus from France has been exaggerated, but the revocation of the Edict of Nantes is still seen as the most deplorable example of Louis' absolutism. Bossuet never outwardly condoned violent persecution by the Church itself, but he hailed Louis' move as the proper exercise of a divine injunction. God gave his temporal princes powers which he denied the Church, was Bossuet's reply to the objections of a Protestant pastor to the persecution which ensued from the revocation. In his *History of Variations of the Protestant Churches,* in 1688, he repeated the meaning of the *Discourse on Universal History:* God is justified in his punishment of heretics who destroy the unity of the Church and who interfere with its destiny as the only valid religious institution for mankind.

When we consider the *Discourse* as a historical work, apart from its theological and political purposes, and contrast it with the work conducted by Mabillon and other Benedictine scholars, we are obliged to conclude that the *Discourse* was reversionary as well as parochial. Bossuet accepted the Bible as an unquestionable historical authority and never examined any of his sources critically, in the manner suggested by Mabillon's *On Diplomatics,* which was published in the same year as the *Discourse.* Bossuet even went so far as to suppress the 1678 book of the critic Richard Simon on the *Historical Criticism of the Old Testament.* The *Discourse,* as we can see in our selections from the section "The Continuity of Religion," is largely the Biblical stories retold, with added power and poetry.

It is just that poetry—that sublime style—which has so often been praised and which gave the *Discourse* its popularity. Bossuet's writing, not only in the *Discourse,* but in his grandiloquent *Funeral Orations* and in his other sermons, is a fine example of the "grand style" characteristic of the Age of Louis XIV.

When Bossuet became embroiled in the dispute over the Quietist or mystical doctrines which became popular at Louis' court late in his reign, he claimed that he had "God, Truth, and the King" on his side. Perhaps he did; but by the time of the Sun King's death in 1715, the world of Versailles was in shambles. The last wars of Louis XIV had ended in defeat as well as in misery for much of the population. Bossuet's prose might endure, but the universe upon which he had based his teaching was coming to an end.

Selected Bibliography

Robert Flint in *Historical Philosophy in France, French Belgium and Switzerland* (1894), 216–234, has the best critical discussion in English of Bossuet as a historian. The only other accessible work in English is the recent *Bossuet* (1963) by E. E. Reynolds, but it is superficial, apologetic, and journalistic. The two volumes of Thérèse Goyet's *Humanisme de Bossuet* (1965) are a detailed and dispassionate investigation of Bossuet's intellectual background in Biblical and classical literature. Unfortunately, Gustave Lanson's *Bossuet* (1894) does not do his critical sense justice, but he does show great sensitivity to Bossuet's art.

DISCOURSE ON UNIVERSAL HISTORY

THE CONTINUITY OF RELIGION

Creation and the Early Ages.

Religion and the history of God's chosen people are the greatest and most useful of all subjects that can be proposed to man. It is beautiful to contemplate the different conditions of God's people, under the law of nature and the patriarchs; under Moses and the written law; under David and the prophets; from the return out of captivity until Jesus Christ; and, finally, under Jesus Christ himself, that is, under the law of grace and the Gospel; in the ages that awaited the coming of the Messiah, and in those in which he appeared; in the ages when the worship of God was reduced to one people, and in those in which, in accordance with the ancient prophecies, this cult was spread over all the earth; and finally, in the ages when men, still weak and coarse, needed the support of temporal rewards and punishments; and in those ages when the faithful, better instructed, needed only to live by faith, having their hearts set upon eternal values, and, in the hope of possessing them, suffered all the evils that could have possibly tried their patience.

Certainly, My Lord,[1] nothing can be conceived more worthy of God, than to have, first, chosen a people who should be a living example of his eternal providence; a people whose good or ill fortune should depend upon their piety, and whose condition should testify to the wisdom and justice of him who governed them. This is how God began, and this he made manifest in the Jewish people. But after having established, with so many tangible proofs, this immutable foundation with which he alone governs as he pleases all the events of this life, it was time to raise men's minds to higher notions, and to send Jesus Christ, to whom it was reserved to reveal to the new nation, gathered from all the nations of the world, the secrets of the life to come.

Discourse on Universal History, Paris: 1966, pp. 149–163, 338–349. Victor Wexler has translated the selections for this volume.
[1]My Lord is *monseigneur,* the Dauphin, Louis XIV's only surviving, legitimate son, for whose moral instruction this *Discourse* was written [trans.].

You can easily follow the history of these two nations, and observe how Jesus Christ unites them; since he has been, whether expected or not, in all ages, the consolation and hope of the children of God.

See then religion ever uniform, or, rather, ever the same from the beginning of the world. The same God has always been acknowledged the author, and the same Christ, the savior of mankind.

Thus you will see that there is nothing older among men than the religion you profess, and that it is not without reason that your ancestors should have made it their greatest glory to be its protectors.

What testimony it is of its truth to find, that, in ages when profane histories have nothing to tell us but fables, or at most confused and half-forgotten facts, Scripture, beyond doubt the oldest book in the world, carries us back by so many specific events, and by the very succession of things to their true principle, that is, to God, who made everything; and shows us so distinctly the creation of the universe, that of man in particular, the happiness of his first condition, the causes of his miseries and frailties, the corruption of the world and the deluge, the origin of arts and nations, the distribution of land, and, finally, the propagation of mankind and other matters of like importance, of which human histories speak but confusedly, and oblige us to seek elsewhere for authoritative sources.

Just as the antiquity of religion gives it such authority, its uninterrupted and unaltered progression during so many ages, and in spite of so many intervening obstacles, makes manifest that the hand of God sustains it.

What is there more wonderful than to see religion subsisting upon the same foundations since the beginning of the world; neither undergoing destruction or alteration by the idolatry and impiety which on all sides surrounded it, nor by the hands of the tyrants who have persecuted it, or by the heretics and infidels who have tried to corrupt it, or by the cowards who have betrayed it, or by its unworthy followers who have dishonored it with their crimes; subsisting without change, despite even the passage of time, which alone can destroy all human things.

If we consider what idea religion, whose antiquity we revere, gives us of its object, that is, of the first being, we shall confess that this object is beyond all human conception and worthy to be regarded as having come from God himself.

The God whom the Jews and Christians have always worshipped has nothing in common with the imperfect and vice-ridden divinities whom the rest of the world adored. Our God is one, infinite, perfect, and is alone worthy to punish wickedness and to reward virtue, because he alone is holiness itself.

He is infinitely above that first cause and that first mover whom the philosophers knew but yet did not worship. Those philosophers who have been the furthest from knowing him have described to us a God who, finding eternal and independent matter co-existent with himself, put it in operation and fashioned it in the manner of a common artisan, constrained in his work by the form of that matter which he did not make. These philosophers were never able to comprehend that if matter is of itself, it did not have to attain its perfection from a foreign hand, and that, if God is infinite and perfect, he needed but himself and his own almighty will to make whatsoever he pleased. But the God of our fathers, the God of Abraham, the God whose wonders Moses has recorded, not only put the world in order, but also made it entirely both in its matter and in its form. Before he gave existence to other things, he alone possessed it. He is represented to us as the one who has made all things, and has made them by his word, and without trouble; and the performance of so great works costs him but a single word, that is, he need only will it.

And to pursue the history of the creation, from where we have begun it, Moses has taught us that this mighty architect whose works cost him so little, was pleased to perform them in several turns and to create the universe in six days, to show that he does not act by necessity or by a blind impetuosity, as some philosophers have imagined. The sun bursts forth at once, without reserve, all the rays it has; but God, who acts with understanding and with a sovereign liberty, applies his strength where he pleases, and as much as he pleases, and as in making the world by his word he shows that nothing causes him difficulty, so by making it in several turns, he demonstrates that he is master of his matter, of his action, of his whole undertaking and that he has, in acting, no other rule than his own will, always right in itself.

God's manner of acting lets us also see that every thing proceeds immediately from his hand. These nations and philosophers who believed that the earth mixed with water, with the help, if you will, of the heat of the sun, had produced, of itself and by its own fruitfulness, the plants and animals, were grossly mistaken. Scripture has made us understand that the elements of nature are sterile if the word of God does not render them fruitful. Neither the earth, nor the water, nor the air, would ever have had the plants and animals we see in them, if God, who had made and prepared matter, had not also formed it by his almighty will, and given to every thing its very own seed for multiplication in all ages.

Those who see the birth and growth of plants from the sun's heat, might possibly fancy that the sun is their Creator. But Scripture makes us see the earth covered with grass and all types of plants, before the sun was created, that so we may understand that every thing depends on God alone.

It pleased the great artificer to create light, even before he reduced it to the form he gave it in the sun and stars, because he wanted to teach us that those great and glorious luminaries, of which some have wished us to make deities, had of themselves neither that precious and shining matter of which they were composed nor that wonderful form to which we see them reduced.

In short, the account of creation as given by Moses, reveals to us this great secret of true philosophy, that in God alone dwell fecundity and absolute power. Happy, wise, almighty, alone self-sufficient, he acts without necessity, as he acts without need; never constrained or hampered by his own matter, of which he makes what he pleases, because he has given it, by his will alone, its very being. By this sovereign right he turns it, he fashions it, he moves it, without effort; everything depends directly upon him; and if, according to the order established in nature, one thing depends on another, as, for instance, the birth and growth of plants on the heat of the sun, it is because this same God, who made all the parts of the universe, desired to link them to one another and to display his wisdom by this wonderful linking of parts.

But all that holy Scripture teaches us concerning the creation of the universe, is nothing in comparison with what it says of the creation of man.

Until now God had done all by commanding: "Let there be light. Let there be a firmament in the midst of the waters. Let the waters that are under heaven, be gathered together into one place, and let the dry land appear. Let the earth bring forth. . . . Let there be great lights to divide the day and the night. Let the waters bring forth the moving creature having life and the fowl that may fly over the earth. Let the earth bring forth the living creature after its kind."[2] But when it is a question of producing man, Moses ascribes to God a different mode of expression: "Let us make man," says he, "in our image and likeness."[3]

It is no longer that imperious and dominating word but one more mild, though no less effective. God holds council in himself: God arouses himself as it were to show us that the work he is about to undertake surpasses all the works he had till then performed.

Let us make man. God has spoken within himself; he has spoken to someone who creates as well as he, to someone of whom man is the creation and image; he speaks to another self; he speaks to him by whom all things were made, to the one of whom it says in his Gospel, "For what things soever he doeth, these also doeth the son likewise."[4] In speaking

---

[2]Genesis, I, 3; Bossuet paraphrases from the first twenty verses of Chapter I of Genesis. In this translation, all biblical quotations conform to the King James version.

[3]Genesis, I, 26.

to his son, or with his son, he speaks at the same time with the almighty spirit, for they are equal and co-eternal beings.

It is an unheard of thing in all Scriptural language that anyone but God has ever spoken of himself in the plural number, saying, "Let us make." God himself does not speak thus more than two or three times in Scripture, and this extraordinary language begins to appear when there is question of creating man.

When God changes his manner of speaking and, in some way, of acting, it is not that he changes in himself, but he shows us that he is going to begin, following eternal counsels, a new order of things.

Thus man, so highly exalted above the other creatures whose generation Moses had described to us, is produced in an entirely new way. The Trinity begins to declare itself by making a reasonable creature, whose intellectual operations are an imperfect image of those eternal operations by which God is productive in himself.

The very counsel which God uses now indicates that the creature which is about to be made is the only one that can act by counsel and understanding. What is to follow is no less extraordinary. Till then we had not seen, in the history of Genesis, the hand of God applied to corruptible matter. To form the body of man, God takes earth,[5] and that earth molded by his hand, receives the most beautiful shape that has yet appeared in the world. This man stands erect, his head raised, his gaze directed toward heaven, and this conformation, particular to him, shows him his origin and the place toward which he must strive.

This particular attention which God pays when he is making man, shows us that he has a particular regard for him, even though all his creations stem directly from this same wisdom.

But the manner in which he produces the soul is much more wonderful: he does not form it from matter; he breathes it from above: it is a breath of life that comes from himself.

When he created the beasts, he said, "Let the waters bring forth the moving creature," and in this manner he created the sea monsters and every moving creature that has life that was to fill the waters. He said also, "Let the earth bring forth the living creature after its kind, cattle, and moving things, and beasts of the earth."[6]

Thus were born the souls of brutish and beastial life, to which God gives no other action than some bodily motions. God calls them forth from the womb of the waters and of the earth; but that soul, whose life was to be an imitation of his own, who was to live as himself by reason and understanding, who was to be united to him by contemplating and

[4]John, V, 19.
[5]Genesis, II, 7.
[6]Genesis, I, 24. Again Bossuet paraphrases from Genesis.

loving him, and who for this reason was made in his image, could not be derived from matter. God, in fashioning matter, may well form a beautiful body, but turn or fashion it how he will, he never will find in it his own image and likeness. The soul, made in his image, and happy in possessing that image, must be produced by a new creation: it must come from above; and this is what is meant by the *breath of life*[7] which God draws from his mouth.

Let us recall that Moses proposes to mortal men, by sensible images, pure and intellectual truths. Let us not imagine that God breathes in the manner of animals. Let us not imagine that our soul is rarefied air, or thin vapor. The breath which comes from God and which bears the image of God, is neither air nor vapor. Let us not imagine that our soul is a portion of the divine nature, as some philosophers have dreamed. God is not a whole that can be divided. Though God should have parts, they are created; for the Creator, the uncreated being could not be composed of created parts. The soul is made that it is not part of the divine nature but only a substance made in the image and likeness of the divine nature, a substance that shall always be united to him that formed it. This is the meaning of that divine breath; this is what this spirit of life represents to us.

See, then, man formed. God then forms out of him the companion he wishes to give him. All men spring from one marriage, in order to be forever one and the same family, however dispersed or multiplied.

Our first parents, thus formed, are placed in that delightful garden called Paradise. God owed it to himself to make his image happy.

He gives a precept to man to let him know he has a master; a precept relating to a sensible thing, because man was made with senses; an easy precept, because he wished to render his life comfortable as long as it was innocent.

Man does not keep a commandment of so easy observance: he listens to the tempting spirit, and to himself, instead of listening only to God; his fall is inevitable; but we must consider it in its origin as well as in its consequences.

God had, at the beginning, made his angels pure spirits, distinct from all matter. He who makes nothing but what is good, had created them all in holiness, and they had it in their power to secure their felicity by a voluntary submission to their Creator. But whatever is drawn from nothingness is defective. A part of those angels allowed themselves to be seduced by self-love. Woe to the creature that delights in itself and not in God! It loses in a moment all its gifts. How strange is the effect of sin!

---

[7]Genesis, II, 7.

Those spirits of light became spirits of darkness; all their light turned to malicious cunning. Malignant desire now took place of charity; their natural greatness was now nothing but pride; their happiness was changed into the dismal consolation of getting themselves companions in their misery, and their former happy exercises changed to the wretched task of tempting men. The most perfect of them all,[8] who had also been the most proud, proved the most evil, and the most miserable. Man, *whom God had made a little lower than the angels,*[9] by uniting him to a body, became an object of jealousy to so perfect a spirit;[10] he wished to draw man into his rebellion that he might afterwards involve him in his destruction. The spiritual creatures had, as God himself, sensible means to communicate with man, who resembled them in the principal part of his being. The evil spirits, whom God was willing to use to test the fidelity of mankind, had not lost the means of maintaining this intercourse with our nature, no more than they had lost a certain dominion which had been given them at first over material creation. The devil used power against our first parents. God permitted him to speak to them in the form of a serpent, as the serpent was best suited to represent wickedness as well as the torment of this evil spirit, as we shall see in what follows. The devil fears not that he will horrify them by taking this shape. All the animals had been brought to the feet of Adam in the same way, to receive a suitable name from him and to recognize the master God had given them.[11] Thus none of the animals aroused horror in man, because, in the state in which man was created, no animal could harm him.

Let us listen to how the devil speaks to man, and let us penetrate the substance of his devices. He addresses himself to Eve as the weaker, but in the person of Eve, he speaks to her husband as well as to her. "Hath God said, ye shall not eat of every tree of the garden?"[12] If he has made you reasonable creatures, you ought to know the reason of everything; this fruit is not poison. "Ye shall not surely die."[13] See how the spirit of revolt begins. The command is discussed, and obedience is brought into doubt. "Ye shall be as gods,"[14] free and independent, happy in yourselves, and wise by yourselves. "You will know good and evil"; nothing shall be unfathomable to you. By these means the spirit raises itself against the Creator's order, and above his rule. Eve, half won over, looked at the fruit

---

[8]Bossuet alludes to Satan, who was an archangel before his fall.
[9]Psalms, VIII, 6.
[10]Again, the allusion is to Satan.
[11]Genesis, II, 19, 20.
[12]Genesis, III, 1.
[13]Genesis, III, 4.
[14]Genesis, III, 5.

whose beauty promised *an excellent taste.*[15] Seeing that God had united in man a soul and body, she thought that on behalf of man he might possibly have also attached supernatural qualities to plants and intellectual gifts to sensible objects. After eating of this beautiful fruit, she presented some of it to her husband. See him dangerously attacked. Her example and a desire to please her add strength to the temptation; he comes under the spell of the tempter, who is now so powerfully abetted. A mistaken curiosity, a flattering thought of pride, the secret pleasure of acting of one's self and according to one's own thoughts allure and blind him; he desires to make a dangerous trial of his liberty, and he tastes, with the forbidden fruit, the pernicious sweetness of satisfying his mind; the senses mix their allurements with this new charm, he follows them, he submits to them, he makes himself their slave—he who was before their master.

At the same time everything changes for him. The earth no longer smiles upon him as it did before; he shall have no more from it but by persistent labor; the sky no longer appears serene; the animals, all of which, even the most odious and fierce, used to afford him an innocent pastime, now assume hideous forms. God, who had made everything for his happiness, in a moment turns everything into his punishment. He is now a burden to himself who had loved himself so well. The rebellion of his senses makes him observe something shameful in himself.[16] This is no more that first work of the Creator, in which everything was beautiful; sin has made a new work which must be hidden. Man can no longer bear his shame, and would like to cover it from his own eyes. But God becomes still more unbearable to him. That great God, who had made him in his likeness and had given him senses as a necessary help to his understanding, was pleased to show himself to him in tangible form. But man can now no longer endure his presence. He seeks the deepest recesses of the woods,[17] to hide himself from the presence of him who formerly was his whole happiness. His conscience accuses him even before God speaks. His sorry excuses complete his confusion. He must die; the consolation of immortality is taken from him, and a more dreadful death, namely, that of the soul, foreshadows that bodily death to which he is condemned.

But see our own sentence pronounced in his. God, who had resolved to reward man's obedience in all his posterity, condemned and smote him, as soon as he revolted, not only in his own person, but also in all his children, the most vital and dearest part of himself; we are all cursed from the outset; our birth is tainted and infected in its source.

---

[15]Genesis, III, 6.
[16]Genesis, III, 7.
[17]Genesis, III, 8.

Let us not examine here those terrible rules of divine justice, by which the human race is cursed in its origin. Let us adore the judgments of God, who looks upon all men as one single man from whom he means to make all come forth. Let us also look upon ourselves as degraded by our rebellious father, as stigmatized forever by the sentence that dooms him, as banished with him and excluded from the Paradise in which he was to give birth to us.

The rules of human justice may help us to enter into the depths of divine justice, of which they are a shadow; but they can never help us discover the bottom of that abyss. Let us believe that the justice as well as mercy of God will not be measured by the standards of men, and that both have effects far more extensive and intimate.

But while God's severities upon mankind terrify us, let us admire how he turns our eyes toward a more agreeable object in foretelling our future deliverance, from the day of our fall. In the guise of a serpent,[18] whose crooked creeping was a lively image of the dangerous insinuations and fallacious devices of the evil spirit, God made our mother Eve see at once the hateful character and the just punishment of her vanquished enemy. The serpent was to be the most hated of all animals, as the devil is the most accursed of all creatures. As the serpent creeps on its breast, so the devil, justly cast down from heaven where he had been created, can no longer stand up. The earth, on which, it is said, the serpent feeds, signifies the low thoughts which the devil inspires in us; and the devil himself has only low thoughts, since all his thoughts are but sin. In the eternal enmity between all mankind and the devil, we learn that victory will be ours, since in this enmity we are shown a blessed seed by which our conqueror was to have his head crushed, signifying that his pride was to be brought low, and his empire destroyed over the whole earth.

This blessed seed was Jesus Christ, the son of a virgin; that Jesus Christ, in whom alone Adam had not sinned, because he was to spring from Adam in a divine manner, conceived not by man, but by the Holy Ghost. It was, therefore, by this divine seed, or through the woman who would bear it, in accordance with the many teachings of this passage, that the fall of mankind was to be restored and that power was to be taken away from that worldly prince, *who can find nothing of his own in Jesus Christ.*[19]

But before giving us the Savior, it was necessary that mankind should, by long experience, know the need it had of such a help. Man was, therefore, left to himself: his inclinations became corrupt, his dissolute living went beyond all bounds, and iniquity covered the whole face of the earth.

---

[18]Genesis, III, 14, 15.
[19]John, XIV, 30.

Then God meditated a vengeance, which he willed should never be blotted out from men's memories—the universal flood. The memory of the deluge and of the wickedness which brought it on still lingers among all nations.

Let men no longer think that the world moves by itself and that what has been shall always be. God, who has made all things, and by whom all things subsist, is about to drown both man and beast, that is, he is about to destroy the most beautiful part of his work.

He needed only himself to destroy what he had made by his word; but he deems it more worthy of him to use his own creatures as the instrument of his vengeance, and he calls the waters to ravage the earth covered with wickedness.

In the destruction, however, one just man was found. Before saving him from the deluge of waters, God had preserved him with divine grace from the deluge of iniquity. His family was spared to repopulate the earth, which was going to be one immense solitude. By the care of that just man, God saved the animals, so that man may understand that they are made for him and that he is to use them for the glory of their Creator.

God did more; and as if to repent for having wreaked such a rigorous justice on mankind, he solemnly promised never again to send a deluge to flood the whole earth; and he deigned to make this pledge not only with *man,* but also *with all animals, whether of the earth or of the air,*[20] to show that his providence extends to everything that has life. The rainbow then appeared. God chose pleasing, agreeably diversified colors, on a cloud filled with a mild dew rather than with an unpleasant rain, as an eternal testimony that the rains he would send in the future would never cause a universal flood. Since that time, the rainbow appears in the heavenly visions as one of the principal ornaments of the throne of God,[21] and conveys an idea of his mercy.

The world is renewed, and the earth once more emerges from the womb of the waters; but in this new world there remains an eternal impression of the divine vengeance. All nature was stronger and more vigorous before the flood. By that immense quantity of water which God brought upon the earth, and by its long presence on it, the essence of the earth was altered; the air, laden with excessive moisture, strengthened the causes of corruption; and the original constitution of the universe was weakened. Human life, which before would run to nearly a thousand years, gradually decreased; herbs and fruits had no longer their former strength, and men needed more substantial food than the flesh of animals.

---

[20]Genesis, IX, 9, 10, etc.
[21]Ezekiel, I, 28; Revelations, IV, 3.

Thus disappeared and gradually vanished the remains of the first creation, and changed nature warned man that God was no longer the same
to him since he had been provoked by so many crimes.

Moreover, the long life of the first men recorded in the annals of God's
chosen people, was not unknown to other nations; and their ancient traditions have preserved its memory.[22] But now as death approached, it
caused men to feel a speedier vengeance; and as they daily plunged
deeper and deeper into wickedness, they had to be, so to speak, plunged
deeper into their punishment every day.

Their change of diet alone might have intimated to them how much
their state was growing worse, since while becoming weaker, they at the
same time became more voracious and bloodthirsty.

Before the time of the deluge, the food that men found without violence
in the fruits which fell of their own accord, and in the herbs which dried
so fast, was, no doubt, some remnant of the primitive innocence and of
the mildness of which we were formed. Now, in order to feed ourselves
we must spill blood, in spite of the horror it naturally arouses in us; and
all the refinements we use to cover our tables are hardly sufficient to
disguise the carcases we must devour to satisfy ourselves.

But that is the smallest part of our misfortunes. Life, already short-
ened, is still more abridged by the violence which was introduced among
mankind. Man, who in the primitive times spared the lives of beasts, now
grows accustomed not to spare even that of his fellows. In vain did God,
immediately after the deluge, forbid the shedding of human blood; in
vain did he preserve some vestiges of the primeval mildness of our nature, by preserving the blood of beasts when he allowed man to eat their
flesh.[23] Murders multiplied without measure. It is true, that before the
flood Cain had sacrificed his brother out of jealousy.[24] Lamech, sprung
from Cain, had committed the second murder,[25] and we may believe that
more murders were committed after those damnable examples. But wars
were not yet invented. It was after the deluge that those ravagers of
provinces appeared, called conquerors, who, incited by the sole glory of
command, have exterminated so many innocent persons. Nimrod, a
cursed spawn of Ham who was cursed by his father, began to make war,
merely to establish an empire for himself.[26] From that time, ambition
was wantonly sported with the lives of men. Men even came to kill each
other without hating each other, and the height of glory and the most

---

[22]Bossuet here refers to several ancient authors who wrote of the history of the
Jews.
[23]Genesis, IX, 3.
[24]Genesis, IV, 8.
[25]Genesis, IV, 23.
[26]Genesis, X, 9.

noble of all arts, was to put one another to death.

A hundred years or so after the deluge, God struck mankind with another scourge through the confusion of tongues. The common language spoken by the first men and taught by Adam to his children, remained a social bond at the inevitable dispersion of the family of Noah throughout the habitable world. But this vestige of ancient concord perished at the Tower of Babel. Perhaps the children of Adam, always incredulous, had not given enough faith to the promise and assurance of God that there would be no more general flood, and had, therefore, prepared themselves a refuge against a similar occurrence by building that solid and superb edifice. Perhaps they merely wished to immortalize themselves by this great work before scattering abroad into all lands, as is stated in Genesis.[27] But God did not permit them to raise this tower, as they hoped, to the clouds; nor to threaten heaven by the erection of that bold structure. God brought confusion among them, by making them forget their first language. It was at this place, therefore, that the children of Adam became divided in languages and in nations. The name Babel, which means confusion, is forever associated with that tower in testimony of that confusion; it is also a perpetual reminder to mankind that pride is the source of divisiveness and strife among men.

Such were the beginnings of the world, as the history of Moses represents them to us—beginnings happy at first, but afterwards filled with infinite evil. With regard to God, who does all things, which are always admirable, we learn, by contemplating them, to consider the universe and mankind as always under the hand of the Creator, brought out of nothingness by his word, preserved by his goodness, governed by his wisdom, punished by his justice, delivered by his mercy, and always subject to his power.

This is not the universe as philosophers have conceived it, formed, according to some, by a fortuitous concourse of atoms; or, according to the wisest of them, furnished its author with its matter, and which consequently neither depends on him in the essence of its being, nor in its first estate, and which binds him to certain laws, which he himself cannot violate.

Moses, and our ancient fathers, whose traditions Moses has collected, give us other notions. The God he has declared to us, has a very different power: he can do and undo just as he pleases; he gives laws to nature, and abrogates them when he will.

If, in order to make himself known in times when the greatest part of men had forgot him, he wrought astonishing miracles, and forced nature

---

[27]Genesis, XI, 4, 7.

to break her most constant laws, he, by so doing, continued to demonstrate that he was her absolute master, and that his will is the only bond that maintains the order of the world.

And this was just what men had forgotten: the stability of so beautiful an order served now only to persuade them that this order had always existed and that it was from itself. Consequently they were prompted to worship either the world in general, or the stars, the elements, and all those great bodies which compose it. God has therefore demonstrated to mankind a goodness worthy of himself in reversing, upon remarkable occasions, that order which not only no longer impressed them, because they grew used to it, but which even prompted them, so grossly were they blinded, to imagine eternity and independence elsewhere than in God.

The history of God's chosen people is attested to by its own development, and by the religion, both of those who wrote it and of those who have preserved it with so much care. This history has maintained the memory of those miracles, as in a faithful record, and gives us thereby a true idea of the supreme dominion of God, almighty master of his creatures, whether holding them subject to the general laws he has established, or giving them others when he judges it necessary by some surprising stroke to awaken sleeping mankind.

Here is the God, whom Moses has proposed to us in his writings as the only one we ought to serve; here is the God whom the patriarchs worshipped before Moses; in a word, the God of Abraham, Isaac, and Jacob; to whom our father Abraham was willing to offer up his only son; of whom Melchisedech, prefiguring Jesus Christ, was high priest; to whom our father Noah made sacrifices, upon coming out of the ark; whom the just Abel acknowledged in offering to him his most precious possession; whom Seth, given to Adam in place of Abel, made known to his children, who are also called the children of God; whom Adam himself showed to his descendants, as him out of whose hands he had lately come, and who alone could put an end to the woes of his unhappy posterity.

Beautiful is the philosophy which gives us such pure ideas of the author of our being! Beautiful is the tradition that preserves the memory of his glorious works! How holy the people of God, since by an uninterrupted succession, from the beginning of the world down to our days, they have always preserved so holy a tradition and philosophy!

Continuity of the Catholic Church. Her Manifest Victory over All Sects.

What consolation to the children of God! What assurance of the truth when they see that they go back, without interruption, from the present

Pope,[1] who so worthily fills at this time the first see of the Church, to Saint Peter, appointed by Jesus Christ the chief of the Apostles; and then through the high priests that served under the law,[2] they go back to Aaron and Moses; and then finally to the patriarchs and to the origin of the world! What continuity, what tradition, what wonderful concatenation! If our mind, naturally uncertain, and become, by its uncertainties, the sport of its own reasonings, has need, in questions that regard salvation, to be fixed and determined by some certain authority, what greater authority can there be than that of the Catholic Church, which centers in itself all the authority of the ages, as well as the ancient traditions of mankind from its first origin?

Thus the society, which Jesus Christ, who was expected through all former ages, at last founded upon the rock, and where Saint Peter and his successors must, by his orders, preside, justifies itself by its own continuity, and bears in its eternal duration the mark of the hand of God.

It is also this succession, which no heresy, no sect, no other society but God's Church alone has ever been able to attain. False religions have imitated the Church in a great many things, and especially by saying, like her, that it was God who founded them; but this assertion in their mouth is but an empty boast. For if God created mankind, and if by creating it in his own image, he did not scorn to teach it the means of serving and pleasing him, then any sect which does not show its succession from the beginning of the world is not of God.

Here, at the feet of the Church, fall down all the societies and sects which men have established within or outside of Christianity. For instance, the false prophet of the Arabs might well call himself "sent of God," and, after deceiving supremely ignorant nations, he might take advantage of the divisions in his part of the world to extend, by force of arms, a wholly sensual religion; but he neither dared to pretend that he had been expected, nor indeed could he claim, either for his person, or for his religion, a real or apparent connection with past ages. To evade this, he found a new expedient. Lest people should be inclined to search the Scriptures of the Chrstians for evidence for his mission like the evidence which Jesus Christ found in the Scriptures of the Jews, he said that both Christians and Jews had falsified their books. Six hundred years after Jesus Christ, his ignorant followers took his word for it and he proclaimed himself, not only without any previous testimony, but even without either himself or his adherents daring to suppose or to promise any visible miracle that might have authorized his mission. In

---

[1]Innocent XI (1676–1689)
[2]By "the law," Bossuet means Mosaic law.

like manner the heresiarchs who founded new sects among the Christians, might well render faith easier and at the same time less dutiful by denying the mysteries that surpass the senses. They might well dazzle men by their eloquence, and by a show of piety, move them by their passions, win them over by their interests, allure them by novelty and libertinage, whether of the mind or even of the senses; in a word, they were easily able to deceive either themselves or others, for nothing is more natural to man than to be deceived. Besides that they could not even boast of having wrought any one miracle in public, nor have they been able to reduce their religion to positive facts of which their followers were witnesses. There is also one unfortunate fact for them which they have never been able to palliate, namely, that of their newness. It will always be visible to the eyes of the whole world that they and the sect they established broke off from that great body of that ancient Church which Jesus Christ founded, where Saint Peter and his successors held the first places, and in which all sects found this succession established. The moment of the separation will always be so fixed that the heretics themselves shall not be able to disown it, and shall not dare so much as to attempt to derive themselves from the source by a continuity that never has known interruption. This is the inevitable weakness of all the sects that men have established. No one can change past ages, nor give himself predecessors, nor pretend to possess them. The Catholic Church alone fills all preceding ages with a continuity that cannot be contested. The law of Moses is the forerunner of the Gospel; Moses and the patriarchs are of one with Jesus Christ who was expected, who came, who was acknowledged by a posterity as lasting as the world, this is the character of the Messiah in whom we believe, "Jesus Christ, the same yesterday, today, and for ever."[3]

Thus, besides the advantage the Church of Christ has of being alone founded upon miraculous and divine facts that were written openly, and without fear of being belied, at the very time they happened, there is also an everlasting miracle in favor of those who did not live in those times, a miracle which confirms the truth of all the others: the continuity of religion ever victorious over the errors that have endeavored to destroy it. To this you may add the fact of another permanent continuity: the visible and continual chastisement of the Jews, who have not received the Christ promised to their fathers.

They continue, nevertheless, to wait for him, and their ever disappointed expectation is a part of their punishment. They still look for him, and thus show that he is still expected. Condemned by their own books,

---

[3]Hebrews, XIII, 8.

they establish the truth of religion; they bear, so to speak, its whole course written upon their forehead. At one view we see what they have been, why they are as we see them, and for what they are reserved.

Thus, four or five authentic facts, clearer than the light of the sun, show our religion to be as ancient as the world. They consequently demonstrate that it has no other author than him who founded the universe, who holding all things in his hand, was alone able to begin and carry on a design that encompasses all ages.

We must, therefore, no longer wonder, as we usually do, that God proposes that we believe so many things so worthy of him and at the same time impenetrable to human understanding. We should rather wonder that, since faith is built upon so sure and so manifest an authority, there should still remain any blind and incredulous persons in the world.

Our unruly passions, our fondness for our senses, and our indomitable pride, are the causes of our blindness and unbelief. We prefer to risk everything rather than to restrain ourselves; we prefer to continue in our ignorance, than to confess it; we choose rather to gratify a vain curiosity and to indulge our disobedient minds in the liberty of thinking what we please, rather than to bend under the yoke of divine authority.

Hence it is that there are so many unbelievers, and that God permits it to be so for the instruction of his children. Without the blind, without the savage, without the infidels, that remain in the very bosom of Christianity, we should not sufficiently realize the deep corruption of our nature, nor the abyss from which Jesus Christ has lifted us. If his sacred truth were not challenged, we should not see the miracle that makes it stand fast amidst so much contradiction, and we should eventually forget that we are saved by grace. Now the incredulity of some humbles others; and the rebels who oppose the designs of God make that power conspicuous, whereby independently of anything else, he accomplishes the promises he has made to his Church.

Why, then, do we delay our submission? Do we wait till God shall work new miracles; till he render them useless by continuing them; till he accustom our eyes to them, as they are to the course of the sun and all the other wonders of nature? Or do we wait till the unbelievers and the obstinate are silent; till good men and libertines[4] bear equal testimony to the truth; till everybody agrees to prefer it to his passion, and till false learning, admired merely for its novelty, ceases to delude mankind? Is it not enough that we see that none can fight religion without betraying, by wild deviations, that their senses are faulty and that they no longer hold out but through presumption or ignorance? Shall not the Church, victori-

---

[4]*Libertin* in seventeenth-century French meant freethinker.

ous over ages and errors, be able to overcome the pitiful arguments brought against her in our minds; and shall not the divine promises, which we daily see accomplished in her, have power to raise us above the senses?

And let none tell us that those promises still remain in suspense, and that, as they extend to the end of the world, it will only be at the end of the world that we shall be able to boast of having seen their accomplishment. For, on the contrary, what is past assures us of what is to come. So many ancient predictions, so visibly accomplished, prove to us that there is nothing that shall not be accomplished; and that the Church, against whom the gates of hell, according to the promise of the Son of God, never can prevail, shall stand fast till the end of time, since Jesus Christ, who is true in everything, has set no other limits to her duration.

The same promises assure us of a future life. God, who has shown himself so faithful in accomplishing what concerns this world, will be no less so in accomplishing what concerns the next, of which all we see is but a preparation; and the Church shall be ever immovable and invincible upon earth until her children be gathered in, and she be transported entire into heaven, which is her true dwelling place.

For those who shall be excluded from that heavenly city, eternal rigor is reserved; and after having lost through their own fault a blissful eternity, nothing shall remain for them but an eternity of woe.

Thus the counsels of God end in an immutable state; his promises and threats are equally certain; and what he carries out in time assures of what he commands us to hope or fear in eternity.

This is what you learn from the continuity of religion outlined before your eyes. It conducts you through time to eternity. You see a certain order in all the designs of God, and a visible mark of his power in the perpetual duration of his people. You can see that the Church has an everlasting stock, from which none can separate without being lost; and that those who are united to this root produce works worthy of their faith, and assure themselves of eternal life.

Study then, My Lord, with particular attention this continuity of the Church, which so clearly assures you of all the promises of God. Whatever breaks this chain, whatever breaks away from this continuity, whatever starts up of itself and comes not in virtue of the promises made to the Church from the beginning of the world, ought to excite your horror. Use all your powers to recall into this unity whatever has strayed from it, and to make men listen to the Church, through whom the Holy Ghost pronounces his oracles.

The glory of your ancestors is not only never to have forsaken her, but to have ever supported her, and to have thereby merited to be called her eldest sons, which is doubtless the most glorious of all their titles.

I need not speak to you of Clovis, Charlemagne, or Saint Louis. Consider only the time in which you live, and of what father[5] God has caused you to be born. A king so great in everything, distinguishes himself more by his faith than by his other admirable qualities. He protects religion, both at home and abroad, and to the ends of the world. His laws are one of the strongest bulwarks of the Church. His authority, revered as much for his personal merit as for the majesty of his sceptre, is never better supported than when it defends the cause of God. Blasphemy is no longer heard; impiety trembles before him: he is the king pointed out by Solomon, who scattereth away all evil with his look.[6] If he attacks heresy in so many ways, and even more than did ever his predecessors, it is not that he fears for his throne; everything is quiet at his feet, and his arms are dreaded over the whole earth; but it is that he loves his people, and that seeing himself exalted by the hand of God to a power that nothing in the universe can equal, he knows no more glorious use of it than to make it subservient to the healing of the wounds of the Church.

Imitate, then, My Lord, so noble an example, and hand it down to your descendants. Recommend to their care the Church even more than that great empire which your ancestors have governed for so many centuries. Let your august house, the most exalted in the world, be the first to defend the rights of God, and to extend through the universe the reign of Jesus Christ, who makes that house prevail with so much glory.

---

[5]The reference is, of course, to Louis XIV.
[6]Proverbs, XX, 8.

Charles Rollin

1661—1741

10

After William Robertson had completed his *History of Scotland* he wrote to David Hume, in 1759, asking him to recommend a new subject for historical investigation. Hume urged his friend in the direction of ancient history, because the popular *Ancient History* by Charles Rollin, which had been widely circulated both in the original French and in English translation since the 1730's, had to be replaced by the work of a critical historian. Rollin's success, Hume answered Robertson, "might encourage you, nor need you be in the least intimidated by his merit. That author has no other merit but a certain facility and sweetness of narration, but has loaded his work with fifty puerilities." When compared with the ridicule and charges of plagiarism which Rollin's *Ancient History* elicited from Voltaire, Hume's criticism seems generous.

Rollin was an austere, pious teacher who had been principal of the Collège of Beauvais, and twice the rector of the University of Paris, before he was forced to retire from official service. He jeopardized his career as an educator because of his association with the Jansenists. During the last half of the seventeenth century, the Jansenists acquired great notoriety for their severe moral teachings and for their criticism of the easy road to salvation which, they charged, the Jesuits and the official Gallican Church establishment guaranteed the faithful. In his last years, Louis XIV dedicated himself to the destruction of this group of "Calvinistic Catholics": their home at Port-Royal des Champs was demolished in 1710, and in 1713, their precepts were anathemetized by the papal bull *Unigenitus,* which Louis had prevailed upon the pope to decree.

The Jansenists who survived into the reign of Louix XV were still regarded as subversive. In the early 1720's, a small group of them gathered at the cemetery of Saint Médard in Paris, where miraculous cures were said to be worked over the tomb of a saintly Jansenist deacon. The fanatical band soon became known as the Convulsionaries, for their ceremonies degenerated into weird incantations where the participants threw themselves into fires and battered themselves to demonstrate their faith and prove their immunity. Their scandalous behavior caused the government to outlaw all further miracles at Saint Médard. When the police disbanded the Convulsionaries, Rollin was discovered among them.

The multivolume *Ancient History,* and the *Roman History* which followed it, were written during Rollin's retirement; like their author, they were naïve and superstitious. Bossuet's *Discourse on Universal History* was an exercise in the providential conception of history, but it was also an eloquent work by a creditable Biblical and classical scholar. Rollin's histories were childlike, almost animistic in their effusive sentimentality. In Rollin's view, God not only directed profane history but the study of history had no other value than to inspire readers with awe of God's power to punish the wicked and reward the virtuous. Rollin did not intend to impart learning to his audience; he sought rather to excite them into a frenzied acceptance of Biblical prophecies, which are, as he said, "literally fulfilled in all their points" in his histories.

Rollin's sententious rhetoric and crude didacticism often degenerate into simple vulgarity. Montesquieu noted that Rollin spoke "heart to heart." Indeed he did, and this, no doubt, accounted for the vogue that his work enjoyed in the eighteenth century, when the philosophical historians Hume, Voltaire, and Gibbon were writing histories we can still read with pleasure and profit today.

Selected Bibliography

Rollin and his histories have not attracted the attention of modern scholars. But his *Treatise on Education,* written from 1726 to 1728, just before he began the *Ancient History,* was a relatively progressive document. He advocated the study of French as a worthy subject which should not be subordinated to the study of Latin, and he encouraged greater room in the university curriculum for science. Albert Charles Gaudin provides a complete explication of the *Treatise on Education* in his immaturely written *Educational Views of Charles Rollin* (1939). In mid-nineteenth century, Sainte-Beuve was fascinated by the story of the Jansenists. He has a sane and sympathetic discussion of Rollin's life and writings in his *Causeries du Lundi* (1852), available in the 1934 edition, VI, 261–282. Sainte-Beuve's estimation of Rollin is tainted by his contempt for the materialistic values of his own generation, which he contrasts to Rollin's "idealism." There is a sentimental summary of Rollin's life by James Bell in his edition of the *Ancient History* (1845).

ANCIENT HISTORY

Fall of Babylon

After having seen the predictions of everything that was to happen to the impious Babylon, it is now time to come to the fulfilment of those prophecies; and to resume our narrative of the taking of that city.

As soon as Cyrus saw that the ditch, which they had long worked upon, was finished, he began to think seriously upon the execution of his vast design, which as yet he had communicated to nobody. Providence soon furnished him with as fit an opportunity for this purpose as he could desire. He was informed that in the city a great festival was to be celebrated; and that the Babylonians, on occasion of that solemnity, were accustomed to pass the whole night in drinking and debauchery.

Belshazzar himself was more concerned in this public rejoicing than any other, and gave a magnificent entertainment to the chief officers of the kingdom and the ladies of the court. When flushed with wine, he ordered the gold and silver vessels which had been taken from the temple of Jerusalem to be brought out; and, as an insult upon the God of Israel, he, his whole court, and all his concubines, drank out of these sacred vessels. God, who was provoked at such insolence and impiety, at the same instant made him sensible who it was that he affronted, by a sudden apparition of a hand, writing certain characters upon the wall. The king, terribly surprised and frighted at this vision, immediately sent for all his wise men, his diviners, and astrologers, that they might read the writing to him, and explain the meaning of it. But they all came in vain, not one of them being able to expound the matter, nor even to read the characters. It is probably in relation to this occurrence that Isaiah, after having foretold to Babylon that she shall be overwhelmed with calamities which she did not expect, adds, "Stand now with thine enchantments, and with the multitude of thy sorceries. Let now the astrologers, the star-gazers, the monthly prognosticators, stand up, and save thee from these things that shall come upon thee." Isa. xlvii, 12, 13. The queen-mother Nitocris (a princess of great merit), coming upon the noise of this prodigy into the banqueting-room, endeavoured to compose the mind of the king, her son, advising him to send for Daniel, with whose abilities in such matters she was well acquainted, and whom she had always employed in the government of the state.

Daniel was therefore immediately sent for, and spoke to the king with a freedom and liberty becoming a prophet. He put him in mind of the dreadful manner in which God had punished the pride of his grandfather Nebuchadnezzar, and the flagrant abuse he made of his power, when he acknowledged no law but his own will, and thought himself empowered to exalt and to abase, to inflict destruction and death wheresoever he would, only because such was his will and pleasure. "And thou his son (says he to the king) hast not humbled thine heart, though thou knewest all this, but hast lifted up thyself against the Lord of heaven; and they have brought the vessels of his house before thee, and thou and thy lords, thy wives and thy concubines, have drunk wine in them; and thou hast praised the gods of silver and gold, of brass, iron, wood, and stone, which see not, nor hear, nor know: and the God in whose hand thy breath is, and whose are all thy ways, hast thou not glorified. Then was the part of the hand sent from him, and this writing was written: MENE, TEKEL, UPHARSIN. This is the interpretation of the thing: MENE, God hath numbered thy kingdom and finished it: TEKEL, thou art weighed in the balances, and art found wanting: PERES, thy kingdom is divided, and given to the Medes and Persians." This interpretation, one would think, should have aggravated the consternation of the company; but they found means to dispel their fears, probably upon a persuasion that the calamity was not denounced as present or immediate, and that time might furnish them with expedients to avert it. This however is certain, that, for fear of disturbing the general joy of the present festival, they put off the discussion of serious matters to another time, and sat down again to their banquet, and continued their revellings to a very late hour.

Cyrus, in the mean time, well informed of the confusion that was generally occasioned by this festival, both in the palace and the city, had posted a part of his troops on that side where the river entered into the city and another part on that side where it went out; and had commanded them to enter the city that very night, by marching along the channel of the river, as soon as ever they found it fordable. Having given all necessary orders, and exhorted his officers to follow him, by representing to them that he marched under the guidance of the gods, in the evening he made them open the great receptacles, or ditches, on both sides of the city, above and below, that the water of the river might run into them. By this means the Euphrates was quickly emptied, and its channel became dry. Then the two forementioned bodies of troops, according to their orders, went into the channel, the one commanded by Gobryas, and the other by Gadatas, and advanced without meeting any obstacle. The invisible guide, who had promised to open all the gates to Cyrus, made the general negligence and disorder of that riotous night subservient to his design, by leaving open the gates of brass, which were made to shut up the descents from the quays to the river, and which alone, if they had not been left open, were sufficient to have defeated the whole enterprise. Thus did these two bodies of troops penetrate into the very heart of the city without any opposition, and meeting together at the royal palace, according to their agreement, surprised the guards, and cut them to pieces. Some of the company that were within the palace opening the doors to know what noise it was they heard without, the soldiers rushed in, and quickly made themselves masters of it. And meeting the king, who came up to them sword in hand, at the head of those that were in the way to succour him, they killed him and put all those that attended him to the sword. The first thing the conquerors did afterwards was to thank the gods for having at last punished that impious king. These words are Xenophon's, and are very worthy of attention, as they so perfectly agree with what the Scriptures have recorded of the impious Belshazzar.

The taking of Babylon put an end to the Babylonian empire, after a duration of two hundred and ten years from the beginning of the reign of Nabonassar. Thus was the power of that proud city abolished, just fifty years after she had destroyed the city of Jerusalem and her temple. And herein were accomplished those predictions which the prophets Isaiah, Jeremiah, and Daniel, had denounced against her, and of which we have already given a particular account. There is still one more, the most important and the most incredible of them all, and yet the Scripture has set it down in the strongest terms, and marked it out with the greatest exactness; a prediction literally fulfilled in all its points; the proof still actually subsists, is the most easy to be verified, and indeed of a nature not to be contested. What I mean is the prediction of so total and absolute a ruin of Babylon that not the least remains or traces should be left of it.

David Hume

11

M. Hume proves by example that the
writing of history belongs by right
to the philosophers, exempt from
prejudice and from passion.
> Friedrich Melchior Grimm,
> *Correspondance littéraire,*
> March, 1763.

The small italicized rubric under the entry "David Hume" in the British
Museum library catalogue reads *historian.* The appellation historian may
strike students of Hume today as a curious misnomer, because of Hume's
justified reputation as the most brilliant of British empirical philosophers
whose *Treatise on Human Nature* is regarded as a seminal work in the history
of British philosophy and the most significant specimen in the corpus of
Hume's writings. The critics of Hume's time, however, either ignored Hume
as a formal philosopher or scorned his philosophical works as skeptical or
atheistical, without bothering to penetrate the meaning of those works, which
was, in any case, beyond most of them. But, as a historian, Hume found the
audience, the fame—and the fortune—he sought. His complete *History of
England,* which appeared in 1762, was the most popular, and the best,
English history written in the eighteenth century. More important than this is
that fact that as a historian Hume made his intentions as a philosopher, or
more precisely, as a philosophe, clear.

In his six-page autobiography, *My Own Life,* Hume maintained that it was
upon his election, in 1752, as librarian to the Faculty of Advocates in Edinburgh that he "formed the plan of writing the *History of England.*" This office
did provide him with many of the sources necessary for the *History,* but his
project of writing a history as part of his study of "the science of man" dated
from the time of the first publication of the *Treatise,* in 1739, and there are

225

several series of extant manuscript notes for the *History,* which he wrote in the mid-1740's. Hume composed the *History of England* backward, that is, the two volumes on Stuart England appeared in 1754 and 1757; in 1759 two more volumes, on Tudor England, were published; and in 1762 he completed his work by adding the final two volumes on the early history from the time of the invasion of Julius Caesar to the establishment of the Tudor dynasty. In each of these sets of volumes, Hume criticized traditional views of English history, and made great advances toward writing the first thoroughly modern history of England. We have taken passages from each of these volumes to demonstrate Hume's achievements, and to show how he integrated his philosophical principles into his history.

Hume's description of the Norman Conquest of England, and the introduction of feudal law by William the Conqueror, was intended as a critique of the myth of the ancient constitution, whereby the seventeenth-century lawyer-parliamentarians (Edward Coke was the most famous) defended their encroachment on the prerogatives of the Stuart monarchy. Coke and his allies in the House of Commons claimed that the demands they presented to the king were legitimized by an "ancient constitution," and guaranteed by the immemorial rights of the Commons. Hume saw no evidence for this ancient constitution or for these immemorial rights of the Commons. The uncivilized state of ancient Britain, according to Hume, allowed little room for any liberty at all. Hume followed Sir Robert Brady, who during the seventeenth-century Restoration revealed that the pseudo-historical arguments of the Whigs, as the parliamentary party in opposition to the Stuarts were then called, were based on the fallacy of anachronism. Brady showed that the Norman Conquest altered the legal system of England, and made the entire kingdom little more than a large feudal domain. How then could the Whigs, with any truth, maintain that the Commons had always been victorious over the king, and that they were merely restoring their ancient rights which the Stuarts were attempting to usurp? Brady's discoveries went unnoticed after the Glorious Revolution of 1688, which initiated the supremacy of the Whig party in England. It was Hume who popularized Brady's critical interpretation of the English Middle Ages during the eighteenth century. The philosopher who refused to admit the possibility of any unexaminable first causes was naturally inclined to dispute the existence of an ancient constitution which could in no way be documented.

From the Tudor volumes, we reproduce the description of the Spanish Armada, and of the imperious Queen Elizabeth, who was loved by the populace, and feared by the House of Commons. Hume delighted in denouncing English chauvinism in these volumes. The English had made something of a romantic legend out of the story of the defeat of the Spanish Armada —Hume reduced the story to credible proportions. When Hume discussed the unprecedented extent of Queen Elizabeth's arbitrary powers, he further dispelled the mythical Whig interpretation, which was based, in part, on the theory that Elizabeth's Stuart successors were the most arbitrary monarchs that England had ever known.

Hume's volume on the early Stuarts was the most controversial. Here his anti-Whiggism takes on its most aggressive and pronounced form. Hume follows Clarendon in the portrayal of Charles I as a martyr during his trial and at his execution. Hume is less sentimental than Clarendon; his sympathy for the ill-fated Stuarts is not founded on the impiety of the parliamentarians, but rather on his understanding of the history of the English constitution, which he had drawn throughout his *History* in terms opposed to the Whig interpretation. To Hume, it was the parliamentarians, not the Stuart monarchs, who were the dangerous innovators. Hume became famous for the generous tear he shed here for Charles I.

In the final selection, from the Appendix to the second Stuart volume, Hume reviewed his interpretation of the constitutional history of England, and declared that in spite of the terror wrought by the seventeenth-century civil war, Englishmen should accept the liberties they then obtained, because they were now able to live happily and peacefully under a new constitution. The Whigs were wrong historically, this had to be stressed, but Hume did not want to subvert a government that was the envy of Europeans and Americans who were now fighting for their liberties. The Appendix, which is a prototype piece of cultural history, ends on a eulogy of Sir Isaac Newton, whom Hume admired above all other philosophers.

After the publication of the *History of England,* Hume's life was happy and fulfilled. He traveled to France in the service of the English ambassador and was received at the French Court, where he was told of the King's admiration for his *History.* He even became something of a darling of the literary salons of Paris. James Boswell, who could detect greatness in others even if he was not capable of it himself, called Hume "the greatest writer in Britain." Hume spent his last years in the new town section of Edinburgh, on St. David Street, a street thus named for one who, despite his relentless iconoclasm, was the best loved of all philosophes.

Selected Bibliography

Ernest Campbell Mossner's *The Life of David Hume* (1954) is complete but perfunctory in the discussion of Hume's philosophy. Norman Kemp Smith's *The Philosophy of David Hume* (1941) is an incisive interpretation of Hume as a philosopher. It was Kemp Smith who made obsolete the popular notion that Hume was a mechanistic philosopher by showing the strong influence of Francis Hutcheson on Hume's *Treatise.* John Passmore's *Hume's Intentions* (1952; reprint, 1968) is a more general explanation of Hume as a philosopher. The only extended work on Hume as a historian is Professor Giuseppe Giarrizzo's *David Hume politico e storio* (1962). Giarrizzo's excellent book has been carefully reviewed by Duncan Forbes in the *Historical Journal,* VI: 2 (1962), 280–295. Mr. Forbes' article is itself a highly suggestive résumé of Hume's historical and political thought. H. R. Trevor-Roper's review of Giarrizzo in *History and Theory,* III: 3 (1963), 381–389, is also helpful in understanding Hume as a historian. Forbes has edited the first volume of Hume's *History of Great Britain* (1970), and has provided it with an excellent "Introduction."

HISTORY OF ENGLAND

William the Conqueror

But the seeming clemency of William towards the English leaders proceeded only from artifice, or from his esteem of individuals: His heart was hardened against all compassion towards the people; and he scrupled no measure, however violent or severe, which seemed requisite to support his plan of tyrannical administration. Sensible of the restless disposition of the Northumbrians, he determined to incapacitate them ever after from giving disturbance, and he issued orders for laying entirely waste that fertile country, which for the extent of sixty miles lies between the Humber and the Tees. The houses were reduced to ashes by the merciless Normans; the cattle seized and driven away; the instruments of husbandry destroyed; and the inhabitants compelled either to seek for a subsistence in the southern parts of Scotland, or if they lingered in England, from a reluctance to abandon their ancient habitations, they perished miserably in the woods from cold and hunger. The lives of a hundred thousand persons are computed to have been sacrificed to this stroke of barbarous policy, which, by seeking a remedy for a temporary evil, thus inflicted a lasting wound on the power and populousness of the nation.

But William finding himself entirely master of a people who had given him such sensible proofs of their impotent rage and animosity, now resolved to proceed to extremities against all the natives of England, and to reduce them to a condition in which they should no longer be formidable to his government. The insurrections and conspiracies in so many parts of the kingdom, had involved the bulk of the landed proprietors, more or less, in the guilt of treason; and the king took advantage of executing against them, with the utmost rigour, the laws of forfeiture and attainder. Their lives were indeed commonly spared; but their estates were confiscated, and either annexed to the royal demesnes, or conferred with the most profuse bounty on the Normans and other foreigners. While the king's declared intention was to depress, or rather

History of England, London: 1790, Vol. I, pp. 251–260; Vol. V, pp. 339–348; Vol. VII, pp. 135–152; Vol. VIII, pp. 319–334.

entirely extirpate, the English gentry, it is easy to believe that scarcely the form of justice would be observed in these violent proceedings; and that any suspicions served as the most undoubted proofs of guilt against a people thus devoted to destruction. It was crime sufficient in an Englishman to be opulent, or noble, or powerful; and the policy of the king, concurring with the rapacity of foreign adventurers, produced almost a total revolution in the landed property of the kingdom. Ancient and honourable families were reduced to beggary; the nobles themselves were every where treated with ignominy and contempt; they had the mortification of seeing their castles and manors possessed by Normans of the meanest birth and lowest stations; and they found themselves carefully excluded from every road which led either to riches or preferment.

As power naturally follows property, this revolution alone gave great security to the foreigners; but William, by the new institutions which he established, took also care to retain for ever the military authority in those hands which had enabled him to subdue the kingdom. He introduced into England the feudal law, which he found established in France and Normandy, and which, during that age, was the foundation both of the stability and of the disorders in most of the monarchial governments of Europe. He divided all the lands of England, with very few exceptions, besides the royal demesnes, into baronies; and he conferred these, with the reservation of stated services and payments, on the most considerable of his adventurers. These great barons, who held immediately of the crown, shared out a great part of their lands to other foreigners, who were denominated knights or vassals, and who paid their lord the same duty and submission in peace and war, which he himself owed to his sovereign. The whole kingdom contained about 700 chief tenants, and 60,215 knights-fees; and as none of the native English were admitted into the first rank, the few who retained their landed property were glad to be received into the second, and under the protection of some powerful Norman, to load themselves and their posterity with this grievous burthen, for estates which they had received free from their ancestors. The small mixture of English which entered into this civil or military fabric (for it partook of both species), was so restrained by subordination under the foreigners, that the Norman dominion seemed now to be fixed on the most durable basis, and to defy all the efforts of its enemies.

The better to unite the parts of the government, and to bind them into one system, which might serve both for defense against foreigners, and for the support of domestic tranquillity, William reduced the ecclesiastical revenues under the same feudal law; and though he had courted the church on his invasion and accession, he now subjected it to services which the clergy regarded as a grievous slavery; and as totally unbefitting their profession. The bishops and abbots were obliged, when required, to furnish to the king, during war, a number of knights or military tenants, proportioned to the extent of property possessed by each see or abbey; and they were liable, in case of failure, to the same penalties which were exacted from the laity. The pope and the ecclesiastics exclaimed against this tyranny, as they called it; but the king's authority was so well established over the army, who held every thing from his bounty, that superstition itself, even in that age, when it was most prevalent, was constrained to bend under his superior influence.

But as the great body of the clergy were still natives, the king had much reason to dread the effects of their resentment: He therefore used the precaution of expelling the English from all the considerable dignities, and of advancing foreigners in their place. The partiality of the Confessor towards the Normans had been so great, that aided by their superior learning, it had promoted them to many of the sees in England; and even before the period of the conquest, scarcely more than six or seven of the prelates were natives of the country. But among these was Stigand, archbishop of Canterbury; a man who, by his address and vigour, by the greatness of his family and alliances, by the extent of his possessions, as well as by the dignity of his office, and his authority among the English, gave jealousy to the king. Though William had on his accession affronted this prelate, by employing the archbishop of York to officiate at his consecration, he was careful on other occasions to load him with honours and caresses, and to avoid giving him farther offence till the opportunity should offer of effecting his final destruction. The suppression of the late rebellions, and the total subjection of the English, made him hope that an attempt against Stigand, however violent, would be covered by his great successes, and be overlooked amidst the other important revolutions which affected so deeply the property and liberty of the kingdom. Yet, notwithstanding these great advantages, he did not think it safe to violate the reverence usually paid to the primate; but under cover of a new superstition, which he was the great instrument of introducing into England.

The doctrine which exalted the papacy above all human power, had gradually diffused itself from the city and court of Rome; and was, during that age, much more prevalent in the southern than in the northern kingdoms of Europe. Pope Alexander, who had assisted William in his conquests, naturally expected that the French and Normans would import into England the same reverence for his sacred character with which they were impressed in their own country; and would break the spiritual as well as civil independency of the Saxons, who had hitherto conducted their ecclesiastical government with an acknowledgment indeed of primacy in the see of Rome, but without much idea of its title to dominion or authority. As soon, therefore, as the Norman prince seemed fully established on the throne, the pope dispatched Ermenfroy, bishop of Sion, as his legate into England; and his prelate was the first that had ever appeared with that character in any part of the British islands. The king, though he was probably led by principle to pay this submission to Rome, determined, as is usual, to employ the incident as a means of serving his political purposes, and of degrading those English prelates who were become obnoxious to him. The legate submitted to become the instrument of his tyranny; and thought that the more violent the exertion of power, the more certainly did it confirm the authority of that court from which he derived his commission. He summoned, therefore, a council of the prelates and abbots at Winchester; and being assisted by two cardinals, Peter and John, he cited before him Stigand, archbishop of Canterbury, to answer for his conduct. The primate was accused of three crimes; the holding of the see of Winchester, together with that of Canterbury; the officiating in the pall of Robert his predecessor; and the having received his own pall from Benedict IX who was afterwards deposed for simony, and for intrusion into the papacy. These crimes of Stigand were mere pretences; since the first had been a practice not unusual in England and was never any where subjected to a higher penalty than a resignation of one of the sees; the second was a pure ceremonial; and as Benedict was the only pope who then officiated, and his acts were never repealed, all the prelates of the church, especially those who lay at a distance, were excusable for making their applications to him. Stigand's ruin, however, was resolved on, and was prosecuted with great severity. The legate degraded him from his dignity: The king confiscated his estate, and cast him into prison, where he continued in poverty and want during the remainder of his life. Like rigour was exercised against the other English prelates: Agelric, bishop of Selesey, and Agelmare of Elmham, were deposed by the legate, and imprisoned by the king. Many considerable abbots shared the same fate: Egelwin, bishop of Durham, fled the kingdom: Wulstan of Worcester, a man of an inoffensive character, was the only English prelate that escaped this general proscription, and remained in possession of his dignity. Aldred, archbishop of York, who had set the crown on William's head, had died a little before of grief and vexation, and had left his malediction to that prince on account of the breach of his coronation oath, and of the extreme tyranny with which he saw he was determined to treat his English subjects.

It was a fixed maxim in this reign, as well as in some of the subsequent, that no native of the island should ever be advanced to any dignity, ecclesiastical, civil, or military. The king, therefore, upon Stigand's deposition, promoted Lanfranc, a Milanese monk, celebrated for his learning and piety, to the vacant see. This prelate was rigid in defending the prerogatives of his station; and after a long process before the pope, he obliged Thomas, a Norman monk, who had been appointed to the see of York, to acknowledge the primacy of the archbishop of Canterbury. Where ambition can be so happy as to cover its enterprises, even to the person himself, under the appearance of principle, it is the most incurable and inflexible of all human passions. Hence Lanfranc's zeal in promoting the interests of the papacy, by which he himself augmented his own authority, was indefatigable; and met with proportionable success. The devoted attachment to Rome continually increased in England; and being favoured by the sentiments of the conquerors, as well as by the monastic establishments formerly introduced by Edred and Edgar, it soon reached the same height at which it had, during some time, stood in France and Italy. It afterwards went much farther; being favoured by that very remote situation which had at first obstructed his progress; and being less checked by knowledge and a liberal education, which were still somewhat more common in the southern countries.

The prevalence of this superstitious spirit became dangerous to some of William's successors, and incommodious to most of them: But the arbitrary sway of this king over the English, and his extensive authority over the foreigners, kept him from feeling any immediate inconveniencies from it. He retained the church in great subjection, as well as his lay subjects; and would allow none, of whatever character, to dispute his sovereign will and pleasure. He prohibited his subjects from acknowledging any one for pope whom he himself had not previously received: He required that all the ecclesiastical canons, voted in any synod, should first be laid before him, and be ratified by his authority: Even bulls or letters from Rome could not legally be produced, till they received the same sanction: and none of his ministers or barons, whatever offences they were guilty of, could be subjected to spiritual censures till he himself had given his consent to their excommunication. These regulations were worthy of a sovereign, and kept united the civil and ecclesiastical powers, which the principles introduced by this prince himself had an immediate tendency to separate.

But the English had the cruel mortification to find that their king's authority, however acquired or however extended, was all employed in their oppression; and that the scheme of their subjection, attended with every circumstance of insult and indignity, was deliberately formed by the prince, and wantonly prosecuted by his followers. William had even entertained the difficult project of totally abolishing the English language; and for that purpose, he ordered that in all schools throughout the kingdom the youth should be instructed in the French tongue; a practice which was continued from custom till after the reign of Edward III and was never indeed totally discontinued in England. The pleadings in the supreme courts of judicature were in French: The deeds were often drawn in the same language: The laws were composed in that idiom: No other tongue was used at court: It became the language of all fashionable company; and the English themselves, ashamed of their own country, affected to excel in that foreign dialect. From this attention of William, and from the extensive foreign dominions long annexed to the crown of England, proceeded that mixture of French which is at present to be found in the English tongue, and which composes the greatest and best part of our language. But amidst those endeavours to depress the English nation, the king, moved by the remonstrances of some of his prelates, and by the earnest desires of the people, restored a few of the laws of king Edward; which, though seemingly of no great importance towards the protection of general liberty, gave them extreme satisfaction, as a memorial of their ancient government, and an unusual mark of complaisance in their imperious conquerors.

Queen Elizabeth

The Spanish Armada was ready in the beginning of May; but, the moment it was preparing to sail, the marquess of Santa Croce, the admiral, was seized with a fever, of which he soon after died. The vice-admiral, the duke of Paliano, by a strange concurrence of accidents, at the very same time suffered the same fate; and the king appointed for admiral the duke of Medina Sidonia, a nobleman of great family, but unexperienced in action, and entirely unacquainted with sea-affairs. Alcarede was appointed vice-admiral. This misfortune, besides the loss of so great an officer as Santa Croce, retarded the sailing of the Armada, and gave the English more time for their preparations to oppose them. At last the Spanish fleet, full of hopes and alacrity, set sail from Lisbon; but next day met with a violent tempest, which scattered the ships, sunk some of the smallest, and forced the rest to take shelter in the Groine, where they waited till they could be refitted. When news of this event was carried to England, the queen concluded that the design of an invasion was disappointed for this summer; and, being always ready to lay hold on every pretence for saving money, she made Walsingham write to the admiral, directing him to lay up some of the larger ships, and to discharge the seamen: But lord Effingham, who was not so sanguine in his hopes, used the freedom to disobey these orders; and he begged leave to retain all the ships in service, though it should be at his own expence. He took advantage of a north wind, and sailed towards the coast of Spain, with an intention of attacking the enemy in their harbours; but, the wind changing to the south, he became apprehensive lest they might have set sail, and, by passing him at sea, invade England, now exposed by the absence of the fleet. He returned, therefore, with the utmost expedition to Plymouth, and lay at anchor in that harbour.

Meanwhile, all the damages of the Armada were repaired; and the Spaniards with fresh hopes set out again to sea, in prosecution of their enterprise. The fleet consisted of a hundred and thirty vessels, of which near a hundred were galleons, and were of greater size than any ever before used in Europe. It carried on board nineteen thousand two hundred and ninety-five soldiers, eight thousand four hundred and fifty-six mariners, two thousand and eighty-eight galley-slaves, and two thousand six hundred and thirty great pieces of brass ordnance. It was victualled for six months; and was attended by twenty lesser ships, called caravals, and ten salves with six oars apiece.

The plan formed by the king of Spain was, that the Armada should sail to the coast opposite to Dunkirk and Newport; and having chased away all English or Flemish vessels, which might obstruct the passage (for it was never supposed they could make opposition), should join themselves with the duke of Parma, should thence make sail to the Thames, and having landed the whole Spanish army, thus complete at one blow the entire conquest of England. In prosecution of this scheme, Philip gave orders to the duke of Medina, that, in passing along the channel, he should sail as near the coast of France as he could with safety; that he should by this policy avoid meeting with the English fleet; and, keeping in view the main enterprise, should neglect all smaller successes, which might prove an obstacle, or even interpose a delay, to the acquisition of a kingdom. After the Armada was under sail, they took a fisherman, who informed them that the English admiral had been lately at sea, had heard of the tempest which scattered the Armada, had retired back into Plymouth, and, no longer expecting an invasion this season, had lain up his ships, and discharged most of the seamen. From this false intelligence the duke of Medina conceived the great facility of attacking and destroying the English ships in harbour; and he was tempted by the prospect of so decisive an advantage to break his orders, and make sail directly for Plymouth: A resolution which proved the safety of England. The Lizard was the first land made by the Armada, about sunset; and as the Spaniards took it for the Ram-head near Plymouth, they bore out to sea with an intention of returning next day, and attacking the English navy. They were descried by Fleming, a Scottish pirate, who was roving in those seas, and who immediately set sail to inform the English admiral of their approach: Another fortunate event which contributed extremely to the safety of the fleet. Effingham had just time to get out of port, when he saw the Spanish Armada coming full sail towards him, disposed in the form of a crescent, and stretching the distance of seven miles from the extremity of one division to that of the other.

The writers of that age raise their style by a pompous description of this spectacle; the most magnificent that had ever appeared upon the ocean; infusing equal terror and admiration into the minds of all beholders. The lofty masts, the swelling sails, and the towering prows of the Spanish galleons, seem impossible to be justly painted but by assuming the colours of poetry; and an eloquent historian of Italy, in imitation of Camden, has asserted, that the Armada, though the ships bore every sail, yet advanced with a slow motion; as if the ocean groaned with supporting, and the winds were tired with impelling, so enormous a weight. The truth, however, is, that the largest of the Spanish vessels would scarcely pass for third rates in the present navy of England: yet were they so ill framed, or so ill governed, that they were quite unwieldy, and could not sail upon a wind, nor tack on occasion, nor be managed in stormy weather by the seamen. Neither the mechanics of ship-building, nor the experience of mariners, had attained so great perfection as could serve for the security and government of such bulky vessels; and the English, who had already had experience how unserviceable they commonly were, beheld without dismay their tremendous appearance.

Effingham gave orders not to come to close fight with the Spaniards; where the size of the ships, he suspected, and the numbers of the soldiers, would be a disadvantage to the English; but to cannonade them at a distance, and to wait the opportunity which winds, currents, or various accidents, must afford him, of intercepting some scattered vessels of the enemy. Nor was it long before the event answered expectation. A great ship of Biscay, on board of which was a considerable part of the Spanish money, took fire by accident; and while all hands were employed in extinguishing the flames, she fell behind the rest of the Armada: The great galleon of Andalusia was detained by the springing of her mast: And both these vessels were taken, after some resistance, by sir Francis Drake. As the Armada advanced up the channel, the English hung upon its rear, and still infested it with skirmishes. Each trial abated the confidence of the Spaniards, and added courage to the English; and the latter soon found, that even in close fight the size of the Spanish ships was no advantage to them. Their bulk exposed them the more to the fire of the enemy; while their cannon, placed too high, shot over the heads of the English. The alarm having now reached the coast of England, the nobility and gentry hastened out with their vessels from every harbour, and reinforced the admiral. The earls of Oxford, Northumberland, and Cumberland, sir Thomas Cecil, sir Robert Cecil, sir Walter Raleigh, sir Thomas Vavafor, sir Thomas Gerrard, sir Charles Blount, with many others, distinguished themselves by this generous and disinterested service of their country. The English fleet, after the conjunction of those ships, amounted to a hundred and forty sail.

The Armada had now reached Calais, and cast anchor before that place; in expectation that the duke of Parma, who had gotten intelligence of their approach, would put to sea and join his forces to them. The English admiral practiced here a successful stratagem upon the Spaniards. He took eight of his smaller ships, and, filling them with all combustible materials, sent them one after another into the midst of the enemy. The Spaniards fancied that they were fireships of the same contrivance with a famous vessel which had lately done so much execution in the Schelde near Antwerp; and they immediately cut their cables, and took to flight with the greatest disorder and precipitation. The English fell upon them next morning while in confusion; and, besides doing great damage to other ships, they took or destroyed about twelve of the enemy.

By this time it was become apparent, that the intention for which these preparations were made by the Spaniards, was entirely frustrated. The vessels provided by the duke of Parma, were made for transporting soldiers, not for fighting; and that general, when urged to leave the harbour, positively refused to expose his flourishing army to such apparent hazard; while the English not only were able to keep the sea, but seemed even to triumph over their enemy. The Spanish admiral found, in many encounters, that while he lost so considerable a part of his own navy, he had destroyed only one small vessel of the English; and he foresaw, that by continuing so unequal a combat, he must draw inevitable destruction on all the remainder. He prepared therefore to return homewards; but as the wind was contrary to his passage through the channel, he resolved to sail northwards, and, making the tour of the island, reach the Spanish harbours by the ocean. The English fleet followed him during some time; and had not their ammunition fallen short, by the negligence of the offices in supplying them, they had obliged the whole Armada to surrender at discretion. The duke of Medina had once taken that resolution; but was diverted from it by the advice of his confessor. This conclusion of the enterprise would have been more glorious to the English; but the event proved almost equally fatal to the Spaniards. A violent tempest overtook the Armada after it passed the Orkneys: The ships had already lost their anchors, and were obliged to keep to sea: The mariners unaccustomed to such hardships, and not able to govern such unwieldy vessels, yielded to the fury of the storm, and allowed their ships to drive either on the western isles of Scotland, or on the coast of Ireland, where they were miserably wrecked. Not a half of the navy returned to Spain; and the seamen as well as soldiers who remained, were so overcome with hardships and fatigue, and so dispirited by their discomfiture, that they filled all Spain with accounts of the desperate valour of the English, and of the tempestuous violence of that ocean which surrounds them.

Such was the miserable and dishonourable conclusion of an enterprise which had been preparing for three years, which had exhausted the revenue and force of Spain, and which had long filled all Europe with anxiety or expectation. Philip, who was a slave to his ambition, but had an entire command over his countenance, no sooner heard of the mortifying event which blasted all his hopes, than he fell on his knees, and rendering thanks for that gracious dispensation of Providence, expressed his joy that the calamity was not greater. The Spanish priests, who had so often blest this holy crusade, and foretold its infallible success, were somewhat at a loss to account for the victory gained over the catholic monarch by excommunicated heretics and an execrable usurper: But they at last discovered, that all the calamities of the Spaniards had proceeded from their allowing the infidel Moors to live among them.

Soon after the defeat and dispersion of the Spanish Armada, the queen summoned a new parliament; and received from them a supply of two subsidies and four fifteenths, payable in four years. This is the first instance that subsidies were doubled in one supply; and so unusual a concession was probably obtained from the joy of the present success, and from the general sense of the queen's necessities. Some members objected to this heavy charge, on account of the great burthen of loans which had lately been imposed upon the nation.

Elizabeth foresaw, that this house of commons, like all the foregoing, would be governed by the puritans; and therefore, to obviate their enterprises, she renewed at the beginning of the session her usual injunction, that the parliament should not on any account presume to treat of matters ecclesiastical. Notwithstanding this strict inhibition, the zeal of one Damport moved him to present a bill to the commons for remedying spiritual grievances, and for restraining the tyranny of the ecclesiastical commission, which were certainly great: But when Mr. secretary Woley reminded the house of her majesty's commands, no one durst second the motion; the bill was not so much as read; and the speaker returned it to Damport without taking the least notice of it. Some members of the house, notwithstanding the general submission, were even committed to custody on account of this attempt.

The imperious conduct of Elizabeth appeared still more clearly in another parliamentary transaction. The right of purveyance was an ancient prerogative, by which the officers of the crown could at pleasure take provisions for the household from all the neighbouring counties, and could make use of the carts and carriages of the farmers; and the price of these commodities and services was fixed and stated. The payment of the money was often distant and uncertain; and the rates, being fixed before the discovery of the West Indies, were much inferior to the present market price; so that purveyance, besides the slavery of it, was always regarded as a great burthen, and, being arbitrary and casual, was liable to great abuses. We may fairly presume, that the hungry courtiers of Elizabeth, supported by her unlimited power, would be sure to render this prerogative very oppressive to the people; and the commons had, last session, found it necessary to pass a bill for regulating these exactions: But the bill was lost in the house of peers. The continuance of the abuses begat a new attempt for redress; and the same bill was now revived, and again sent up to the house of peers, together with a bill for some new regulations in the court of exchequer. Soon after the commons received a message from the upper house, desiring them to appoint a committee for a conference. At this conference, the peers informed them, that the queen, by a message delivered by lord Burleigh, had expressed her displeasure, that the commons should presume to touch on her prerogative. If there were any abuses, she said, either in imposing purveyance, or in the practice of the court of exchequer, her majesty was both able and willing to provide due reformation; but would not permit the parliament to intermeddle in these matters. The commons, alarmed at this intelligence, appointed another committee to attend the queen, and endeavour to satisfy her of their humble and dutiful intentions. Elizabeth gave a gracious reception to the committee: She expressed her great *inestimable loving care* towards her loving subjects; which, she said, was greater than of her own self, or even than any of them could have of themselves. She told them, that she had already given orders for an inquiry into the abuses attending purveyance, but the dangers of the Spanish invasion had retarded the progress of the design; that she had as much skill, will, and power to rule her household as any subjects whatsoever to govern theirs, and needed as little the assistance of her neighbours; that the exchequer was her chamber, consequently more near to her than even her household, and therefore the less proper for them to intermeddle with; and that she would of herself, with advice of her council and the judges, redress every grievance in these matters, but would not permit the commons, by laws moved without her privity, to bereave her of the honour attending these regulations. The issue of this matter was the same that attended all contests between Elizabeth and her parliaments. She seems even to have been more imperious in this particular than her predecessors; at least her more remote ones: For they often permitted the abuses of purveyance to be redressed by law. Edward III, a very arbitrary prince, allowed ten several statutes to be enacted for that purpose.

In so great awe did the commons stand of every courtier, as well as of the crown, that they durst use no freedom of speech which they thought would give the least offence to any of them. Sir Edward Hobby shewed in the house his extreme grief, that by some great personage, not a member of the house, he had been sharply rebuked for speeches delivered in parliament: He craved the favour of the house, and desired that some of the members might inform that great personage of his true meaning and intention in these speeches. The commons, to obviate these inconveniencies, passed a vote that no one should reveal the secrets of the house.

Charles I

Charles himself was assured, that the period of his life was now approaching; but notwithstanding all the preparations which were making, and the intelligence which he received, he could not, even yet, believe that his enemies really meant to conclude their violences by a public trial and execution. A private assassination he every moment looked for; and though Harrison assured him, that his apprehensions were entirely groundless, it was by that catastrophe, so frequent with dethroned princes, that he expected to terminate his life. In appearance, as well as in reality, the king was now dethroned. All the exterior symbols of sovereignty were withdrawn, and his attendants had orders to serve him without ceremony. At first, he was shocked with instances of rudeness and familiarity, to which he had been so little accustomed. *Nothing so contemptible as a despised prince!* was the reflection which they suggested to him. But he soon reconciled his mind to this, as he had done to his other calamities.

All the circumstances of the trial were now adjusted; and the high court of justice fully constituted. It constituted of 133 persons as named by the commons; but there scarcely ever sat above 70: So difficult was it, notwithstanding the blindness of prejudice and the allurements of interest, to engage men of any name or character in that criminal measure. Cromwell, Ireton, Harrison, and the chief officers of the army, most of them of mean birth, were members, together with some of the lower house and some citizens of London. The twelve judges were at first appointed in the number: But as they had affirmed, that it was contrary to all the ideas of English law to try the king for treason, by whose authority all accustions for treason must necessarily be conducted; their names, as well as those of some peers, were afterwards struck out. Bradshaw, a lawyer, was chosen president. Coke was appointed solicitor for the people of England. Dorislaus, Steele, and Aske, were named assistants. The court sat in Westminster hall.

It is remarkable, that, in calling over the court, when the crier pronounced the name of Fairfax, which had been inserted in the number, a voice came from one of the spectators, and cried, *He has more wit than to be here.* When the charge was read against the king, *In the name of the people of England;* the same voice exclaimed, *Not a tenth part of them.* Axtel the officer, who guarded the court, giving orders to fire into the box whence these insolent speeches came; it was discovered, that lady Fairfax was there, and that it was she who had had the courage to utter them. She was a person of noble extraction, daughter of Horace, lord Vere of Tilbury; but being seduced by the violence of the times, she had long seconded her husband's zeal against the royal cause, and was now, as well as he, struck with abhorrence at the fatal and unexpected consequence of all his boasted victories.

The pomp, the dignity, the ceremony of this transaction corresponded to the greatest conception that is suggested in the annals of human kind; the delegates of a great people sitting in judgment upon their supreme magistrate, and trying him for his misgovernment and breach of trust. The solicitor, in the name of the commons, represented, that Charles Stuart, being admitted king of England, and *entrusted* with a limited power; yet nevertheless, from a wicked design to erect an unlimited and tyrannical government, had traitorously and maliciously levied war against the present parliament, and the people whom they represented, and was therefore impeached as a tyrant, traitor, murderer, and a public and implacable enemy to the commonwealth. After the charge was finished, the president directed his discourse to the king, and told him, that the court expected his answer.

The king, though long detained a prisoner, and now produced as a criminal, sustained, by his magnanimous courage, the majesty of a monarch: With great temper and dignity, he declined the authority of the court, and refused to submit himself to their jurisdiction. He represented, that having been engaged in treaty with his two houses of parliament, and having finished almost every article, he had expected to be brought to his capital in another manner, and ere this time, to have been restored to his power, dignity, revenue, as well as to his personal liberty: That he could not now perceive any appearance of the upper house, so essential a member of the constitution; and had learned, that even the commons, whose authority was pretended, were subdued by lawless force, and were bereaved of their liberty: That he himself was their NATIVE HEREDITARY KING; nor was the whole authority of the state, though free and united, entitled to try him, who derived his dignity from the Supreme Majesty of heaven: That, admitting those extravagant principles which levelled all orders of men, the court could plead no power delegated by the people; unless the consent of every individual, down to the meanest and most ignorant peasant, had been previously asked and obtained: That he acknowledged, without scruple, that he had a *trust* committed to him, and one most sacred and inviolable; he was entrusted with the liberties of his people, and would not now betray them, by recognizing a power founded on the most atrocious violence and usurpation: That having taken arms, and frequently exposed his life in defence of public liberty, of the constitution, of the fundamental laws of the kingdom, he was willing, in this last and most solemn scene, to seal with his blood those precious rights for which, though in vain, he had so long contended: That those who arrogated a title to sit as his judges, were born his subjects, and born subjects to those laws, which determined, *That the king can do no wrong:* That he was not reduced to the necessity of sheltering himself under this general maxim, which guards every English monarch, even the least deserving; but was able, by the most satisfactory reasons, to justify those measures, in which he had been engaged: That to the whole world, and even to them, his pretended judges, he was desirous, if called upon in another manner, to prove the integrity of his conduct, and assert the justice of those defensive arms, to which, unwillingly and unfortunately, he had had recourse: But that, in order to preserve a uniformity of conduct, he must at present forego the apology of his innocence; lest, by ratifying an authority, no better founded than that of robbers and pirates, he be justly branded as the betrayer, instead of being applauded as the martyr, of the constitution.

The president, in order to support the majesty of the people, and maintain the superiority of his court above the prisoner, still inculcated, that he must not decline the authority of his judges; that they overruled his objections; that they were delegated by the people, the only source of every lawful power; and that kings themselves acted but in trust from that community, which had invested this high court of justice with its jurisdiction. Even according to those principles, which in his present situation he was perhaps obliged to adopt, his behaviour in general will appear not a little harsh and barbarous; but when we consider him as a subject, and one too of no high character, addressing himself to his unfortunate sovereign, his style will be esteemed, to the last degree, audacious and insolent.

Three times was Charles produced before the court, and as often declined their jurisdiction. On the fourth, the judges having examined some witnesses, by whom it was proved that the king had appeared in arms against the forces commissioned by the parliament; they pronounced sentence against him. He seemed very anxious, at this time, to be admitted to a conference with the two houses; and it was supposed, that he intended to resign the crown to his son: But the court refused compliance, and considered that request as nothing but a delay of justice.

It is confessed, that the king's behaviour, during this last scene of his life, does honour to his memory; and that, in all appearances before his judges, he never forgot his part either as a prince or as a man. Firm and intrepid, he maintained, in each reply, the utmost perspicuity and justness both of thought and expression: Mild and equable, he rose into no passion at that unusual authority which was assumed over him. His soul, without effort or affectation, seemed only to remain in the situation familiar to it, and to look down with contempt on all the efforts of human malice and iniquity. The soldiers, instigated by their superiors, were brought, though with difficulty, to cry aloud for justice: *Poor souls!* said the king to one of his attendants; *for a little money they would do as much against their commanders.* Some of them were permitted to go the utmost length of brutal insolence, and to spit in his face, as he was conducted along the passage to the court. To excite a sentiment of piety was the only effect which this inhuman insult was able to produce upon him.

The people, though under the rod of lawless unlimited power, could not forbear, with the most ardent prayers, pouring forth their wishes for his preservation; and, in his present distress, they avowed *him,* by their generous tears for their monarch, whom, in their misguided fury, they had before so violently rejected. The king was softened at this moving scene, and expressed his gratitude for their dutiful affection. One soldier too, seized by contagious sympathy, demanded from heaven a blessing on oppressed and fallen majesty: His officer, overhearing the prayer, beat him to the ground in the king's presence. *The punishment, methinks, exceeds the offence:* This was the reflection which Charles formed on that occasion.

As soon as the intention of trying the king was known in foreign countries, so enormous an action was exclaimed against by the general voice of reason and humanity; and all men, under whatever form of government they were born, rejected this example, as the utmost effort of undisguised usurpation, and the most heinous insult on law and justice. The French ambassador, by orders from his court, interposed in the king's behalf: The Dutch employed their good offices: The Scots exclaimed and protested against the violence: The queen, the prince, wrote pathetic letters to the parliament. All solicitations were found fruitless with men whose resolutions were fixed and irrevocable.

Four of Charles's friends, persons of virtue and dignity, Richmond, Hertford, Southampton, Lindesey, applied to the commons. They represented that they were the king's counsellors, and had concurred, by their advice, in all those measures which were now imputed as crimes to their royal master: That in the eye of the law, and according to the dictates of common reason, they alone were guilty, and were alone exposed to censure for every blameable action of the prince: And that they now presented themselves, in order to save, by their own punishment, that precious life which it became the commons themselves, and every subject, with the utmost hazard, to protect and defend. Such a generous effort tended to their honour; but contributed nothing towards the king's safety.

The people remained in that silence and astonishment which all great passions, when they have not an opportunity of exerting themselves, naturally produce in the human mind. The soldiers being incessantly plied with prayers, sermons, and exhortations, were wrought up to a degree of fury, and imagined, that in the acts of the most extreme disloy-alty towards their prince, consisted their greatest merit in the eye of heaven.

Three days were allowed the king between his sentence and his execu-tion. This interval he passed with great tranquillity, chiefly in reading and devotion. All his family that remained in England were allowed access to him. It consisted only of the princess Elizabeth and the duke of Glocester; for the duke of York had made his escape. Glocester was little more than an infant: The princess, notwithstanding her tender years, shewed an advanced judgment; and the calamities of her family had made a deep impression upon her. After many pious consolations and advices, the king gave her in charge to tell the queen, that, during the whole course of his life, he had never once, even in thought, failed in his fidelity towards her; and that his conjugal tenderness and his life should have an equal duration.

To the young duke too, he could not forbear giving some advice, in order to season his mind with early principles of loyalty and obedience towards his brother, who was so soon to be his sovereign. Holding him on his knee, he said, "Now they will cut off thy father's head." At these words the child looked very stedfastly upon him. "Mark, child! what I say: They will cut off my head! and perhaps make thee a king: But mark what I say, thou must not be a king, as long as thy brothers Charles and James are alive. They will cut off thy brothers' heads, when they can catch them! And thy head too they will cut off at last! Therefore, I charge thee, do not be made a king by them!" The duke, sighing, replied, "I will be torn in pieces first!" So determined an answer, from one of such tender years, filled the king's eyes with tears of joy and admiration.

Every night, during this interval, the king slept sound as usual; though the noise of workmen, employed in framing the scaffold, and other preparations for his execution, continually resounded in his ears. The morning of the fatal day he rose early; and calling Herbert, one of his attendants, he bade him employ more than usual care in dressing him, and preparing him for so great and joyful a solemnity. Bishop Juxon, a man endowed with the same mild and steady virtues by which the king himself was so much distinguished, assisted him in his devotions, and paid the last melancholy duties to his friend and sovereign.

The street before Whitehall was the place destined for the execution: For it was intended, by choosing that very place, in sight of his own palace, to display more evidently the triumph of popular justice over royal majesty. When the king came upon the scaffold, he found it so surrounded with soldiers, that he could not expect to be heard by any of the people: He addressed, therefore, his discourse to the few persons who were about him; particularly colonel Tomlinson, to whose care he had lately been committed, and upon whom, as upon many others, his amiable deportment had wrought an entire conversion. He justified his own innocence in the late fatal wars, and observed that he had not taken arms till after the parliament had inlisted forces; nor had he any other object in his warlike operations, than to preserve that authority entire, which his predecessors had transmitted to him. He threw not, however, the blame upon the parliament; but was more inclined to think that ill-instruments had interposed, and raised in them fears and jealousies with regard to his intentions. Though innocent towards his people, he acknowledged the equity of his execution in the eyes of his Maker; and observed, that an unjust sentence, which he had suffered to take effect, was now punished by an unjust sentence upon himself. He forgave all his enemies, even the chief instruments of his death; but exhorted them and the whole nation to return to the ways of peace, by paying obedience to their lawful sovereign, his son and successor. When he was preparing himself for the block, bishop Juxon called to him: "There is, sir, but one stage more, which though turbulent and troublesome, is yet a very short one. Consider, it will soon carry you a great way; it will carry you from earth to heaven; and there you shall find, to your great joy, the prize to which you hasten, a crown of glory." "I go," replied the king, "from a corruptible to an incorruptible crown; where no disturbance can have place." At one blow was his head severed from his body. A man in a vizor performed the office of executioner: Another, in a like disguise, held up to the spectators the head streaming with blood, and cried aloud, *This is the head of a traitor!*

It is impossible to describe the grief, indignation, and astonishment, which took place, not only among the spectators, who were overwhelmed with a flood of sorrow, but throughout the whole nation, as soon as the report of this fatal execution was conveyed to them. Never monarch, in the full triumph of success and victory, was more dear to his people, than his misfortunes and magnanimity, his patience and piety, had rendered this unhappy prince. In proportion to their former delusions, which had animated them against him, was the violence of their return to duty and affection; while each reproached himself, either with active disloyalty towards him, or with too indolent defence of his oppressed cause. On weaker minds, the effect of these complicated passions was prodigious. Women are said to have cast forth the untimely fruit of their womb: Others fell into convulsions, or sunk into such a melancholy as attended them to their grave: Nay, some, unmindful of themselves, as though they could not, or would not survive their beloved prince, it is reported, suddenly fell down dead. The very pulpits were bedewed with unsuborned tears; those pulpits, which had formerly thundered out the most violent imprecations and anathemas against him. And all men united in their detestation of those hypocritical parricides, who, by sanctified pretences, had so long disguised their treasons, and in this last act on iniquity had thrown an indelible stain upon the nation.

A fresh instance of hypocrisy was displayed the very day of the king's death. The generous Fairfax, not content with being absent from the trial, had used all the interest which he yet retained, to prevent the execution of the fatal sentence; and had even employed persuasion with his own regiment, though none else would follow him, to rescue the king from his disloyal murderers. Cromwell and Ireton, informed of this intention, endeavoured to convince him that the Lord had rejected the king; and they exhorted him to seek by prayer some direction from heaven on this important occasion: But they concealed from him that they had already signed the warrant for the execution. Harrison was the person appointed to join in prayer with the unwary general. By agreement, he prolonged his doleful cant, till intelligence arrived, that the fatal blow was struck. He then rose from his knees, and insisted with Fairfax, that this event was a miraculous and providential answer, which heaven had sent to their devout supplications.

It being remarked, that the king, the moment before he stretched out his neck to the executioner, had said to Juxon, with a very earnest accent, the single word REMEMBER; great mysteries were supposed to be concealed under that expression; and the generals vehemently insisted with the prelate, that he should inform them of the king's meaning. Juxon told them, that the king, having frequently charged him to inculcate on his son the forgiveness of his murderers, had taken this opportunity, in the last moment of his life, when his commands, he supposed, would be regarded as sacred and inviolable, to reiterate that desire; and that his mild spirit thus terminated its present course, by an act of benevolence towards his greatest enemies.

The character of this prince, as that of most men, if not of all men, was mixed; but his virtues predominated extremely above his vices, or, more properly speaking, his imperfections: For scarce any of his faults rose to that pitch as to merit the appellation of vices. To consider him in the most favourable light, it may be affirmed that his dignity was free from pride, his humanity from weakness, his bravery from rashness, his temperance from austerity, his frugality from avarice: All these virtues, in him, maintained their proper bounds, and merited unreserved praise. To speak the most harshly of him, we may affirm that many of his good qualities were attended with some latent frailty, which, though seemingly inconsiderable, was able, when seconded by the extreme malevolence of his fortune, to disappoint them of all their influence: His beneficent disposition was clouded by a manner not very gracious; his virtue was tinctured with superstition; his good sense was disfigured by a deference to persons of a capacity inferior to his own; and his moderate temper exempted him not from hasty and precipitate resolutions. He deserves the epithet of a good, rather than of a great man; and was more fitted to rule in a regular established government, than either to give way to the encroachments of a popular assembly, or finally to subdue their pretensions. He wanted suppleness and dexterity sufficient for the first measure: He was not endowed with the vigour requisite for the second. Had he been born an absolute prince, his humanity and good sense had rendered his reign happy and his memory precious: Had the limitations on prerogative been in his time quite fixed and certain, his integrity had made him regard, as sacred, the boundaries of the constitution. Unhappily, his fate threw him into a period when the precedents of many former reigns favoured strongly of arbitrary power, and the genius of the people ran violently towards liberty. And if his political prudence was not sufficient to extricate him from so perilous a situation, he may be excused; since even after the event, when it is commonly easy to correct all errors, one is at a loss to determine what conduct, in his circumstances, could have maintained the authority of the crown, and preserved the peace of the nation. Exposed without revenue, without arms, to the assault of furious, implacable, and bigoted factions, it was never permitted him, but with the most fatal consequences, to commit the smallest mistake; a condition too rigorous to be imposed on the greatest human capacity.

Some historians have rashly questioned the good faith of this prince: But, for this reproach, the most malignant scrutiny of his conduct, which, in every circumstance is now thoroughly known, affords not any reasonable foundation. On the contrary, if we consider the extreme difficulties to which he was so frequently reduced, and compare the sincerity of his professions and declarations; we shall avow, that probity and honour ought justly to be numbered among his most shining qualities. In every treaty, those concessions which he thought he could not in conscience maintain, he never could, by any motive or persuasion, be induced to make. And though some violations of the petition of right may perhaps be imputed to him; these are more to be ascribed to the necessity of his situation, and to the lofty ideas of royal prerogative, which, from former established precedents, he had imbibed, than to any failure in the integrity of his principles.

This prince was of a comely presence; of a sweet, but melancholy aspect. His face was regular, handsome, and well complexioned; his body strong, healthy, and justly proportioned; and being of a middle stature, he was capable of enduring the greatest fatigues. He excelled in horsemanship and other exercises; and he possessed all the exterior, as well as many of the essential qualities, which form an accomplished prince.

The tragical death of Charles begat a question, whether the people, in any case, were entitled to judge and to punish their sovereign; and most men, regarding chiefly the atrocious usurpation of the pretended judges and the merit of the virtuous prince who suffered, were inclined to condemn the republican principle as highly seditious and extravagant: But there still were a few who, abstracting from the particular circumstance of this case, were able to consider the question in general, and were inclined to moderate, not contradict, the prevailing sentiment. Such might have been their reasoning. If ever, on any occasion, it were laudable to conceal truth from the populace, it must be confessed, that the doctrine of resistance affords such an example; and that all speculative reasoners ought to observe, with regard to this principle, the same cautious silence, which the laws in every species of government have ever prescribed to themselves. Government is instituted in order to restrain the fury and injustice of the people; and being always founded on opinion, not on force, it is dangerous to weaken, by these speculations, the reverence which the multitude owe to authority, and to instruct them beforehand, that the case can ever happen, when they may be freed from their duty of allegiance. Or should it be found impossible to restrain the license of human disquisitions, it must be acknowledged, that the doctrine of obedience ought alone to be *inculcated,* and that the exceptions, which are rare, ought seldom or never to be mentioned in popular reasonings and discourses. Nor is there any danger, that mankind, by this prudent reserve, should universally degenerate into a state of abject servitude. When the exception really occurs, even though it be not previously expected and descanted on, it must, from its very nature, be so obvious and undisputed, as to remove all doubt, and overpower the restraint, however great, imposed by teaching the general doctrine of obedience. But between resisting a prince and dethroning him, there is a wide interval; and the abuses of power, which can warrant the latter violence, are greater and more enormous than those which will justify the former. History, however, supplies us with examples even of this kind; and the reality of the supposition, though, for the future, it ought ever to be little looked for, must, by all candid inquirers, be acknowledged in the past. But between dethroning a prince and punishing him, there is another very wide interval; and it were not strange, if even men of the most enlarged thought should question, whether human nature could ever in any monarch reach that height of depravity, as to warrant, in revolted subjects, this last act of extraordinary jurisdiction. That illusion, if it be an illusion, which teaches us to pay a sacred regard to the persons of princes, is so salutary, that to dissipate it by the formal trial and punishment of a sovereign, will have more pernicious effects upon the people, than the example of justice can be supposed to have a beneficial influence upon princes, by checking their career of tyranny. It is dangerous also, by these examples to reduce princes to despair, or bring matters to such extremities against persons endowed with great power, as to leave them no resource, but in the most violent and most sanguinary counsels. This general position being established, it must however be observed, that no reader, almost of any party or principle, was ever shocked, when he read in ancient history, that the Roman senate voted Nero, their absolute sovereign, to be a public enemy, and, even without trial, condemned him to the severest and most ignominious punishment; a punishment from which the meanest Roman citizen was, by the laws, exempted. The crimes of that bloody tyrant are so enormous, that they break through all rules; and extort a confession, that such a dethroned prince is no longer superior to his people, and can no longer plead, in his own defence, laws, which were established for conducting the ordinary course of administration. But when we pass from the case of Nero to that of Charles, the great disproportion, or rather total contrariety, of character immediately strikes us; and we stand astonished, that, among a civilized people, so much virtue could ever meet with so fatal a catastrophe. History, the great mistress of wisdom, furnishes examples of all kinds; and every prudential, as well as moral precept, may be authorised by those events, which her enlarged mirror is able to present to us. From the memorable revolutions which passed in England during this period, we may naturally deduce the same useful lesson, which Charles himself, in his later years, inferred, that it is dangerous for princes, even from the appearance of necessity, to assume more authority than the laws have allowed them. But it must be confessed, that these events furnish us with another instruction, no less natural, and no less useful, concerning the madness of the people, the furies of fanaticism, and the danger of mercenary armies.

In order to close this part of the British history, it is also necessary to relate the dissolution of the monarchy in England: That event soon followed upon the death of the monarch. When the peers met, on the day appointed in their adjournment, they entered upon business, and sent down some votes to the commons, of which the latter deigned not to take the least notice. In a few days, the lower house passed a vote, that they would make no more addresses to the house of peers, nor receive any from them; and that that house was useless and dangerous, and was therefore to be abolished. A like vote passed with regard to the monarchy;

and it is remarkable, that Martin, a zealous republican, in the debate on this question, confessed, that, if they desired a king, the last was as proper as any gentleman in England. The commons ordered a new great seal to be engraved, on which that assembly was represented, with this legend, ON THE FIRST YEAR OF FREEDOM, BY GOD'S BLESSING, RESTORED, 1648. The forms of all public business were changed, from the king's name, to that of the keepers of the liberties of England. And it was declared high treason to proclaim, or any otherwise acknowledge, Charles Stuart, commonly called prince of Wales.

The commons intended, it is said, to bind the princess Elizabeth apprentice to a button-maker: The duke of Glocester was to be taught some other mechanical employment. But the former soon died; of grief, as is supposed, for her father's tragical end: The latter was, by Cromwell, sent beyond sea.

The king's statue, in the Exchange, was thrown down; and on the pedestal these words were inscribed: EXIT TYRANNUS, REGUM ULTIMUS; *The tyrant is gone, the last of the kings.*

James II: Appendix

Thus have we seen, through the whole course of four reigns, a continual struggle maintained between the crown and the people: Privilege and prerogative were ever at variance: And both parties, beside the present object of dispute, had many latent claims, which, on a favourable occasion, they produced against their adversaries. Governments too steady and uniform, as they seldom are free, so are they, in the judgment of some, attended with another sensible inconvenience: They abate the active powers of men; depress courage, invention, and genius; and produce an universal lethargy in the people. Though this opinion may be just, the fluctuation and contest, it must be allowed, of the English government were, during these reigns, much too violent both for the repose and safety of the people. Foreign affairs, at that time, were either entirely neglected, or managed to pernicious purposes: And in the domestic administration there was felt a continued fever, either secret or manifest; sometimes the most furious convulsions and disorders. The revolution forms a new epoch in the constitution; and was probably attended with consequences more advantageous to the people, than barely freeing them from an exceptionable administration. By deciding many important questions in favour of liberty, and still more by that great precedent of deposing one king, and establishing a new family, it gave such an ascendant to popular principles, as has put the nature of the English constitution beyond all controversy. And it may justly be affirmed, without any danger of exaggeration, that we, in this island, have ever since enjoyed, if not the best system of government, at least the most entire system of liberty, that ever was known amongst mankind.

To decry with such violence, as is affected by some, the whole line of Stuart; to maintain, that their administration was one continued encroachment on the *incontestable* rights of the people; is not giving due honour to that great event, which not only put a period to their hereditary succession, but made a new settlement of the whole constitution. The inconveniences suffered by the people under the two first reigns of that family (for in the main they were fortunate), proceeded in a great measure from the unavoidable situation of affairs; and scarcely any thing could have prevented those events, but such vigour of genius in the sovereign, attended with such good fortune, as might have enabled him entirely to overpower the liberties of his people. While the parliaments, in those reigns, were taking advantage of the necessities of the prince, and attempting every session to abolish, or circumscribe, or define, some prerogative of the crown, and innovate in the usual tenor of government: What could be expected, but that the prince would exert himself in defending, against such inveterate enemies, an authority which, during the most regular course of the former English government, had been exercised without dispute or controversy? And though Charles II in 1672, may with reason be deemed the aggressor, nor is it possible to justify his conduct; yet there were some motives, surely, which could engage a prince so soft and indolent, and at the same time so judicious, to attempt such hazardous enterprises. He felt that public affairs had reached a situation at which they could not possibly remain without some farther innovation. Frequent parliaments were become almost absolutely necessary to the conducting of public business; yet these assemblies were still, in the judgment of the royalists, much inferior in dignity to the sovereign, whom they seemed better calculated to counsel than control. The crown still possessed considerable power of opposing parliaments; and had not as yet acquired the means of influencing them. Hence a continual jealousy between these parts of the legislature: Hence the inclination mutually to take advantage of each other's necessities: Hence the impossibility, under which the king lay, of finding ministers, who could at once be serviceable and faithful to him. If he followed his own choice in appointing his servants, without regard to their parliamentary interest, a refractory session was instantly to be expected: If he chose them from among the leaders of popular assemblies, they either lost their influence with the people, by adhering to the crown, or they betrayed the crown, in order to preserve their influence. Neither Hambden, whom Charles I was willing to gain at any price; nor Shaftesbury, whom Charles II after the popish plot, attempted to engage in his counsels, would renounce their popularity for the precarious, and, as they esteemed it, deceitful favour of the prince. The root of their authority they still thought to lie in the parliament; and as the power of that assembly was not yet uncontrollable, they still resolved to augment it, though at the expence of the royal prerogatives.

It is no wonder that these events have long, by the representations of faction, been extremely clouded and obscured. No man has yet arisen, who has paid an entire regard to truth, and has dared to expose her, without covering or disguise, to the eyes of the prejudiced public. Even that party amongst us, which boasts of the highest regard to liberty, has not possessed sufficient liberty of thought in this particular, nor has been able to decide impartially of their own merit, compared with that of their antagonists. More noble perhaps in their ends, and highly beneficial to mankind; they must also be allowed to have often been less justifiable in the means, and in many of their enterprises to have payed more regard to political than to moral considerations. Obliged to court the favour of the populace, they found it necessary to comply with their rage and folly; and have even, on many occasions, by propagating calumnies, and by promoting violence, served to infatuate, as well as corrupt that people, to whom they made a tender of liberty and justice. Charles I was a tyrant, a papist, and a contriver of the Irish massacre: The church of England was relapsing fast into idolatry: Puritanism was the only true religion, and the covenant the favourite object of heavenly regard. Through these delusions, the party proceeded, and, what may seem wonderful, still to the increase of law and liberty; till they reached the imposture of the popish plot, a fiction which exceeds the ordinary bounds of vulgar credulity. But however singular these events may appear, there is really nothing altogether new in any period of modern history: And it is remarkable, that tribunitian arts, though sometimes useful in a free constitution, have usually been such as men of probity and honour could not bring themselves either to practise or approve. The other faction, which, since the revolution, has been obliged to cultivate popularity, sometimes found it necessary to employ like artifices.

The whig party, for a course of near seventy years, has, almost without interruption, enjoyed the whole authority of government; and no honours or offices could be obtained but by their countenance and protection. But this event, which in some particulars, has been advantageous to the state, has proved destructive to the truth of history, and has established many gross falsehoods, which it is unaccountable how any civilized nation could have embraced with regard to its domestic occurences. Compositions the most despicable, both for style and matter, have been extolled, and propagated, and read; as if they had equalled the most celebrated remains of antiquity. And forgetting that a regard to liberty, though a laudable passion, ought commonly to be subordinate to a reverence for established government, the prevailing faction has celebrated only the partisans of the former, who pursued as their object the perfection of civil society, and has extolled them at the expence of their antagonists, who maintained those maxims that are essential to its very existence. But extremes of all kinds are to be avoided; and though no one will ever please either faction by moderate opinions, it is there we are most likely to meet with truth and certainty.

We shall subjoin to this general view of the English government, some account of the state of the finances, arms, trade, manners, arts, between the restoration and revolution.

The revenue of Charles II as settled by the long parliament, was put upon a very bad footing. It was too small, if they intended to make him independent in the common course of his administration: It was too large, and settled during too long a period, if they resolved to keep him in entire dependence. The great debts of the republic, which were thrown upon that prince; the necessity of supplying the naval and military stores, which were entirely exhausted; that of repairing and furnishing his palaces: All these causes involved the king in great difficulties immediately after his restoration; and the parliament was not sufficiently liberal in supplying him. Perhaps too he had contracted some debts abroad; and his bounty to the distressed cavaliers, though it did not correspond either to their services or expectations, could not fail, in some degree, to exhaust his treasury. The extraordinary sums granted the king during the first years, did not suffice for these extraordinary expences; and the excise and customs, the only constant revenue, amounted not to nine hundred thousand pounds a year, and fell much short of the ordinary burdens of government. The addition of hearth money in 1662, and of another two branches in 1669 and 1670, brought up the revenue to one million three hundred fifty-eight thousand pounds, as we learn from lord Danby's account: But the same authority informs us, that the yearly expence of government was at that time one million three hundred eighty-seven thousand seven hundred and seventy pounds; without mentioning contingencies, which are always considerable, even under the most prudent administration. Those branches of revenue, granted in 1669 and 1670, expired in 1680, and were never renewed by parliament: They were computed to be above two hundred thousand pounds a year. It must be allowed, because asserted by all contemporary authors of both parties, and even confessed by himself, that king Charles was somewhat profuse and negligent. But it is likewise certain, that a very rigid frugality was requisite to support the government under such difficulties. It is a familiar rule in all business, that every man should be payed in proportion to the trust reposed in him, and to the power which he enjoys; and the nation soon found reason, from Charles's dangerous connexions with

France, to repent their departure from that prudential maxim. Indeed, could the parliaments in the reign of Charles I have been induced to relinquish so far their old habits, as to grant that prince the same revenue which was voted to his successor, or had those in the reign of Charles II conferred on him as large a revenue as was enjoyed by his brother, all the disorders in both reigns might easily have been prevented, and probably all reasonable concessions to liberty might peaceably have been obtained from both monarchs. But these assemblies, unacquainted with public business, and often actuated by faction and fanaticism, could never be made sensible, but too late and by fatal experience, of the incessant change of times and situations. The French ambassador informs his court, that Charles was very well satisfied with his share of power, could the parliament have been induced to make him tolerable easy in his revenue.

If we estimate the ordinary revenue of Charles II at one million two hundred thousand pounds a year during his whole reign, the computation will rather exceed than fall below the true value. The convention parliament, after all the sums which they had granted the king towards the payment of old debts, threw, the last day of their meeting, a debt upon him amounting to one million seven hundred forty-three thousand two hundred sixty-three pounds. All the extraordinary sums which were afterwards voted him by parliament, amounted to eleven millions four hundred forty-three thousand four hundred and seven pounds; which, divided by twenty-four, the number of years which that king reigned, make four hundred seventy-six thousand eight hundred and eight pounds a year. During that time, he had two violent wars to sustain with the Dutch; and in 1678, he made expensive preparations for a war with France. In the first Dutch war, both France and Denmark were allies to the United Provinces, and the naval armaments in England were very great: So that it is impossible he could have secreted any part, at least any considerable part, of the sums which were then voted him by parliament.

To these sums we must add about one million two hundred thousand pounds, which had been detained from the bankers on shutting up the Exchequer in 1672. The king payed six per cent for this money during the rest of his reign. It is remarkable, that notwithstanding this violent breach of faith, the king, two years after, borrowed money at eight per cent; the same rate of interest which he had payed before that event. A proof that public credit, instead of being of so delicate a nature as we are apt to imagine, is, in reality, so hardy and robust, that it is very difficult to destroy it.

The revenue of James was raised by the parliament to about one million eight hundred and fifty thousand pounds; and his income, as duke of York, being added, made the whole amount to two millions a year; a sum well proportioned to the public necessities, but enjoyed by him in too independent a manner. The national debt at the revolution amounted to one million fifty-four thousand nine hundred twenty-five pounds.

The militia fell much to decay during these two reigns, partly by the policy of the kings, who had entertained a diffidence of their subjects, partly by that ill-judged law which limited the king's power of mustering and arraying them. In the beginning, however, of Charles's reign, the militia was still deemed formidable. De Wit having proposed to the French king an invasion of England during the first Dutch war, that monarch replied, that such an attempt would be entirely fruitless, and would tend only to unite the English. In a few days, said he, after our landing, there will be fifty thousand men at least upon us.

Charles, in the beginning of his reign, had in pay near five thousand men, of guards and garrisons. At the end of his reign he augmented this number to near eight thousand. James, on Monmouth's rebellion, had on foot about fifteen thousand men; and when the prince of Orange invaded him, there were no fewer than thirty-thousand regular troops in England.

The English navy, during the greater part of Charles's reign, made a considerable figure, for number of ships, valour of the men, and conduct of the commanders. Even in 1678, the fleet consisted of eighty-three ships; besides thirty, which were at that time on the stocks. On the king's restoration he found only sixty-three vessels of all sizes. During the latter part of Charles's reign, the navy fell somewhat to decay, by reason of the narrowness of the king's revenue: But James, soon after his accession, restored it to its former power and glory; and before he left the throne carried it much farther. The administration of the admiralty under Pepys, is still regarded as a model for order and economy. The fleet at the revolution consisted of one hundred seventy-three vessels of all sizes; and required forty-two thousand seamen to man it. That king, when duke of York, had been the first inventor of sea-signals. The military genius, during these two reigns, had not totally decayed among the young nobility. Dorset, Mulgrave, Rochester, not to mention Ossory, served on board the fleet, and were present in the most furious engagements against the Dutch.

The commerce and riches of England did never, during any period, increase so fast as from the restoration to the revolution. The two Dutch wars, by disturbing the trade of that republic, promoted the navigation of this island; and after Charles had made a separate peace with the States, his subjects enjoyed, unmolested, the trade of Europe. The only disturbance which they met with, was from a few French privateers who infested the channel; and Charles interposed not in behalf of his subjects with sufficient spirit and vigour. The recovery or conquest of New York and the Jerseys was a considerable accession to the strength and security of the English colonies; and together with the settlement of Pennsylvania and Carolina, which was effected during that reign, extended the English empire in America. The persecutions of the dissenters, or, more properly speaking, the restraints imposed upon them, contributed to augment and people these colonies. Dr. Davenant affirms, that the shipping of England more than doubled during these twenty-eight years. Several new manufactures were established; in iron, brass, silk, hats, glass, paper, etc. One Brewer, leaving the Low Countries, when they were threatened with a French conquest, brought the art of dying woollen cloth into England, and by that improvement, saved the nation great sums of money. The increase of coinage during these two reigns was ten millions two hundred sixty-one thousand pounds. A board of trade was erected in 1670; and the earl of Sandwich was made president. Charles revived and supported the charter of the East-India company; a measure whose utility is by some thought doubtful: He granted a charter to the Hudson's Bay company; a measure probably hurtful.

We learn from sir Josiah Child, that in 1688 there were on the Change more men worth 10,000 pounds than there were in 1650 worth a thousand; that 500 pounds with a daughter was, in the latter period, deemed a larger portion than 2000 in the former; that gentlewomen, in those earlier times, thought themselves well cloathed in a serge gown, which a chambermaid would, in 1688, be ashamed to be seen in; and that, besides the great increase of rich clothes, plate, jewels, and household furniture, coaches were in that time augmented a hundred fold.

The duke of Buckingham introduced from Venice the manufacture of glass and crystal into England. Prince Rupert was also an encourager of useful arts and manufactures: He himself was the inventor of etching.

The first law for erecting turnpikes was passed in 1662: The places of the turnpikes were Wadesmill, Caxton, and Stilton: But the general and great improvement of highways took not place till the reign of George II.

In 1663, was passed the first law for allowing the exportation of foreign coin and bullion.

In 1667 was concluded the first American treaty between England and Spain: This treaty was made more general and complete in 1670. The two states then renounced all right of trading with each other's colonies; and the title of England was acknowledged to all the territories in America, of which she was then possessed.

The French king, about the beginning of Charles's reign, laid some impositions on English commodities: And the English, partly displeased with this innovation, partly moved by their animosity against France, retaliated, by laying such restraints on the commerce with that kingdom as amounted almost to a prohibition. They formed calculations, by which they persuaded themselves that they were losers a million and a half, or near two millions a-year, by the French trade. But no good effects were found to result from these restraints; and in king James's reign they were taken off by parliament.

Lord Clarendon tells us, that in 1665, when money, in consequence of a treaty, was to be remitted to the bishop of Munster, it was found, that the whole trade of England could not supply above 1000 pounds a month to Frankfort and Cologne, nor above 20,000 pounds a month to Hamburgh: These sums appear surprisingly small.

At the same time that the boroughs of England were deprived of their privileges, a like attempt was made on the colonies. King James recalled the charters, by which their liberties were secured; and he sent over governors invested with absolute power. The arbitrary principles of that monarch appear in every part of his administration.

The people, during these two reigns, were, in a great measure, cured of that wild fanaticism, by which they had formerly been so much agitated. Whatever new vices they might acquire, it may be questioned, whether, by this change, they were, in the main, much losers in point of morals. By the example of Charles II and the cavaliers, licentiousness and debauchery became prevalent in the nation. The pleasures of the table were much pursued. Love was treated more as an appetite than a passion. The one sex began to abate of the national character of chastity, without being able to inspire the other with sentiment or delicacy.

The abuses in the former age, arising from overstrained pretensions to piety, had much propagated the spirit of irreligion; and many of the ingenious men of this period lie under the imputation of deism. Besides wits and scholars by profession, Shaftesbury, Halifax, Buckingham, Mulgrave, Sunderland, Essex, Rochester, Sidney, Temple, are supposed to have adopted these principles.

The same factions which formerly distracted the nation, were revived, and exerted themselves in the most ungenerous and unmanly enterprises against each other. King Charles, being in his whole deportment a model of easy and gentleman-like behaviour, improved the politeness of the nation; as much as faction, which of all things is most destructive to that virtue, could possibly permit. His courtiers were long distinguishable in England by their obliging and agreeable manners.

Till the revolution, the liberty of the press was very imperfectly enjoyed in England, and during a very short period. The star-chamber, while that court subsisted, put effectual restraints upon printing. On the suppression of that tribunal in 1641, the long parliament, after their rupture with the king, assumed the same power with regard to the licensing of books; and this authority was continued during all the period of the republic and protectorship. Two years after the restoration, an act was passed reviving the republican ordinances. This act expired in 1679; but was revived in the first of king James. The liberty of the press did not even commence with the revolution. It was not till 1694 that the restraints were taken off; to the great displeasure of the king and his ministers, who, seeing no where, in any government, during present or past ages, any example of such unlimited freedom, doubted much of its salutary effects, and probably thought, that no books or writings would ever so much improve the general understanding of men, as to render it safe to entrust them with an indulgence so easily abused.

In 1677, the old law for burning heretics was repealed; a prudent measure, while the nation was in continual dread of the return of popery.

Amidst the thick cloud of bigotry and ignorance which overspread the nation, during the commonwealth and protectorship, there were a few sedate philosophers, who, in the retirement of Oxford, cultivated their reason, and established conferences for the mutual communication of their discoveries in physics and geometry. Wilkins, a clergyman, who had married Cromwell's sister, and was afterwards bishop of Chester, promoted these philosophical conversations. Immediately after the restoration, these men procured a patent, and having enlarged their number, were denominated the *Royal Society*. But this patent was all they obtained from the king. Though Charles was a lover of the sciences, particularly chemistry and mechanics; he animated them by his example alone, not by his bounty. His craving courtiers and mistresses, by whom he was perpetually surrounded, engrossed all his expence, and left him neither money nor attention for literary merit. His contemporary, Lewis, who fell short of the king's genius and knowledge in this particular, much exceeded him in liberality. Besides pensions conferred on learned men throughout all Europe, his academies were directed by rules, and supported by salaries: A generosity which does great honour to his memory; and, in the eyes of all the ingenious part of mankind, will be esteemed an atonement for many of the errors of his reign. We may be surprised that this example should not be more followed by princes; since it is certain that that bounty, so extensive, so beneficial, and so much celebrated, cost not this monarch so great a sum as is often conferred on one useless overgrown favourite or courtier.

But though the French academy of sciences was directed, encouraged, and supported by the sovereign, there arose in England some men of superior genius who were more than sufficient to cast the balance, and who drew on themselves and on their native country the regard and attention of Europe. Besides Wilkins, Wren, Wallis, eminent mathematicians; Hooke, an accurate observer by microscopes; and Sydenham, the restorer of true physic; there flourished during this period a Boyle and a Newton; men who trod with cautious, and therefore the more secure steps, the only road which leads to true philosophy.

Boyle improved the pneumatic engine invented by Otto Guericke, and was thereby enabled to make several new and curious experiments on the air, as well as on other bodies: His chemistry is much admired by those who are acquainted with that art: His hydrostatics contain a greater mixture of reasoning and invention with experiment than any other of his works; but his reasoning is still remote from that boldness and temerity which had led astray so many philosophers. Boyle was a great partisan of the mechanical philosophy; a theory which, by discovering some of the secrets of nature, and allowing us to imagine the rest, is so agreeable to the natural vanity and curiosity of men. He died in 1691, aged 65.

In Newton this island may boast of having produced the greatest and rarest genius that ever rose for the ornament and instruction of the species. Cautious in admitting no principles but such as were founded on experiment; but resolute to adopt every such principle, however new or unusual: From modesty, ignorant of his superiority above the rest of mankind; and thence less careful to accommodate his reasonings to common apprehensions: More anxious to merit than acquire fame: He was, from these causes, long unknown to the world; but his reputation at last broke out with a lustre, which scarcely any writer, during his own lifetime, had ever before attained. While Newton seemed to draw off the veil from some of the mysteries of nature, he shewed at the same time the imperfections of the mechanical philosophy; and thereby restored her ultimate secrets to that obscurity in which they ever did and ever will remain. He died in 1727, aged 85.

William Robertson

12

During the five-year period from 1753 to 1758, in which William Robertson composed his *History of Scotland,* he often consulted David Hume, as well as many other authorities on Scottish history, in an effort to make his work as accurate as possible. Hume was delighted to assist Robertson, whom he regarded as the most reasonable member of the General Assembly of the Presbyterian Kirk, where Robertson had been a delegate since 1746. Robertson's *History of Scotland* was concerned mainly with the sixteenth century, the time of the Scottish Reformation and the infamous Mary Stuart, Queen of Scots. Although the Presbyterian minister, Robertson, could not be as critical or as sardonic in his discussion of that thunderous reformer, John Knox, as was the skeptic David Hume, the two historians agreed that the true story of the Queen of Scots had to be exposed. Hume and Robertson were central figures among the group of Scottish literati who, in the 1750's, were trying to discredit the remaining supporters of the reactionary Jacobite party, who revered Mary as a patroness saint. The literati, members of the Select Society, and promoters of the *Edinburgh Review* of 1755, wanted to promote the union of Scotland and England and to purge their language of Scotticisms in order to bring Scotland into the European Republic of Letters.

It was in 1745, to defend Edinburgh from the Jacobite army of the Stuart Pretender, that Robertson left his study and his Kirk for the only time in his life. When he was elected to the General Assembly in 1746, he was determined to be a spokesman for the Moderate party. Robertson was a sincere, conscientious minister and a true believer, but he was also convinced that religious fanaticism was a dangerous weapon of Scottish nationalism. His lifetime career in the Assembly was distinguished by his articulate opposition to both of these reactionary ideals of the Evangelical, or "high-flying," party.

Robertson adorned his *History of Scotland* with elaborate footnotes and appendixes in order to authenticate his case against the Queen of Scots, who was, to both Hume and Robertson, a deceitful conspirator and murderess. Robertson's reputation as a good historian is largely based on the energy he expended in collecting and deciphering manuscripts. Before the publication of Robertson's *History of Scotland,* Hume reproached Robertson for not consulting the original version of certain letters produced as evidence against Mary during her trial for conspiracy against Elizabeth Tudor, her cousin, and Queen of England. But once Robertson's *History* was for sale, Hume had nothing but praise for it. He wrote to Robertson in March, 1759, that whatever their minor differences of opinion and historical methods might have been, they could now be heroes together in the fight against Jacobitism, which Hume once called the "most terrible *ism* of them all."

Robertson's *History* was at least as popular as Hume's Tudor volumes, which appeared in the same year, 1759. Robertson had the additional good fortune of securing the patronage of another Scotsman, Lord Bute, who after George III's accession to the throne in 1760, became the most influential politician in Great Britain. With Bute's support, Robertson became Principal of the University of Edinburgh in 1762, and in the following year was appointed Historiographer Royal for Scotland by His Majesty. Robertson was Principal until 1792, when he resigned. It was probably the longest (and most successful) career as a university administrator that a man of letters has ever enjoyed. While Hume encouraged Robertson to write an ancient history as his next production, the king and Bute requested a history of England. Robertson decided, however, to broaden his study of the sixteenth century. In 1769 appeared the *History of the Reign of the Emperor Charles V.*

The outstanding feature of this history of the Hapsburg Emperor was the introductory volume, which is a schematic history of the Middle Ages in Europe. His description of this period has both the virtues and the faults of Enlightenment historiography on the Middle Ages: it is an excellent synthesis, based on vast research, but Robertson fails to treat this period as anything more than a pre-history to the modern era. Robertson followed Voltaire's periodization of history into ages of learning and reason and ages of ignorance and barbarism, but he went even further than Voltaire and Hume by denying the existence of learning even in the medieval monasteries. Robertson's account of the "Dark Ages" was justly criticized by the English historian, S. R. Maitland, in the nineteenth century.

In order to be able to discuss the Spanish discovery and conquest of the Americas, Robertson spent eight more years gathering a wide array of sources including the reports of Spanish missionaries and explorers, who had been to the New World. The result was the *History of America,* published in 1777. Robertson's *America* has stood the test of time better than any of his other works. It was an original and fair-minded discussion of Spanish colonization, as well as a vivid and entertaining description of the Indian tribes which were discovered in America. Robertson was concerned to show that the popular notions about the rape and ruthless rule of America by the Spanish conquerors were far from the whole truth. Along with the horrendous stories of the seizure of Puerto Rico, he spoke of the humanity of the Spanish missionaries, and of the concern of the Crown for the welfare of the native population.

Our selection comes from Book IV of the *History of America*. Here, Robertson anticipated Gibbon's application of Montesquieu's sociology to the writing of history by examining the effect of geography on the temperament of peoples and their history. Robertson's analysis of "the bodily constitution of the Americans," or of "the qualities of their minds," may strike us as crude, if not at times ludicrous, but it represents a laudable effort to expand the study of history in such a way that the whole fabric of human society might be understood.

When, in 1770, David Hume wrote from Edinburgh to William Strahan, his friend and publisher in London, he noted with a deserved sense of pride and accomplishment that "this is the historical age, and this the historical nation." Hume knew well how far he and Robertson, whom he singled out in his letter for praise, had gone toward writing the first modern works in English historiography. From the perspective of two hundred years, we can only corroborate his opinion.

Selected Bibliography

Robertson has not received the attention he deserves from contemporary scholars. There exists no extensive, modern study of his life or his work. J. B. Black in the *Art of History* (1926), 117–143, makes many pertinent observations on Robertson as a historian, while R. A. Humphreys treats the *History of America* in some detail in a published lecture entitled "William Robertson and his *History of America*" (1954). Professor D. B. Horn's article "Principal William Robertson, D.D., Historian," in the *University of Edinburgh Journal*, XVIII (1956), 155–68, is a summary of Robertson's goals as an educator, minister, and historian. The scholarly article by Manfred Schlenke, "Kulturgeschichte oder politische Geschichte in der Geschichtsschreibung des 18. Jahrhunderts," in the *Archiv für Kulturgeschichte* XXXVII (1955), 60–97, has the particular virtue of considering the political program implicit in Robertson's histories.

HISTORY OF AMERICA

View of America when first Discovered

In order to conduct this inquiry with greater accuracy, it should be rendered as simple as possible. Man existed as an individual before he became the member of a community; and the qualities which belong to him under his former capacity should be known, before we proceed to examine those which arise from the latter relation. This is peculiarly necessary in investigating the manners of rude nations. Their political union is so incomplete, their civil institutions and regulations so few, so simple, and of such slender authority, that men in this state ought to be viewed rather as independent agents, than as members of a regular society. The character of a savage results almost entirely from his sentiments or feelings as an individual, and is but little influenced by his imperfect subjection to government and order. I shall conduct my researches concerning the manner of the Americans in this natural order, proceeding gradually from what is simple to what is more complicated.

I shall consider, I. The bodily constitution of the Americans in those regions now under review. II. The qualities of their minds. III. Their domestic state. IV. Their political state and institutions. V. Their system of war, and public security. VI. The arts with which they were acquainted. VII. Their religious ideas and institutions. VIII. Such singular detached customs as are not reducible to any of the former heads. IX. I shall conclude with a general review and estimate of their virtues and defects.

I. The bodily constitution of the Americans.—The human body is less affected by climate than that of any other animal. Some animals are confined to a particular region of the globe, and cannot exist beyond it; others, though they may be brought to bear the injuries of a climate foreign to them, cease to multiply when carried out of that district which nature destined to be their mansion. Even such as seem capable of being naturalized in various climates, feel the effect of every remove from their proper station, and gradually dwindle and degenerate from the vigour and perfection peculiar to their species. Man is the only living creature

---

History of America, London: 1851, Book IV, pp. 274–300.

whose frame is at once so hardy and so flexible, that he can spread over the whole earth, become the inhabitant of every region, and thrive and multiply under every climate. Subject, however, to the general law of nature, the human body is not entirely exempt from the operation of climate; and when exposed to the extremes either of heat or cold, its size or vigour diminishes.

The first appearance of the inhabitants of the New World filled the discoverers with such astonishment, that they were apt to imagine them a race of men different from those of the old hemisphere. Their complexion is of a reddish brown, nearly resembling the colour of copper. The hair of their heads is always black, long, coarse, and uncurled. They have no beard, and every part of their body is perfectly smooth. Their persons are of a full size, extremely straight, and well proportioned. Their features are regular, though often distorted by absurd endeavours to improve the beauty of their natural form, or to render their aspect more dreadful to their enemies. In the islands, where four-footed animals were both few and small, and the earth yielded her productions almost spontaneously, the constitution of the natives, neither braced by the active exercises of the chase, nor invigorated by the labour of cultivation, was extremely feeble and languid. On the continent, where the forests abound with game of various kinds, and the chief occupation of many tribes was to pursue it, the human frame acquired greater firmness. Still, however, the Americans were more remarkable for agility than strength. They resembled beasts of prey, rather than animals formed for labour. They were not only averse to toil, but incapable of it; and when roused by force from their native indolence, and compelled to work, they sunk under tasks which the people of the other continent would have performed with ease. This feebleness of constitution was universal among the inhabitants of those regions in America which we are surveying, and may be considered as characteristic of the species there.

The beardless countenance and smooth skin of the American seems to indicate a defect of vigour, occasioned by some vice in his frame. He is destitute of one sign of manhood and of strength. This peculiarity, by which the inhabitants of the New World are distinguished from the people of all other nations, cannot be attributed, as some travellers have supposed, to their mode of subsistence. For though the food of many Americans be extremely insipid, as they are altogether unacquainted with the use of salt, rude tribes in other parts of the earth have subsisted on aliments equally simple, without this mark of degradation, or any apparent symptom of a diminution in their vigour.

As the external form of the Americans leads us to suspect that there is some natural debility in their frame, the smallness of their appetite for food has been mentioned by many authors as a confirmation of this suspicion. The quantity of food which men consume varies according to the temperature of the climate in which they live, the degree of activity which they exert, and the natural vigour of their constitutions. Under the enervating heat of the torrid zone, and when men pass their days in indolence and ease, they require less nourishment than the active inhabitants of temperate or cold countries. But neither the warmth of their climate, nor their extreme laziness, will account for the uncommon defect of appetite among the Americans. The Spaniards were astonished with observing this, not only in the islands, but in several parts of the continent. The constitutional temperance of the natives far exceeded, in their opinion, the abstinence of the most mortified hermits; while, on the other hand, the appetite of the Spaniards appeared to the Americans insatiably voracious; and they affirmed, that one Spaniard devoured more food in a day than was sufficient for ten Americans.

A proof of some feebleness in their frame, still more striking, is the insensibility of the Americans to the charms of beauty, and the power of love. That passion which was destined to perpetuate life, to be the bond of social union, and the source of tenderness and joy, is the most ardent in the human breast. Though the perils and hardships of the savage state, though excessive fatigue, on some occasions, and the difficulty at all times of procuring subsistence, may seem to be adverse to this passion, and to have a tendency to abate its vigour, yet the rudest nations in every other part of the globe seem to feel its influence more powerfully than the inhabitants of the New World. The negro glows with all the warmth of desire natural to his climate; and the most uncultivated Asiatics discover that sensibility, which from their situation on the globe, we should expect them to have felt. But the Americans are, in an amazing degree, strangers to the force of this first instinct of nature. In every part of the New World the natives treat their women with coldness and indifference. They are neither the objects of that tender attachment which takes place in civilized society, nor of that ardent desire conspicuous among rude nations. Even in climates where this passion usually acquires its greatest vigour, the savage of America views his female with disdain, as an animal of a less noble species. He is at no pains to win her favour by the assiduity of courtship, and still less solicitous to preseve it by indulgence and gentleness. Missionaries themselves, notwithstanding the austerity of monastic ideas, cannot refrain from expressing their astonishment at the dispassionate coldness of the American young men in their intercourse with the other sex. Nor is this reserve to be ascribed to any opinion which they entertain with respect to the merit of female chastity. That is an idea too refined for a savage, and suggested by a delicacy of sentiment and affection to which he is a stranger.

But in inquiries concerning either the bodily or mental qualities of particular races of men, there is not a more common or more seducing error, than that of ascribing to a single cause those characteristic peculiarities, which are the effect of the combined operation of many causes. The climate and soil of America differ, in so many respects, from those of the other hemisphere, and this difference is so obvious and striking, that philosophers of great eminence have laid hold on this as sufficient to account for what is peculiar in the constitution of its inhabitants. They rest on phsycial causes alone, and consider the feeble frame and languid desire of the Americans, as consequences of the temperament of that portion of the globe which they occupy. But the influences of political and moral causes ought not to have been overlooked. These operate with no less effect than that on which many philosophers rest as a full explanation of the singular appearances which have been mentioned. Wherever the state of society is such as to create many wants and desires, which cannot be satisfied without regular exertions of industry, the body accustomed to labour becomes robust and patient of fatigue. In a more simple state, where the demands of men are so few and so moderate, that they may be gratified, almost without any effort, by the spontaneous productions of nature, the powers of the body are not called forth, nor can they attain their proper strength. The natives of Chili and of North America, the two temperate regions in the New World, who live by hunting, may be deemed an active and vigorous race, when compared with the inhabitants of the isles, or of those parts of the continent where hardly any labour is requisite to procure subsistence. The exertions of a hunter are not, however, so regular, or so continued, as those of persons employed in the culture of the earth, or in the various arts of civilized life, and though his agility may be greater than theirs, his strength is on the whole inferior. If another direction were given to the active powers of man in the New World, and his force augmented by exercise, he might acquire a degree of vigour which he does not in his present state possess. The truth of this is confirmed by experience. Wherever the Americans have been gradually accustomed to hard labour, their constitutions become robust, and they have been found capable of performing such tasks, as seemed not only to exceed the powers of such a feeble frame as has been deemed peculiar to their country, but to equal any effort of the natives, either of Africa, or of Europe.

The same reasoning will apply to what has been observed concerning their slender demand for food. As a proof that this should be ascribed as much to their extreme indolence, and often total want of occupation, as to anything peculiar in the physical structure of their bodies, it has been observed, that in those districts, where the people of America are obliged to exert any unusual effort of activity, in order to procure subsistence, or wherever they are employed in severe labour, their appetite is not inferior to that of other men, and, in some places, it has struck observers as remarkably voracious.

The operation of political and moral causes is still more conspicuous, in modifying the degree of attachment between the sexes. In a state of high civilization, this passion, inflamed by restraint, refined by delicacy, and cherished by fashion, occupies and engrosses the heart. It is no longer a simple instinct of nature; sentiment heightens the ardour of desire, and the most tender emotions of which our frame is susceptible, soothe and agitate the soul. This description, however, applies only to those, who, by their situation, are exempted from the cares and labours of life. Among persons of inferior order, who are doomed by their condition to incessant toil, the dominion of this passion is less violent; their solicitude to procure subsistence, and to provide for the first demand of nature, leaves little leisure for attending to its second call. But if the nature of the intercourse between the sexes varies so much in persons of different rank in polished societies, the condition of man, while he remains uncivilized, must occasion a variation still more apparent. We may well suppose, that, amidst the hardships, the dangers, and the simplicity of savage life, where subsistence is always precarious and often scanty, where men are almost continually engaged in the pursuit of their enemies, or in guarding against their attacks, and where neither dress nor reserve are employed as arts of female allurement, that the attention of the Americans to their women would be extremely feeble, without imputing this solely to any physical defect or degradation in their frame.

It is accordingly observed, that in those countries of America, where, from the fertility of the soil, the mildness of the climate, or some farther advances which the natives have made in improvement, the means of subsistence are more abundant, and the hardships of savage life are less severely felt, the animal passion of the sexes becomes more ardent. Striking examples of this occur among some tribes seated on the banks of great rivers well stored with food, among others who are masters of hunting-grounds abounding so much with game, that they have a regular and plentiful supply of nourishment with little labour. The superior degree of security and affluence which these tribes enjoy, is followed by their natural effects. The passions implanted in the human frame by the hand of nature acquire additional force; new tastes and desires are formed; the women, as they are more valued and admired, become more attentive to dress and ornament; the men, beginning to feel how much of their own happiness depends upon them, no longer disdain the arts of winning their favour and affection. The intercourse of the sexes becomes very different from that which takes place among their ruder countrymen; and as hardly any restraint is imposed on the gratification of desire, either by religion, or laws, or decency, the dissolution of their manners is excessive.

Notwithstanding the feeble make of the Americans, hardly any of them are deformed, or mutilated, or defective in any of their senses. All travellers have been struck with this circumstance, and have celebrated the uniform symmetry and perfection of their external figure. Some authors search for the cause of this appearance in their physical condition. As the parents are not exhausted or over-fatigued with hard labour, they suppose that their children are born vigorous and sound. They imagine, that, in the liberty of savage life, the human body naked and unconfined from its earliest age, preserves its natural form; and that all its limbs and members acquire a juster proportion, than when fettered with artificial restraints, which stint its growth and distort its shape. Something, without doubt, may be ascribed to the operation of these causes; but the true reasons of this apparent advantage, which is common to all savage nations, lie deeper, and are closely interwoven with the nature and genius of that state. The infancy of man is so long and so helpless, that it is extremely difficult to rear children among rude nations. Their means of subsistence are not only scanty, but precarious. Such as live by hunting must range over extensive countries, and shift often from place to place. The care of children, as well as every other laborious task, is devolved upon the women. The distresses and hardships of the savage life, which are often such as can hardly be supported by persons in full vigour, must be fatal to those of more tender age. Afraid of undertaking a task so laborious, and of such long duration, as that of rearing their offspring, the women, in some parts of America, procure frequent abortions by the use of certain herbs, and extinguish the first sparks of that life which they are unable to cherish. Sensible that only stout and well-formed children have force of constitution to struggle through such a hard infancy, other nations abandon or destroy such of their progeny as appear feeble or defective, as unworthy of attention. Even when they endeavour to rear all their children without distinction, so great a proportion of the whole number perishes under the rigorous treatment which must be their lot in the savage state, that few of those who laboured under any original frailty attain the age of manhood. Thus, in polished societies, where the means of subsistence are secured with certainty, and acquired with ease; where the talents of the mind are often of more importance than the powers of the body; children are preserved notwithstanding their defects or deformity, and grow up to be useful citizens. In rude nations, such persons are either cut off as soon as they are born, or, becoming a burden to themselves and to the community, cannot long protract their lives. But in those provinces of the New World where, by the establishment of the Europeans, more regular provision has been made for the subsistence of its inhabitants, and they are restrained from laying violent hands on their children, the Americans are so far from being eminent for any superior perfection in their form, that one should rather suspect some peculiar imbecility in the race, from the extraordinary number of individuals who are deformed, dwarfish, mutilated, blind or deaf.

How feeble soever the constitution of the Americans may be, it is remarkable, that there is less variety in the human form throughout the New World, than in the ancient continent. When Columbus and the other discoverers first visited the different countries of America which lie within the torrid zone, they naturally expected to find people of the same complexion with those in the corresponding regions of the other hemisphere. To their amazement, however, they discovered that America contained no negroes; and the cause of this singular appearance became as much the object of curiosity, as the fact itself was of wonder. In what part or membrane of the body that humour resides which tinges the complexion of the negro with a deep black, it is the business of anatomists to inquire and describe. The powerful operation of heat appears manifestly to be the cause which produces this striking variety in the human species. All Europe, a great part of Asia, and the temperate countries of Africa, are inhabited by men of a white complexion. All the torrid zone in Africa, some of the warmer regions adjacent to it, and several countries in Asia, are filled with people of a deep black colour. If we survey the nations of our continent, making our progress from cold and temperate countries towards those parts which are exposed to the influence of vehement and unremitting heat, we shall find that the extreme whiteness of their skin soon begins to diminish; that its colour deepens gradually as we advance; and, after passing through all the successive gradations of shade, terminates in an uniform unvarying black. But in America, where the agency of heat is checked and abated by various causes, which I have already explained, the climate seems to be destitute of that force which produces such wonderful effects on the human frame. The colour of the natives of the torrid zone in America is hardly of a deeper hue than that of the people in the more temperate parts of their continent. Accurate observers, who had an opportunity of viewing the Americans in very different climates, and in provinces far removed from each other, have been struck with the amazing similarity of their figure and aspect.

But though the hand of nature has deviated so little from one standard in fashioning the human form in America, the creation of fancy hath been various and extravagant. The same fables that were current in the ancient continent, have been revived with respect to the New World, and

America too has been peopled with human beings of monstrous and fantastic appearance. The inhabitants of certain provinces were described to be pigmies of three feet high; those of others to be giants of an enormous size. Some travellers published accounts of people with only one eye; others pretended to have discovered men without heads, whose eyes and mouths were planted in their breasts. The variety of nature in her productions is, indeed, so great, that it is presumptuous to set bounds to her fertility, and to reject indiscriminately every relation that does not perfectly accord with our own limited observation and experience. But the other extreme, of yielding a hasty assent, on the slightest evidence, to whatever has the appearance of being strange and marvellous, is still more unbecoming a philosophical inquirer; as, in every period, men are more apt to be betrayed into error, by their weakness in believing too much, than by their arrogance in believing too little. In proportion as science extends, and nature is examined with a discerning eye, the wonders which amused ages of ignorance disappear. The tales of credulous travellers concerning America are forgotten; the monsters which they describe have been searched for in vain; and those provinces where they pretend to have found inhabitants of singular forms, are now known to be possessed by people no wise different from the other Americans.

Though those relations may, without discussion, be rejected as fabulous, there are other accounts of varieties in the human species in some parts of the New World, which rest upon better evidence, and merit more attentive examination. This variety has been particularly observed in three different districts. The first of these is situated in the isthmus of Darien, near the centre of America. Lionel Wafer, a traveller possessed of more curiosity and intelligence than we should have expected to find in an associate of bucaneers, discovered there a race of men few in number, but of a singular make. They are of low stature, according to his description, of a feeble frame, incapable of enduring fatigue. Their colour is a dead milk white; not resembling that of fair people among Europeans, but without any tincture of a blush or sanguine complexion. Their skin is covered with a fine hairy down of a chalky white; the hair of their heads, their eye-brows, and eye-lashes, are of the same hue. Their eyes are of a singular form, and so weak, that they can hardly bear the light of the sun; but they see clearly by moonlight, and are most active and gay in the night. No race similar to this has been discovered in any other part of America. Cortes, indeed, found some persons exactly resembling the white people of Darien, among the rare and monstrous animals which Montezuma had collected. But as the power of the Mexican empire extended to the provinces bordering on the isthmus of Darien, they were probably brought thence. Singular as the appearance of those people may be, they cannot be considered as constituting a distinct species.

Among the negroes of Africa, as well as the natives of the Indian Islands, nature sometimes produces a small number of individuals, with all the characteristic features and qualities of the white people of Darien. The former are called *Albinos* by the Portuguese, the latter *Kackerlakes* by the Dutch. In Darien the parents of those *whites* are of the same colour with the other natives of the country; and this observation applies equally to the anomalous progeny of the negroes and Indians. The same mother who produces some children of a colour that does not belong to the race, brings forth the rest with the complexion peculiar to her country. One conclusion may then be formed with respect to the people described by Wafer, the *Albinos* and the *Kackerlakes;* they are a degenerated breed, not a separate class of men; and from some disease or defect of their parents, the peculiar colour and debility which mark their degradation are transmitted to them. As a decisive proof of this, it has been observed, that neither the white people of Darien, nor the Albinos of Africa, propagate their race: their children are of the colour and temperament peculiar to the natives of their respective countries.

The second district that is occupied by inhabitants differing in appearance from the other people of America, is situated in a high northern latitude, extending from the coast of Labrador towards the pole, as far as the country is habitable. The people scattered over those dreary regions, are known to the Europeans by the name of *Esquimaux.* They themselves, with that idea of their own superiority, which consoles the rudest and most wretched nations, assume the name of *Keralit* or *Men.* They are of a middle size, and robust, with heads of a disproportioned bulk, and feet as remarkably small. Their complexion, though swarthy, by being continually exposed to the rigour of a cold climate, inclines to the European white, rather than to the copper colour of America, and the men have beards which are sometimes bushy and long. From these marks of distinction, as well as from one still less equivocal, the affinity of their language to that of the Greenlanders, which I have already mentioned, we may conclude, with some degree of confidence, that the Esquimaux are a race different from the rest of the Americans.

We cannot decide with equal certainty concerning the inhabitants of the third district, situated at the southern extremity of America. These are the famous *Patagonians,* who, during two centuries and a half, have afforded a subject of controversy to the learned, and an object of wonder to the vulgar. They are supposed to be one of the wandering tribes, which occupy that vast but least known region of America, which extends from the river de la Plata to the straits of Magellan. Their proper station is in that part of the interior country, which lies on the banks of the river Negro; but in the hunting season, they often roam as far as the straits which separate Tierra del Fuego from the main land. The first accounts of this people were brought to Europe by the companions of Magellan, who described them as a gigantic race, above eight feet high, and of strength in proportion to their enormous size. Among several tribes of animals, a disparity in bulk as considerable may be observed. Some large breeds of horses and dogs exceed the more diminutive races in stature and strength, as far as the Patagonian is supposed to rise above the usual standard of the human body. But animals attain the highest perfection of their species only in mild climates, or where they find the most nutritive food in greatest abundance. It is not then in the uncultivated waste of the Magellanic regions, and among a tribe of improvident savages, that we should expect to find man possessing the highest honours of his race, and distinguished by a superiority of size and vigour, far beyond what he has reached in any other part of the earth. The most explicit and unexceptionable evidence is requisite, in order to establish a fact repugnant to those general principles and laws, which seem to affect the human frame in every other instance, and to decide with respect to its nature and qualities. Such evidence has not hitherto been produced. Though several persons to whose testimony great respect is due, have visited this part of America since the time of Magellan, and have had interviews with the natives; though some have affirmed, that such as they saw were of gigantic stature, and others have formed the same conclusion, from measuring their footsteps, or from viewing the skeletons of their dead; yet their accounts vary from each other in so many essential points, and are mingled with so many circumstances, manifestly false or fabulous, as detract much from their credit. On the other hand, some navigators, and those among the most eminent of their order, for discernment and accuracy, have asserted that the natives of Patagonia, with whom they had intercourse, though stout and well made, are not of such extraordinary size as to be distinguished from the rest of the human species. The existence of this gigantic race of men seems then, to be one of those points in natural history, with respect to which a cautious inquirer will hesitate, and will choose to suspend his assent until more complete evidence shall decide, whether he ought to admit a fact, seemingly inconsistent with what reason and experience have discovered concerning the structure and condition of man, in all the various situations in which he has been observed.

In order to form a complete idea with respect to the constitution of the inhabitants of this and the other hemisphere, we should attend not only to the make and vigour of their bodies, but consider what degree of health they enjoy, and to what period of longevity they usually arrive. In the simplicity of the savage state, when man is not oppressed with labour, or enervated by luxury, or disquieted with care, we are apt to imagine, that this life will flow on almost untroubled by disease or suffering, until his days be terminated in extreme old age, by the gradual decays of nature. We find, accordingly, among the Americans, as well as among other rude people, persons, whose decrepit and shrivelled form seems to indicate an extraordinary length of life. But as most of them are unacquainted with the art of numbering, and all of them as forgetful of what is past, as they are improvident of what is to come, it is impossible to ascertain their age, with any degree of precision. It is evident that the period of their longevity must vary considerably, according to the diversity of climates, and their different modes of subsistence. They seem, however, to be everywhere exempt from many of the distempers which afflict polished nations. None of the maladies, which are the immediate offspring of luxury, ever visited them; and they have no names in their languages by which to distinguish this numerous train of adventitious evils.

But whatever be the situation in which man is placed, he is born to suffer; and his diseases, in the savage state, though fewer in number, are like those of the animals whom he nearly resembles in his mode of life, more violent and more fatal. If luxury engenders and nourishes distempers of one species, the rigour and distresses of savage life bring on those of another. As men in this state are wonderfully improvident, and their means of subsistence precarious, they often pass from extreme want to exuberant plenty, according to the vicissitudes of fortune in the chase, or in consequence of the various degrees of abundance with which the earth affords to them its productions, in different seasons. Their inconsiderate gluttony in the one situation, and their severe abstinence in the other, are equally pernicious. For, though the human constitution may be accustomed by habit, like that of animals of prey, to tolerate long famine, and then to gorge voraciously, it is not a little affected by such sudden and violent transitions. The strength and vigour of savages are at some seasons impaired by what they suffer from scarcity of food; at others they are afflicted with disorders arising from indigestion and a superfluity of gross aliment. These are so common, that they may be considered as the unavoidable consequence of their mode of subsisting, and cut off considerable numbers in the prime of life. They are likewise extremely subject to consumptions, to pleuritic, asthmatic, and paralytic disorders, brought on by the immoderate hardships and fatigue which they endure in hunting and in war; or owing to the inclemency of the seasons to which they are conntinually exposed. In the savage state, hardships and fatigue violently assault the constitution. In polished societies, intemperance undermines it. It is not easy to determine which of them operates with most fatal effect, or tends most to abridge human life. The influence of the former is certainly most extensive. The pernicious consequences of luxury reach only a few members in any community; the distresses of savage life are felt by all. As far as I can judge, after very minute inquiry, the general period of human life is shorter among savages, than in well-regulated and industrious societies.

One dreadful malady, the severest scourge with which, in this life, offended heaven chastens the indulgence of criminal desire, seems to have been peculiar to the Americans. By communicating it to their conquerors, they have not only amply avenged their own wrongs, but, by adding this calamity to those which formerly embittered human life, they have, perhaps, more than counterbalanced all the benefits which Europe has derived from the discovery of the New World. This distemper, from the country in which it first raged, or from the people by whom it was supposed to have been spread over Europe, has been sometimes called the Neapolitan, and sometimes the French disease. At its first appearance, the affection was so malignant, its symptoms so violent, its operation so rapid and fatal, as to baffle all the efforts of medical skill. Astonishment and terror accompanied this unknown affliction in its progress, and men began to dread the extinction of the human race by such a cruel visitation. Experience, and the ingenuity of physicians, gradually discovered remedies of such virtue as to cure or to mitigate the evil. During the course of two centuries and a half, its virulence seems to have abated considerably. At length, in the same manner with the leprosy, which raged in Europe for some centuries, it may waste its force and disappear; and, in some happier age, this western infection, like that from the East, may be known only by description.

II. After considering what appears to be peculiar in the bodily constitution of the Americans, our attention is naturally turned towards the powers and qualities of their minds. As the individual advances from the ignorance and imbecility of the infant state to vigour and maturity of understanding, something similar to this may be observed in the progress of the species. With respect to it, too, there is a period of infancy, during which several powers of the mind are not unfolded, and all are feeble and defective in their operation. In the early ages of society, while the condition of man is simple and rude his reason is but little exercised, and his desires move within a very narrow sphere. Hence arise two remarkable characteristics of the human mind in this state. Its intellectual powers are extremely limited; its emotions and efforts are few and languid. Both these distinctions are conspicuous among the rudest and most unimproved of the American tribes, and constitute a striking part of their description.

What, among polished nations, is called speculative reasoning or research, is altogether unknown in the rude state of society, and never becomes the occupation or amusement of the human faculties, until man be so far improved as to have secured, with certainty, the means of subsistence, as well as the possession of leisure and tranquillity. The thoughts and attention of a savage are confined within the small circle of objects immediately conducive to his preservation or enjoyment. Everything beyond that, escapes his observation, or is perfectly indifferent to him. Like a mere animal, what is before his eyes interests and affects him; what is out of sight, or at a distance, makes little impression. There are several people in America whose limited understandings seem not to be capable of forming an arrangement for futurity; neither their solicitude nor their foresight extend so far. They follow blindly the impulse of the appetite which they feel, but are entirely regardless of distant consequences, and even of those removed in the least degree from immediate apprehension. While they highly prize such things as serve for present use, or minister to present enjoyment, they set no value upon those which are not the object of some immediate want. When, on the approach of the evening, a Caribbee feels himself disposed to go to rest, no consideration will tempt him to sell his hammock. But, in the morning, when he is sallying out to the business or pastime of the day, he will part with it for the slightest toy that catches his fancy. At the close of winter, while the impression of what he has suffered from the rigour of the climate is fresh in the mind of the North American, he sets himself with vigour to prepare materials for erecting a comfortable hut to protect him against the inclemency of the succeeding season; but, as soon as the weather becomes mild, he forgets what is past, abandons his work, and never thinks of it more, until the return of cold compels him, when too late, to resume it.

If in concerns the most interesting, and seemingly the most simple, the reason of man, while rude and destitute of culture, differs so little from the thoughtless levity of children, or the improvident instinct of animals, its exertions in other directions cannot be very considerable. The objects towards which reason turns, and the disquisitions in which it engages, must depend upon the state in which man is placed, and are suggested by his necessities and desires. Disquisitions, which appear the most necessary and important to men in one state of society, never occur to those in another. Among civilized nations, arithmetic, or the art of numbering, is deemed an essential and elementary science; and in our continent, the invention and use of it reaches back to a period so remote as is beyond the knowledge of history. But among savages, who have no property to estimate, no hoarded treasures to count, no variety of objects or multiplicity of ideas to enumerate, arithmetic is a superfluous and useless art. Accordingly, among some tribes in America it seems to be quite unknown. There are many who cannot reckon farther than three; and have no denomination to distinguish any number above it. Several can proceed as far as ten, others to twenty. When they would convey an idea of any number beyond these, they point to the hair of their head, intimating that it is equal to them, or with wonder declare it to be so great that it cannot be reckoned. Not only the Americans, but all nations, while extremely rude, seem to be unacquainted with the art of computation. As soon, however, as they acquire such acquaintance or connexion with a variety of objects, that there is frequent occasion to combine or divide them, their knowledge of numbers increases, so that the state of this art among any people may be considered as one standard, by which to estimate the degree of their improvement. The Iroquois, in North America, as they are much more civilized than the rude inhabitants of Brazil, Paraguay, or Guiana, have likewise made greater advances in this respect; though even their arithmetic does not extend beyond a thousand, as in their petty transactions they have no occasion for any higher number. The Cherokee, a less considerable nation on the same continent, can reckon only as far as a hundred, and to that extent have names for the several numbers; the smaller tribes in their neighbourhood can rise no higher than ten.

In other respects, the exercise of the understanding among rude nations is still more limited. The first ideas of every human being must be such as he receives by the senses. But, in the mind of man, while in the savage state, there seem to be hardly any ideas but what enter by this avenue. The objects around him are presented to his eye. Such as may be subservient to his use, or can gratify any of his appetites, attract his notice; he views the rest without curiosity or attention. Satisfied with considering them under that simple mode in which they appear to him, as separate and detached, he neither combines them so as to form general classes, nor contemplates their qualities apart from the subject in which they inhere, nor bestows a thought upon the operations of his own mind concerning them. Thus he is unacquainted with all the ideas which have been denominated *universal,* or *abstract,* or *of reflection.* The range of his understanding must, of course, be very confined, and his reasoning powers be employed merely on what is sensible. This is so remarkably the case with the ruder nations of America, that their languages, as we shall afterwards find, have not a word to express anything but what is material or corporeal. *Time, space, substance,* and a thousand other terms, which represent abstract and universal ideas, are altogether unknown to them. A naked savage, cowering over the fire in his miserable cabin, or stretched under a few branches which afford him a temporary shelter, has as little inclination as capacity for useless speculation. His thoughts extend not beyond what relates to animal life; and when they are not directed towards some of its concerns, his mind is totally inactive. In situations where no extraordinary effort either of ingenuity or labour is requisite, in order to satisfy the simple demands of nature, the powers of the mind are so seldom roused to any exertion, that the rational faculties continue almost dormant and unexercised. The numerous tribes scattered over the rich plains of South America, the inhabitants of some of the islands, and of several fertile regions on the continent, come under this description. Their vacant countenance, their staring unexpressive eye, their listless inattention, and total ignorance of subjects, which seem to be the first which should occupy the thoughts of rational beings, made such impression upon the Spaniards, when they first beheld those rude people, that they considered them as animals of an inferior order, and could not believe that they belonged to the human species. It required the authority of a papal bull to counteract this opinion, and to convince them that the Americans were capable of the functions, and entitled to the privileges of humanity. Since that time, persons more enlightened and impartial than the discoverers or conquerors of America, have had an opportunity of contemplating the most savage of its inhabitants, and they have been astonished and humbled, with observing how nearly man, in this condition, approaches to the brute creation. But in severer climates, where subsistence cannot be procured with the same ease, where men must unite more closely, and act with greater concert, necessity calls forth their talents, and sharpens their invention, so that the intellectual powers are more exercised and improved. The North American tribes and the natives of Chili, who inhabit the temperate regions in the two great districts of America, are people of cultivated and enlarged understandings, when viewed in comparison with some of those seated in the islands, or on the banks of the Maragnon and Orinoco. Their occupations are more various, their system of policy, as well as of war, more complex, their arts more numerous. But even among them, the intellectual powers are extremely limited in their operations, and, unless when turned directly to those objects which interest a savage, are held in no estimation. Both the North Americans and Chilese, when not engaged in some of the functions belonging to a warrior or hunter, loiter away their time in thoughtless indolence, unacquainted with any other subject worthy of their attention, or capable of occupying their minds. If even among them reason is so much circumscribed in its exertions, and never arrives, in its highest attainments, at the knowledge of those general principles and maxims, which serve as the foundation of science, we may conclude, that the intellectual powers of man in the savage state are destitute of their proper object, and cannot acquire any considerable degree of vigour and enlargement.

From the same causes, the active efforts of the mind are few, and, on most occasions, languid. If we examine into the motives which rouse men to activity in civilized life, and prompt them to persevere in fatiguing exertions of their ingenuity or strength, we shall find that they arise chiefly from acquired wants and appetites. These are numerous and importunate; they keep the mind in perpetual agitation, and, in order to gratify them, invention must be always on the stretch, and industry must be incessantly employed. But the desires of simple nature are few, and where a favourable climate yields almost spontaneously what suffices to gratify them, they scarcely stir the soul, or excite any violent emotion. Hence the people of several tribes in America waste their life in a listless indolence. To be free from occupation, seems to be all the enjoyment towards which they aspire. They will continue whole days stretched out in their hammocks, or seated on the earth in perfect idleness, without changing their posture, or raising their eyes from the ground, or uttering a single word.

Such is their aversion to labour, that neither the hope of future good, nor the apprehension of future evil, can surmount it. They appear equally indifferent to both, discovering little solicitude, and taking no precautions to avoid the one, or to secure the other. The cravings of hunger may rouse them; but as they devour, with little distinction, whatever will appease its instinctive demands, the exertions which these occasion are of short duration. Destitute of ardour, as well as variety of desire, they feel not the force of those powerful springs which give vigour to the movements of the mind, and urge the patient hand of industry to persevere in its efforts. Man, in some parts of America, appears in a form so rude, that we can discover no effects of his activity, and the principle of understanding which should direct it, seems hardly to be unfolded. Like the other animals, he has no fixed residence; he has erected no habitation to shelter him from the inclemency of the weather; he has taken no measures for securing certain subsistence; he neither sows nor reaps; but roams about as led in search of the plants and fruits which the earth brings forth in succession; and in quest of the game which he kills in the forests, or of the fish which he catches in the rivers.

This description, however, applies only to some tribes. Man cannot continue long in this state of feeble and uninformed infancy. He was made for industry and action, and the powers of his nature, as well as the necessity of his condition, urge him to fulfil his destiny. Accordingly, among most of the American nations, especially those seated in rigorous climates, some efforts are employed, and some previous precautions are taken, for securing subsistence. The career of regular industry is begun, and the laborious arm has made the first essays of its power. Still, however, the improvident and slothful genius of the savage state predominates. Even among those more improved tribes, labour is deemed ignominious and degrading. It is only to work of a certain kind that a man will deign to put his hand. The greater part is devolved entirely upon the women. One half of the community remains inactive, while the other is oppressed with the multitude and variety of its occupations. Thus their industry is partial, and the foresight which regulates it is no less limited. A remarkable instance of this occurs in the chief arrangement with respect to their manner of living. They depend for their subsistence, during one part of the year, on fishing; during another, on hunting; during a third, on the produce of their agriculture. Though experience has taught them to foresee the return of those various seasons, and to make some provision for the respective exigencies of each, they either want sagacity to proportion this provision to their consumption, or are so incapable of any command over their appetites, that, from their inconsiderate waste, they often feel the calamities of famine as severely as the rudest of the savage tribes. What they suffer one year does not augment their industry, or render them more provident to prevent similar distresses. This inconsiderate thoughtlessness about futurity, the effect of ignorance and the cause of sloth, accompanies and characterizes man in every stage of savage life; and, by a capricious singularity in his operations, he is then least solicitous about supplying his wants, when the means of satisfying them are most precarious, and procured with the greatest difficulty.

Voltaire

13

No matter how historians may differ in their interpretations of the Western Enlightenment, they are agreed that François-Marie Arouet, known to his contemporaries and to us as Voltaire, is the most representative writer of his age. The vast body of Voltaire's works, which includes virtually every known literary genre—some invented by Voltaire himself—demonstrates the values for which all the philosophes lived and to which they directed their work. To achieve such a distinction, especially when there are so many qualified rivals, one must live long and passionately, work tirelessly, court and correspond with the great.

Voltaire's long career can be said to begin with his education at Louis-le-Grand. Voltaire was sent to this Jesuit *collège* by his bourgeois parents so that he might make the right connections and, later as a lawyer, rise from bourgeois ranks into the nobility of the robe. The Jesuits, for their part, wanted their gifted pupil to use the excellent classical training they had given him for the same pious ends they cherished, but the pupil defied both parents and teachers: he would gain status, but as a poet; he would remain devoted to the classics, yet never use them as mere guides to the secrets of Christianity. Like his admirer, David Hume, he refused to subordinate learning to legalism or confine the study of ethics to accepted religious doctrine.

Voltaire's trip to England in 1726 is often considered the first step in the making of a philosopher out of a poet. But as important as his English experience was, we can detect his philosophy in his early poetry; in his lengthy *Henriade* (1728), his hatred of the religious persecution of the sixteenth century, and his love of tolerance; in the brief *Epitre à Uranie* (1722), his anti-Christian Deism; even his letters from Holland dated in 1722 anticipate his praise of cosmopolitan culture. Philosophy was already the heart of the philosophe's poetry.

England was necessary, however, for the writing of what has been called "the first bomb dropped on the Old Regime." Fully aware of the power and meaning of the *Philosophical Letters,* Voltaire tried to keep the work from general circulation; but by June 1734, the Parlement of Paris had ordered the offensive work burned and its author arrested. The authorities were right to fear this paean to English society. Voltaire stayed out of the Bastille only by staying out of Paris. While he extolled the religious tolerance and liberty of the English, he condemned the bigoted Church hierarchy and the suppression of elementary freedoms in his own country. When he praised the free pursuit of commerce and the egalitarian system of taxation he thought he found in England, he touched the *privilégiés* of France to the quick. He had, in fact, openly criticized the injustices which would ultimately bring France to revolution. Even in his preference for the British empirical philosophers over the French rationalists, he scored away at native prejudice.

The years Voltaire spent with his mistress, Madame du Châtelet, at her chateau of Cirey, were years of great intellectual production. Philosophe and bluestocking experimented in physics, popularized Newtonian metaphysics, and pioneered in Biblical criticism; and, what is most important for us, at Cirey Voltaire began the first modern works of French historiography. He had conceived of his *Age of Louis XIV* as early as 1732, and wrote and revised it throughout the decade at Cirey; he published it first in 1751, but then waited until 1768 to proclaim it a finished work. All that labor was not wasted: students today find his study of seventeenth-century French culture an indispensable mine of information carefully assimilated from hundreds of memoirs and state archives. Voltaire's aim in this history was to depict the spirit of an age, and he succeeded. The recording of the wars and the diplomatic intrigues of the time, while not at all ignored, serves merely as an introduction to a celebration of the complex administrative machinery of Louis' France, as well as of the art and literature which made this period the greatest in the history of French culture. Indeed, it is the invention of cultural history that makes *The Age of Louis XIV* the starting point of modern historiography.

In the *Essay on the Customs and the Spirit of Nations,* written expressly for Madame du Châtelet but first published in 1756, Voltaire replaces the Christian view of the past, which had been eloquently stated by Bossuet and popularized by Rollin, with the wholly secular view of universal history. In Voltaire's hands, history is no longer the story of a chosen people in a small corner of the globe; the Bible can no longer be the ultimate historical authority when entire civilizations predate all Biblical literature and extend far beyond the geography known to the Christians or the Jews. In his discussion of the Chaldeans, Indians, Hindus, and Chinese, Voltaire shows sacred history to be deficient in both time and space. From 1753 to 1768, the *Essay on Customs* was reprinted no fewer than sixteen times. However much historical knowledge has advanced beyond Voltaire, it was he who showed the literate public that profane history was the history of man, and the proper subject of historical study.

After Madame du Châtelet's death in 1749, Voltaire became the irascible courtier to Frederick the Great of Prussia. He soon learned that despots simply cannot be enlightened, and by the mid-1750's he settled in the neighborhood of Geneva. He found the Calvinistic republic, in its way, as much in need of reform as the monarchial government of France or the militaristic regime of Prussia. From his lovely country house at Les Délices, Voltaire launched a polemical campaign against the legal, political, and religious abuses of the old regime everywhere—a campaign which grew more intense as he grew older. In the 1760's, his final residence, Ferney, in France, became the capital of the Western Enlightenment.

The variety of Voltaire's literary productions during his last twenty years is unified by their purpose: work on behalf of humanity. In verse or in prose, in plays or in short stories, or in articles on history or philosophy, he railed at religious bigotry and at the legalized cruelty of the existing judicial systems. Two masterpieces of this period stand out as examples of the art which we can still delight in today, when some of the evils he sought to destroy have been eliminated. *Candide* (1759) has never been surpassed in all the enormous literature of social satire, and the *Philosophical Dictionary* (1764) endures as a biting critique of Christian theology. Neither work can be condensed: they deserve their reputations and their wide audiences for their wit as much as for their morality.

By the time of his death in 1778, Voltaire was famous for his efforts on behalf of persecuted Frenchmen, but he was refused a ceremonious burial in the Catholic Church. When his remains were moved to the Panthéon during the French Revolution, a new order sought to do justice to the poet who had risked his reputation and his security to help the victims of the old.

Selected Bibliography

The best introduction to Voltaire is Gustave Lanson's *Voltaire* (1906; translated by Robert A. Wagoner, 1966). In his introduction to this edition of Lanson's sensible biography, Peter Gay has shown that Lanson's work is dated only where documents, which were not available to him, have added to our knowledge of Voltaire's political thinking as well as of his love life. Gay has integrated this new information into his own *Voltaire's Politics* (1959); the result is a picture of Voltaire as a practical political thinker who adapted his program for reform for each political environment he experienced. Theodore Besterman, one of the most devoted and admiring contemporary students of Voltaire, has recently published a lengthy biography, *Voltaire* (1969).

J. H. Brumfitt has made Voltaire's career as a historian the object of a careful and scholarly study, but the conclusion to *Voltaire Historian* (1958) is not as appreciative or as felicitous as it should be; considering Voltaire's contributions to historiography, it seems unfair to dub him "an indifferent devotee of Clio the muse." Brumfitt continues his exegesis of Voltaire as a historian in "History and Propaganda in Voltaire" in *Studies on Voltaire and the Eighteenth Century*, XXIV (1963), 271–287.

THE AGE OF LOUIS XIV

INTRODUCTION

It is not the life of Louis XIV that we propose to write; we have a wider aim in view. We shall endeavour to depict for posterity, not the actions of a single man, but the spirit of men in the most enlightened age the world has even seen.

Every age has produced its heroes and statesmen; every nation has experienced revolutions; every history is the same to one who wishes merely to remember facts. But the thinking man, and what is still rarer, the man of taste, numbers only four ages in the history of the world; four happy ages when the arts were brought to perfection and which, marking an era of the greatness of the human mind, are an example to posterity.

The first of these ages, to which true glory belongs, is that of Philip and Alexander, or rather of Pericles, Demosthenes, Aristotle, Plato, Apelles, Phidias, Praxiteles; and this honour was confined within the limits of Greece, the rest of the known world being in a barbarous state.

The second age is that of Caesar and Augustus, distinguished moreover by the names of Lucretius, Cicero, Livy, Virgil, Horace, Ovid, Varro and Vitruvius.

The third is that which followed the taking of Constantinople by Mahomet II. The reader may remember that the spectacle was then witnessed of a family of mere citizens in Italy accomplishing what should have been undertaken by the kings of Europe. The scholars whom the Turks had driven from Greece were summoned by the Medici to Florence; it was the hour of Italy's glory. The fine arts had already taken on new life there; and the Italians honoured them with the name of virtue as the early Greeks had characterised them with the name of wisdom. Everything conduced to perfection. The arts, for ever transplanted from Greece to Italy, fell on favourable ground, where they flourished immediately. France, England, Germany and Spain, in their turn, desired the

The Age of Louis XIV translated by Martyn P. Pollack, Introduction by Ernest Rhys, New York: E. P. Dutton & Co., Inc. 1961, pp. 3–19, 320–381. Preface Copyright © 1961. Reprinted by permission.

possession of these fruits; but either they never reached these countries or they degenerated too quickly.

Francis I encouraged scholars who were scholars and nothing else: he had architects, but neither a Michael Angelo nor a Palladio; it was in vain that he endeavoured to found Schools of Painting, for the Italian painters whom he employed made no French disciples. A few epigrams and fables made up the whole of our poetry. Rabelais was the only prose writer in fashion in the age of Henry II.

In a word, the Italians alone possessed everything, if one except music, which had not yet been brought to perfection, and experimental philosophy, equally unknown everywhere, and which Galileo at length brought to men's knowledge.

The fourth age is that which we call the age of Louis XIV; and it is perhaps of the four the one which most nearly approaches perfection. Enriched with the discoveries of the other three it accomplished in certain departments more than the three together. All the arts, it is true, did not progress further than they did under the Medici, under Augustus or under Alexander; but human reason in general was brought to perfection.

Rational philosophy only came to light in this period; and it is true to say that from the last years of Cardinal Richelieu to those which followed the death of Louis XIV, a general revolution took place in our arts, minds and customs, as in our government, which will serve as an eternal token of the true glory of our country. This beneficent influence was not merely confined to France; it passed over into England, and inspired a profitable rivalry in that intellectual and fearless nation; it imported good taste into Germany, and the sciences into Russia; it even revived Italy, who had begun to languish, and Europe has owed both her manners and the social spirit to the court of Louis XIV.

It must not be assumed that these four ages were exempt from misfortunes and crimes. The attainment of perfection in those arts practised by peaceful citizens does not prevent princes from being ambitious, the people from being mutinous, nor priests and monks from becoming sometimes turbulent and crafty. All ages resemble one another in respect of the criminal folly of mankind, but I only know of these four ages so distinguished by great attainments.

Prior to the age which I call that of Louis XIV, and which began almost with the founding of the Académie française, the Italians looked upon all those north of the Alps as barbarians; it must be confessed that to a certain extent the French deserved the insult. Their fathers joined the romantic courtesy of the Moors to Gothic coarseness. They practised scarcely any of the fine arts, which proves that the useful arts were neglected; for when one has perfected the necessary things, one soon discovers the beautiful and agreeable; and it is not to be wondered that painting, sculpture, poetry, oratory and philosophy were almost unknown to a nation which, while possessing ports on the Atlantic Ocean and the Mediterranean, yet had no fleet, and which, though inordinately fond of luxury, had but a few coarse manufactures.

The Jews, the Genoese, the Venetians, the Portuguese, the Flemish, the Dutch, the English, in turn carried on the trade of France, who was ignorant of its first principles. When Louis XIII ascended the throne he did not possess a ship; Paris did not contain four hundred thousand inhabitants, and could not boast of four fine buildings; the other towns of the kingdom resembled those market towns one sees south of the Loire. The whole of the nobility, scattered over the country in their moat-surrounded castles, oppressed the people, who were engaged in tilling the land. The great highways were well-nigh impassable; the towns were without police, the state without money, and the government nearly always without credit among foreign nations. The fact must not be concealed that after the decadence of Charlemagne's descendants France had continued more or less in this state of weakness simply because she had hardly ever enjoyed good government.

If a state is to be powerful, either the people must enjoy a liberty based on its laws, or the sovereign power must be affirmed without contradiction. In France, the people were enslaved until the time of Philip Augustus; the nobles were tyrants until the time of Louis XI, and the kings, continually engaged in upholding their authority over that of their vassals, had neither the time to think of the welfare of their subjects nor the power to make them happy.

Louis XI did a great deal for the royal power, but nothing for the happiness and glory of the nation. Francis I inaugurated commerce, navigation, letters and the arts; but he did not succeed in making them take root in France, and they all perished with him. Henri-Quatre was about to redeem France from the calamities and barbarity into which she had been plunged by twenty years of dissension, when he was assassinated in his capital, in the midst of the people to whom he was on the point of bringing prosperity. Cardinal Richelieu, occupied with the humbling of the House of Austria, Calvinism and the nobles, did not possess a sufficiently secure position to reform the nation; but at least he inaugurated the auspicious work.

Thus for nine hundred years the genius of France had almost continually been cramped under a gothic government, in the midst of partitions and civil wars, having neither laws nor fixed customs, and changing every two centuries a language ever uncouth; her nobles undisciplined and acquainted solely with war and idleness; her clergy living in disorder and ignorance; and her people without trade, sunk in their misery.

The French also had no share in the great discoveries and wonderful inventions of other nations; printing, gunpowder, glassmaking, telescopes, the proportional compass, pneumatic machines, the true system of the universe—in such things they had no concern; they were engaged in tournaments while the Portuguese and Spaniards discovered and conquered new worlds to the east and west. Charles V was already lavishing on Europe the treasures of Mexico before a few subjects of Francis I discovered the uncultivated regions of Canada; but even from the slight accomplishments of the French at the beginning of the sixteenth century, one could see what they are capable of when they are led.

We propose to show what they became under Louis XIV.

Do not let the reader expect here, more than in the description of earlier centuries, minute details of wars, of attacks on towns taken and retaken by force of arms, surrendered and given back by treaties. A thousand events interesting to contemporaries are lost to the eyes of posterity and disappear, leaving only to view great happenings that have fixed the destiny of empires. Every event that occurs is not worth recording. In this history we shall confine ourselves to that which deserves the attention of all time, which paints the spirit and the customs of men, which may serve for instruction and to counsel the love of virtue, of the arts and of the fatherland.

The state of France and the other European States before the birth of Louis XIV has already been described:[1] we shall here relate the great political and military events of his reign. The internal government of the kingdom, the most important matter for the people at large, will be treated separately. To the private life of Louis XIV, to the peculiarities of his court and of his reign, a large part will be devoted. Other chapters will deal with the arts, the sciences, and the progress of the human mind in this age. Finally, we shall speak of the Church, which has been joined to the government for so long a period, sometimes disturbing it, at other times invigorating it, and which, established for the teaching of morality, often surrenders herself to politics and the passions of mankind.

EUROPEAN STATES BEFORE LOUIS XIV

Already for a long time one could regard Christian Europe (except Russia) as a sort of great republic divided into several states, some monarchical, others of a mixed character; the former aristocratic, the latter popular, but all in harmony with each other, all having the same substratum of religion, although divided into various sects; all possessing the

---

[1] In Voltaire's *Essay on Customs* (*Essai sur les Mœurs*).

same principles of public and political law, unknown in other parts of the world. In obedience to these principles the European nations do not make their prisoners slaves, they respect their enemies' ambassadors, they agree as to the pre-eminence and rights of certain princes, such as the Emperor, kings and other lesser potentates, and, above all, they are at one on the wise policy of maintaining among themselves so far as possible an equal balance of power, ceaselessly carrying on negotiations, even in wartime, and sending each to the other ambassadors or less honourable spies, who can acquaint every court with the designs of any one of them, give in a moment the alarm to Europe, and defend the weakest from invasions which the strongest is always ready to attempt.

Since the time of Charles V the balance inclined to the side of the House of Austria. Towards the year 1630 this powerful House was mistress of Spain, Portugal, and the treasures of America; the Netherlands, the Milanese States, the Kingdom of Naples, Bohemia, Hungary, even Germany (one may say) had become her patrimony; and since so many states had become united under a single head of this House, it is credible that all Europe would at last have been subdued.

Germany

The German Empire is France's most powerful neighbour: it has a greater expanse, is not so rich in bullion perhaps, but more prolific in vigorous men inured to hard labour. The German nation is ruled in almost the same manner as France under the first kings of the House of Capet, who were the chiefs often ill-obeyed of a few great vassals and a large number of petty ones. Today, sixty free towns, known as imperial towns, nearly as many secular sovereigns, nearly forty ecclesiastical princes, either abbots or bishops, nine electors, among whom today one can count four kings, and finally the Emperor, the chief of these potentates, form this great Germanic body, which, thanks to German stolidity, has survived until the present day, with almost as much order as there was formerly confusion in the French government.

Each member of the Empire has his rights, his privileges, his duties; and the hardly acquired knowledge of so many laws, often disputed, has given rise to what is known in Germany as *the Study of Public Law,* for which the German nation is famed.

By himself the Emperor would be no more powerful and rich than a Venetian doge, for Germany, being divided into towns and principalities, allows the head of so many states only a highly-honoured pre-eminence, without possessions, without money, and consequently without power.

He does not possess a single village in virtue of being Emperor. Nevertheless, this dignity, often as empty as it was supreme, had become so powerful in the hands of the Austrians, that it was often feared that they would transform what was a republic of princes into an absolute monarchy.

Two parties at that time divided Christian Europe, as they still do to-day, and especially Germany.

The first is that of the Catholics, more or less subjected to the Pope; the second is that of the enemies of the spiritual and temporal rule of the Pope and the Catholic prelates. The adherents of this party are called by the general name of Protestants, although they are made up of Lutherans, Calvinists, and others, who hate one another almost as much as they hate Rome. In Germany, Saxony, part of Brandenburg, the Palatinate, part of Bohemia, Hungary, the State of the House of Brunswick, Würtemberg and Hesse, observe the Lutheran religion, which is known as *evangelistic*. All the imperial free towns have embraced this sect, which seemed more suitable than the Catholic religion to people who were jealous of their liberty.

The Calvinists, scattered among the strongest party, the Lutherans, form only a moderate party; the Catholics compose the rest of the Empire and with the House of Austria as their head were undoubtedly the most powerful.

Not only Germany, but all the Christian States were still bleeding from the wounds they had received in numerous religious wars, a madness peculiar to Christians and unknown to pagans, the unfortunate result of a dogmatic spirit so long introduced into all classes of society. Few indeed are the points of difference which have resulted in civil war; and foreign nations (perhaps our own descendants) will find it hard to understand how our fathers were at one another's throats for so many years whilst at the same time preaching forbearance.

I have in a former work pointed out how Ferdinand was about to transform the German aristocracy into an absolute monarchy, and how he was on the point of being dethroned by Gustavus Adolphus. His son Ferdinand III who inherited his policy, and like him directed wars from the shelter of his study, reigned during the minority of Louis XIV.

Germany was far from being at that time so flourishing as she afterwards became; luxury was a thing unknown, and the comforts of life were very rare even among the greatest nobles. It was not until 1686 that they were introduced by French refugees who set up their manufactures there. This fertile and populous country lacked trade and money: the seriousness of their customs and the peculiar sluggishness of the Germans debarred them from those pleasures and agreeable arts which Italian acuteness had cultivated for so many years, and which French industry from that time began to bring to perfection. The Germans, rich at home, were poor abroad; and this poverty, added to the difficulty of mobilising so many different peoples under the same standard at such short notice, rendered it almost impossible, as to-day, for them to carry on war for any length of time against their neighbours. Hence the French have nearly always made war on imperial soil against the Emperors. The difference of government and of national genius seems to render the French more adapted for attack and the Germans for defence.

Spain

Spain, ruled by the elder branch of the House of Austria, had, after the death of Charles V, inspired more terror than the German nation. The Kings of Spain were immeasurably more powerful and rich. The mines of Mexico and Potosi apparently supplied whatever was necessary to buy the freedom of Europe. This generation saw the scheme of a monarchy, or rather of a universal superiority over Christian Europe, begun by Charles V, and continued by Philip II.

The greatness of Spain under Philip III was nothing more than that of a vast body without substance, having more fame than power.

Philip IV, heir to his father's weakness, lost Portugal by carelessness, Rousillon through the weakness of his forces, and Catalonia by the abuse of despotism. Such kings could not for long be successful in their wars against France. If they gained certain advantages from the divisions and mistakes of their enemies, they lost them by their own incapacity. More-over, they governed a people whose privileges allowed them to be dis-loyal; the Castilians had the right of not fighting outside their own country; the Aragonese ceaselessly contested their liberty against the Royal Council, and the Catalonians, who regarded their kings as their enemies, would not suffer them even to raise troops in their provinces.

Nevertheless, united with the empire, Spain was a formidable factor in the balance of Europe.

Portugal

Portugal at this time again became a separate kingdom; John, Duke of Braganza, a prince commonly thought weak, had snatched this province from a king weaker than himself. The Portuguese cultivated commerce out of necessity as Spain neglected it out of pride; in 1641 they leagued themselves with France and Holland against Spain. This revolution in Portugal was worth more to France than the winning of the most decisive victories. The French ministry, which had contributed nothing to the event, reaped without effort the greatest advantage that one can have over an enemy, that of seeing her attacked by an irreconcilable power.

Portugal, shaking off the yoke of Spain, expanding her trade and increasing her power, recalls to mind the case of Holland, who enjoyed the same advantages in quite a different way.

The United Provinces

This small state, consisting of seven united provinces, a country abounding in pasture land but barren of grain, unhealthy, and almost swamped by the sea, had presented for nearly fifty years an almost unique example in the world of what love of liberty and indefatigable labour can accomplish. These far from wealthy people, numerically small, far less disciplined in war than the poorest Spanish troops, and who as yet counted for nothing in Europe, withstood the whole forces of their master and tyrant Philip II, evaded the schemes of various princes who wished to aid them in order to subdue them, and laid the foundations of a power that we have witnessed counterbalance the might of Spain herself. Despair, engendered by tyranny, first armed them; liberty exalted their courage and the princes of the House of Orange made them into excellent soldiers. Scarcely had they conquered their masters than they established a form of government which so far as it is possible maintains equality, the most natural right of men.

This state of so peculiar a nature was from its commencement closely allied with France: interest united them, they had the same enemies, and the great Henri-Quatre and Louis XIII had been the allies and protectors of Holland.

England

England, much more powerful, assumed the supremacy of the seas and claimed to set a balance among the states of Europe; but Charles I, who had reigned since 1625, far from being able to support the weight of this balance already felt the sceptre slipping from his grasp; he had wished to make his power independent of the laws of England and to change the religion of Scotland. Too obstinate to abandon his designs and too weak to execute them, a good husband, a good master, a good father, an honest man, but an ill-advised monarch, he became involved in a civil war, which, as we have shown elsewhere, at length caused him to lose his throne and his life on the scaffold in the course of an almost unprecedented revolution.

The civil war, begun during the minority of Louis XIV, prevented England for a time from interesting herself in the concerns of her neighbours; she lost alike her prosperity and her reputation; her trade was suspended; and other nations believed her to be buried beneath her own ruins, until suddenly she became more formidable than ever under the sway of Cromwell, who ruled her, the Bible in one hand and a sword in the other, wearing the mask of religion on his face, and disguising in his government the crimes of a usurper under the qualities of a great king.

Rome

This balance, which England had long flattered herself she had preserved among kings by her power, the court of Rome endeavoured to maintain by her policy. Italy was divided as to-day into several sovereignties; that which the Pope possesses is large enough to make him respected as a prince and too small to make him formidable. The nature of his government does not tend to populate the country, which has indeed little money and trade; his spiritual authority, always somewhat involved with the temporal, is destroyed and abhorred by one-half of Christendom; and if by the other half he is regarded as a father, he has children who sometimes oppose him with both reason and success. The rule of France has been to regard him as a sacred but overreaching person, whose feet one must kiss, but whose hands one must sometimes bind. In all Catholic countries one may still see traces of the steps taken by the court of Rome towards a universal monarchy. All princes of the Catholic religion on their accession send to the Pope embassies of obedience, as they are called. Every crowned head has a cardinal in Rome who takes the name of protector. All bishoprics receive their bulls from the Pope, and in these bulls he addresses them as if he conferred such dignities by his power alone. All Italian, Spanish and Flemish bishops are pronounced bishops by divine permission and *that of the Holy See.* About the year 1682, many French prelates rejected this formula, unknown to earlier centuries; and in our time, in 1754, we have seen a bishop (Stuart Fitz-James, Bishop of Soissons) brave enough to omit it in a decree which deserves to be handed down to posterity; a decree, or rather a unique instruction, wherein it is expressly stated what no pontiff had yet dared to say, that all men, even unbelievers, are our brothers.

In fine, the Pope has preserved certain prerogatives in all Catholic countries which he certainly would not now obtain had time not previously given them to him. There is no kingdom in which there are not many benefices under his nomination, and as tribute he receives the first-year revenues of the consistorial benefices.

The monks, whose superiors are resident at Rome, are still the immediate subjects of the Pope, and are scattered throughout every state. Custom, which is all-powerful, and which is the cause of the world being ruled by abuses as well as by laws, has sometimes prevented princes from entirely removing danger, especially when it was related to matters considered as sacred. To take an oath to anyone but one's sovereign is a crime of high treason in the layman; it is an act of religion in the monk. The difficulty of knowing to what extent such a foreign sovereignty should be obeyed, the ease of allowing oneself to be won over, the pleasure of throwing off a natural yoke in order to accept one chosen by oneself, the spirit of disorder, the evil of the times, have only too often prompted whole religious orders to serve Rome against their own country.

The enlightened spirit that has prevailed in France for the last century and which has been diffused among nearly all classes has been the best remedy for this evil. Good books on this matter are of real service to kings and peoples, and one of the great changes thus brought about in our customs under Louis XIV is the conviction which the monks are beginning to have, that they are subjects of the king before being servants of the Pope.

Jurisdiction, that essential mark of sovereignty, still rests with the Roman pontiff. In spite of all the liberties of the Gallic Church, even France permits a final right of appeal to the Pope in certain ecclesiastical cases.

If one wishes to annul a marriage, to marry one's cousin or one's niece, to be released from one's vows, it is still to Rome and not to one's bishop that application must be made; to Rome where favours are bought and individuals from every country obtain dispensations at varying prices.

The right to confer these advantages, regarded by many people as the result of the most intolerable abuses, and by others as the relics of the most sacred rights, is always cunningly maintained. Rome looks after her credit with as much policy as the Roman republic employed in conquering half the known world.

Never did a court know better how to conduct itself in conformity with men and with the times. The popes are nearly always Italians grown old in the conduct of affairs, free from any blinding passions; their council is formed of cardinals of similar characters, all emboldened with the same spirit. From this council mandates are issued that extend to China and America; in this respect it embraces the whole world, and it could sometimes be said of it what a foreigner once said of the Roman senate: "I have seen a Council of Kings." The majority of our writers have justifiably cried out against the ambition of this court, but I do not know of one of them who has done sufficient justice to its prudence. I know of no nation that could have maintained so long in Europe so many prerogatives that were continually being challenged; any other court would have lost them, either by pride or weakness, by over-eagerness or indolence, but Rome, rarely failing to employ at the appropriate moment now firmness and now tact, has kept everything that was humanly possible for her to keep. We see her raging under the hand of Charles V, violent towards Henri III of France, by turns the enemy and friend of Henri IV, cunning with Louis XIII, openly opposed to Louis XIV at the time when he was to be feared, and often the secret enemy of the Emperors whom she distrusted more than the Turkish Sultans.

Rome retains to-day a few rights, many pretensions, a statecraft and patience, which is all that is left of her ancient power which six centuries ago attempted to bring the empire, nay all Europe, under the tiara.

Naples is an extant example of that right which the popes once seized with such ingenuity and magnificence, that of creating and bestowing kingdoms; but the King of Spain, the possessor of that state, left to the Roman court only the honour and the danger of having too powerful a vassal.

For the rest, the papal state was enjoying a prosperous peace, which had only been broken by the little war of which I have spoken elsewhere between the Cardinals Barberini, the nephews of Pope Urban VIII, and the Duke of Parma.

The Rest of Italy

The other provinces of Italy were occupied with various interests. Venice feared the Turks and the emperor; she was hard put to defend her mainland states from the claims of Germany and from the invasion of the Sultan. She was no longer that Venice once the mistress of the world's trade, who a hundred and fifty years before had aroused the envy of so many kings. The wisdom of her government remained, but the loss of her enormous trade deprived her of nearly all her power, and the city of Venice thus remained by reason of her situation invincible, but by reason of her decadence unable to make fresh conquests.

The State of Florence was enjoying peace and prosperity under the rule of the Medici; literature, the arts, and polite manners, which the Medici had created, still flourished. Tuscany, at that time, was to Italy what Athens had been to Greece.

Savoy, torn by civil war and overrun by French and Spanish troops, was at length completely united on the side of France, and contributed towards the weakening of the Austrian power in Italy.

The Swiss preserved as they do to-day their liberty without attempting to oppress others. They hired their forces to neighbours richer than themselves; they were poor, they were unacquainted with the sciences and arts which luxury had created, but they were prudent and happy.

The Northern States

The northern European states, Poland, Sweden, Denmark and Russia, were like the other powers continually suspicious of one another or openly at war. One might witness in Poland then as to-day the customs and government of the Goths and Franks—an elective king, nobles sharing his power, an enslaved people, weak infantry and a cavalry recruited from the nobles, no fortified towns and practically no trade. These people were attacked now by the Swedes or Russians, now by the Turks. The Swedes, constitutionally a still freer nation, admitting even peasants to the states-general, but at that time more under the subjection of their kings than Poland, were victorious nearly everywhere; Denmark, at one time formidable to Sweden, was now no longer so to any state; and her real greatness only commenced under her two kings, Frederick III and Frederick IV.

Russia was still in a state of barbarism.

The Turks

The Turks were no longer what they had been under the Selims, the Mahomets and the Solymans; effeminacy corrupted the seraglio, but did not banish cruelty. The Sultans were at one and the same time the most despotic of rulers in their seraglio and the least assured of their thrones and their lives. Osman and Ibrahim met their death by strangulation. Mustapha was twice deposed. Shaken by these shocks, the Turkish Empire was, moreover, attacked by the Persians; but, when the Persians allowed her breathing space and palace revolutions were at an end, that empire became formidable to Christendom; for, from the mouth of the Dnieper as far as the Venetian States, Russia, Hungary, Greece and the islands of the Mediterranean became in turn the prey of the Turkish forces; and from the year 1644 onwards they steadily prosecuted a war in Candia which was disastrous to the Christians. Such were the state of affairs, the forces and the aims of the chief European nations at the time of the death of Louis XIII, King of France.

The Situation in France

France, allied to Sweden, Holland, Savoy and Portugal, and possessing the goodwill of other neutral countries, was waging a war against the Empire and Spain, ruinous to both sides and disastrous to the House of Austria. It resembled many other wars that have been waged for centuries by Christian princes, in which millions of men are sacrificed and provinces laid waste in order finally to obtain a few small frontier towns whose possession is rarely worth the cost of conquest.

Louis XIII's generals had taken Roussillon. The Catalonians were about to go over to the side of France, the protectress of the liberty for which they fought against their own kings; but these triumphs did not prevent our enemies from taking Corbie in 1636 and advancing as far as Pontoise. Half the inhabitants of Paris had fled from fear, and Cardinal Richelieu, deep in his vast schemes for the humbling of the Austrian power, had been reduced to taxing the gates of Paris for each one to provide a lackey to go to the war and drive the enemy back from the gates of the capital. The French had thus done much damage to the Spaniards and Germans, and had suffered no less themselves.

The Forces of France After the Death of Louis XIII and the Manners of the Time

The wars had produced famous generals such as Gustavus Adolphus, Wallenstein, the Duke of Weimar, Piccolomini, Jean de Vert, the Marshal of Guébriant, the Princes of Orange and the Count d'Harcourt. Certain ministers of state had been no less conspicuous. The chancellor Oxenstiern, the Count-Duke of Olivares, and above all, Cardinal Richelieu, had attracted the attention of Europe. No century has lacked famous statesmen and warriors, for politics and warfare seem unhappily to be the two most natural professions to man, and he must always be either bargaining or fighting. The most fortunate is considered the greatest, and public opinion often ascribes to merit the happy chances of fortune.

War was not then waged as we have seen it waged in the time of Louis XIV: armies were not so numerous; after the siege of Metz, for instance, by Charles V, no general found himself at the head of fifty thousand men; towns were besieged and defended with fewer cannon than are used to-day, and the art of fortification was still in its infancy. Pikes and arquebuses were used, and the sword which has become useless in our time was employed a great deal. The old international rule of declaring war by a herald was still in use. Louis XIII was the last to observe this custom, when in 1635 he sent a herald-at-arms to Brussels to declare war upon Spain.

It is common knowledge that nothing was more usual at that time than to see priests in command of armies; the Cardinal Infant of Spain, the Cardinal of Savoy, Richelieu, La Valette, Sourdis, Archbishop of Bordeaux, Cardinal Theodore Trivulzio, commandant of the Spanish cavalry, had all donned the cuirass and fought in person. A Bishop of Mende had been many times an army commissary. The popes sometimes threatened these warrior priests with excommunication. Pope Urban VIII, when vexed with France, told Cardinal de la Valette that he would deprive him of his cardinal's hat if he did not lay down his arms; but once reconciled to France he overwhelmed him with benedictions.

Ambassadors, no less ministers of peace than ecclesiastics, made no difficulty about serving in the armies of allied powers, in whose service they were employed. Charnace, sent from France into Holland, commanded a regiment there in 1637, and later even the ambassador, d'Estrades, became a colonel in their service.

France had only about 80,000 foot-soldiers available in all. The navy, neglected for centuries, was restored a little by Cardinal Richelieu, but ruined again by Mazarin. Louis XIII had only about 45,000,000 livres of ordinary revenue; but money was at 26 livres to the mark; these 45,-000,000 would amount to about 85,000,000 to-day, when the arbitrary value of the silver mark has risen to as much as 49½ livres, and that of pure silver to 54 livres 17 sous; a value that public interest and justice alike demand should never be changed.

Commerce, to-day spread widely abroad, was then in very few hands. The policing of the kingdom was wholly neglected, a sure proof of a far from prosperous administration. Cardinal Richelieu, mindful of his own greatness, which was itself bound up with that of the state, had begun to make France formidable abroad, but had not yet been able to bring prosperity to her at home. The great highways were neither kept in repair nor policed, and they were infested with brigands; the streets of Paris, narrow, badly paved and covered with filth, were overrun with thieves. The parliamentary registers show that the city watch was at that time reduced to forty-five badly paid men, who, to crown all, totally neglected their work.

Since the death of Francis II France had been continually torn by civil wars or factions. The yoke had never been borne easily and voluntarily. The nobles had been bred up in the midst of conspiracies; such was indeed the art of the court, as since it has been that of pleasing the sovereign.

This spirit of discord and faction spread from the court to the smaller towns, and pervaded every community in the kingdom; everything was disputed, because there was nothing fixed, and even in the parishes of Paris the people were continually coming to blows; processions fought one another for the honour of their respective banners. More than once the canons of Notre-Dame were seen at grips with their brethren of the Sainte-Chapelle; members of parliament and of the chambers of accounts fought each other for pride of place in Notre-Dame on the day that Louis XIII placed his kingdom under the protection of the Virgin Mary.

Practically every commune in the kingdom was armed, practically every person was inspired by the passion for duelling. This gothic barbarism, sanctioned once by kings themselves, and become a part of the national character, contributed to the depopulation of the country as much as civil or foreign wars. It is not too much to say that in the course of twenty years, ten of which had been troubled by war, more French gentlemen were killed at the hands of their own countrymen than at the hands of their enemies.

We shall say nothing here with regard to the cultivation of the arts and sciences; that part of the history of our customs will be found in its proper place. We shall merely remark that the French nation was steeped in ignorance, not excepting those who held that they were not of the people.

People consulted astrologers, and, what is more, believed them. Every memoir of that period, from President de Thou's History onward, is prodigal of prophecies. The serious and austere Duke de Sully solemnly describes those which were made to Henri IV. This credulity, the most infallible sign of ignorance, was so universal that care was taken to have an astrologer hidden near the bedchamber of Anne of Austria at the birth of Louis XIV.

What is hardly credible, but which is nevertheless vouched for by the abbé, Vittorio Siri, a very well-informed contemporary writer, is that Louis XIII was surnamed the *Just* from his infancy, because he was born under the sign of Libra.

The same ignorance which popularised the absurd phantom of judicial astrology gave credit to the belief in possession by the devil and sorcery; it was made a point of religion, and there was scarcely a priest who did not exorcise devils. The courts of justice, presided over by magistrates who ought to have been more enlightened than the vulgar herd, were occupied in judging sorcerers. The memory of Cardinal Richelieu will always be stained by the death of the celebrated curé of Loudun, Urbain Grandier, who was condemned to the stake as a magician, by a decree of the council. One is shocked that the minister and judges should have had the ignorance to believe in the devils of Loudun, or the barbarity to have condemned an innocent man to the flames. Posterity will always remember with amazement that the Maréchale d'Ancre was burnt as a sorceress in the Place de la Grève.

One may still see in a copy of some registers of *Le Châtelet* the record of a trial begun in 1610, concerning a horse who had been laboriously trained by his master to perform very much like a modern circus animal; it was proposed to burn both master and horse.

We have said enough here to show in a general way the customs and the spirit of the age preceding that of Louis XIV.

This lack of enlightenment in all classes of society favoured superstitious practices even in the most upright which brought disgrace upon religion. The Calvinists, confusing the rational Catholic religion with the abuses emanating from it, became only the more determined in their hatred of our church.

As was typical of all the reformers, they opposed to our popular superstitions, often intimately allied to debauchery, a fierce austerity and harsh manners; thus the partisan spirit tore and debased France; and the social spirit that to-day makes this nation so renowned and so attractice was entirely unknown. There were no houses where men of ability might gather together for the purpose of communicating knowledge, no academies, no regular theatres. In short, customs, laws, the arts, society, religion, peace and war, were as nothing to what they afterwards became in the century known as the *Age of Louis XIV.* . . .

INTERNAL GOVERNMENT JUSTICE, TRADE, POLICE, LAWS, MILITARY DISCIPLINE, NAVAL AFFAIRS, ETC.

One owes this much justice to public men who have benefited their own age, to consider the point from which they started in order to perceive more clearly the changes they wrought in their country. Posterity owes them eternal gratitude for the examples they gave, even though such examples have been surpassed. Such lawful glory is their only reward. It is certain that the love of such glory inspired Louis XIV, at the time of his taking the government into his own hands, in his desire to improve his kingdom, beautify his court and perfect the arts.

Not only did he impose upon himself the duty of regularly transacting affairs with each of his ministers, but any well-known man could obtain a private audience with him and any citizen was free to present petitions and projects to him. The petitions were first received by a master of requests who wrote his recommendations in the margin; and they were then despatched to the ministerial offices. Projects were examined in council if they were thought worthy of such attention, and their authors were on more than one occasion admitted to discuss their proposals with the ministers in the king's presence. There was thus a channel between the throne and the nation which existed notwithstanding the absolute power of the monarch.

Louis XIV trained and inured himself to work; work which was the more arduous to him as he was new to it and the allurement of pleasures might easily distract him. He wrote the first despatches to his ambassadors. The more important letters were often revised by his own hand, and he made it a habit to read every document which bore his name.

Colbert had scarcely restored the finances of the country after the fall of Fouquet, when the king rescinded all the taxes owing for the years 1647 to 1658—in particular, three millions of poll-taxes. Certain burdensome duties were removed by payment of five hundred thousand crowns a year. The Abbé de Choisi seemed thus much misinformed or very prejudiced when he said that the receipts had not decreased. They were undoubtedly decreased by such abatements and increased as a result of better methods of collection.

It was due to the efforts of the first president of Bellièvre, assisted by the benefactions of the Duchess d'Aiguillon and a few citizens, that the general hopsital was founded. The king enlarged it and had others built in all the principal towns of the kingdom.

The great highways hitherto impassable were no longer neglected and became gradually what they are to-day under Louis XV—the admiration of foreigners. Leaving Paris in any direction one may now travel from fifty to sixty miles to various places near at hand on well-paved roads bordered by trees. The roads constructed by the ancient Romans were more lasting, but not so wide and beautiful.

Colbert's genius was chiefly directed to commerce, which was as yet undeveloped and whose fundamental principles were as yet unknown. The English, and to a still greater extent the Dutch, carried nearly all the trade of France in their ships. The Dutch especially loaded up in our ports with French produce and distributed it throughout Europe. In 1662 the king took steps to exempt his subjects from a tax known as *freight duty,* which was payable by all foreign ships; and allowed the French every facility for transporting their own goods themselves at lower charges. It was then that maritime trade sprang up. The council of commerce which is still in existence was established, and the king presided over it every fortnight. Dunkirk and Marseilles were declared free ports, a privilege which soon attracted the trade of the Levant to Marseilles and that of the North to Dunkirk.

A West India company was formed in 1664 and an East India company was established in the same year. Previous to this the luxury of France had been entirely dependent upon the industry of Holland. The supporters of the old system of economy, timid, ignorant and narrow-minded, vainly declaimed against a system of commerce by which money, which is imperishable, was continually being exchanged for perishable goods. They did not reflect that these wares from the Indies, which had become indispensable, would have been much dearer if bought from a foreign country. It is true that more money is sent to the East Indies than is received from them, and that Europe is thus impoverished. But the bullion itself comes from Peru and Mexico, being the price paid for our wares at Cadiz, and more of this money remains in France than is absorbed by the East Indies.

The king gave more than six millions of present-day money to the company; and urged wealthy people to interest themselves in it. The queens, princes and all the court provided two millions in the currency of the time, and the higher courts furnished twelve hundred thousand livres; financiers, two millions; the company of merchants, six hundred and fifty thousand livres. Thus the whole nation supported their ruler.

This company exists to the present day; for although the Dutch took Pondicherry in 1694 with the result that trade with the Indies declined from that time, it received a fresh impetus under the regency of the Duke of Orleans. Pondicherry then became the rival of Batavia, and this Indian company, founded under extremely adverse conditions by the great Colbert, re-established in our time by remarkable efforts, was for some years one of the principal resources of the kingdom. In 1669 the king also formed a Northern company; he contributed to its funds as to the Indian company. It was then clearly shown that there is nothing derogatory in trade, since the most influential houses took an interest in such establishments, following the example of their monarch.

The West India company was no less encouraged than the others, the king supplying a tenth part of the total funds.

He gave thirty francs for every ton exported and forty for every ton imported. All who built ships in national ports received five livres for every ton of carrying capacity.

One cannot be too much astonished that the Abbé de Choisi should have condemned these institutions in his *Memoirs*, which must not be relied upon. We perceive to-day all that Colbert in his capacity as minister did for the good of the nation, but it was not perceived at the time; he worked for ungrateful people. Paris resented his interference in suppressing certain revenues of the town hall acquired very cheaply since 1656, and the fall in the value of bank-notes, which had been lavishly poured out under the preceding ministry, much more than it appreciated what he had done for the common good. There were more merchants than good citizens. Few persons had any views on the public welfare. It is well known how private interests blind the eyes and cramp the mind; I am speaking not only of the interests of a merchant, but those of a company, those of a town. The rude answer given by a merchant, named Haxon, when consulted by Colbert, was still widely quoted in my youth: "You found the carriage overturned on one side and you have upset it on the other"; and this anecdote is to be found in Moreri. It was left for the spirit of philosophy, introduced at a very late period into France, to amend the prejudices of the people, before complete justice could be at length accorded to the memory of that great man. He had the same exactitude as the Duke de Sulli and possessed much wider views. The one could merely organise, the other could build up great institutions. After the Peace of Vervins, the only difficulty Sulli had to overcome was the maintenance of a rigid and strict economy; Colbert was obliged to provide at a moment vast resources for the wars of 1667 and 1672. Henri IV assisted Sulli with his economy reforms, while the extravagance of Louis XIV continually thwarted Colbert's efforts.

Nevertheless, there is little that was not either re-established or created in his time. In 1665, visible proof of a liberal circulation was forthcoming when the interest on the loans of the king and private individuals was reduced to five per cent. He wanted to enrich France and increase her population. People in the country were encouraged to marry by exempting those who had done so by the age of twenty from paying poll-tax for a period of five years; and every head of a family of ten children was exempt for the remainder of his life, since he gave more to the state by the product of his children's work than he would have done by paying taxes. Such a law should never have been repealed.

Each year of this ministry, from 1663 to 1672, was marked by the establishment of some manufacture. Fine stuffs, which had hitherto come from England and Holland, were now manufactured at Abbeville. The king advanced to the manufacturer two thousand livres for each loom at work, in addition to considerable grants. In the year 1669 there were 44,200 wool looms at work in the kingdom. Fine silk manufactures produced more than fifty millions in the currency of the time, and not only were the profits much greater than the outlay on the necessary silk, but the growing of mulberry trées enabled the manufacturers to dispense with foreign silk for the weaving of their material.

In 1666 glass began to be made as fine as that of Venice, which had hitherto supplied the whole of Europe, and soon French glass attained a splendour and beauty which have never been surpassed elsewhere. The carpets of Turkey and Persia were excelled at La Savonnerie. The tapestries of Flanders yielded to those of Les Gobelins. At that time more than eight hundred workmen were employed in the vast Gobelin works, and three hundred of them were actually lodged there; the finest painters directed the work, which was executed either from their designs or copied from those of the old Italian masters. It was in the precincts of the Gobelins that inlaid work was also produced—a delightful kind of mosaic work—and the art of marquetry was brought to perfection.

Besides the fine tapestry factory at Les Gobelins another was established at Beauvais. The first manufacturer in the town employed six hundred workmen, and the king made him a present of sixty thousand livres. Sixteen hundred girls were employed in making lace; thirty of the best operatives in Venice were engaged, and two hundred from Flanders; and they were presented with thirty-six thousand livres to encourage them.

The manufactures of Sedan cloth and of Aubusson tapestry, which had deteriorated and dwindled, were again set going. Rich stuffs, in which silk was interwoven with gold and silver, were made at Lyons and Tours, with a fresh outburst of industry.

It is well known that the ministry bought from England the secret of that ingenious machine by which stockings can be made ten times more quickly than with the needle. Tin, steel, fine crockery-ware, morocco leather, which had always been brought from foreign countries, were now worked in France. But certain Calvinists, who possessed secrets of tin and steel smelting, carried them away with them in 1686, and shared them and many others with foreign nations.

Every year the king bought about eight hundred thousand livres' worth of works of art, manufactured in his kingdom, and gave them away as presents.

The city of Paris was very far from being what it is to-day. The streets were unlighted, unsafe and dirty. It was necessary to find money for the constant cleaning of the streets, for lighting them every night with five thousand lamps, completely paving the whole city, building two new gates and repairing the old ones, keeping the permanent guard, both foot and mounted, to ensure the safety of the citizens. The king charged himself with everything, drawing upon funds for such necessary expenses. In 1667 he appointed a magistrate whose sole duty was to superintend the police. Most of the large cities of Europe have imitated these examples long afterwards, but none has equalled them. There is no city paved like Paris, and Rome is not even illuminated.

In every sphere matters tended to become so perfect that the second-lieutenant of police in Paris earned a reputation in the performance of his duties which placed him on a level with those who did honour to their age; he was a man capable of anything. He was afterwards in the ministry, and would have made a good general in the army. The position of second-lieutenant of police was beneath his birth and capabilities; yet in filling that post he earned much greater reputation then when occupying an uneasy and transient office in the ministry towards the end of his life.

It should be here pointed out that M. d'Argenson was not by any means the only member of ancient chivalry who performed the office of a magistrate. France is almost the only country in Europe where the old nobility has so often donned the robe. Nearly all other countries, swayed by a relic of Gothic barbarism, are unaware of the greatness of this profession.

From 1661 the king was ceaseless in his building at the Louvre, Saint-Germain and Versailles. Following his example private individuals erected thousands of dwellings in Paris as magnificent as they were comfortable. Their number increased to such an extent that in the environs of the Palais-Royal and St. Sulpice two new towns sprang up in Paris, both vastly superior to the old. It was about this time that those magnificent spring carriages with mirrors were invented, so that a citizen of Paris could ride through the streets of that great city in greater luxury than the first Roman triumvirs along the road to the Capitol. Inaugurated in Paris, the custom soon spread throughout the whole of Europe, and, become general, it is no longer a luxury.

Louis XIV took delight in architecture, gardens, and sculpture, his delight being for all that was grand and imposing. From 1664 the Comptroller-General Colbert, who was in charge of buildings, a duty properly belonging to the ministry of arts, devoted himself to the carrying out of his master's plans. The Louvre must first be finished, and François Mansard, one of the greatest French architects of all time, was chosen to construct the immense buildings that had been projected. He declined to proceed, unless he were allowed to alter certain parts already built which appeared to him defective. These doubts he cast on the scheme, to alter which would have entailed too great an expense, were the cause of his services being dispensed with. The cavalier Bernini was summoned from Rome, famous already for the colonnade surrounding the parvis of St. Peter's, the equestrian statue of Constantine, and the Navonna fountain. An equipage was provided for his journey. He was brought to Paris as a man come to do honour to France. He received, in addition to the five louis a day for the eight months he remained, a present of fifty thousand crowns and a pension of two thousand, and five hundred for his son. This generosity of Louis XIV towards Bernini was yet greater than the munificence accorded to Raphael by Francis I. In gratitude Bernini afterwards cast at home the equestrian statue of the king which now stands at Versailles. But once arrived in Paris with so much pomp as the only man worthy to work for Louis XIV, he was not a little astonished to see the design of the façade of the Louvre on the Saint-Germain-l'Auxerrois side, which when finished shortly afterwards became one of the most imposing architectural monuments to be found in the world. Claude Perrault was the draughtsman, and it was executed by Louis Levau and Dorbay. He invented machines for conveying the stone blocks, fifty-two feet long, which form the pediment of this majestic building.

Men sometimes seek very far afield for what they have at home. Not a Roman palace has an entrance comparable to that of the Louvre, for which we are indebted to that Perrault upon whom Boileau dared to try to pour ridicule. In the opinion of travellers, those famous *vineyards* are not comparable to the Château de Maisons, which was built at such small cost by François Mansard. Bernini was magnificently remunerated, but did not deserve his rewards: he merely drew up plans which were never executed.

After building the Louvre, the completion of which is greatly to be desired, founding a town at Versailles close to the palace which cost so many millions, building Trianon, Marli, and beautifying so many other buildings, the king had completed building the Observatory, begun in 1666, at the time that he founded the Academy of Sciences. But the work glorious for its utility, its vastness and the difficulties of its construction, was the Languedoc canal, which connected the two seas, and finds an outlet in the port of Cette, built for that purpose. All these undertakings were begun after 1664 and were continued uninterruptedly until 1681. The founding of the Invalides and its chapel, the finest in Paris, the building of Saint-Cyr, the last of the edifices to be erected by that monarch, would alone suffice to hallow his memory. Four thousand soldiers and a large number of officers, who find consolation in their old age and relief for their wounds and needs in the former of those great institutions; two hundred and fifty girls of noble birth who receive in the latter an education worthy of their high position, are so many witnesses to the glory of Louis XIV.

The institution of Saint-Cyr will be surpassed by the one which Louis XV is about to found for the education of five hundred noblemen, but so far from causing Saint-Cyr to be forgotten, it will remind one of it; the art of doing good is thus brought to perfection.

Louis XIV resolved at the same time to do greater things, of more general utility as they were more difficult of accomplishment, and one of these was the remodelling of the laws. He instructed the chancellor Séguier, Lamoignon, Talon, Bignon and, above all, the state councillor, Pussort, to set to work. He was sometimes present at their meetings. The year 1667 marked the epoch of his earliest statutes as it did his earliest conquests. The civil code appeared first to be followed by the law of rivers and forests, and later statutes concerning every kind of manufacture; the criminal code, the laws of commerce and the marine laws were passed in annual succession. A new kind of justice was even introduced in favour of the negroes in French colonies, a people who had not hitherto possessed the rights of mankind.

A sovereign need not possess a profound knowledge of jurisprudence; but the king was well versed in the principal laws; he entered into their spirit, and knew when either to enforce or modify them as occasion demanded. He often passed judgment on his subjects' law-suits, not only in the council of the state secretaries, but in that one bearing the name of the *council of the parties*. Two judgments of his have become famous, in which he decided against himself.

The first case, which was tried in 1680, was an action between himself and certain private individuals in Paris who had erected buildings on his land. He gave judgment that the houses should remain to them with the land belonging to him, which he made over to them.

The other one concerned a Persian, named Roupli, whose merchandise had been seized by the clerks of his farms in 1687. His decision was that all should be returned to him, and he added a present of three thousand crowns. Roupli carried back to his own country his admiration and gratitude. When the Persian ambassador, Mehemet Rixabeg, came afterwards to Paris, it was discovered that he had long known of that action by the fame which it had spread abroad.

The suppression of duelling was one of the greatest services rendered to the counrty. Formerly such duels had been sanctioned by kings, even by parliament and by the Church, and though forbidden since the days of Henri IV, the pernicious practice was more prevalent than ever. The famous combat of the La Frettes in 1663, when eight combatants were engaged, determined Louis XIV to pardon such duels no longer. His well-timed severity gradually reformed the nation and even neighbouring nations, who conformed to our wise customs after having copied our bad ones. At the present day the number of duels in Europe is a hundred times less than in the time of Louis XIII.

Legislator of his people, he was no less so of his armies. It is astonishing that before his time the troops had no uniform dress. It was he who in the first year of his administration decreed that each regiment should be distinguished by the colour of their uniform, or by different badges—a regulation which was soon adopted by all other nations. It was he who organised the brigadiers and gave the king's household troops the status they hold at the present day. He formed a company of musketeers from Cardinal Mazarin's guards and fixed the number of men for the two companies at five hundred, whom he furnished with the uniform they still wear to-day.

During this reign the post of High Constable was abolished, and after the death of the Duke of Épernon there were no more colonels-general of infantry; they were too much the master; he resolved to be the only master, and deserved to be so. Marshal Grammont, a mere colonel in the French guards under the Duke d'Épernon, and taking his orders from this brigadier-general, now only took them from the king, and was the first to bear the title of colonel of the guards; Louis himself appointed these colonels to the head of their regiments, presenting them with his own hands a gold gorget with a pike, and afterwards a spontoon, when the use of pikes was abolished. In the king's regiment, which is of his creation, he founded the grenadiers, at first to the number of four to each company; afterwards, he formed a company of grenadiers in each infantry regiment, and provided the French guards with two of them; at the present day there is one in every infantry battalion in the army. He greatly enlarged the corps of dragoons and gave them a brigadier-general. Nor must be forgotten the institution of breeding-studs in 1667. Heretofore, they had been absolutely neglected, and they were of great assistance in providing mounts for the cavalry; an important resource which has since been too much neglected.

The use of the bayonet attached to the end of the musket originated with him. Before his time they were sometimes employed, but only a few of the regiments fought with this weapon. There was no regular practice and no drill, all being left to the will of the general. Pikes were considered to be the most formidable weapon. The Fusiliers, founded in 1671, were the first regiment to employ bayonets and to be drilled in the use of that weapon.

The use to which artillery is put at the present day is entirely due to him. He established schools at Douai, and later at Metz and at Strasburg, and the artillery regiment found itself at last provided with officers who were nearly all capable of efficiently conducting a siege. All the magazines in the country were well stocked and eight thousand hundredweights of powder were distributed amongst them every year. He formed a regiment of bombardiers and hussars; before his time hussars were only to be found among the enemy.

In 1688 he established thirty militia regiments, furnished and equipped by the communes. These regiments were trained for war, but they did not neglect the tilling of the land.

Companies of cadets were maintained at most of the frontier towns; they were taught mathematics, drawing, and all manner of drill, and carried out the duties of soldiers. This system was pursued for ten years. At length the difficulties in the way of training insubordinate youths proved too great; but the corps of engineers, formed by the king and for which he drew up regulations which still obtain, will last for ever. Under Louis XIV the art of fortifying towns was brought to perfection by Marshal Vauban and his pupils, whose works surpassed those of Count Pagan. He constructed or rebuilt one hundred and fifty fortresses.

For the maintenance of military discipline, he created inspectors-general, and afterwards superintendents, who reported on the condition of the troops, and their reports showed whether the commissaries had carried out their duties.

He founded the Order of Saint Louis, and this honourable distinction was often more sought after than wealth itself. The Hôtel des Invalides crowned the efforts he made to be worthy of the faithful service of his subjects.

It was by such efforts that, from the year 1672, he possessed one hundred and eighty thousand regular troops, and increasing his forces proportionately to the increase in the number and power of his enemies he had at length as many as four hundred and fifty thousand men under arms, including the marines.

Before that time no such powerful armies had been seen. His enemies were able to put in the field armies almost as large, but to do so their forces were compelled to be united. He showed what France could do unaided, and had always, if not great success, at any rate great resources.

He was the first to give displays of war maneuvers and mimic warfare in times of peace. In 1698 seventy thousand troops were mustered at Compiègne. They performed all the operations of a campaign, the display being intended for the benefit of his three grandsons. The luxurious accompaniments of this military school made of it a sumptuous fête.

He was as assiduous in his efforts to secure the sovereignty of the seas as he had been to form numerous and well-trained armies upon land, even before war was declared. He began by repairing the few ships that Cardinal Mazarin had left to rot in the ports. Others were bought from Holland and Sweden, and in the third year of his government he despatched his maritime forces in an attempt to take Jijeli on the coast of Africa. In 1665 the Duke of Beaufort began to clear the seas of pirates, and two years later France had sixty warships in her ports. This was only a beginning, but while in the midst of making new regulations and fresh efforts, he was already conscious of his strength, and would not allow his ships to dip their flag to the English. It was in vain that King Charles II's council insisted on this right, which the English had acquired long since by reason of their power and labours. Louis XIV wrote to his ambassador, Count D'Estrades, in these terms: "The King of England and his chancellor may see what forces I possess, but they cannot see my heart. I care for nothing apart from my honour."

He only said what he was determined to uphold, and in fact the English surrendered their claims and submitted to a natural right and Louis XIV's firmness. Equal conditions obtained between the two nations on the seas. But while insisting upon equality with England, Louis maintained his superiority over Spain. By reason of the formal precedence conceded in 1662, he compelled the Spanish admirals to dip their flag to his ships.

Meanwhile the work of establishing a navy capable of upholding such arrogant sentiments progressed everywhere. The town and port of Rochefort were built at the mouth of the Charente. Seamen of all classes were enrolled, some of whom were placed on merchant vessels and others distributed among the royal fleets. In a short time sixty thousand were enrolled.

Building commissions were set up in the ports so that ships might be constructed on the best possible lines. Five naval arsenals were built at Brest, Rochefort, Toulon, Dunkirk and Hâvre-de-Grâce. In 1672, there were 60 ships of the line and 40 frigates. In 1681, there were 198 ships of war, counting the auxiliaries and 30 galleys in the port of Toulon, either armed or about to be so; 11,000 of the regular troops served on the ships, and 3000 on the galleys. One hundred sixty-six thousand men of all classes were enrolled for the various services of the navy. During the succeeding years there were a thousand noblemen or young gentlemen in this service, carrying out the duties of soldiers on board ship, and learning everything in harbour to do with the art of navigation and tactics; they were the marine guards, having the same rank at sea as the cadets on land. They had been formed in 1672, but in small numbers; they have since proved themselves a school which has produced the finest ships' officers in the navy.

As yet no officer in the marine corps had been made a Marshal of France, a proof that this vital part of France's forces had been neglected. Jean d'Estrées was made the first marshal in 1681. It seems that one of Louis XIV's great objects was to stir up rivalry for this honour in all classes, without which there is no initiative.

The French fleets held the advantage in every naval battle fought until the engagement of La Hogue in 1692, when Count de Tourville, obeying the orders of the court, attacked with forty ships a fleet of ninety English and Dutch ships; he was forced to yield to superior numbers and lost fourteen ships of the first class, which ran aground and were burnt in order to prevent them falling into the enemy's hands. In spite of this set-back the naval forces still held their own; but they deteriorated during the war of the succession. Subsequently Cardinal Fleury neglected to repair their losses during the leisure of a prosperous peace—the very time in which to re-establish them.

The naval forces greatly assisted in protecting trade. The colonies of Martinique, San Domingo and Canada, hitherto languishing, now flourished, and with unhoped-for success; for from 1635 to 1665 these settlements had been a burden upon the nation.

In 1664, the king established a colony at Cayenne and soon afterwards another in Madagascar. He sought by every means to redress the folly and misfortunes which France had brought upon herself by ignoring the sea, while her neighbours were founding empires at the ends of the world.

It will be seen by this cursory glance what great changes Louis XIV brought about in the state; and that such changes were useful since they are still in force. His ministers vied with each other in their eagerness to assist him. The details, indeed the whole execution of such schemes was doubtless due to them, but his was the general organisation. There can be no shadow of doubt that the magistrates would never have reformed the laws, the finances of the country would not have been put on a sound basis, nor discipline introduced into the army, nor a regular police force instituted throughout the kingdom; there would have been no fleets, no encouragement accorded to the arts; all these things would never have been peacefully and steadily accomplished in such a short period and under so many different ministers, had there not been a ruler to conceive of such great schemes, and with a will strong enough to carry them out.

His own glory was indissolubly connected with the welfare of France, and never did he look upon his kingdom as a noble regards his land, from which he extracts as much as he can that he may live in luxury. Every king who loves glory loves the public weal; he had no longer a Colbert nor a Louvois, when about 1698 he commanded each comptroller to present a detailed description of his province for the instruction of the Duke of Burgundy. By this means it was possible to have an exact record of the whole kingdom and a correct census of the population. The work was of the greatest utility, although not every comptroller had the ability and industry of M. de Lamoignon of Baville. Had the comptroller of every province carried out the king's intent so well as the magistrate of Languedoc with regard to the numbering of the population, this collection of records would have been one of the finest achievements of the age. Some of them are well done, but a general scheme was lacking since the same orders were not issued to each comptroller. It is to be wished that each one had given in separate columns a statement of the number of inhabitants of each estate, such as nobles, citizens, labourers, artisans, workmen, cattle of all kinds, fertile, mediocre, and poor land, all clergy, both orthodox and secular, their revenues, and those of the towns and communes.

In most of the records submitted all these details are confused; the matter is not well thought out and inexact; one must search, often with great difficulty for the needed information such as a minister should have ready to hand and be able to take in at a glance so as to ascertain with ease the forces, needs and resources at his disposal. The scheme was excellent, and had it been methodically carried out would have been of the greatest utility.

The foregoing is a general account of what Louis XIV did or attempted to do in order to make his country more flourishing. It seems to me that one can hardly view all his works and efforts without some sense of gratitude, nor without being stirred by the love for the public weal which inspired them. Let the reader picture to himself the condition to-day, and he will agree that Louis XIV did more good for his country than twenty of his predecessors together; and what he accomplished fell far short of what he might have done. The war which ended with the Peace of Ryswick began the ruin of that flourishing trade established by his minister Colbert, and the war of the succession completed it.

Had he devoted the immense sums which were spent on the aqueducts and works at Maintenon for conveying water to Versailles—works which were interrupted and rendered useless—to beautifying Paris and completing the Louvre; had he expended on Paris a fifth part of the money spent in transforming nature at Versailles, Paris would be in its entire length and breadth as beautiful as the quarter embracing the Tuileries and the Pont-Royal; it would have become the most magnificent city in the world.

It is a great thing to have reformed the laws, but justice has not been powerful enough to suppress knavery entirely. It was thought to make the administration of justice uniform; it is so in criminal cases, in commercial cases and in judicial procedure; it might also be so in the laws which govern the fortunes of private citizens.

It is in the highest degree undesirable that the same tribunal should have to give decisions on more than a hundred different customs. Territorial rights, doubtful, burdensome or merely troublesome to the community, still survive as relics of a feudal government which no longer exists; they are the rubbish from the ruins of a gothic edifice.

We do not claim that the different classes of the nation should all be subject to the same law. It is obvious that the customs of the nobility, clergy, magistrates and husbandmen must all be different, but it is surely desirable that each class should be subject to the same law throughout the kingdom; that what is just or right in Champagne should not be deemed unjust or wrong in Normandy. Uniformity in every branch of administration is a virtue; but the difficulties that beset its achievement are enough to frighten the boldest statesman. It is to be regretted that Louis XIV did not dispense more readily with the dangerous expedient of employing tax-farmers, an expedient to which he was driven by the continual advance drawings he made on his revenues, as will be seen in the chapter on finance.

Had he not thought that his mere wish would suffice to compel a million men to change their religion, France would not have lost so many citizens. Nevertheless, this country, in spite of the shocks and losses she has sustained, is still one of the most flourishing in the world, since all the good that Louis XIV did for her still bears fruit, and the mischief which it was difficult not to do in stormy times has been remedied. Posterity, which passes judgment on kings, and whose judgment they should continually have before them, will acknowledge, weighing the greatness and defects of that monarch, that though too highly praised during his lifetime, he will deserve to be so for ever, and that he was worthy of the statue raised to him at Montpellier, bearing a Latin inscription whose meaning is *To Louis the Great after his death*. A statesman, Don Ustariz, who is the author of works on the finance and trade of Spain, called Louis XIV *a marvel of a man*.

All these changes that we have mentioned in the government and all classes of the nation inevitably produced a great change in customs and manners. The spirit of faction, strife and rebellion which had possessed the people since the time of Francis II, was transformed into a rivalry to serve their king. With the great landowning nobles no longer living on their estates, and the governors of the provinces no longer having important posts at their command, each man desired to earn his sovereign's favour alone: and the state became a perfect whole with all its powers centralised.

It was by such means that the court was freed from the intrigues and conspiracies which had troubled the state for so many years. There was but a single plot under the rule of Louis XIV, which was instigated in 1674 by La Truaumont, a Norman nobleman, ruined by debauchery and debts, and aided and abetted by a man of the House of Rohan, master of the hounds of France, of great courage but little discretion.

The arrogance and severity of the Marquis de Louvois had irritated him to such a point that on leaving him one day he entered M. Caumartin's house, quite beside himself, and throwing himself on a couch, exclaimed: "Either Louvois dies . . . or I do." Caumartin thought that this outburst was only a passing fit of anger, but the next day, when the same young man having asked him if he thought the people of Normandy were satisfied with the government, he perceived signs of dangerous plans. "The times of the Fronde have passed away," he told him; "believe me, you will ruin yourself, and no one will regret you." The chevalier did not believe him, and threw himself headlong into the conspiracy of La Truaumont. The only other person to enter into the plot was a chevalier of Préaux, a nephew of La Truaumont, who, beguiled by his uncle, won over his mistress, the Marquise de Villiers. Their object and hope was not and could not have been to raise a new party in the kingdom; they merely aimed at selling and delivering Quillebeuf into the hands of the Dutch and letting the enemy into Normandy. It was rather a base and poorly contrived piece of treachery than a conspiracy. The torture of all the guilty parties was the only result of this senseless and useless crime, which to-day is practically forgotten.

The only risings in the provinces were feeble disorders on the part of the populace, which were easily suppressed. Even the Huguenots remained quiet until their houses of worship were pulled down. In a word, the king succeeded in transforming a hitherto turbulent people into a peace-loving nation, who were dangerous only to their foes, after having been their own enemies for more than a hundred years. They acquired softer manners without impairing their courage.

The houses which all the great nobles built or bought in Paris, and their wives who lived there in fitting style, formed schools of gentility, which gradually drew the youth of the city away from the tavern life which was for so long the fashion, and which only encouraged reckless debauchery. Manners depend upon such little things that the custom of riding on horseback in Paris tended to produce frequent brawls, which ceased when the practice was discontinued.

Propriety, due in large part to the ladies who gathered circles of society in their *salons,* made wits more agreeable, and reading in the long run made them more profound. Treason and great crimes, such as bring no disgrace upon men in times of sedition and intrigue, were now hardly known. The enormities of the Brinvilliers and the Voisins were merely passing storms in an otherwise clear sky, and it would be as unreasonable to condemn a nation for the notorious crimes of a few individuals, as it would be to canonise a people for the reforms of a La Trappe.

Hitherto all the various professions could be recognised by their characteristic failings. The military and the youths who intended to take up the profession of arms were of a hotheaded nature; men of law displayed a forbidding gravity, to which their custom of always going about in their robes, even at court, contributed not a little. It was the same with university graduates and with physicians. Merchants still wore their short robes at their assemblies and when they waited upon ministers, and the greatest merchants were as yet but unmannerly men; but the houses, theatres, and public promenades, where everyone began to meet in order to partake of more refined pleasures, gradually gave to all citizens almost the same outward appearance. It is noticeable at the present day, even behind a counter, how good manners have invaded all stations of life. The provinces in time also experienced the effects of these changes.

We have finally come to enjoy luxury only in taste and convenience. The crowd of pages and liveried servants has disappeared, to allow greater freedom in the interior of the home. Empty pomp and outward show have been left to nations who know only how to display their magnificence in public and are ignorant of the art of living. The extreme ease which obtains in the intercourse of society, affable manners, simple living and the culture of the mind, have combined to make Paris a city which, as regards the harmonious life of the people, is probably vastly superior to Rome and Athens during the period of their greatest splendour.

These ever-present advantages, always at the service of every science, every art, taste or need; so many things of real utility combined with so many others merely pleasant and coupled with the freedom peculiar to Parisians, all these attractions induce a large number of foreigners to travel or take up their residence in this, as it were, birthplace of society. The few natives who leave their country are those who, on account of their talents, are called elsewhere, and are an honour to their native land; or they are the scum of the nation who endeavour to profit by the consideration which the name of France inspires; or they may be emigrants

VOLTAIRE

who place their religion even before their country, and depart elsewhere to meet with misfortune or success, following the example of their forefathers who were expelled from France by that irreparable insult to the memory of the great Henri IV—the revocation of his perpetual law of the Edict of Nantes; or finally they are officers dissatisfied with the ministry, culprits who have escaped the vigorous laws of a justice which is at times ill-administered, a thing which happens in every country in the world.

People complain at no longer seeing that pride of bearing at court. There are certainly no longer petty autocrats, as at the time of the Fronde, under Louis XIII, and in earlier ages; but true greatness has come to light in that host of nobles so long compelled in former times to demean themselves by serving overpowerful subjects. To-day one sees gentlemen, citizens who would formerly have considered themselves honoured to be servants to these noblemen, now become their equals and very often their superiors in the military service.

The more that services rendered are accounted above titles of nobility, the more flourishing is the condition of the state.

The age of Louis XIV has been compared with that of Augustus. It is not that their power and individual events are comparable; Rome and Augustus were ten times more considered in the world than Louis XIV and Paris, but it must be remembered that Athens was the equal of the Roman Empire in all things whose value is not dependent upon might and power.

We must also bear in mind that there is nothing in the world to-day to compare with ancient Rome and Augustus, yet Europe taken as a whole is vastly superior to the whole of the Roman Empire. In the time of Augustus there was but a single nation, while at the present day there are several nations, all civilised, warlike, and enlightened, who cultivate arts unknown to the Greeks and Romans; and of these nations, there is none that has shone more brilliantly in every sphere for nearly a century, than the nation moulded to a great extent by Louis XIV.

FINANCE AND PUBLIC ADMINISTRATION

If Colbert's administration be compared with all preceding administrations, posterity will cherish the memory of that man, whose body the maddened populace wished to tear in pieces after his death. The French certainly owe their industries and trade to him, and consequently that wealth whose sources are sometimes diminished in time of war, but which always become again abundant in time of peace. Nevertheless, in 1702, people were so ungrateful as to charge Colbert with the general depression which was beginning to make itself felt in every department of the state. About that time a certain Bois-Guillebert, a lieutenant-general in the bailiwick of Rouen, published a work entitled *Description of France* in two small volumes, in which he claimed that everything had been on the decline since 1660. This was exactly contrary to the truth. France had never been in such a flourishing state as from the death of Cardinal Mazarin to the war of 1689, and even during that war the body of the state, though beginning to feel distress, was sustained by the vigour which Colbert had infused into every limb. The author of the *Description* maintained that since 1660 the landed property of the kingdom had diminished in value by fifteen hundred millions. Nothing was more false nor more improbable. However, these captious arguments convinced those who wished to be so that the absurd paradox was true. The same thing happens in England, where at her most flourishing periods there are hundreds of pamphlets published proving that the state is ruined. It was, however, easier in France than elsewhere to discredit the ministry of finance in the minds of the people. This ministry is the most hated for the simple reason that taxes are always hated: moreover, as many prejudices and as much ignorance prevailed in general in financial matters as in philosophy.

Instruction has been so long delayed that even in our days, in 1718, one hears parliament in a body tell the Duke of Orleans that "the intrinsic value of the silver mark is twenty-five livres"; as if there were any real and intrinsic value other than that of weight and standard; and the Duke of Orleans, though an extremely well-educated man, had not sufficient intelligence to refute this mistake of parliament.

Colbert brought both knowledge and genius to the administration of the finance department. Like the Duke de Sulli, he began by putting a stop to fraudulent practices and pilferings which were enormous. The collecting of taxes was simplified as far as possible, and by exercising an economy which was little short of miraculous, he increased the king's treasury and at the same time reduced the poll-tax. It will be seen from the memorable decree of 1664, that a sum of one million in contemporary currency of the period was annually devoted to the encouragement of manufactures and maritime trade. So little did he neglect agriculture, which had hitherto been abandoned to the rapacity of tax-farmers, that when English merchants offered to his brother, M. Colbert de Crossi, French ambassador in London, in 1667, to supply France with Irish cattle and salted provisions for the colonies, the comptroller-general replied that for the last four years they had been re-selling them to foreign countries.

To succeed in establishing such an admirable system of administration it was necessary to create a court of justice and bring about certain sweeping reforms. He was obliged to cancel more than eight millions of municipal stock, acquired at an extremely low price, the holders receiving the same price that they themselves had paid. Such various changes required decrees. Since the time of Francis I parliament had had the right to examine them. It was proposed to have them registered simply by the chamber of accounts; but the old method of procedure prevailed; and in 1664 the king himself went to parliament to supervise the passing of his decrees.

He never forgot the Fronde, the proscription of a cardinal, his first minister, and the other decrees authorising the seizure of the royal funds, and the plundering of the goods and money of citizens attached to the crown. All these abuses having begun by protestations against decrees concerning state revenues, in 1667 the king decreed that parliament should make no protest after the lapse of a week, having once recorded their allegiance. The edict was renewed in 1673, and accordingly, during the whole course of his administration, he suffered no protest from any judicial court, except in the fateful year of 1709, when the parliament of Paris vainly protested against the injury which the minister of finance did to the state by varying the price of gold and silver.

Nearly all citizens were convinced that had parliament, knowing the causes of such things, confined itself to bringing to the close attention of the king, the misfortunes and the needs of the people, the dangers of taxation and the still greater danger of such taxes being sold to farmers who both deceived the king and oppressed the people, the right of making remonstrances would have become an inviolable resource of the state, a check on the rapacity of financiers, and a perpetual warning to ministers. But the strange abuses of so wholesome a remedy had so exasperated Louis XIV that he saw nothing but the abuses and condemned the remedy. His indignation reached such a pitch that in 1669, on 13 August, he again attended parliament in person for the purpose of revoking the privileges of nobility, previously granted to all higher courts in 1664, during his minority.

But in spite of this decree, registered in the presence of the king, the custom has remained of allowing all whose fathers have held a judicial office in a higher court for twenty years, or who had died in office, to enjoy such privileges of nobility.

In thus humbling a body of magistrates, he desired to encourage both the nobles who defend the country and the farmers who supply it with food. Already in a decree of 1666 he had granted an annuity of two thousand francs, worth at the present day nearly four thousand, to every gentleman who had twelve children, and a thousand francs to those who had ten. Half of this gratuity was guaranteed to all the inhabitants of towns who were exempted from paying poll-tax, and, of those who were taxable, every father of a family who had or who had had ten children was free from all taxes.

It is true that Colbert did not do all that he could have done, still less all that he wished to do. Men's minds were not yet sufficiently enlightened, and in a great kingdom there are always great abuses. The arbitrary poll-tax, the multiplicity of dues, the custom duties payable from one province to another, which make the people of one part of France strangers and even enemies to another, the different standards of weight from town to town, and twenty other ills in the body politic, could not be cured.

The greatest mistake attributed to that minister is that of not daring to encourage the export of wheat. No wheat had been exported to foreign countries for many years. Its cultivation had been neglected during the stormy period of Richelieu's ministry, and it was still more neglected during the civil wars of the Fronde. In 1661 famine completed the desolation of the land, which nature, however, aided by labour, is always ready to repair. In that disastrous year the parliament of Paris passed a decree which, while in principle appearing just, proved nearly as fatal in its consequences as all the decrees wrung from that body during the civil wars. Merchants were forbidden, under the severest penalties, from entering into any association for the marketing of wheat, and individuals were prohibited from hoarding it. What was good in a time of temporary famine became harmful in the long run, and discouraged all farming whatsoever. To have annulled such a decree at a critical and unfavourable moment would have meant a revolution among the lowest class.

The minister was reduced to the necessity of buying dearly from foreign countries the very wheat which the French had formerly sold to them in years of plenty. The people had food, but at great cost to the state; the order which Colbert had introduced into the country finances, however, rendered this loss a light one.

The fear of another famine closed all French ports to the exportation of wheat. Each provincial comptroller, moreover, prided himself on opposing the passage of wheat from his own to a neighbouring province. Even in prosperous times wheat could only be sold by permission of the council. This fatal regulation appeared justified by past experience. Every member of the council feared that any trading in wheat would compel them once more to repurchase that necessary commodity at a high cost from other nations, which the self-interest and shortsightedness of the growers would incline to sell very cheaply.

Thus the peasant farmer, still more timorous than the council, feared to be ruined if he raised a commodity from which he could hope to obtain no great profit, and the land was consequently not so well tilled as it should have been. The fact that all the other departments of the administration were in a flourishing state prevented Colbert from applying a remedy to the defect in the principal department of all.

It is the only blot on his ministry, and it is a great one; but what excuses it and proves how unpopular is the task of eradicating such prejudices inherent in French administration and how difficult is the task of doing right, is the fact that this defect, thought apparent to all intelligent citizens, was not remedied by any minister for fully a hundred years, until the memorable epoch of 1764, when a more enlightened comptroller-general relieved France from profound distress by restoring to her free trade in wheat, with restrictions almost identical with those commonly in use in England.

About 1672, in order to provide for the expenses of wars, buildings and entertainments, Colbert was obliged to renew what he had at first intended to abolish for ever, namely, the farming of taxes, government stocks, sale of new offices, increase of pledges on crown property, in a word, everything which maintains the state for a certain length of time, but encumbers it for centuries.

He went beyond the limits he had prescribed for himself: for from all his writings which remain one can perceive that he was convinced that the wealth of a nation lies in the number of its inhabitants, in the cultivation of the land, in industry and trade; and it is thus obvious that the king, possessing very few estates of his own and being only the trustee for the property of his subjects, really became rich only by taxes which are easily collected and equally distributed.

Colbert was so afraid of delivering the state into the hands of tax-farmers that a short time after the dissolution of the Court of Justice, which he had had instituted against them, he sanctioned a decree of the council which ordained the death penalty against anyone who should advance money on new taxes. By this comminatory decree, which was never printed, he sought to intimidate the cupidity of business men. But soon afterwards he was obliged to utilise their services without even repealing the decree; the king was urgent, and prompt measures were necessary.

This expedient, brought to France from Italy by Catherine de Medici, had so corrupted the government by its fatal facility, that, after having been suppressed during the prosperous reign of Henri IV, it reappeared during the whole of Louis XIII's reign, and infected especially the latter years of Louis XIV.

In short, while Sully enriched the state by wise economy, being supported by a king as parsimonious as he was brave, a soldier king who rode at the head of his army, and a father to his people; Colbert sustained the state in spite of the extravagance of a pompous master who was lavish of everything that would make his reign more brilliant.

It is recorded that on Colbert's death, when the king proposed to appoint Le Pelletier Minister of Finance, Le Tellier said to him: "Sire, he is not fitted for that post." "Why?" asked the king. "He is not hard-hearted enough," replied Le Tellier. "But," replied the king, "I have no wish that my people should be treated harshly." The new minister was certainly well-meaning and just, but in 1688, when the country was again plunged into war and had to contend against the League of Augsburg, that is to say, against nearly the whole of Europe, he found himself saddled with a burden which even Colbert found too heavy, and his first resource was the easy and fatal expedient of borrowing and creating government stocks. In the next place he proposed to cut down luxuries, which, in a kingdom full of manufactures, is to cut down industry and the circulation of money, and which only a nation that obtains its luxuries from abroad should do.

Orders were given that all solid silver ornaments, which were to be seen in large numbers of the houses of great noblemen—a sure sign of affluence—were to be delivered up to the Mint. The king set the example, and parted with all his silver tables, candelabra, fine solid silver couches, and all his other furniture, which were masterpieces of carving from the hands of Ballin, an artist unique of his kind, and all executed from designs by Lebrun. They had cost ten millions; they produced three. The wrought silver ornaments of private individuals yielded three more millions. The resource was slight.

Then the ministry committed one of those huge blunders which has only been lately rectified; it altered the currency, changed the standards of the new coinage, giving a value to the crown out of all proportion to that of the quarter; the result was that as quarters were increased in value and crowns diminished, all quarters passed over into foreign countries; there they were coined as crowns, and thus a profit was made by sending them back again to France. A country must indeed be sound at heart to be still powerful after having sustained such blows so often. Ignorance was as yet rife; finance, like physics, was still a science based on idle conjecture. Tax-farmers were so many charlatans who cheated the ministry, and they cost eighty millions to the state. It takes twenty years of toil and drudgery to repair such losses.

By 1691 and 1692 the state finances were consequently considerably disorganised. Those who attributed the reduction in the sources of wealth to the extravagance of Louis XIV on his palaces, the arts, and his entertainments, were unaware that expenditure which encourages industry, so far from impoverishing, actually enriches a state. It is war that inevitably impoverishes the public treasure, unless it be replenished with the spoils of a defeated enemy. But I know of no nation that has enriched itself by its victories since the ancient Romans. Italy in the sixteenth century owed her riches to her trade. Holland would never have existed long as a power had she confined herself to capturing the Spanish silver fleet, without drawing the means of her subsistence from the East Indies. England has always impoverished herself by war even when defeating the French fleets; and trade alone has enriched her. The Algerians, who have practically nothing save what they gain from piracy, are a very wretched people.

Among the European nations a few years of war place the victor in almost as desperate a situation as the vanquished. War is a gulf in which all channels of prosperity are swallowed up. Ready money, the source of all prosperity and all misfortune, raised with so much trouble in the provinces, finds its way into the coffers of a hundred contractors and a hundred of their partisans, who advance the capital and purchase by such advances the right of plundering the nation in the sovereign's name. Private individuals, upon this looking upon the government as their enemy, conceal their money, and a deficient circulation weakens the resources of the kingdom.

No hasty remedy can take the place of a settled and stable economic scheme, established long since. The poll-tax was instituted in 1695. It was abolished at the Peace of Ryswick and immediately restored. In 1696, Pontchartrain, the comptroller-general, sold letters of nobility for two thousand crowns apiece; five hundred individuals bought them, but the resource was temporary while the disgrace was permanent. All nobles, both old and new, were forced to register their coats-of-arms and to pay for the permission to seal their letters with their heraldic arms. Special and illegal tax-gatherers dealt with this affair and advanced money. The ministry almost without exception employed such petty expedients in a country which could have furnished greater ones.

The ministry did not venture to levy the *dixième* (that is, a tenth part of the individual's total income) until 1710. But this tax, following in the wake of so many other oppressive taxes, was so much resented that it was not vigorously enforced. The government derived no more than twenty-five millions yearly from it at forty francs to the mark.

Colbert had made slight changes in the cash value of the currency. It is better not to change it at all. Gold and silver, the bases of exchange, should be invariable standards. He had only increased the cash value of the silver mark from twenty-six francs to twenty-seven or twenty-eight, and during the last years of Louis XIV his successors raised the imaginary value of this coin to forty livres; a fatal proceeding by which the king was relieved for a moment only to be ruined the next; for instead of receiving one silver mark he now received little more than half. A man owing twenty-six livres in 1668 would pay one mark, and in 1710 a man owing forty livres would pay very much the same amount, i.e. one mark. The lowered values unsettled what little trade there remained as much as the increased values had done.

A paper currency would have proved an adequate expedient, but such paper money should be introduced in a time of prosperity, and can then hold its own in difficult times.

In 1706 the minister Chamillart began to use a certain kind of paper money for payments; notes were issued from the Mint in exchange for used coin, and notes known as *billets de subsistance et d'ustensiles* were also given to persons in payment for the billeting of troops; but as this paper money was refused by the king's treasury, it was discredited almost as soon as it appeared. The government was reduced to continue borrowing heavily and pledging four years of crown revenue in advance.

What were known as extraordinary measures were continually being adopted; ridiculous offices were created which were always bought by those eager to avoid payment of the poll-tax; for this tax being considered degrading in France, and all men being vain by nature, the bait of freeing them from this ignominy will always dupe them; and the high wages attached to such newly-created posts tempt people to buy them in difficult times, not stopping to think they will be abolished in more prosperous days.

Thus in 1707 the posts of overseers of the king's vine-dressers and vine-brokers were instituted, and these produced 180,000 livres. The offices of royal recorders and of sub-deputies to the comptrollers of provinces were created; likewise king's councillor comptrollers for the superintendence of the storing of timber, superintendents of police, officers of royal barbers and wig-makers, controller-overseers of fresh butter-making, tasters of salted butter. We smile at such follies now; but they were wept for then.

The comptroller-general, Desmarets, a nephew of the illustrious Colbert, who succeeded Chamillart in 1708, was unable to remedy an evil which everything tended to make incurable.

Nature conspired with misfortune to crush the state. The bitter winter of 1709 compelled the king to remit nine millions of poll-tax to the people at a time when he could not pay his troops. The scarcity of food was such that it cost forty-five millions to feed the army. The expenditure of the year 1709 amounted to two hundred and twenty-one millions, and the ordinary revenue of the king did not produce forty-nine. It was consequently necessary to ruin the state to preserve it from its enemies. Disorder increased to such an extent and so little was done to check it, that long after peace was signed at the beginning of 1715, the king was obliged to pledge thirty-two millions of notes, in exchange for eight millions in cash, and at his death he left two thousand six hundred million livres of debts, at twenty livres to the mark, to which the currency was at that time reduced, and which amounts to about four thousand five hundred million livres in our currency of 1760.

It is astonishing but nevertheless true that this enormous debt would not have been an impossible burden to bear had trade been in a flourishing condition, paper money honoured, and had there existed solid companies as security for the money, as in Sweden, England, Venice and Holland; for when a powerful state is in debt to no one but itself, confidence and the circulation of money are sufficent to remove it, but France at that time was far from possessing sufficient resources to set such a huge complicated machine in motion, whose very weight was crushing her.

In the course of his reign Louis XIV spent eighteen milliards, which amounts on an average to a yearly expediture of three hundred and thirty millions, compensation being made for the rise and fall in the value of money.

Under the great Colbert's administration the ordinary revenues of the crown only amounted to one hundred and seventeen millions at twenty-seven livres, and afterwards twenty-eight livres, to the silver mark. Thus the whole of the surplus expenditure was provided by extraordinary measures. Colbert, the greatest enemy of this baneful expedient, was obliged to make use of it, in order to obtain the money promptly. During the war of 1672 he borrowed eight hundred millions in present-day currency. Scarcely any of the old crown lands were left to the king. They have been declared the inalienable property of the crown by every parliament in the kingdom, and yet they have nearly all of them been transfered. At the present day the king's revenue is vested in that of his subjects: it is a perpetual interchange of debts and payments.

The king owes his subjects annually more millions in cash in the form of dividends on municipal stock, than any king has ever received from crown lands.

To gain an idea of this enormous increase in taxes, debts, wealth, circulation of money, and at the same time of disorganisation and misery, which France and other countries have experienced, one has only to consider that on the death of Francis I the state was in debt to the extent of about thirty thousand livres for perpetual municipal stock, and that at the present day the debt amounts to more than forty-five millions.

Those who have sought to compare the revenue of Louis XIV and Louis XV have found that, with regard to the fixed and current revenue alone, Louis XIV was much more wealthy in 1683, at the time of Colbert's death, with one hundred and seventeen millions of revenue than his successor

in 1730 with nearly two hundred millions, and this is entirely borne out
by a consideration merely of the fixed and ordinary revenues of the
crown, since one hundred and seventeen millions in specie at twenty-
eight livres to the mark are worth more than two hundred millions at
forty-nine livres, which was the amount of the king's revenue in 1730;
moreover, one must take into account the losses caused by the borrowings
of the crown; the king's revenues, however—that is to say, the state revenues—were afterwards increased, and an understanding of finance
affairs was so far improved that during the disastrous war of 1741 the
country was never for a moment insolvent. The expedient of establishing
sinking-funds has been resorted to in imitation of the English; it has
become necessary to adopt some part of their financial system as also of
their philosophy; and were it possible to introduce into an essentially
monarchic state those circulating notes, which at least double the wealth
of England, the government of France would attain to the last degree of
perfection, but a perfection perhaps too near abuse under a monarchical
system.

In 1683 there was a silver coinage to the value of about five hundred
millions in the kingdom; and in 1730 about twelve hundred millions
according to present-day reckoning. But under Cardinal Fleury's ministry the metallic currency was nearly double of that during Colbert's
administration. It would therefore appear that France was only about a
sixth part richer in circulating wealth after Colbert's death. True, she
has a much greater wealth of manufactured gold and silver wares for
purposes of utility and luxury. In 1690, there were only a hundred millions' worth of such articles in present-day currency, but by the year 1730
they were worth as much as the coinage in circulation. Nothing shows
more plainly how trade, whose sources were first opened by Colbert, has
grown when once the channels necessarily closed in time of war have
again been opened. The industries of the country have been perfected,
despite the emigration of so many skilled workmen driven from their
country by the revocation of the Edict of Nantes, and these industries are
daily increasing. The nation is capable of accomplishing as great and
even greater things than were achieved under Louis XIV, because initiative and commerce always become invigorated when they are encouraged.

To see the affluence of private individuals, the enormous number of
comfortable houses in Paris and in the provinces, the quantity of carriages, the commodities and refinements known under the general name
of luxury, one would think that there was twenty times as much wealth
as formerly; but all this is rather the product of ingenious labour than of
great wealth. It costs but little more to-day to be housed comfortably than
it did to be housed wretchedly under Henri IV.

A beautiful mirror of French manufacture now decks our houses at far less cost than the little mirrors we formerly bought from Venice. Our beautiful and ornamental stuffs are much cheaper than those formerly imported from abroad, and also of better quality.

In fact, it is not gold and silver that ensure the comforts of life, but industrial initiative. A people who possessed nothing beside those precious metals would be very wretched; a people who lacked those metals, but successfully cultivated all the products of the land, would indeed be rich. France possesses this advantage, together with a larger quantity of precious metals than it is necessary to put into circulation.

As skilled labour was brought to greater perfection in the towns, it spread into the country districts as well. Complaints will always be raised about the conditions of the tillers of the land. They are heard in every country in the world and are nearly always the murmurings of the idle rich, who condemn the government much more than they sympathise with the people. It is true that in almost every country, if those who pass their days in rustic toil had the leisure to complain, they would rebel against the exactions which deprive them of a part of their livelihood. They would express their detestation of being compelled to pay taxes which they have not imposed upon themselves and to carry the burden of the state without sharing in the advantages enjoyed by other citizens. It is not within the province of history to enquire how much the people should contribute to the state without being oppressed, or to mark the precise point, always a difficult matter, between the just carrying out of laws and their abuse, between taxation and robbery; but history should point out how impossible it is for a town to flourish unless the surrounding country is also flourishing; for it is undoubtedly the country which feeds the towns. On certain days one hears, in every town in France, reproaches made by those whose profession permits them to declaim in public against the various kinds of commodities which come under the name of luxuries. It is obvious that such luxuries can only be supplied by the skilled labour of the workers in the fields, and is always dearly paid for.

More vines were planted and were better cultivated; new wines unknown before were produced, such as those of Champagne, which were given the colour, body and strength of those of Burgundy, and big profits are repeated from their sale in foreign countries; this increase in the production of wines led also to the making of brandies. Extraordinary developments were made in the cultivation of gardens, vegetables and fruits, and the provision trade with the American colonies was largely augmented as a result; the complaints which have ever been raised of the misery of the countryside now ceased to have any ground for justification.

Besides, in these vague complaints no distinction is made between growers, peasant farmers and labourers. The last live simply by the work of their hands; and thus it is in all countries of the world, where the majority must exist by manual toil. But there is hardly a kingdom in the world where the husbandman and farmer live under more comfortable conditions than in certain provinces of France; England alone can dispute the claim. The proportionate poll-tax, substituted in place of the arbitrary one in certain provinces, has still further helped to consolidate the prosperity of those farmers in possession of ploughs, vineyards and gardens. The farm-labourer, the workman, work because forced to do so by necessity; it is the lot of man. The greater number of such men are bound to be poor, but they need not be wretched.

The middle classes enriched themselves by industry. Ministers and courtiers became less wealthy, since while the amount of money in circulation had increased by nearly a half, salaries and pensions remained the same, and the price of food and commodities had almost doubled; in every country in Europe the same thing happened. Titles and fees remained everywhere on the old footing. An elector, receiving the investiture of his states, pays only what his predecessors paid at the time of the Emperor Charles IV in the fourteenth century, and no more than a single crown is due to the Emperor's secretary for his services in that ceremony.

What is still more extraordinary is that while everything has increased, the sum total of the currency, the quantity of gold and silver bullion, the price of commodities, nevertheless the soldier's pay has remained the same as it was two hundred years ago; foot-soldiers receive five sous in cash just as they did in the time of Henri IV. Not one of all these ignorant men, who sell their lives so cheaply, is aware that, taking into account the raising of the currency and the high prices of food and commodities, he is receiving about two-thirds less than the soldiers of Henri IV. If he knew it and demanded an increase of two-thirds of his pay, he would have to be given it; in that event every European power would maintain but one-third of its present troops, the forces would remain in the same proportion, and agriculture and manufactures would profit by it.

It should further be observed that, owing to the increasing profits of trade and the decrease in real value of all high official appointments, there is less wealth than formerly among the great and more among the middle class; the result has been to lessen the distance between classes. Formerly the poor had no other alternative but to serve the great; to-day industry has opened a thousand paths that were unknown a century ago. Thus, however state finances may be administered, France possesses an incalculable treasure in the labours of nearly twenty millions of inhabitants.

Science

This happy age, which saw the birth of a revolution in the human mind, gave at its commencement no signs of such a destiny; to begin with philosophy, there seemed no likelihood in the time of Louis XIII that it would extricate itself from the chaos in which it was plunged. The Inquisition in Italy, Spain and Portugal had linked philosophical errors with religious dogmas; the civil wars in France and the Calvinist disputes were not more calculated to elevate human reason than was the fanaticism in England at the time of Cromwell. No sooner did a canon of Thorn resuscitate the ancient planetary system of the Chaldeans, so long buried in oblivion, than its truth was condemned at Rome; and the Brotherhood of the Holy Office, composed of seven cardinals, having pronounced the movement of the earth, without which there can be no true science of astronomy, not merely heretical, but absurd, and the great Galileo having asked forgiveness, at the age of seventy, for having spoken the truth, there seemed no likelihood that truth could be established upon earth.

Chancellor Bacon had pointed out the way from afar; Galileo had discovered the laws of falling bodies; Torricelli was on the point of discovering the weight of the air surrounding us, and various experiments had been made at Magdeburg. Ignoring these few attempts, the schools persisted in their folly, and the world in its ignorance. Then came Descartes; he did the opposite to what he should have done; instead of studying Nature, he sought to interpret her. He was the greatest geometrician of his age; but geometry leaves the mind where it finds it. Descartes' geometry was too much given to flights of fancy. He who was the foremost among mathematicians wrote scarcely anything else but philosophic romances. A man who scorned to make experiments, who never quoted Galileo, who thought to build without materials, could erect but an imaginary structure.

All that was romantic in his book succeeded, while the scraps of truth intermingled in these new extravagances were at first contested. But at length this modicum of truth prevailed, thanks to the system he had introduced. Before him no one had had a thread in the labyrinth; he at least provided one which others made use of, when he himself had gone astray. It was much to destroy the delusions of Peripateticism, though it was by the introduction of others. Each strove for mastery; each fell in due season, leaving reason to raise itself on their ruins. About 1655, Cardinal Leopold de' Medici had founded a society for making experiments in Florence, under the name of del Cimento. In that country of the arts it was already felt that one could only understand anything of the vast edifice of Nature by examining it piece by piece. After Galileo's death, and from the time of Torricelli, this Academy rendered great services.

In England under Cromwell's sombre rule, a few philosophers met together for the purpose of seeking truth in peace, while elsewhere fanaticism suppressed all truth. Recalled to the throne of his forefathers by a repentant and fickle nation, Charles II presented letters patent to this budding academy; but this was the government's only gift. The Royal Society, or rather the Free Society of London, worked for the honour of working. We owe to this body the discoveries on the nature of light, the principle of gravitation, the aberrations of fixed stars, astronomical geometry, and a hundred other discoveries, which would justify one in calling this age the Age of the English, as well as the Age of Louis XIV.

In 1666 M. Colbert, jealous of this new glory, and anxious that France should share it, at the request of several scholars obtained permission from Louis XIV to found an Academy of Science. Like the English society and the French Academy, it was a free institution until 1699. By offering liberal annuities, Colbert attracted Domenico Cassini from Italy, Huygens from Holland and Roemer from Denmark. Roemer determined the velocity of the solar rays; Huygens discovered the ring and one of the satellites of Saturn, and Cassini the other four. We owe to Huygens, if not the original invention of pendulum clocks, at any rate the correct principles underlying the regularity of their movements, principles which he deduced from a wonderful geometrical system.

By the rejection of every system a certain amount of knowledge in every branch of true physics was gradually acquired. People were astonished to see a system of chemistry which did not profess either to search for the philosopher's stone or to prolong life beyond the natural limits; a system of astronomy which did not predict future events, and a system of medicine which was independent of the phases of the moon. Putrefaction was no longer thought to breed spontaneously insects and plants.

There was an end of miracles when Nature was better understood and she was studied in all her productions.

Geography was astonishingly developed. The observatory built by Louis XIV's orders was hardly finished, when, in 1669, Domenico Cassini and Picard set to work to determine the meridian line. In 1683 it was continued as far as Roussillon. This was the most glorious achievement of astronomy and was sufficient in itself to immortalise the age.

In 1672 scientists were sent to Cayenne to make some useful observations. On this voyage there was first originated the notion of the oblateness of the earth's sphere, which was afterwards proved by the great Newton; this led the way for those more famous voyages which have since rendered Louis XV's reign illustrious.

In 1700 Tournefort was sent out to the Levant, the object of his voyage being to collect plants for the royal garden, hitherto neglected, but now restored to its proper state in which it has become worthy of the curiosity of Europe. The royal library, already numerous, was enriched by more than thirty thousand volumes under Louis XIV, and this example has been so well followed in our days that it now contains more than one hundred and eighty thousand volumes. The law school, which had been closed for a century, was reopened. Chairs were founded in every university in France for the teaching of French law. It seemed right that others should not be taught, and that the admirable Roman laws, embodied with those of the country, should form the whole jurisprudence of the nation.

The publishing of journals originated during this reign. It is well known that the *Journal des Savants,* first issued in 1665, was the forerunner of all similar works, which at the present day circulate all over Europe, and into which, as into the most useful things, too many abuses have crept.

The Academy of Belles-Lettres, first formed in 1663 by some members of the French Academy for the purpose of having medallions struck to commemorate and hand down to posterity the achievements of Louis XIV, became useful to the public when it was no longer solely occupied with its monarch, and began to undertake researches into antiquity, and exercise a judicious criticism on ideas and events. It did very much for history what the Academy of Sciences did for physics; it dissipated error.

The spirit of learning and criticism which spread from place to place imperceptibly destroyed much of the prevalent superstition. To this dawn of reason was due the king's declaration in 1672, which forbade tribunals hearing simple accusations of sorcery. No one would have dared to do this in the reign of Henri IV or Louis XIII, and while people have still been tried for sorcery since 1672, judges have as a usual rule only condemned the accused as blasphemers, or in certain cases as poisoners in addition.

It had hitherto been very common to try sorcerers by throwing them bound into the water; if they floated, they were judged guilty. Many of the judges in the provinces had ordered such trials, and they long continued among the common people. Every shepherd was a sorcerer, and amulets and charmed rings were worn in the towns. Hazel twigs were definitely thought to have the power of revealing the sources of springs, treasures and thieves, and in more than one province of Germany the belief in their efficacy is still strong. There was hardly a person who did not have his horoscope cast. People spoke of nothing but magic secrets; almost everything was illusion. Solemn treatises were written on these subjects by scholars and magistrates, among whom was to be found a group of demonologists. There were tests by which real magicians could be distinguished, and those really possessed, from impostors; in short, up to that period hardly anything had been adopted from antiquity save its errors.

Superstitious notions were so deeply rooted in men's minds that even as late as 1680 people were alarmed at comets. Scientists hardly dared to controvert this universal dread. Jacques Bernouilli, one of the greatest mathematicians in Europe, when questioned about these comets by prejudiced persons, replied that a comet's head could not be a sign of divine wrath, because the head remains unchanged, but that the tail might certainly mean such a thing.

Yet in point of fact neither the head nor the tail remains unchanged. It was left to Bayle to write his famous book against popular superstition, a book which, read in the light of human reason of today, seems less caustic than when it first appeared.

One would not think that sovereigns would be under any obligation to philosophers. Yet it is true that the philosophic spirit which has penetrated practically every class of society save the lowest, has done much to promote the rights of sovereigns. Disputes which would once have produced excommunications, interdicts and schisms, have had no such effect. It has been said that the peoples would be happy could they have philosophers for kings, but it is also true to say that kings are so much the happier when many of their subjects are philosophers.

It must be admitted that this spirit of reason, which is beginning to control education in the large towns, was powerless to prevent the frenzied acts of the fanatics of the Cevennes or to prevent the populace of Paris from rioting before a tomb at Saint-Medard, or to settle disputes as bitter as they were frivolous between men who should have known better; but before this century such disputes would have brought about disturbances in the state; the greatest citizens would have believed in the miracles of Saint-Medard, and fanaticism, so far from being confined to the regions of the Cevennes, would have spread to the towns.

All branches of science and literature were utilised in this century, and so many writers contributed to extend the enlightenment of the human spirit that those who would have been accounted marvellous in former ages, were now lost in the crowd. Their individual glory is slight on account of their number, but the glory of their age is all the greater.

Literature and the Arts

The philosophy of reason did not make such great progress in France as in England and in Florence, and while the Academy of Sciences contributed greatly to the enlightenment of the human mind, it did not place France in front of other nations. All the great discoveries and the great truths originated elsewhere.

But in rhetoric, poetry, culture, didactic or merely amusing books, the French were the legislators of Europe. There was no longer taste in Italy. True rhetoric was everywhere unknown, religion ridiculously expounded in the pulpit and cases absurdly argued in the courts.

Preachers quoted Virgil and Ovid; barristers, St. Augustine and St. Jerome. The genius had not yet been found to give to the French language the turn of phrase, the numbers, the propriety of style and the dignity it afterwards possessed. A few verses of Malherbe showed only that it was capable of grandeur and force; but this was all. Men of talent who could write excellently in Latin, such as President de Thou and a certain chancellor de L'Hospital, wrote but indifferently in their own language, which proved to be a refractory medium in their hands. French was as yet but noteworthy for a certain simple directness which had constituted the sole merit of Joinville, Amyot, Marot, Montaigne, Regnier and the *Satire Ménippée*. This naïveté was very near to carelessness and coarseness.

Jean de Lingendes, Bishop of Mâcon, unknown to-day, since he omitted to publish his works, was the first orator to speak in the grand style. His sermons and funeral orations, though stained with the rust of his time, were a model of later orators, who imitated and surpassed him. The funeral oration on Charles Emmanuel, Duke of Savoy, surnamed "the Great" by his countrymen, delivered by Lingendes in 1630, contained such grand flights of eloquence, that long afterwards Fléchier took the whole of the exordium, as well as the text and several considerable passages, to embellish his famous funeral oration on the Vicomte de Turenne.

At this period Balzac gave number and harmony to prose. It is true that his letters were bombastic effusions; he wrote thus to the first Cardinal de Retz: "You have just grasped the sceptre of kings and the rose-coloured livery." Speaking of the perfumed waters, he wrote thus to Boisrobert, from Rome: "I am curing myself by swimming in my chamber in the midst of perfumes." With all these faults, he charmed the ear. Rhetoric has such power on men that Balzac was praised in his day for having discovered that small, neglected, but necessary branch of art which consists in the harmonious choice of words, even although he often employed it out of place.

Voiture gave some idea of the airy charm of the epistolary style, which is not the best since it consists of nothing more than wit. His two volumes of letters are a jumble of conceits containing not a single instructive letter, not one which comes from the heart, not one that paints the manners of the time and the characters of men; they show not so much the use of wit as its abuse.

The language gradually became more refined and took on a permanent form. The change was due to the French Academy, and above all to

Vaugelas. His *Translation of Quintius Curtius,* which appeared in 1646, was the first good book to be written in a pure form, and there are few of its expressions and idioms which have become obsolete.

Olivier Patru, who followed him closely, did much to rule and purify the language, and though not considered to be deeply versed in the law, he displayed a conciseness, clarity, propriety and elegance of diction in his speeches, such as had never before been known at the Bar.

One of the works which most contributed to form the taste of the nation and give it a spirit of nicety and precision was the little collection of *Maxims* by François, Duke de La Rochefoucauld. Although there is but one real truth expressed in this book, namely, that "self-love is the main-spring of every action," yet the thought is presented under so many various aspects, that it is nearly always striking. It is not so much a book as materials to embellish a book. The little collection was read with eagerness; and it accustomed people to think and to express their thoughts in a vivid, concise and elegant manner. It was a merit which no other writer had had before in Europe, since the revival of letters.

The first book of genius, however, to appear in prose, was the collection of *Provincial Letters,* in 1656. Every variety of style is to be found there. After the lapse of a century, there is not a single word which has undergone that alteration of meaning which so often changes a living language. To this work must be ascribed the moment when the language became fixed. The Bishop of Lucon, son of the celebrated Bussi, told me that when he asked the Bishop of Meaux what book he would rather have written had he not written his own, Bossuet replied: *"The Provincial Letters."* They have lost much of their pertinence now that the Jesuits have been suppressed and the objects of their disputes come into contempt.

The good taste which distinguishes this book from beginning to end, and the vigour of the final letters, did not at first reform the loose, slovenly, incorrect and disconnected style which for long afterwards characterised the writings and speeches of nearly all authors, preachers and barristers.

One of the first to display a reasoned eloquence in the pulpit was Bourdaloue, about 1668. It was a new departure. After him came other pulpit orators, such as Massillon, Bishop of Clermont, who brought to their addresses greater elegance and finer and more penetrating descriptions of the manners of the age; but not one of them eclipsed him. His style was vigorous rather than florid, without any touch of fancy, so that it seemed that he was more inclined to convince people than to touch their hearts, and he never sought to please.

One may sometimes wish that in banishing bad taste from the pulpit which it degraded, he had also done away with the practice of preaching from a text. For, to speak at some length on a quotation of a line or two, to strain oneself to keep the whole of the sermon centred on those two lines, seems a work unworthy of the solemn office of a minister. The text becomes a sort of device, or rather enigma, which is unravelled by the sermon. The Greeks and the Romans were ignorant of such a practice. It was introduced during the decadence of letters, and course of time has hallowed it.

The custom of dividing all subjects under two or three headings, some of which, such as a question of morals require no division, and others, such as matters of controversy, require many more, remains a tiresome custom, which Bourdaloue found in common use and with which he himself complied.

He had been preceded by Bossuet, afterwards Bishop of Meaux. Bossuet, who became so great a man, was affianced in his youth to Mlle. Desvieux, a girl of remarkably fine character. His talent for theology, and that remarkable gift of eloquence which characterised it, showed themselves at such an early age that his parents and friends persuaded him to give himself to the Church alone. Mlle. Desvieux herself urged him to this course, preferring the glory that he was sure to obtain to the happiness of living with him. He had preached when quite young in 1662 before the king and queen-mother, long before Bourdaloue was known. His sermons, aided by a noble and impressive delivery, the first to be heard at court that approached the sublime manner, met with such great success that the king wrote to his father, the comptroller of Soissons, to congratulate him on possessing such a son.

However, on Bourdaloue's appearance, Bossuet was no longer considered the foremost preacher. He was already himself given to the composition of funeral orations, a kind of oratory which requires an imagination and majestic dignity which approaches poetry, from which art, indeed, something must always be borrowed, though with discretion, when one aspires to the sublime. The funeral oration on the queen-mother, which he delivered in 1667, brought him the bishopric of Condon; but the oration was not worthy of him, and, like his sermons, was not printed. The funeral panegyric on the Queen of England, widow of Charles I, which he delivered in 1669, appears in every detail a masterpiece. The subjects of such pieces of rhetoric are happy in proportion to the misfortunes which the dead experienced. They may be compared to tragedies where it is the misfortunes of the principal characters that interest us most. The funeral panegyric of *Madame*, carried off in the flower of life, who actually breathed her last in his arms, gained the greatest and rarest of triumphs, that of drawing tears from the eyes of courtiers. He was obliged to stop after the words: "O ill-fated, horrible night! when suddenly, like a clap of thunder, echoed the dire news:

Madame is dying. *Madame* is dead. . . ." The listeners burst into sobs, and the orator's voice was lost amidst the sighs and weeping of the congregation.

The French were the only people who succeeded in this kind of oratory. Some time afterwards, the same man introduced a new style, which could hardly have succeeded save in his own hands. He applied the art of oratory to history itself, a literary genre which would seem incapable of admitting it. His *Discourse on Universal History,* written for the Dauphin's education, has neither precedent nor imitators. While the system which he adopts to reconcile the Jewish chronology with that of other nations has met with certain opposition among scholars, his style has met with nothing but admiration. The lofty vigour with which he describes the manners and customs, the government, the rise and fall of great empires, is astonishing, as are the vigorous, true and lively strokes with which he paints and passes judgment on the nations.

Nearly all the works which added lustre to this age were of a king unknown to the ancients. *Télémaque* is of the number. Fénelon, the pupil and friend of Bossuet, and afterwards against his will his rival and enemy, wrote this singular book, which resembles now a novel and now a poem, and in which a modulated prose takes the place of verse. Apparently his aim was to treat the novel as Bossuet had treated history, lending it a fresh dignity and charm and, above all, drawing from fiction a moral beneficial to mankind, and hitherto entirely overlooked in nearly all fictitious compositions. It has been thought that he wrote the book to serve as an exercise for the instruction of the Duke of Burgundy and other French princes, whose tutor he was, in the same way as Bossuet had written his *Universal History* for the education of Monseigneur. But his nephew, the Marquis de Fénelon, who inherited the graces of that celebrated man and who was killed at the Battle of Raucoux, assured me to the contrary. It would certainly have been unseemly for a priest to have taught the loves of Calypso and Eucharis as his first lessons to the royal princes.

This work was not written until he had retired to his archbishopric of Cambrai. Full of classical learning and endowed with a lively and sensitive imagination, he invented a style which could belong to none other than himself, and which flowed easily and fluently. I have seen the original manuscript, and there are not ten erasures in it. He wrote it in three months, in the midst of his unfortunate disputes on Quietism, little suspecting how superior such recreation was to his more learned occupation. It is said that a servant stole a copy of the manuscript and had it printed. If that is so, the Archbishop of Cambrai owes the great reputation he has in Europe to that dishonest act, but to that act was also due the loss of any hope of favour at court for ever.

People pretend to discern in *Télémaque* a veiled criticism of Louis XIV's government. Sesostris, displaying too much pomp in the hour of triumph, Idomeneus revelling in luxury at Salentini and forgetting the necessities of life, were thought to represent the king, although after all it is impossible for anyone to indulge in superfluous luxury except by a superabundance of the products of the needful arts.

In the eyes of malcontents the Marquis de Louvois seemed represented under the name of Protesilas, vain, harsh and proud, an enemy of the great captains who served the state but not the minister.

The Allies who had united against Louis XIV in the war of 1688, and later caused his throne to totter in the war of 1701, joyfully recognised him in the character Idomeneus, whose arrogance disgusted all his neighbours. These allusions made a profound impression, aided, as they were, by a harmonious style, which insinuates in so delicate a manner the advantages of peace and moderation. Foreigners and even the French themselves, weary of so many wars, saw with malicious relief a satire in a book written for the purpose of inculcating virtue. Innumerable editions were brought out. I have myself seen forty in the English language. It is true that after the death of that monarch, who had been so feared, so envied, so respected by all, and so hated by a few, when human malice had at length surfeited its appetite for those alleged allusions which cast a slur upon his conduct, the critics of a sterner taste treated *Télémaque* with some severity. They blamed its wearisomeness, its details, its too little connected adventures, and its oft-repeated and little-varied descriptions of country life, but this book has always been considered one of the finest monuments of a brilliant age.

The *Characters* of La Bruyère may be regarded as a production of a unique kind. No examples of such a work are to be found in the classics any more than of *Télémaque*. The public were struck by a style at once rapid, terse and vigorous, by picturesque expressions, in a word, by a totally new use of the language which did not, however, break its rules; and the numerous allusions contained in the work crowned its success. When La Bruyère showed the manuscript of his work to M. de Malezieu, the latter said to him: "Here is something which will bring you many readers and many enemies." When the generation that was attached in this book had passed away, its reputation declined. Nevertheless, as there are some books which belong to all time and to all countries, it is probable that it will never be forgotten. *Télémaque* had some imitators; the *Characters* of La Bruyère had many more. It is easier to write short descriptions of things that strike us, than to compose a lengthy work of imagination which is both pleasing and instructive.

The delicate art of introducing charm into a philosophical work was as yet an innovation; of which the first example was *La Pluralité des*

Mondes of Fontenelle, and a dangerous one, since the true dress of philosophy is method, clarity and, above all, truth. The fact that this work is partly based on the chimerical hypothesis of Descartes' vortices is sufficient to preclude it from being ranked among the classics by posterity.

Among these literary novelties mention should be made of the works of Bayle, who compiled a kind of dictionary of logic. It was the first work of its kind in which one may learn how to think. One must abandon to the fate of all second-rate books the articles in this collection which contain such unimportant facts as are alike unworthy of Bayle, of a serious reader and of posterity. For the rest, in thus counting Bayle among the authors who gave lustre to the age of Louis XIV, though he was a refugee in Holland, I am but conforming to a decree of the parliament of Toulouse, which proclaimed the validity of his will in France despite the rigour of the laws, and expressly stated "that such a man could not be regarded as a foreigner."

This is no time to expatiate upon the large number of good books which were produced in this age; we shall only dwell on those works which are characterised by new or remarkable genius, and which distinguish this age from others. The eloquence of Bossuet and Bourdaloue, for example, was not and could not be that of a new Cicero, it was of a new order and excellence. If there is anything to approach the Roman orator it is the three memorials composed by Pellisson for Fouquet. They are in the same manner as some of Cicero's orations, a medley of legal matters and state affairs, judiciously treated with an art that never obtrudes and diffused with passages of touching eloquence.

Historians there were, but no Livy. The style of the *Conspiracy of Venice* is comparable to that of Sallust. It is obvious that the Abbé of Saint-Réal had taken that writer for his model, and it is possible that he has surpassed him. All the other writings which we have just mentioned seem of a new creation. It is that above all which distinguishes this illustrious age; for, as for scholars and commentators, the sixteenth and seventeenth centuries had produced them in shoals; but true genius in any genre had not yet been developed.

Who would think that such masterpieces of prose would probably never have been written, had they not been preceded by poetry? Yet such is the progress of the human spirit in every nation, verses were everywhere the earliest children of genius and the first masters of eloquence.

Nations do not differ from the individual. Plato and Cicero began by writing poetry. People knew by heart the few fine stanzas of Malherbe, when it was not possible to quote a noble and sublime passage of prose, and in all probability if Pierre Corneille had not lived the genius of prose-writers would not have been developed.

Corneille is the more highly to be admired in that when he began to compose his tragedies he had but wretched models to guide him; that these models were admired made it still more difficult for him to choose the right path, and to dishearten him still further they were approved by Cardinal Richelieu, the patron of men of letters, though not of good taste. He remunerated such wretched scribblers as are customarily importunate, and, with an arrogance of mind which well became him in other affairs, he was inclined to disdain those in whom he perceived with a certain envy signs of real genius, such as will never bow the knee to idle patronage. It is rare indeed that a powerful man, himself an artist, is seen to give his protection to the artists who best deserve it.

Corneille had to contend with his age, his rivals, and Cardinal Richelieu. I do not propose to repeat here what has been written about *The Cid;* I shall merely remark that the Academy, in passing judgment between Corneille and Scudéri, was over-mindful of Cardinal Richelieu's good favour when it censured the love of Chimène. To love her father's murderer and yet seek to revenge that murder was admirable. To have made her master her love would have been to break one of the fundamental laws of the tragic art, which is chiefly concerned with conflicts of the heart, but at that time the art was itself unknown to all except the author.

The Cid was not the only work of Corneille which Cardinal Richelieu sought to depreciate. The Abbé d'Aubignac tells us that that minister disapproved also of *Polyeucte.*

The Cid was after all a highly embellished imitation of *Guillem de Castro,* and in several passages a translation. *Cinna,* which followed it, was unique. I knew an old servant of the house of Condé, who told me that the great Condé, at the age of twenty, being present at the first performance of *Cinna,* shed tears at these words of Augustus:

> I am the world's great master and my own;
> I am, I will be. Memory and time
> Shall this last, greatest victory record.
> I triumph over wrath too justly rous'd,
> And latest age the conquest shall applaud
> Cinna, let us be friends; 'tis I who ask it.

They were the tears of a hero. The great Corneille causing the great Condé to weep with admiration constitutes a truly commemorative epoch in the history of the human spirit.

The number of plays unworthy of his genius which he composed years later did not prevent the nation from regarding him as a great man, just as the faults of Homer have never prevented his being sublime. It is the privilege of true genius, and especially of the genius who opens up a new avenue of thought, to make mistakes with impunity.

Corneille had formed himself alone; but Louis XIV, Colbert, Sophocles and Euripides all contributed to form Racine. An ode which he composed at the age of eighteen on the occasion of the king's marriage brought him a present which he had not expected, and this decided him to become a poet. His reputation was steadily increased, while that of Corneille has suffered a slight eclipse. The reason is that Racine in all his works after *Alexandre* is always elegant, always correct, always true; he speaks to the heart; and Corneille not infrequently fails in all these respects. Racine was far in advance of both the Greeks and Corneille in his knowledge of the passions, and carried the music of his verse and the elegance of his style to the highest perfection attainable. These men taught the nation to think, to feel, and to express their thoughts. Their audiences, whom they alone had enlightened, at length became relentless critics of the very men who had instructed them.

In the time of Cardinal Richelieu there were few persons in France competent to detect the faults of *The Cid;* yet in 1702, when *Athalie,* a masterpiece of the theatre, was performed at the house of the Duchess of Burgundy, the courtiers thought themselves sufficiently qualified to condemn it. Time has avenged the author; but the great man died without enjoying the success of his finest work. A numerous party long took pride in being prejudiced against Racine. Mme. de Sévigné, the first letter-writer of her age, who had no rival in the sprightly recounting of trifles, always thought that Racine *would not go far.*

She judged him like coffee, of which she said: "People will soon grow tired of it." Reputations can ripen by the passage of time alone.

By the singular good-fortune of the age Molière was the contemporary of Corneille and Racine. It is not true to say that when Molière appeared he found the stage entirely lacking in good comedies. Corneille himself had presented *Le Menteur (The Liar),* a play of character and intrigue, borrowed like *The Cid* from the Spanish theatre; and Molière had written but two of his great masterpieces, when Quinault presented to the public *La Mère Coquette (The Mother as Coquette),* a comedy of both character and intrigue, and indeed a model of intrigue. It appeared in 1664; and was the first comedy in which those who were afterwards known as Marquises were caricatured. The majority of the great lords at the Court of Louis XIV were eager to imitate the grand air, the majesty and dignity of their masters. Those who were in a lower position copied the haughty manners of their betters, until at last there were many who carried this air of superiority and overweening conceit to the highest point of absurdity.

The failing lasted long. Molière attacked it often and contributed to rid the public of such self-important mediocrities, as well as of the affectation of the *précieuses* (affected young women), the pedantry of the *femmes savantes* (learned ladies), and the robe and Latin jargon of the doctors. Molière was, one may say, the legislator over the good manners of society. I am speaking here only of the service he rendered to his age; his other merits are sufficiently well known.

Such an age was worthy of the consideration of future ages; an age in which the heroes of Corneille and Racine, the characters of Molière, the symphonies of Lulli, all of them novelties to the nation, and (since we are here concerned only with the arts) the eloquence of Bossuet and Bourdaloue, were appreciated by Louis XIV, by *Madame* noted for her good taste, by such men as Condé, Turenne, Colbert and a host of eminent men in every department of life. There will never again be such an era in which a Duke de La Rochefoucauld, the author of the *Maxims,* after discoursing with a Pascal and an Arnauld, goes to the theatre to witness a play of Corneille.

Boileau attained to the level of these great men, not with his early satires, for posterity will not give a second glance to the *Embarras de Paris,* and to the names of the Cassaignes and Cotins, but by the exquisite epistles with which he has instructed posterity, and especially by the *Art Poétique,* in which Corneille could have found much to learn.

La Fontaine, far less chaste in style, and far less faultless in his language, but unique in the simplicity and grace which are typical of his work, placed himself by the simplest of writings almost on a level with these sublime writers.

As the originator of a wholly new style, rendered but more difficult by its apparent ease, Quinault was worthy to be placed among his illustrious contemporaries. It is well known how unjustly Boileau sought to disparage him.

Boileau had never sacrificed on the altar of the Graces; and all his life he attempted, though in vain, to belittle a man whose true worth was recognised by them alone. The sincerest praise that we can give a poet is to remember his verses: whole scenes from Quinault are known by heart, a tribute which no Italian opera could obtain. French music has retained a simplicity which is no longer appreciated by other nations; but the natural and beautiful simplicity, which is so frequently and charmingly shown in Quinault, still delights everyone in Europe who is conversant with our language and possesses a cultured taste.

Were a poem like *Armide* or *Atys* to be discovered in antiquity, with what idolatry would it be received! But Quinault was a modern.

All these great men were known and protected by Louis XIV, with the exception of La Fontaine. His excessive simplicity of life, which was carried to the length of personal negligence, caused him to be slighted by a court whose favours he did not seek; but he was welcomed by the Duke of Burgundy and received kindnesses from that prince in his old age. Despite his genius, he was almost as artless as the heroes of his fables. A priest of the Oratory, named Pouget, took great credit to himself for having treated that man of such guileless character, as though he were speaking to the Marquise de Brinvilliers or La Voisin. His tales are all borrowed from Poggio, Ariosto and the Queen of Navarre. If desire be dangerous, pleasantries do not make it so. His admirable fable of the *Animals Afflicted with the Plague*, who accuse themselves of their misdeeds, might be applied to La Fontaine himself. All is pardoned to the lions, wolves and bears, and an innocent animal is sacrificed for having eaten a blade or two of grass.

In the company of these men of genius, who will be the delight and instruction of future ages, there sprang up a host of schools of pretty wits who produced innumerable elegant works of minor importance, that contribute to the amusement of cultured people, just as there have been many pleasing painters whom one would not put beside such painters as Poussin, Lesueur, Lebrun, Lemoine and Vanloo.

But towards the end of Louis XIV's reign two men rose above the crowd of mediocre talents and acquired great reputations. The one was La Motte Houdar, a man of a wise and generous rather than of a lofty spirit, a careful and methodical prose-writer, but often lacking favour and grace in his poetry, and even that correctness which it is only permissible to sacrifice for the sublime. At first he wrote fine stanzas rather than fine odes. His talent deteriorated soon afterwards; but many beautiful fragments which remain to us in more than one genre, will place him for ever above the rank of authors that may be ignored. He proved that in the art of letters a writer of the second rank may yet do good service.

The other was Rousseau, a man of less intellect, less delicacy and less ease than La Motte, but with a greater talent for the art of versifying. His odes were imitations of La Motte, but they excelled in elegance, in variety, and in fancy. His psalms equalled in grace and harmony the sacred songs of Racine. His epigrams are more highly finished than those of Marot. He was far less successful in opera, which requires delicacy of feeling, in comedies, in which humour is indispensable, and in moral epistles, which must delineate the truth; for he lacked all those qualities. Thus he failed in those branches which were foreign to him.

He would have corrupted the French language if others had imitated the Marotic style which he employed in serious works. But fortunately his adulteration of the purity of our language with the outworn forms of two centuries earlier proved only a passing phase. Some of his epistles are rather strained imitations of Boileau, but are not based on sufficiently clear ideas or acknowledged truths: "Truth alone can please."

This genius degenerated considerably in foreign countries, whether age and misfortunes had impaired his talents, or whether, his principal merit consisting in the choice of words and happy turns of phrase, a merit more rare and necessary in a great writer than might be thought, he was no longer within reach of the same assistance. Far from his native country, he might count among his misfortunes the lack of any severe critics.

His continued ill-fortune was the outcome of an ungovernable self-pride, too near inclined to jealousy and spite. His fate cannot but be a striking lesson to every man of talent; but he is to be considered here only as a writer who contributed not a little to the honour of letters.

Scarcely any great genius arose after the halcyon days of these great writers, and towards the time of the death of Louis XIV Nature herself seemed to be reposing.

The path was difficult at the beginning of the age because no one had yet trodden it; it is difficult to-day because it has been beaten flat. The great men of the past age taught us how to think and speak; they told us things which we knew not. Those who succeed them can hardly say anything that is not known already. In short, a kind of distaste has arisen from a very surfeit of masterpieces.

Thus the age of Louis XIV suffered the same fate as those of Leo X, Augustus and Alexander. The ground which in those illustrious periods produced so many fruits of genius had been long prepared. Both moral and physical causes have been searched in vain to provide reason for this slow fecundity, followed by a long period of sterility. The true reason is that among nations who cultivate the fine arts many years must elapse before language and taste become purified. Once these first steps have been made men of genius begin to appear; rivalry and public favour incite fresh efforts and stimulate all talents. Each artist seizes upon the natural beauties which are proper to his particular genre. Any man who thoroughly examines the theory of the arts of pure genius must know, if he has anything of talent himself, that the prime beauties, the great natural opportunities which are suited to the nation for which the author is working are few in number. The subjects available and their appropriate elaboration have much narrower limits than might be thought. The Abbé Dubos, a man of great judgment, who wrote a treatise on poetry and printing about the year 1714, was of the opinion that in the whole of French history there was but a single subject for an epic poem, the destruction of the League by Henri-Quatre. He should have added that since embellishments of the epic theme, such as were well suited to the Greeks, the Romans and the Italians of the fifteenth and sixteenth centuries are prohibited among the French, and the gods of fable, oracles, invulnerable heroes, monsters, sorceries, metamorphoses and romantic adventures no longer held to be fit subjects, the beauties appropriate to the epic poem are confined within a very narrow circle. If, therefore, it happens that any artist seizes upon the only embellishments suited to the times, the subject and the nation, and who carries out what others have attempted, those who come after him will find the ground already occupied.

It is the same with the art of tragedy. It is a mistake to believe that the great tragic passions and emotions can be infinitely varied in new and striking ways. Everything has its limits.

High comedy has no less its own. In human nature there are at the most a dozen characters that are really comic and that are marked by striking qualities. The Abbé Dubos, lacking talent, believes that men of talent can discover a whole host of new characters; but nature would first have to make them. He imagines that the little differences that distinguish one man from another can be as successfully treated as the fundamental qualities. It is true that there are numberless shades of differences, but the number of brilliant colours is small; and it is these primary colours of which a great artist does not fail to make use.

The eloquence of the pulpit, and especially funeral orations, provide a case in point. Moral truths once eloquently expressed, descriptions of human misery and human weaknesses, of the vanity of greatness and the ravages of death, once painted by able fingers, and all becomes commonplace. One is reduced to imitating them or going astray. An adequate number of fables having once been written by a La Fontaine, any additions to them can but point the same moral and relate almost the same adventures. Genius can thus flourish but in a single age and must then degenerate.

The other branches of literature whose subject-matter is, as it were, being continually renewed, such as history and natural science, which require only hard work, judgment and common sense, can more easily maintain their position; and the plastic arts such as painting and sculpture can avoid degeneration when those in power, like Louis XIV, take care to employ only the best artists. For in painting and in sculpture, the same subjects can be treated a hundred times; artists still paint the Holy Family, though Raphael expended all the genius of his art on this subject; but one would not be permitted to treat again the themes of *Cinna,* *Andromaque, L'Art Poétique* and *Tartuffe.*

It must be noted that, the past age having enlightened the present, it has become so easy to write mediocre stuff that we have been flooded out with books and, what is worse, with serious though useless books; but among this multitude of mediocre writing an evil becomes a necessity in a city at once large, wealthy and idle, in which one party of citizens being continually occupied in entertaining the other, there have appeared, from time to time, excellent works of history, of reflection or of that light literature which is the recreation of all sorts of minds.

Of all the nations, France has produced the greatest number of such works. Its language has become the language of Europe; everything has contributed to this end; the great writers of the age of Louis XIV, and their successors the exiled Calvinist ministers, who brought their eloquence and logic into foreign countries; above all, a Bayle, who, writing his works in Holland, has had them read by every nation; a Rapin de Thoyras, who has written in French the only good history of England; a Saint-Evremond, whose acquaintance was sought by every person of the Court of London: the Duchess de Mazarin, to please whom was everyone's ambition; Mme d'Olbreuse, later Duchess von Zell, who carried with her into Germany all the graces of her country. The social spirit is the natural heritage of the French; it is a merit and a pleasure of which other nations have felt the need. The French language is of all languages that which expresses with the greatest ease, exactness and delicacy all subjects of conversation which can arise among gentlefolk; and it thus contributes throughout all Europe to one of the most agreeable diversions of life.

The Arts (continued)

The arts which do not solely depend upon the intellect had made but little progress in France before the period which is known as the age of Louis XIV. Music was in its infancy; a few languishing songs, some airs for the violin, the guitar and the lute, composed for the most part in Spain, were all that we possessed. Lulli's style and technique were astonishing. He was the first in France to write bass counterpoint, middle parts and figures. At first some difficulty was experienced in playing his compositions, which now seem so easy and simple. At the present day there are a thousand people who know music, for one who knew it in the time of Louis XIII; and the art has been perfected by this spread of knowledge. To-day, there is no great town which has not its public concerts: yet at that time Paris itself had none; the king's twenty-four violins comprised the sum total of French music.

The familiarity with music and its dependent arts has so increased that towards the end of Louis XIV's reign the practice of dancing figures to music was instituted, so that at the present day it may be truly said that people dance at sight.

There were several very great architects during the regency of Marie de' Medici. She had the Palace of Luxembourg built in the Tuscan style, in honour of her country and for the adornment of our own. The same de Brosse, whose gate of Saint-Gervais is still standing, built a palace for this queen, which she never occupied. Cardinal Richelieu, with all his greatness of mind, was far from having as good taste in such matters as she. The cardinal's palace, which is now the Palais-Royal, is indeed a proof of this. We had great hopes when we saw the fine façade of the Louvre being built, which is such as to make one long to see the palace completed. Many citizens built themselves magnificent houses, more distinguished for the exquisite taste of the interior rather than the exterior, and gratifying the luxury of private individuals even more than adorning the city.

Colbert, the Maecenas of all the arts, founded an Academy of Architecture in 1671. A Vitruvius is not enough, one must have an Augustus to employ him.

Municipal officials should also have an ardour for the arts, an ardour which must be enlightened. Had there been two or three mayors like President Turgot, the city of Paris would not be disgraced by such a badly built and badly situated town hall, by such a small and badly laid-out square, famous only for its gibbets and its bonfires; by the narrowness of the streets in the busiest quarters—in short, by this relic of barbarism in the midst of splendour and in the very home of all the arts.

Painting began with Poussin in the reign of Louis XIII. No account need be taken of the indifferent painters who preceded him. Since his time every age has had its great painters, though not in that profusion which is one of Italy's glories; but without stopping to dwell upon Lesueur, who owned no master, or Lebrun, who rivalled the Italians in design and execution, we have had more than thirty painters who have bequeathed works of art very worthy of regard. Foreigners are beginning to take them from us. The galleries and apartments of one great king I have seen filled with nothing else but French pictures, whose value we should perhaps be loath to recognise. In France I have seen a picture of Santerre refused for twelve thousand livres. There is scarcely to be found in Europe a larger painting than the ceiling of Lemoine at Versailles, and I know not whether there are any more beautiful. Since then we have had Vanloo, considered even in foreign countries as the finest painter of his time.

Not only did Colbert organise the Academy of Painting as it is to-day, but in 1667 he persuaded Louis XIV to establish one in Rome. A palace was purchased in that capital for the residence of the director, and pupils who have won prizes at the Paris Academy are sent there to study, the expenses of their journey and board being defrayed by the king; they there copy ancient works of art, and study the works of Raphael and Michael Angelo. The desire to imitate both ancient and modern Rome is in itself a noble homage to the eternal city, and the homage has still been rendered even since the enormous collections of Italian paintings amassed by the king and the Duke of Orleans, and the masterpieces of sculpture which France has produced, have enabled us to dispense with the necessity of seeking masters abroad.

It is chiefly in sculpture that we have excelled, and in the art of casting colossal equestrian figures in a single mould.

Should posterity discover one day fragments of such works of art as the baths of Apollo, buried under ruins, or exposed to the ravages of the weather in the thickets of Versailles; or the tomb of Cardinal Richelieu in the Sorbonne chapel, too little noticed by the public; or the equestrian statue of Louis XIV made in Paris to grace the city of Bordeaux; or the Mercury which Louis XV presented to the King of Prussia; and many other works of art equal to those that I have mentioned, one cannot but think that these productions of our time would find a place among the finest of Greek antiquity.

We have equalled the ancients in our medallions. Warin was the first to raise this art from mediocrity towards the end of the reign of Louis XIII. Those dies and stamps now arranged in historical order in the corridors of the Louvre gallery are a marvellous sight. They are worth about two millions, and the greater part of them are masterpieces.

The art of engraving precious stones was no less successfully cultivated. That of reproducing pictures, and of perpetuating them by means of copper plates, and thus handing down to posterity all kinds of representations of nature and of art, was still in a very imperfect state in France previous to this age. It is one of the most pleasing and useful of arts. We owe its discovery to the Florentines, who invented it towards the middle of the fifteenth century, and it has made even greater progress in France than in the country of its origin, because a greater number of works of that class were produced there. Collections of royal engravings often formed the most magnificent gift of the king to ambassadors. The chasing of gold and silver, which requires a knowledge of designing, and good taste, was brought to the highest degree of perfection to which it is possible for the skill of man to attain.

Now that we have surveyed all the arts which contribute to the pleasures of the people and the glory of the state, we cannot pass over in silence the most useful of all the arts, and one in which the French excelled all other nations in the world; I mean the art of surgery, whose progress was so rapid and far-famed in this age, that people came to Paris from the ends of Europe for any cure or operation that required exceptional skill. Not only was France almost the only country in which first-rate surgeons were to be found, but it was in that country alone that the requisite instruments were properly made; France provided all her neighbours with them, and I have heard from the mouth of the celebrated Cheseldon, the greatest surgeon in London, that it was he who first began to make in London, in 1715, the instruments of his art. Medicine, which helped to improve surgery, did not reach a higher degree of perfection in France than in England, or under the famous Boerhaave in

Holland; medicine indeed, like natural science, was perfected by making use of the discoveries of our neighbours.

The foregoing is, on the whole, a faithful account of the progress of the human spirit in France during that age which began in the time of Cardinal Richelieu, and ended in our days. It will be with difficulty surpassed, and, if in some ways it be eclipsed, it will remain the model of more fortunate ages, to which it will have given birth.

The Useful Arts and Sciences in Europe During the Reign of Louis XIV

We have sufficiently intimated throughout the whole of this history that the national disasters which fill it, and which followed one another almost without a break, are in the long run erased from the register of time. The details and devices of politics sink into oblivion; but sound laws, institutions, and achievements in the sciences and the arts remain for ever.

The crowd of foreigners who travel to Rome to-day, not as pilgrims, but as men of taste, find few traces of Gergory VII or Boniface VIII; they admire the temples built by men like Bramante and Michael Angelo, the pictures of Raphael and the sculpture of Bernini; if they are men of intelligence, they read Ariosto and Tasso and honour the ashes of Galileo. In England Cromwell's name is but spoken of now and then; people no longer discuss the Wars of the White Rose, but they will study Newton for years at a time, and no one is surprised to read in his epitaph that *he was the glory of the human race,* though one would be much surprised to find in England the memory of any statesman accorded such an honour.

I would gladly have it in my power to do justice to all the great men who, like Newton, gave lustre to their country during the last hundred years. I have called that period the age of Louis XIV, not only because that monarch gave greater encouragement to the arts than all his fellow-kings together, but also because in his lifetime he outlived three generations of the kings of Europe. I have set the limits of this epoch at some years before Louis XIV and some years after him; for it was during this space of time that the human spirit has made most progress.

From 1660 to the present day the English have made greater progress in all the arts than in all preceding ages. I will not here repeat what I have said elsewhere of Milton. It is true that some critics disapprove of his fantastic descriptions, his paradise of fools, his alabaster walls which encircle the earthly paradise; his devils, who transform themselves from giants into pigmies that they may take less room in council, seated in a vast hall of gold erected in hell; his cannons fired from heaven, his

mountains hurled at the heads of foes; his angels on horseback, angels
who are cut in two and their dissevered bodies as quickly joined together
again. His long descriptions and repetitions are considered tedious; it is
said that he has equalled neither Ovid nor Hesiod in his long description
of the way in which the earth, the animals and mankind were created.
His dissertations on astronomy are condemned as too dry and the creations of his fancy as being extravagant, rather than marvellous, and
more disgusting than impressive; such is a long passage upon chaos; the
love of Sin and Death and the children of their incest; and Death, "who
turns up his nose to scent across the immensity of chaos the change that
has come over the earth, like a crow scenting a corpse"—Death, who
smells out the odour of the Fall, who strikes with his petrifying hammer
on cold and dry; and cold and dry with hot and moist, transformed into
four fine army generals, lead into battle their embryonic atoms like light-
armed infantry. Criticism indeed exhausts itself, but never praise. Milton remains at once the glory and wonder of England; he is compared to
Homer, whose defects are as great, and he is preferred to Dante, whose
conceptions are yet more fantastic.

Among the large number of pleasing poets who graced the reign of
Charles II, such as Waller, the Earl of Dorset and the Earl of Rochester,
the Duke of Buckingham and many others, we must single out Dryden,
who distinguished himself in every branch of poetry; his works are full
of details both brilliant and true to nature, lively, vigorous, bold and
passionate, merits in which none of his own nation equals him nor any
of the ancients surpass him. If Pope, who succeeded him, had not written
late in life his *Essay on Man*, he could not be compared to Dryden.

No other nation has treated moral subjects in poetry with greater depth
and vigour than the English; there lies, it seems to me, the greatest merit
of her poets.

There is another kind of elegant writing which requires at once a mind
more cultured and more universal; such was Addison's; he achieved immortal fame with his *Cato*, the only English tragedy written from beginning to end in an elegant and lofty style, and his other moral and critical
works breathe a perfect taste; in all he wrote, sound sense appears
adorned by a lively fancy, and his manner of writing is an excellent
model for any country. Dean Swift left several passages whose like is not
to be found among the writers of antiquity—a Rabelais made perfect.

The English have hardly any examples of funeral orations; it is not
their custom to praise their kings and queens in churches; but pulpit
oratory, which was in London coarse before the reign of Charles II, suddenly improved. Bishop Brunet admits in his *Memoirs* that it was
brought about by imitating the French. Perhaps they have surpassed

their masters; their sermons are less formal, less pretentious and less declamatory than those of the French.

It is, moreover, remarkable that this insular people, separated from the rest of the world and so lately cultured, should have acquired at least as much knowledge of antiquity as the Italians have been able to gather in Rome, which was for so long the meeting-place of the nations. Marsham penetrated the mysteries of ancient Egypt. No Persian had such a knowledge of the Zoroastrian religion as the scholar Hyde. The Turks were unacquainted with the history of Mahomet and the preceding centuries, and its interpretation was left to the Englishman Sale, who turned his travels in Arabia to such good profit.

There is no other country in the world where the Christian religion has been so vigorously attacked and so ably defended as in England. From Henry VIII to Cromwell men argued and fought, like that ancient breed of gladiators who descended into the arena sword in hand and a bandage on their eyes. A few slight differences in creed and dogma were sufficient to cause frightful wars, but from the Restoration to the present day when every Christian tenet has been almost annually attacked, such disputes have not aroused the least disturbance; science has taken the place of fire and sword to silence every argument.

It is above all in philosophy that the English have become the teachers of other nations. It is no mere question of ingenious systems. The false myths of the Greeks should have disappeared long ago and modern myths should never have appeared at all. Roger Bacon broke fresh ground by declaring that Nature must be studied in a new way, that experiments must be made; Boyle devoted his life to making them. This is no place for a dissertation on physics; it is enough to say that after three thousand years of fruitless research, Newton was the first to find and demonstrate the great natural law by which all elements of matter are mutually attracted, the law by which all the stars are held in their courses. He was indeed the first to see the light; before him it was unknown.

His principles of mathematics, which include a system of physics at once new and true, are based on the discovery of the calculus, incorrectly called *infinitesimal,* a supreme effort of geometry, and one which he made at the age of twenty-four. It was a great philosopher, the learned Halley, who said of him "that it is not permitted to any mortal to approach nearer to divinity."

A host of expert geometricians and physicists were enlightened by his discoveries and inspired by his genius. Bradley discovered the aberration of the light of fixed stars, distant at least twelve billion leagues from our small globe.

Halley, whom I have quoted above, though but an astronomer, received the command of one of the king's ships in 1698. It was on this ship that he determined the position of the stars of the Antarctic Pole, and noted the variations of the compass in all parts of the known globe. The voyage of the Argonauts was in comparison but the crossing of a bark from one side of a river to the other. Yet Halley's voyage has been hardly spoken of in Europe.

The indifference we display towards great events become too familiar, and our admiration of the ancient Greeks for trivial ones, is yet another proof of the wonderful superiority of our age over that of the ancients. Boileau in France and Sir William Temple in England obstinately refused to acknowledge such a superiority; they were eager to disparage their own age, in order to place themselves above it: but the dispute between the ancients and the moderns has been at last decided, at any rate in the field of philosophy. There is not a single ancient philosopher whose works are taught to-day to the youth of any enlightened nation.

Locke alone should serve as a good example of the advantage of our age over the most illustrious ages of Greece. From Plato to Locke there is indeed nothing; no one in that interval developed the operations of the human mind, and a man who knew the whole of Plato and only Plato, would know little and that not well.

Plato was indeed an eloquent Greek; his *Apologia of Socrates* stands a service rendered to philosophers of every nation; he should be respected, as having represented ill-fortuned virtue in so honourable a light and its persecutors in one so odious. It was long thought that ethics so admirable could not be associated with metaphysics so false; he was almost made a Father of the Church for his *Ternaire,* which no one has ever understood. But what would be thought to-day of a philosopher who should tell us that one substance is the same as *any other;* that the world is a figure of twelve pentagons; that fire is a pyramid which is connected with the earth by numbers? Would it be thought convincing to prove the immortality and transmigration of the soul by saying that sleep is born of wakefulness and wakefulness of sleep, the living from the dead and the dead from the living? Such reasonings as these have been admired for many centuries, and still more fantastic ideas have since been employed in the education of mankind.

Locke alone has developed the *human understanding* in a book where there is naught but truths, a book made perfect by the fact that these truths are stated clearly.

To complete our review of the superiority of the past century over all others, we may cast our eyes towards Germany and the North. Hevelius of Danzig was the first astronomer to study deeply the planet of the moon; no man before him surveyed the heavens with greater care: and of all the great men that the age produced, none showed more plainly why it should be justly called the age of Louis XIV. A magnificent library that he possessed was destroyed by fire; upon which the King of France bestowed on the astronomer of Danzig a present which more than compensated him for the loss.

Mercator of Holstein was the forerunner of Newton in geometry; and the Bernouillis in Switzerland were worthy pupils of that great man. Leibnitz was for some time regarded as his rival.

The celebrated Leibnitz was born at Leipzig; and died, full of learning, in the town of Hanover; like Newton, worshipping a god, and seeking counsel of no man. He was perhaps the most universal genius in Europe: a historian assiduous in research; a sagacious lawyer, enlightening the study of law with science, foreign to that subject though it seem; a metaphysician sufficiently open-minded to endeavour to reconcile theology with metaphysics; even a Latin poet, and finally a mathematician of sufficient calibre to dispute with the great Newton the invention of the infinitesimal calculus, so that for some time the issue remained uncertain.

It was the golden age of geometry; mathematicians frequently challenged one another, that is to say, they sent each other problems to be solved, almost as the ancient kings of Asia and Egypt are reported to have sent each other riddles to divine. The problems propounded by the geometricians were more difficult than the ancient riddles; and in Germany, England, Italy and France, not one of them was left unsolved. Never was intercourse between philosophers more universal; Leibnitz did much to encourage it. A republic of letters was being gradually established in Europe, in spite of different religions. Every science, every art, was mutually assisted in this way, and it was the academies which formed this republic. Italy and Russia were allied by literature. The Englishman, the German and the Frenchman went to Leyden to study. The celebrated physician Boerhaave was consulted both by the Pope and by the Czar. His greatest pupils attracted the notice of foreigners and thus became to some extent the physicians of the nation; true scholars in every branch drew closer the bonds of this great fellowship of intellect, spread everywhere and everywhere independent. This intercourse still obtains, and is indeed one of the consolations for those ills which political ambition scatters throughout the earth.

Italy throughout this century preserved her ancient glory, though she produced no new Tassos nor Raphaels; it is enough to have produced them once. Men like Chiabrera, and later Zappi and Filicaia, showed that refinement is still a characteristic of that nation. Maffei's *Merope* and the dramatic works of Metastasio are worthy monuments of the age.

The study of true physics, founded by Galileo, was still pursued despite the opposition of an ancient and too hallowed philosophy. Men like Cassini, Viviani, Manfredi, Bianchini, Zanotti and many others spread the same light in Italy which was already lighting other countries; and, while admitting that the chief rays of this beacon came from England, let it be said that Italian teachers at least did not hide their eyes from the gleam.

All branches of literature were cultivated in this ancient home of the arts, and with as great success save in those subjects where a liberty of thought unknown to Italy gives wider scope. This age, above all, was better acquainted with antiquity than all preceding ages. Italy provided more such monuments than all the rest of Europe, and every fresh excavation has but extended the boundaries of knowledge.

We owe this progress to a few learned men, a few geniuses scattered in small numbers in various parts of Europe, nearly all of them unhonoured for many years and often persecuted; they enlightened and consoled the world when it was devastated by war. The names of all those who thus gave lustre to Germany, England and Italy may be found elsewhere. A foreigner is perhaps little able to appreciate the merits of all these illustrious men. It is enough, here, if we have shown that during the past century mankind, from one end of Europe to the other, has been more enlightened than in all preceding ages.

Edward Gibbon

1737—1794

14

Edward Gibbon's *Decline and Fall of the Roman Empire* is regarded not only as the greatest historical achievement of Enlightenment historiography; even more, many modern critics consider it among the greatest historical works in the English language. To this monumental history—over a million and one quarter words in length, spanning 1,300 years, from Rome in the "Age of the Antonines" in the first century to the dawn of the Renaissance, spread over the three continents of the ancient world, and describing the rise of both Christianity and Mohammedanism—Gibbon claims to have devoted twenty years of his life. Yet as we consider his life story, in the memoirs he left to posterity, we must conclude that the passion and energy of his whole life, not merely the work of twenty years, lay in the production of a work which recounts, in the words of its author, "the greatest, perhaps most awful scene in the history of mankind." Whatever the events and frustrations of Gibbon's worldly career, they appear to us as merely shadows cast upon his life and his devotion to learning and language that gave the world the *Decline and Fall.*

Gibbon was a sickly, unhappy child, neglected by his mother, who died when he was ten. From that time, until a stern, impatient father shipped a bookish, introverted son to Magdalen College, Oxford, in 1752, Gibbon noted that "reading—free desultory reading—was the employment and comfort of my solitary hours." The best that Gibbon could say for the Philistine environment he found at Oxford was that it could not tempt him from a vocation he had already found.

In order to reform his wayward son from his adolescent conversion to Catholicism at Oxford, his father banished him to a strict Protestant household in Protestant Switzerland. But even the Calvinists could not keep Gibbon from the experience of what he alone could have termed "the discovery of a sixth sense, the first consciousness of manhood." Unfortunately, his love for Mademoiselle Susan Curchod was short-lived; once again

351

he felt the oppressive hand of his father, and dutifully extinguished the only romantic flame he ever felt. He suffered, yet he kept on reading.

By 1761, after his return to England, Gibbon was ready to publish a preliminary report on his reading, called *An Essay on the Study of Literature.* Written in French, this compact work, whose publication marked for Gibbon "the loss of my literary maidenhead," revealed his knowledge of the ancient historians, his concern with the laws and institutions of the Roman Republic, and most important of all, his consuming interest in the works of Montesquieu, an interest which would later influence the whole design of the *Decline and Fall.* The year 1763 brought peace to Europe and free access to the continent for British travelers. Within a year, Gibbon was in Rome, and the decision of his life was made. It was there, "amidst the ruins of the Capitol" (he wrote with precise detail in his *Autobiography*), "while the barefooted friars were singing their vespers in the temple of Jupiter that the idea of writing the decline and fall of the city first started to my mind."

Shortly before his death in 1776, David Hume was delighted to receive the first volume of the *Decline and Fall.* Gibbon's wish was to follow in the path of Hume and Robertson, and he wrote that Hume's praise "overpaid the labour of ten years." In retrospect, we know that Gibbon's work far surpassed that of both his Scottish predecessors. While he shared with them the commitment to write history in the philosophical spirit, he was able to bring into his work the erudite and pious scholarship of the previous century. When Gibbon was in Paris on his way to Rome, he visited the Academy of Medals and Inscriptions and discovered the writings of the Benedictine monks, Jean Mabillon and Bernard Montfaucon. He saw no need to redo Mabillon's works on medieval manuscripts, or Montfaucon's on Greek paleography; it was enough to make use of their learning, as is evident in the footnotes to the *Decline and Fall.*

The Benedictines drew him to the study of coins and inscriptions; his native curiosity brought him to the works of other seventeenth-century scholars, and for the rest of his life he nourished his antiquarian interests through subscriptions to the learned journals that were being published by the academies in Paris. For his account of the early Church, he relied on the ecclesiastical histories of the friar Caesar Baronius and of the Jansenist Nain de Tillemont; for his description of the Empire in the East, he turned to the work of the French Byzantinist Charles du Fresne Du Cange. The *Decline and Fall* can be seen as the synthesis of two hundred years of research into ancient and medieval history.

The sources for the *Decline and Fall* were in part the erudition of the seventeenth century, but the integral structure reflects the influence of Montesquieu's *Spirit of the Laws,* the most widely read sociological work of the eighteenth century. Montesquieu taught Gibbon that geography and climate affect the character of and the changes in political institutions and legal systems as much as do the traumatic effects of invasion and war. It was Gibbon's aim to expand Montesquieu's sociological history into the study of other social institutions as historical forces, especially religion. His splendid fifteenth and sixteenth chapters on the rise and nature of Christianity made the *Decline and Fall* as scandalous as it was learned. These chapters provoked ill-considered criticism, and elicited in 1779 Gibbon's brilliant *Vindication*.

Gibbon fully accounted for the multiplicity of causes which brought a great civilization to its end; Christianity, however, was not merely one among many: in Gibbon's history, it became the central destructive social force. The Roman Empire described in the opening chapters was a tolerant pagan establishment. The populace loved mundane pleasures, and built strong governments which they defended with admirable courage. Their energies were directed to mechanical arts, conquest, and the creation of civilized law. As the overextended Empire began to decay and suffer from repeated invasion, a new religion offered a despairing people the promise of comfort in a life after death. As a consequence, they neglected to defend their Empire from its enemies with their former ardor, and substituted the hope of an afterlife for the rational pursuit of pleasure and virtue. Thus, Christianity is coordinate with the decline of the Empire, and is indispensable to the explanation of its fall. It is true, of course, that these superbly written chapters are supreme examples of Gibbon's powerful irony; almost every paragraph is both historical observation and pungent anticlerical humor, all of which pleased the philosophes and enraged the believers.

Gibbon was hesitant to terminate the work of a lifetime, yet by June, 1787, after years of delight and hard work—and constant revision—he had to take "an everlasting leave of an old and agreeable companion." Of the remaining seven years of Gibbon's life little needs to be said, except, perhaps, to agree with him that the "life of the historian must be short and precarious," and to vindicate his hope that his *History* would have "a future fate."

Selected Bibliography

The best book on Gibbon is by the historian himself. The *Autobiography* is most readily available in the new, revised edition of 1961. There are two good biographies: a short, incisive one, by G. M. Young, *Gibbon* (1932); and a longer, more detailed one, by Edward M. Low, *Edward Gibbon* (1937). Before writing his book on Hume, Giuseppe Giarrizzo made an equally valuable study of Gibbon, *Edward Gibbon e la cultura europea del Settecento* (1954), where he shows what Gibbon learned from the culture that surrounded him, and how he, in turn, advanced eighteenth-century historiography. There is an excellent article on "Gibbon's Contribution to Historical Method," in *Historia II* (1954), 450–463, by Arnaldo Momigliano which discusses Gibbon's debts to his predecessors and contemporaries. This article is also available in Momigliano's valuable collection of essays,

Studies in Historiography (1966), 40–56. Professor H. R. Trevor-Roper presents some urbane and illuminating comments in his essay, "The Idea of the Decline and Fall of the Roman Empire," in *The Age of Enlightenment: Studies Presented to Theodore Besterman,* ed., W. H. Barber et al. (1967), 413–430, as does J. H. Plumb in his article, "Gibbon and History," in *History Today,* XIV:2 (November, 1969), 737–743.

J. B. Bury, in his "Introduction" to his definitive seven-volume edition of the *Decline and Fall,* published in the last years of the nineteenth century, from which we have drawn our selections, compares Gibbon's work with more recent scholarship. Bury's own notes to this edition, which we include along with Gibbon's footnotes, reveal that for the most part Gibbon's history has been embellished and corroborated by his successors, rather than surpassed. Leo Braudy examines Gibbon's historiographical style in *Narrative Form in History and Fiction: Hume, Fielding and Gibbon* (1970).

DECLINE AND FALL
OF THE ROMAN EMPIRE

The Extent and Military Force of the Empire
in the Age of the Antonines

In the second century of the Christian Era, the empire of Rome comprehended the fairest part of the earth, and the most civilized portion of mankind. The frontiers of that extensive monarchy were guarded by ancient renown and disciplined valour. The gentle, but powerful, influence of laws and manners had gradually cemented the union of the provinces. Their peaceful inhabitants enjoyed and abused the advantages of wealth and luxury. The image of a free constitution was preserved with decent reverence. The Roman senate appeared to possess the sovereign authority, and devolved on the emperors all the executive powers of government. During a happy period of more than fourscore years, the public administration was conducted by the virtue and abilities of Nerva, Trajan, Hadrian, and the two Antonines. It is the design of this and of the two succeeding chapters, to describe the prosperous condition of their empire; and afterwards, from the death of Marcus Antoninus, to deduce the most important circumstances of its decline and fall: a revolution which will ever be remembered, and is still felt by the nations of the earth.

The principal conquests of the Romans were achieved under the republic; and the emperors, for the most part, were satisfied with preserving those dominions which had been acquired by the policy of the senate, the active emulation of the consuls, and the martial enthusiasm of the people. The seven first centuries were filled with a rapid succession of triumphs; but it was reserved for Augustus to relinquish the ambitious design of subduing the whole earth, and to introduce a spirit of moderation into the public councils. Inclined to peace by his temper and situation, it was easy for him to discover that Rome, in her present exalted situation, had much less to hope than to fear from the chance of arms; and that, in the prosecution of remote wars, the undertaking became every day more difficult, the event more doubtful, and the possession more precarious and less beneficial. The experience of Augustus added

Decline and Fall of the Roman Empire edited by J. B. Bury, London: 1896, Vol. I, pp. 1–3; Vol. II, pp. 1–8, 32–70; Vol. IV, pp. 160–169.

weight to these salutary reflections, and effectually convinced him that, by the prudent vigour of his counsels, it would be easy to secure every concession which the safety or the dignity of Rome might require from the most formidable barbarians. Instead of exposing his person and his legions to the arrows of the Parthians, he obtained, by an honourable treaty, the restitution of the standards and prisoners which had been taken in the defeat of Crassus.[1]

His generals, in the early part of his reign, attempted the reduction of Ethiopia and Arabia Felix. They marched near a thousand miles to the south of the tropic; but the heat of the climate soon repelled the invaders and protected the unwarlike natives of those sequestered regions.[2] The northern countries of Europe scarcely deserved the expense and labour of conquest. The forests and morasses of Germany were filled with a hardy race of barbarians, who despised life when it was separated from freedom; and though, on the first attack, they seemed to yield to the weight of the Roman power, they soon, by a signal act of despair, regained their independence, and reminded Augustus of the vicissitude of fortune.[3] On the death of that emperor his testament was publicly read in the senate. He bequeathed, as a valuable legacy to his successors, the advice of confining the empire within those limits which nature seemed to have placed as its permanent bulwarks and boundaries; on the west the Atlantic ocean; the Rhine and Danube on the north; the Euphrates on the east; and towards the south the sandy deserts of Arabia and Africa.[4] . . .

The Progress of the Christian Religion, and the Sentiments, Manners, Numbers, and Condition, of the Primitive Christians

A candid but rational inquiry into the progress and establishment of Christianity may be considered as a very essential part of the history of

---

[1]Dion Cassius (1. liv. p. 736 [8]) with the annotations of Reimar, who has collected all that Roman vanity has left upon the subject. The marble of Ancyra, on which Augustus recorded his own exploits, asserts that *he compelled* the Parthians to restore the ensigns of Crassus.

[2]Strabo (1. xvi. p. 780), Pliny the elder (Hist. Natur. 1. vi. 32, 35 [28, 29]) and Dion Cassius (1. liii. p. 723 [29], and 1. liv. p. 734 [6]) have left us very curious details concerning these wars. The Romans made themselves masters of Mariaba, or Merab, a city of Arabia Felix, well known to the Orientals. They were arrived within three days' journey of the Spice country, the rich object of their invasion.

[3]By the slaughter of Varus and his three legions. See the first book of the Annals of Tacitus. Sueton. in August. c. 23, and Velleius Paterculus, 1. ii. c. 117, etc. Augustus did not receive the melancholy news with all the temper and firmness that might have been expected from his character.

[4]Tacit. Annal, 1. ii. [i. II]. Dion Cassius, 1. lvi. p. 832 [33], and the speech of Augustus himself, in Julian's Caesars. It receives great light from the learned notes of his French translator, M. Spanheim.

the Roman empire. While that great body was invaded by open violence, or undermined by slow decay, a pure and humble religion gently insinuated itself into the minds of men, grew up in silence and obscurity, derived new vigour from opposition, and finally erected the triumphant banner of the cross on the ruins of the Capitol. Nor was the influence of Christianity confined to the period or to the limits of the Roman empire. After a revolution of thirteen or fourteen centuries, that religion is still professed by the nations of Europe, the most distinguished portion of human kind in arts and learning as well as in arms. By the industry and zeal of the Europeans it has been widely diffused to the most distant shores of Asia and Africa; and by the means of their colonies has been firmly established from Canada to Chili, in a world unknown to the ancients.

But this inquiry, however useful or entertaining, is attended with two peculiar difficulties. The scanty and suspicious materials of ecclesiastical history seldom enable us to dispel the dark cloud that hangs over the first age of the church. The great law of impartiality too often obliges us to reveal the imperfections of the uninspired teachers and believers of the gospel; and, to a careless observer, *their* faults may seem to cast a shade on the faith which they professed. But the scandal of the pious Christian, and the fallacious triumph of the Infidel, should cease as soon as they recollect not only *by whom,* but likewise *to whom,* the Divine Revelation was given. The theologian may indulge the pleasing task of describing Religion as she descended from Heaven, arrayed in her native purity. A more melancholy duty is imposed on the historian. He must discover the inevitable mixture of error and corruption which she contracted in a long residence upon earth, among a weak and degenerate race of beings.

Our curiosity is naturally prompted to inquire by what means the Christian faith obtained so remarkable a victory over the established religions of the earth. To this inquiry, an obvious but satisfactory answer may be returned; that it was owing to the convincing evidence of the doctrine itself, and to the ruling providence of its great Author. But, as truth and reason seldom find so favourable a reception in the world, and as the wisdom of Providence frequently condescends to use the passions of the human heart, and the general circumstances of mankind, as instruments to execute its purpose; we may still be permitted, though with becoming submission, to ask not indeed what were the first, but what were the secondary causes of the rapid growth of the Christian church. It will, perhaps, appear that it was most effectually favoured and assisted by the five following causes: I. The inflexible, and, if we may use the expression, the intolerant zeal of the Christians, derived, it is true, from the Jewish religion, but purified from the narrow and unsocial spirit which, instead of inviting, had deterred the Gentiles from embracing the law of Moses. II. The doctrine of a future life, improved by every additional circumstance which could give weight and efficacy to that important truth. III. The miraculous powers ascribed to the primitive church. IV. The pure and austere morals of the Christians. V. The union and discipline of the Christian republic, which gradually formed an independent and increasing state in the heart of the Roman empire.

I. We have already described the religious harmony of the ancient world, and the facility with which the most different and even hostile nations embraced, or at least respected, each other's superstitions. A single people refused to join in the common intercourse of mankind. The Jews, who, under the Assyrian and Persian monarchies, had languished for many ages the most despised portion of their slaves,[1] emerged from obscurity under the successors of Alexander; and, as they multiplied to a surprising degree in the East, and afterwards in the West, they soon excited the curiosity and wonder of other nations.[2] The sullen obstinacy with which they maintained their peculiar rites and unsocial manners seemed to mark them out a distinct species of men, who boldly professed, or who faintly disguised, their implacable hatred to the rest of human kind.[3] Neither the violence of Antiochus, nor the arts of Herod, nor the example of the circumjacent nations, could ever persuade the Jews to associate with the institutions of Moses the elegant mythology of the Greeks.[4] According to the maxims of universal toleration, the Romans protected a superstition which they despised.[5] The polite Augustus condescended to give orders that sacrifices should be offered for his prosper-

---

[1] Dum Assyrios penes, Medosque, et Persas Oriens fuit, despectissima pars servientium. Tacit. Hist. v. 8. Herodotus, who visited Asia whilst it obeyed the last of those empires, slightly mentions the Syrians of Palestine, who, according to their own confession, had received from Egypt the rite of circumcision. See 1. ii. c. 104.

[2] Diodorus Siculus, 1. xl. [2 *sqq.*]. Dion Cassius, 1. xxxvii. p. 121 [c. 17]. Tacit. Hist. v. 1–9. Justin, xxxvi. 2, 3.

[3] Tradidit arcano quaecunque volumine Moses.
        Non monstrare vias eadem nisi sacra colenti
        Quaesitum ad fontem solos deducere verpos. [Juvenal, xiv. 102.]
The letter of this law is not to be found in the present volume of Moses. But the wise, the humane Maimonides openly teaches that, if an idolater fall into the water, a Jew ought not to save him from instant death. See Basnage, Histoire des Juifs, 1. vi. c. 28.

[4] A Jewish sect, which indulged themselves in a sort of occasional conformity, derived from Herod, by whose example and authority they had been seduced, the name of Herodians. But their numbers were so inconsiderable, and their duration so short, that Josephus has not thought them worthy of his notice. See Prideaux's Connection, vol. ii. p. 285.

[5] Cicero pro Flacco, c. 28.

ity in the temple of Jerusalem;[6] while the meanest of the posterity of Abraham, who should have paid the same homage to the Jupiter of the Capitol, would have been an object of abhorrence to himself and to his brethren. But the moderation of the conquerors was insufficient to appease the jealous prejudices of their subjects, who were alarmed and scandalized at the ensigns of paganism, which necessarily introduced themselves into a Roman province.[7] The mad attempt of Caligula to place his own statue in the temple of Jerusalem was defeated by the unanimous resolution of a people who dreaded death much less than such an idolatrous profanation.[8] Their attachment to the law of Moses was equal to their detestation of foreign religions. The current of zeal and devotion, as it was contracted into a narrow channel, ran with the strength, and sometimes with the fury, of a torrent.

This inflexible perseverance, which appeared so odious, or so ridiculous, to the ancient world, assumes a more awful character, since Providence has deigned to reveal to us the mysterious history of the chosen people. But the devout, and even scrupulous, attachment to the Mosaic religion, so conspicuous among the Jews who lived under the second temple, becomes still more surprising, if it is compared with the stubborn incredulity of their forefathers. When the law was given in thunder from Mount Sinai; when the tides of the ocean and the course of the planets were suspended for the convenience of the Israelites; and when temporal rewards and punishments were the immediate consequences of their piety or disobedience; they perpetually relapsed into rebellion against the visible majesty of their Divine King, placed the idols of the nations in the sanctuary of Jehovah, and imitated every fantastic ceremony that was practised in the tents of the Arabs or in the cities of Phoenicia.[9] As the protection of Heaven was deservedly withdrawn from the ungrateful race, their faith acquired a proportionable degree of vigour and purity. The contempo-

---

[6]Philo de Legatione. Augustus left a foundation for a perpetual sacrifice. Yet he approved of the neglect which his grandson Caius expressed towards the temple of Jerusalem. See Sueton. in August. c. 93, and Casaubon's notes on that passage.

[7]See, in particular, Joseph. Antiquitat, xvii. 6 [§2], xviii. 3, and de Bel. Judaic. i. 33 [§2 *sqq.*], and ii. 9 [§2, 3]. Edit. Havercamp.

[8]Jussi a Caio Caesare, effigiem ejus in templo locare arma potius sumpsere. Tacit. Hist. v. 9. Philo and Josephus gave a very circumstantial, but a very rhetorical, account of this transaction, which exceedingly perplexed the governor of Syria. At the first mention of this idolatrous proposal, King Agrippa fainted away; and did not recover his senses till the third day.

[9]For the enumeration of the Syrian and Arabian deities, it may be observed that Milton has comprised, in one hundred and thirty very beautiful lines, the two large and learned syntagmas which Selden had composed on that abstruse subject.

raries of Moses and Joshua had beheld, with careless indifference, the most amazing miracles. Under the pressure of every calamity, the belief of those miracles has preserved the Jews of a later period from the universal contagion of idolatry; and, in contradiction to every known principle of the human mind, that singular people seems to have yielded a stronger and more ready assent to the traditions of their remote ancestors than to the evidence of their own senses.[10]

The Jewish religion was admirably fitted for defence, but it was never designed for conquest; and it seems probable that the number of proselytes was never much superior to that of apostates. The divine promises were originally made, and the distinguishing rite of circumcision was enjoined, to a single family. When the posterity of Abraham had multiplied like the sands of the sea, the Deity, from whose mouth they received a system of laws and ceremonies, declared himself the proper and, as it were, the national God of Israel; and, with the most jealous care, separated his favourite people from the rest of mankind. The conquest of the land of Canaan was accompanied with so many wonderful and with so many bloody circumstances that the victorious Jews were left in a state of irreconcilable hostility with all their neighbours. They had been commanded to extirpate some of the most idolatrous tribes; and the execution of the Divine will had seldom been retarded by the weakness of humanity. With the other nations they were forbidden to contract any marriages or alliances; and the prohibition of receiving them into the congregation, which, in some cases, was perpetual, almost always extended to the third, to the seventh, or even to the tenth generation. The obligation of preaching to the Gentiles the faith of Moses had never been inculcated as a precept of the law, nor were the Jews inclined to impose it on themselves as a voluntary duty. In the admission of new citizens, that unsocial people was actuated by the selfish vanity of the Greeks, rather than by the generous policy of Rome. The descendants of Abraham were flattered by the opinion that they alone were the heirs of the covenant; and they were apprehensive of diminishing the value of their inheritance, by sharing it too easily with the strangers of the earth. A larger acquaintance with mankind extended their knowledge without correcting their prejudices; and, whenever the God of Israel acquired any new votaries, he was much more indebted to the inconstant humour of polytheism than to the active zeal of his own missionaries.[11] The religion

---

[10]"How long will this people provoke me? and how long will it be ere they *believe* me, for all the *signs* which I have shewn among them?" (Numbers, xiv. II.) It would be easy, but it would be unbecoming, to justify the complaint of the Deity, from the whole tenor of the Mosaic history.

[11]All that relates to the Jewish proselytes has been very ably treated by Basnage, Histoire des Juifs, 1. vi. c. 6, 7.

of Moses seems to be instituted for a particular country, as well as for a single nation; and, if a strict obedience had been paid to the order that every male, three times in the year, should present himself before the Lord Jehovah, it would have been impossible that the Jews could ever have spread themselves beyond the narrow limits of the promised land.[12] That obstacle was indeed removed by the destruction of the temple of Jerusalem; but the most considerable part of the Jewish religion was involved in its destruction; and the Pagans, who had long wondered at the strange report of an empty sanctuary,[13] were at a loss to discover what could be the object, or what could be the instruments, of a worship which was destitute of temples and of altars, of priests and of sacrifices. Yet even in their fallen state, the Jews, still asserting their lofty and exclusive privileges, shunned, instead of courting, the society of strangers. They still insisted with inflexible rigour on those parts of the law which it was in their power to practise. Their peculiar distinctions of days, of meats, and a variety of trivial though burdensome observances, were so many objects of disgust and aversion for the other nations, to whose habits and prejudices they were diametrically opposite. The painful and even dangerous rite of circumcision was alone capable of repelling a willing proselyte from the door of the synagogue.[14]

Under these circumstances, Christianity offered itself to the world, armed with the strength of the Mosaic law, and delivered from the weight of its fetters. An exclusive zeal for the truth of religion and the unity of God was as carefully inculcated in the new as in the ancient system; and whatever was now revealed to mankind, concerning the nature and designs of the Supreme Being, was fitted to increase their reverence for that mysterious doctrine. The divine authority of Moses and the prophets was admitted, and even established, as the firmest basis of Christianity. From the beginning of the world, an uninterrupted series of predictions had announced and prepared the long expected coming of the Messiah, who, in compliance with the gross apprehensions of the Jews, had been more frequently represented under the character of a King and Conqueror, than under that of a Prophet, a Martyr, and the Son

---

[12]See Exod. xxiv. 23, Deut. xvi. 16, the commentators, and a very sensible note in the Universal History, vol. i. p. 603, edit. fol.

[13]When Pompey, using or abusing the right of conquest, entered into the Holy of Holies, it was observed with amazement, "Nullâ intus Deûm effigie, vacuam sedem et inania arcana." Tacit. Hist. v. 9. It was a popular saying, with regard to the Jews,

Nil praeter nubes et caeli numen adorant.

[14]A second kind of circumcision was inflicted on a Samaritan or Egyptian proselyte. The sullen indifference of the Talmudists, with respect to the conversion of strangers, may be seen in Basnage, Histoire des Juifs, i. vi. c. 6.

of God. By his expiatory sacrifice, the imperfect sacrifices of the temple were at once consummated and abolished. The ceremonial law, which consisted only of types and figures, was succeeded by a pure and spiritual worship, equally adapted to all climates, as well as to every condition of mankind; and to the initiation of blood was substituted a more harmless initiation of water. The promise of divine favour, instead of being partially confined to the posterity of Abraham, was universally proposed to the freeman and the slave, to the Greek and to the barbarian, to the Jew and to the Gentile. Every privilege that could raise the proselyte from earth to Heaven, that could exalt his devotion, secure his happiness, or even gratify that secret pride which, under the semblance of devotion, insinuates itself into the human heart, was still reserved for the members of the Christian church; but at the same time all mankind was permitted, and even solicited, to accept the glorious distinction, which was not only proffered as a favour, but imposed as an obligation. It became the most sacred duty of a new convert to diffuse among his friends and relations the inestimable blessing which he had received, and to warn them against a refusal that would be severely punished as a criminal disobedience to the will of a benevolent but all-powerful deity.

The enfranchisement of the church from the bonds of the synagogue was a work however of some time and of some difficulty. The Jewish converts, who acknowledged Jesus in the character of the Messiah foretold by their ancient oracles, respected him as a prophetic teacher of virtue and religion; but they obstinately adhered to the ceremonies of their ancestors, and were desirous of imposing them on the Gentiles, who continually augmented the number of believers. These Judaizing Christians seem to have argued with some degree of plausibility from the divine origin of the Mosaic law, and from the immutable perfections of its great Author. They affirmed *that,* if the Being, who is the same through all eternity, had designed to abolish those sacred rites which had served to distinguish his chosen people, the repeal of them would have been no less clear and solemn than their first promulgation: *that,* instead of those freqent declarations, which either suppose or assert the perpetuity of the Mosaic religion, it would have been represented as a provisionary scheme intended to last only till the coming of the Messiah, who should instruct mankind in a more perfect mode of faith and of worship: *that* the Messiah himself, and his disciples who conversed with him on earth, instead of authorizing by their example the most minute observances of the Mosaic law, would have published to the world the abolition of those useless and obsolete ceremonies, without suffering Christianity to remain during so many years obscurely confounded among the sects of the Jewish church. Arguments like these appear to have been used in the defence of the expiring cause of the Mosaic law; but the industry of our learned divines has abundantly explained the ambiguous language of the Old Testament, and the ambiguous conduct of the apostolic teachers. It was proper gradually to unfold the system of the Gospel, and to pronounce, with the utmost caution and tenderness, a sentence of condemnation so repugnant to the inclination and prejudices of the believing Jews. . . .

It is a very ancient reproach, suggested by the ignorance or the malice of infidelity, that the Christians allured into their party the most atrocious criminals, who, as soon as they were touched by a sense of remorse, were easily persuaded to wash away, in the water of baptism, the guilt of their past conduct, for which the temples of the gods refused to grant them any expiation. But this reproach, when it is cleared from misrepresentation, contributes as much to the honour as it did to the increase of the church.[84] The friends of Christianity may acknowledge without a blush that many of the most eminent saints had been before their baptism the most abandoned sinners. Those persons who in the world had followed, though in an imperfect manner, the dictates of benevolence and propriety, derived such a calm satisfaction from the opinion of their own rectitude, as rendered them much less susceptible of the sudden emotions of shame, of grief, and of terror, which have given birth to so many wonderful conversions. After the example of their Divine Master, the missionaries of the gospel disdained not the society of men, and especially of women, oppressed by the consciousness, and very often by the effects, of their vices. As they emerged from sin and superstition to the glorious hope of immortality, they resolved to devote themselves to a life, not only of virtue, but of penitence. The desire of perfection became the ruling passion of their soul; and it is well known that, while reason embraces a cold mediocrity, our passions hurry us, with rapid violence, over the space which lies between the most opposite extremes.

When the new converts had been enrolled in the number of the faithful and were admitted to the sacraments of the church, they found themselves restrained from relapsing into their past disorders by another consideration of a less spiritual, but of a very innocent and respectable nature. Any particular society that has departed from the great body of the nation or the religion to which it belonged immediately becomes the object of universal as well as invidious observation. In proportion to the smallness of its numbers, the character of the society may be affected by the virtue and vices of the persons who compose it; and every member is engaged to watch with the most vigilant attention over his own behaviour and over that of his brethren, since, as he must expect to incur a part of the common disgrace, he may hope to enjoy a share of the common

---

[84]The imputations of Celsus and Julian, with the defence of the fathers, are very fairly stated by Spanheim, Commentaire sur les Césars de Julian, p. 468.

reputation. When the Christians of Bithynia were brought before the tribunal of the younger Pliny, they assured the proconsul that, far from being engaged in any unlawful conspiracy, they were bound by a solemn obligation to abstain from the commission of those crimes which disturb the private or public peace of society, from theft, robbery, adultery, perjury, and fraud.[85] Near a century afterwards, Tertullian, with an honest pride, could boast that very few Christians had suffered by the hand of the executioner, except on account of their religion.[86] Their serious and sequestered life, averse to the gay luxury of the age, insured them to chastity, temperance, economy, and all the sober and domestic virtues. As the greater number were of some trade or profession, it was incumbent on them, by the strictest integrity and the fairest dealing, to remove the suspicions which the profane are too apt to conceive against the appearances of sanctity. The contempt of the world exercised them in the habits of humility, meekness, and patience. The more they were persecuted, the more closely they adhered to each other. Their mutual charity and unsuspecting confidence has been remarked by infidels, and was too often abused by perfidious friends.[87]

It is a very honourable circumstance for the morals of the primitive Christians, that even their faults, or rather errors, were derived from an excess of virtue. The bishops and doctors of the church, whose evidence attests, and whose authority might influence, the professions, the principles, and even the practice, of their contemporaries, had studied the scriptures with less skill than devotion, and they often received in the most literal sense, those rigid precepts of Christ and the apostles to which the prudence of succeeding commentators has applied a looser and more figurative mode of interpretation. Ambitious to exalt the perfection of the gospel above the wisdom of philosophy, the zealous fathers have carried the duties of self-mortification, of purity, and of patience, to a height which it is scarcely possible to attain, and much less to preserve, in our present state of weakness and corruption. A doctrine so extraordinary and so sublime must inevitably command the veneration of the people; but it was ill calculated to obtain the suffrage of those worldly philosophers who, in the conduct of this transitory life, consult only the feelings of nature and the interest of society.[88]

There are two very natural propensities which we may distinguish in

---

[85]Plin. Epist. x. 97.

[86]Tertullian, Apolog. c. 44. He adds, however, with some degree of hesitation, "Aut si [et] aliud, jam non Christianus."

[87]The philosopher Peregrinus (of whose life and death Lucian has left us so entertaining an account) imposed, for a long time, on the credulous simplicity of the Christians of Asia.

[88]See a very judicious treatise of Barbeyrac sur la Morale des Pères.

the most virtuous and liberal dispositions, the love of pleasure and the love of action. If the former be refined by art and learning, improved by the charms of social intercourse, and corrected by a just regard to economy, to health, and to reputation, it is productive of the greatest part of the happiness of private life. The love of action is a principle of a much stronger and more doubtful nature. It often leads to anger, to ambition, and to revenge; but, when it is guided by the sense of propriety and benevolence, it becomes the parent of every virtue; and, if those virtues are accompanied with equal abilities, a family, a state, or an empire may be indebted for their safety and prosperity to the undaunted courage of a single man. To the love of pleasure we may therefore ascribe most of the agreeable, to the love of action we may attribute most of the useful and respectable qualifications. The character in which both the one and the other should be united and harmonized would seem to constitute the most perfect idea of human nature. The insensible and inactive disposition, which should be supposed alike destitute of both, would be rejected, by the common consent of mankind, as utterly incapable of procuring any happiness to the individual, or any public benefit to the world. But it was not in *this* world that the primitive Christians were desirous of making themselves either agreeable or useful.

The acquisition of knowledge, the exercise of our reason or fancy, and the cheerful flow of unguarded conversation, may employ the leisure of a liberal mind. Such amusements, however, were rejected with abhorrence, or admitted with the utmost caution, by the severity of the fathers, who despised all knowledge that was not useful to salvation, and who considered all levity of discourse as a criminal abuse of the gift of speech. In our present state of existence, the body is so inseparably connected with the soul that it seems to be our interest to taste, with innocence and moderation, the enjoyments of which that faithful companion is susceptible. Very different was the reasoning of our devout predecessors; vainly aspiring to imitate the perfection of angels, they disdained, or they affected to disdain, every earthly and corporeal delight.[89] Some of our senses indeed are necessary for our preservation, others for our subsistence, and others again for our information, and thus far it was impossible to reject the use of them. The first sensation of pleasure was marked as the first moment of their abuse. The unfeeling candidate for Heaven was instructed, not only to resist the grosser allurements of the taste or smell, but even to shut his ears against the profane harmony of sounds, and to view with indifference the most finished productions of human art. Gay apparel, magnificent houses, and elegant furniture were sup-

---

[89]Lactant. Institut. Divin. 1. vi. c. 20, 21, 22.

posed to unite the double guilt of pride and of sensuality: a simple and mortified appearance was more suitable to the Christian who was certain of his sins and doubtful of his salvation. In their censures of luxury, the fathers are extremely minute and circumstantial;[90] and among the various articles which excite their pious indignation, we may enumerate false hair, garments of any colour except white, instruments of music, vases of gold or silver, downy pillows (as Jacob reposed his head on a stone), white bread, foreign wines, public salutations, the use of warm baths, and the practice of shaving the beard, which, according to the expression of Tertullian, is a lie against our own faces, and an impious attempt to improve the works of the Creator.[91] When Christianity was introduced among the rich and the polite, the observation of these singular laws was left, as it would be at present, to the few who were ambitious of superior sanctity. But it is always easy, as well as agreeable, for the inferior ranks of mankind to claim a merit from the contempt of that pomp and pleasure, which fortune has placed beyond their reach. The virtue of the primitive Christians, like that of the first Romans, was very frequently guarded by poverty and ignorance.

The chaste severity of the fathers, in whatever related to the commerce of the two sexes, flowed from the same principle; their abhorrence of every enjoyment which might gratify the sensual, and degrade the spiritual, nature of man. It was their favourite opinion that, if Adam had preserved his obedience to the Creator, he would have lived for ever in a state of virgin purity, and that some harmless mode of vegetation might have peopled paradise with a race of innocent and immortal beings.[92] The use of marriage was permitted only to his fallen posterity, as a necessary expedient to continue the human species, and as a restraint, however imperfect, on the natural licentiousness of desire. The hesitation of the orthodox casuists on this interesting subject betrays the perplexity of men, unwilling to approve an institution which they were compelled to tolerate.[93] The enumeration of the very whimsical laws, which they most circumstantially imposed on the marriage-bed, would force a smile from the young, and a blush from the fair. It was their unanimous sentiment that a first marriage was adequate to all the pur-

---

[90]Consult a work of Clemens of Alexandria, intitled the Paedagogue, which contains the rudiments of ethics, as they were taught in the most celebrated of the Christian schools.

[91]Tertullian, de Spectaculis, c. 23. Clemens Alexandrin. Paedagog. 1. iii. c. 8.

[92]Beausobre, Hist. Critique du Manichéisme, 1. vii. c. 3. Justin, Gregory of Nyssa, Augustin, etc., strongly inclined to this opinion.

[93]Some of the Gnostic heretics were more consistent; they rejected the use of marriage.

poses of nature and of society. The sensual connexion was refined into a resemblance of the mystic union of Christ with his church, and was pronounced to be indissoluble either by divorce or by death. The practice of second nuptials was branded with the name of a legal adultery; and the persons who were guilty of so scandalous an offence against Christian purity were soon excluded from the honours, and even from the alms of the church.[94] Since desire was imputed as a crime, and marriage was tolerated as a defect, it was consistent with the same principles to consider a state of celibacy as the nearest approach to the divine perfection. It was with the utmost difficulty that ancient Rome could support the institution of six vestals;[95] but the primitive church was filled with a great number of persons of either sex who had devoted themselves to the profession of perpetual chastity.[96] A few of these, among whom we may reckon the learned Origen, judged it the most prudent to disarm the tempter.[97] Some were insensible and some were invincible against the assaults of the flesh. Disdaining an ignominious flight, the virgins of the warm climate of Africa encountered the enemy in the closest engagement; they permitted priests and deacons to share their bed, and gloried amidst the flames in their unsullied purity. But insulted Nature sometimes vindicated her rights, and this new species of martyrdom served only to introduce a new scandal into the church.[98] Among the Christian ascetics, however (a name which they soon acquired from their painful exercise), many, as they were less presumptuous, were probably more successful. The loss of sensual pleasure was supplied and compensated by spiritual pride. Even the multitude of Pagans were inclined to estimate the merit of the sacrifice by its apparent difficulty; and it was in the praise of these chaste spouses of Christ that the fathers have poured forth

---

[94]See a chain of tradition, from Justin Martyr to Jerome, in the Morale des Pères; c. iv. 6–26.

[95]See a very curious Dissertation on the Vestals, in the Mémoires de l'Académie des Inscriptions, tom. iv. p. 161–227. Notwithstanding the honours and rewards which were bestowed on those virgins, it was difficult to procure a sufficient number; nor could the dread of the most horrible death always restrain their incontinence.

[96]Cupiditatem procreandi aut unam scimus aut nullam. Minucius Felix, c. 31. Justin. Apolog. Major [29]. Athenagoras in Legat. c. 28. Tertullian de Cultu Femin. 1. ii.

[97]Eusebius, 1. vi. 8. Before the fame of Origen had excited envy and persecution, this extraordinary action was rather admired than censured. As it was his general practice to allegorize scripture, it seems unfortunate that, in this instance only he should have adopted the literal sense.

[98]Cyprian Epst. 4, and Dodwell Dissertat. Cyprianic. iii. Something like this rash attempt was long afterwards imputed to the founder of the order of Fontevrault. Bayle has amused himself and his readers on that very delicate subject.

the troubled stream of their eloquence.[99] Such are the early traces of monastic principles and institutions which, in a subsequent age, have counterbalanced all the temporal advantages of Christianity. [100]

The Christians were not less averse to the business than to the pleasures of this world. The defence of our persons and property they knew not how to reconcile with the patient doctrine which enjoined an unlimited forgiveness of past injuries and commanded them to invite the repetition of fresh insults. Their simplicity was offended by the use of oaths, by the pomp of magistracy, and by the active contention of public life, nor could their humane ignorance be convinced that it was lawful on any occasion to shed the blood of our fellow-creatures, either by the sword of justice or by that of war; even though their criminal or hostile attempts should threaten the peace and safety of the whole community.[101] It was acknowledged that, under a less perfect law, the powers of the Jewish constitution had been exercised, with the approbation of Heaven, by inspired prophets and by anointed kings. The Christians felt and confessed that such institutions might be necessary for the present system of the world, and they cheerfully submitted to the authority of their Pagan governors. But, while they inculcated the maxims of passive obedience, they refused to take any active part in the civil administration or the military defence of the empire. Some indulgence might perhaps be allowed to those persons who, before their conversion, were already engaged in such violent and sanguinary occupations;[102] but it was impossible that the Christians, without renouncing a more sacred duty, could assume the character of soldiers, of magistrates, or of princes.[103] This indolent, or even criminal, disregard to the public welfare exposed them to the contempt and reproaches of the Pagans, who very frequently asked, What must be the fate of the empire, attacked on every side by the barbarians, if all mankind should adopt the pusillanimous sentiments of

---

[99]Dupin (Bibliothèque Ecclésiastique, tom. i. p. 195) gives a particular account of the dialogue of the ten virgins, as it was composed by Methodius, bishop of Tyre. The praises of virginity are excessive.

[100]The Ascetics (as early as the second century) made a public profession of mortifying their bodies, and of abstaining from the use of flesh and wine. Mosheim, p. 310.

[101]See the Morale des Pères. The same patient principles have been revived since the Reformation by the Socinians, the modern Anabaptists, and the Quakers. Barclay, the apologist of the Quakers, has protected his brethren by the authority of the primitive Christians, p. 542–549.

[102]Tertullian, Apolog. c. 21, De Idoloatriâ, c. 17, 18. Origen contra Celsum, 1. v. p. 253, [p. 1232, Migne, Patr. G. xi.,] 1. vii. p. 348, [1457,] 1. viii. p. 423–428, [1620, sqq.].

[103]Tertullian (De Coronâ Militis, c. 11) suggests to them the expedient of deserting; a counsel which, if it had been generally known, was not very proper to conciliate the favour of the emperors towards the Christian sect.

the new sect?[104] To this insulting question the Christian apologists returned obscure and ambiguous answers, as they were unwilling to reveal the secret cause of their security; the expectation that, before the conversion of mankind was accomplished, war, government, the Roman empire and the world itself would be no more. It may be observed that, in this instance likewise, the situation of the first Christians coincided very happily with their religious scruples, and that their aversion to an active life contributed rather to excuse them from the service, than to exclude them from the honours, of the state and army.

But the human character, however it may be exalted or depressed by a temporary enthusiasm, will return, by degrees, to its proper and natural level, and will resume those passions that seem the most adapted to its present condition. The primitive Christians were dead to the business and pleasures of the world; but their love of action, which could never be entirely extinguished, soon revived, and found a new occupation in the government of the church. A separate society, which attacked the established religion of the empire, was obliged to adopt some form of internal policy, and to appoint a sufficient number of ministers, intrusted not only with the spiritual functions, but even with the temporal direction, of the Christian commonwealth. The safety of that society, its honour, its aggrandisement, were productive, even in the most pious minds, of a spirit of patriotism, such as the first of the Romans had felt for the republic, and sometimes, of a similar indifference in the use of whatever means might probably conduce to so desirable an end. The ambition of raising themselves or their friends to the honours and offices of the church was disguised by the laudable intention of devoting to the public benefit the power and consideration which, for that purpose only, it became their duty to solicit. In the exercise of their functions, they were frequently called upon to detect the errors of heresy, or the arts of faction, to oppose the designs of perfidious brethren, to stigmatize their characters with deserved infamy, and to expel them from the bosom of a society whose peace and happiness they had attempted to disturb. The ecclesiastical governors of the Christians were taught to unite the wisdom of the serpent with the innocence of the dove; but, as the former was refined, so the latter was insensibly corrupted, by the habits of government. In the church as well as in the world the persons who were placed in any public station rendered themselves considerable by their eloquence and firmness, by their knowledge of mankind, and by their dexterity in business; and, while they concealed from others, and, perhaps, from them-

---

[104]As well as we can judge from the mutiliated representation of Origen (1. viii. p. 423 [1620]), his adversary, Celsus, had urged his objection with great force and candour.

selves, the secret motives of their conduct, they too frequently relapsed into all the turbulent passions of active life, which were tinctured with an additional degree of bitterness and obstinacy from the infusion of spiritual zeal.

The government of the church has often been the subject, as well as the prize, of religious contention. The hostile disputants of Rome, of Paris, of Oxford and of Geneva have alike struggled to reduce the primitive and apostolic model[105] to the respective standards of their own policy. The few who have pursued this inquiry with more candour and impartiality are of opinion[106] that the apostles declined the office of legislation, and rather chose to endure some partial scandals and divisions than to exclude the Christians of a future age from the liberty of varying their forms of ecclesiastical government according to the changes of times and circumstances. The scheme of policy which, under their approbation, was adopted from the use of the first century may be discovered from the practice of Jerusalem, of Ephesus, or of Corinth. The societies which were instituted in the cities of the Roman empire were united only by the ties of faith and charity. Independence and equality formed the basis of their internal constitution. The want of discipline and human learning was supplied by the occasional assistance of the *prophets,*[107] who were called to that function, without distinction of age, of sex, or of natural abilities, and who, as often as they felt the divine impulse, poured forth the effusions of the spirit in the assembly of the faithful. But these extraordinary gifts were frequently abused or misapplied by the prophetic teachers. They displayed them at an improper season, presumptuously disturbed the service of the assembly, and by their pride or mistaken zeal they introduced, particularly into the apostolic church of Corinth, a long and melancholy train of disorders.[108] As the institution of prophets became useless, and even pernicious, their powers were withdrawn and their office abolished. The public functions of religion were solely intrusted to the established ministers of the church, the *bishops* and the *presbyters;* two appellations which, in their first origin, appear to have distinguished the same office and the same order of persons. The name of Presbyter was expressive of their age, or rather of their gravity and wisdom. The title of Bishop denoted their inspection over the

---

[105]The aristocratical party in France, as well as in England, has strenuously maintained the divine origin of bishops. But the Calvinistical presbyters were impatient of a superior; and the Roman Pontiff refused to acknowledge an equal. See Fra Paolo.

[106]In the history of the Christian hierarchy, I have, for the most part, followed the learned and candid Mosheim.

[107]For the prophets of the primitive church, see Mosheim, Dissertationes ad Hist. Eccles. pertinentes, tom. ii. p. 132–208.

[108]See the Epistles of St. Paul, and of Clemens, to the Corinthians.

faith and manners of the Christians who were committed to their pastoral care. In proportion to the respective numbers of the faithful, a larger or smaller number of these *episcopal presbyters* guided each infant congregation with equal authority and with united councils.[109]

But the most perfect equality of freedom requires the directing hand of a superior magistrate; and the order of public deliberations soon introduced the office of a president, invested at least with the authority of collecting the sentiments, and of executing the resolutions, of the assembly. A regard for the public tranquillity, which would so frequently have been interrupted by annual or by occasional elections, induced the primitive Christians to constitute an honourable and perpetual magistracy, and to choose one of the wisest and most holy among their presbyters to execute, during his life, the duties of their ecclesiastical governor. It was under these circumstances that the lofty title of Bishop began to raise itself above the humble appellation of presbyter; and, while the latter remained the most natural distinction for the members of every Christian senate, the former was appropriated to the dignity of its new president.[110] The advantages of this episcopal form of government, which appears to have been introduced before the end of the first century,[111] were so obvious, and so important for the future greatness, as well as the present peace, of Christianity, that it was adopted without delay by all the societies which were already scattered over the empire, had acquired in a very early period the sanction of antiquity,[112] and is still revered by the most powerful churches, both of the East and of the West, as a primitive and even as a divine establishment.[113] It is needless to observe that the pious and humble presbyters who were first dignified with the episcopal

---

[109]Hooker's Ecclesiastical Polity, 1. vii.

[110]See Jerome ad Titum, c. 1, and Epistol. 85 (in the Benedictine edition, 101), and the elaborate apology of Blondel, pro sententiâ Hieronymi. The ancient state, as it is described by Jerome, of the bishop and presbyters of Alexandria receives a remarkable confirmation from the patriarch Eutychius (Annal. tom. i. p. 330, Vers. Pocock), whose testimony I know not how to reject, in spite of all the objections of the learned Pearson in his Vindicae Ignatianae, part i. c. 11.

[111]See the introduction to the Apocalypse. Bishops, under the name of angels, were already instituted in seven cities of Asia. And yet the epistle of Clemens (which is probably of as ancient a date) does not lead us to discover any traces of episcopacy either at Corinth or Rome. [The date of the first letter (the second is spurious) of Clement is generally admitted to be about 100 A.D.; it is an admonition addressed by the Roman to the Corinthian church. The author is supposed by some to be no other than Flavius Clemens, the cousin of Domitian who was put to death by him for ἀθεοτης, by others to be one of his freedmen, (so Lightfoot, who has edited the letter in his Apostolic Fathers).]

[112]Nulla Ecclesia sine Episcopo, has been a fact as well as a maxim since the time of Tertullian and Irenaeus.

[113]After we have passed the difficulties of the first century, we find the episcopal government universally established, till it was interrupted by the republican genius of the Swiss and German reformers.

title could not possess, and would probably have rejected, the power and pomp which now encircles the tiara of the Roman pontiff, or the mitre of a German prelate. But we may define, in a few words, the narrow limits of their original jurisdiction, which was chiefly of a spiritual, though in some instances of a temporal, nature.[114] It consisted in the administration of the sacraments and discipline of the church, the superintendency of religious ceremonies, which imperceptibly increased in number and variety, the consecration of ecclesiastical ministers, to whom the bishop assigned their respective functions, the management of the public fund, and the determination of all such differences as the faithful were unwilling to expose before the tribunal of an idolatrous judge. These powers, during a shórt period, were exercised according to the advice of the presbyteral college, and with the consent and approbation of the assembly of Christians. The primitive bishops were considered only as the first of their equals, and the honourable servants of a free people. Whenever the episcopal chair became vacant by death, a new president was chosen among the presbyters by the suffrage of the whole congregation, every member of which supposed himself invested with a sacred and sacerdotal character.[115]

Such was the mild and equal constitution by which the Christians were governed more than a hundred years after the death of the apostles. Every society formed within itself a separate and independent republic: and, although the most distant of these little states maintained a mutual as well as friendly intercourse of letters and deputations, the Christian world was not yet connected by any supreme authority or legislative assembly. As the numbers of the faithful were gradually multiplied, they discovered the advantages that might result from a closer union of their interest and designs. Towards the end of the second century, the churches of Greece and Asia adopted the useful institutions of provincial synods, and they may justly be supposed to have borrowed the model of a representative council from the celebrated examples of their own country, the Amphictyons, the Achaean league, or the assemblies of the Ionian cities. It was soon established as a custom and as a law that the bishops of the independent churches should meet in the capital of the province at the stated periods of spring and autumn. Their deliberations

---

[114]See Mosheim in the first and second centuries. Ignatius (ad Smyrnaeos, c. 3. etc.) is fond of exalting the episcopal dignity. Le Clerc (Hist. Eccles. p. 569) very bluntly censures his conduct. Mosheim, with a more critical judgment (p. 161), suspects the purity even of the smaller epistles.

[115]Nonne et Laici sacerdotes sumus? Tertullian, Exhort. ad Castitat. c. 7. As the human heart is still the same, several of the observations which Mr. Hume has made on Enthusiasm (Essays, vol. i. p. 76, quarto edit.) may be applied even to real inspiration.

were assisted by the advice of a few distinguished presbyters, and moderated by the presence of a listening multitude.[116] Their decrees, which were styled Canons, regulated every important controversy of faith and discipline; and it was natural to believe that a liberal effusion of the Holy Spirit would be poured on the united assembly of the delegates of the Christian people. The institution of synods was so well suited to private ambition and to public interest that in the space of a few years it was received throughout the whole empire. A regular correspondence was established between the provincial councils, which mutually communicated and approved their respective proceedings; and the Catholic church soon assumed the form, and acquired the strength, of a great federative republic.[117]

As the legislative authority of the particular churches was insensibly superseded by the use of councils, the bishops obtained by their alliance a much larger share of executive and arbitrary power; and, as soon as they were connected by a sense of their common interest, they were enabled to attack, with united vigour, the original rights of their clergy and people. The prelates of the third century imperceptibly changed the language of exhortation into that of command, scattered the seeds of future usurpations, and supplied, by scripture allegories and declamatory rhetoric, their deficiency of force and of reason. They exalted the unity and power of the church, as it was represented in the EPISCOPAL OFFICE, of which every bishop enjoyed an equal and undivided portion.[118] Princes and magistrates, it was often repeated, might boast an earthly claim to a transitory dominion; it was the episcopal authority alone which was derived from the Deity, and extended itself over this and over another world. The bishops were the viceregents of Christ, the successors of the apostles, and the mystic substitutes of the high priest of the Mosaic law. Their exclusive privilege of conferring the sacerdotal character invaded the freedom both of clerical and of popular elections; and if, in the administration of the church, they still consulted the judgment of the presbyters or the inclination of the people, they most carefully inculcated the merit of such a voluntary condescension. The bishops acknowledged the supreme authority which resided in the assembly of their brethren; but, in the government of his peculiar diocese, each of them exacted from

---

[116]Acta Concil. Carthag. apud Cyprian. Edit. Fell, p. 158. This council was composed of eighty-seven bishops from the provinces of Mauritania, Numidia, and Africa; some presbyters and deacons assisted at the assembly; praesente plebis maximâ parte.

[117]Aguntur praeterea per Graecias illas, certis in locis concilia, etc. Tertullian de Jejuniis, c. 13. The African mentions it as a recent and foreign institution. The coalition of the Christian churches is very ably explained by Mosheim, p. 164–170.

[118]Cyprian, in his admired treatise De Unitate Ecclesiae, p. 75–86.

his *flock* the same implicit obedience as if that favourite metaphor had been literally just, and as if the shepherd had been of a more exalted nature than that of his sheep.[119] This obedience, however, was not imposed without some efforts on one side, and some resistance on the other. The democratical part of the constitution was, in many places, very warmly supported by the zealous or interested opposition of the inferior clergy. But their patriotism received the ignominious epithets of faction and schism; and the episcopal cause was indebted for its rapid progress to the labours of many active prelates, who, like Cyprian of Carthage, could reconcile the arts of the most ambitious statesman with the Christian virtues which seem adapted to the character of a saint and martyr.[120]

The same causes which at first had destroyed the equality of the presbyters introduced among the bishops a pre-eminence of rank, and from thence a superiority of jurisdiction. As often as in the spring and autumn they met in provincial synod, the difference of personal merit and reputation was very sensibly felt among the members of the assembly, and the multitude was governed by the wisdom and eloquence of the few. But the order of public proceedings required a more regular and less invidious distinction; the office of perpetual presidents in the councils of each province was conferred on the bishops of the principal city, and these aspiring prelates, who soon acquired the lofty titles of Metropolitans and Primates, secretly prepared themselves to usurp over their episcopal brethren the same authority which the bishops had so lately assumed above the college of presbyters.[121] Nor was it long before an emulation of pre-eminence and power prevailed among the metropolitans themselves, each of them affecting to display, in the most pompous terms, the temporal honours and advantages of the city over which he presided; the numbers and opulence of the Christians who were subject to their pastoral care; the saints and martyrs who had arisen among them, and the purity with which they preserved the tradition of the faith, as it had been transmitted through a series of orthodox bishops from the apostle or the apostolic disciple, to whom the foundation of their church was ascribed.[122] From every cause, either of a civil or of an ecclesiastical nature,

---

[119]We may appeal to the whole tenor of Cyprian's conduct, of his doctrine, and of his Epistles. Le Clerc, in a short life of Cyprian (Bibliothèque Universelle, tom. xii. p. 207–378), has laid him open with great freedom and accuracy.

[120]If Novatus, Felicissimus, etc., whom the bishop of Carthage expelled from his church, and from Africa, were not the most detestable monsters of wickedness, the zeal of Cyprian must occasionally have prevailed over his veracity. For a very just account of these obscure quarrels, see Mosheim, p. 497–512.

[121]Mosheim, p. 269, 574. Dupin, Antiquae Eccles. Disciplin., p. 19, 20.

[122]Tertullian, in a distinct treatise, has pleaded against the heretics the right of prescription, as it was held by the apostolic churches.

it was easy to foresee that Rome must enjoy the respect, and would soon claim the obedience, of the provinces. The society of the faithful bore a just proportion to the capital of the empire; and the Roman church was the greatest, the most numerous, and, in regard to the West, the most ancient of all the Christian establishments, many of which had received their religion from the pious labours of her missionaries. Instead of *one* apostolic founder, the utmost boast of Antioch, of Ephesus, or of Corinth, the banks of the Tiber were supposed to have been honoured with the preaching and martyrdom of the *two* most eminent among the apostles;[123] and the bishops of Rome very prudently claimed the inheritance of whatsoever prerogatives were attributed either to the person or to the office of St. Peter.[124] The bishops of Italy and of the provinces were disposed to allow them a primacy of order and association (such was their very accurate expression) in the Christian aristocracy.[125] But the power of a monarch was rejected with abhorrence, and the aspiring genius of Rome experienced, from the nations of Asia and Africa, a more vigorous resistance to her spiritual, than she had formerly done to her temporal, dominion. The patriotic Cyprian, who ruled with the most absolute sway the church of Carthage and the provincial synods, opposed with resolution and success the ambition of the Roman pontiff, artfully connected his own cause with that of the eastern bishops, and, like Hannibal, sought out new allies in the heart of Asia.[126] If this Punic war was carried on without any effusion of blood, it was owing much less to the moderation than to the weakness of the contending prelates. Invectives and excommunications were *their* only weapons; and these, during the progress of the whole controversy, they hurled against each other with equal fury and devotion. The hard necessity of censuring either a pope, or a saint and martyr, distresses the modern Catholics, whenever they are obliged to relate the particulars of a dispute in which the champions of religion

---

[123]The journey of St. Peter to Rome is mentioned by most of the ancients (see Eusebius, ii. 25), maintained by all the Catholics, allowed by some Protestants (see Pearson and Dodwell de Success. Episcop. Roman.), but has been vigorously attacked by Spanheim (Miscellanea Sacra, iii. 3). According to father Hardouin, the monks of the thirteenth century, who composed the Aeneid, represented St. Peter under the allegorical character of the Trojan hero.

[124]It is in French only that the famous allusion to St. Peter's name is exact. Tu es *Pierre* et sur cette *pierre.*—The same is imperfect in Greek, Latin, Italian, etc., and totally unintelligible in our Teutonic languages.

[125]Irenaeus adv. Haereses, iii. 3. Tertullian de Praescription., c. 36, and Cyprian Epistol. 27, 55, 71, 75. Le Clerc (Hist. Eccles. p. 764) and Mosheim (p. 258, 578) labour in the interpretation of these passages. But the loose and rhetorical style of the fathers often appears favourable to the pretensions of Rome.

[126]See the sharp epistle from Firmilianus, bishop of Caesarea, to Stephen, bishop of Rome, ap. Cyprian Epistol. 75.

indulged such passions as seem much more adapted to the senate or to the camp.[127]

The progress of the ecclesiastical authority gave birth to the memorable distinction of the laity and of the clergy, which had been unknown to the Greeks and Romans.[128] The former of these appellations comprehended the body of the Christian people; the latter, according to the signification of the word, was appropriated to the chosen portion that had been set apart for the service of religion; a celebrated order of men which has furnished the most important, though not always the most edifying, subjects for modern history. Their mutual hostilities sometimes disturbed the peace of the infant church, but their zeal and activity were united in the common cause, and the love of power, which (under the most artful disguises) could insinuate itself into the breasts of bishops and martyrs, animated them to increase the number of their subjects, and to enlarge the limits of the Christian empire. They were destitute of any temporal force, and they were for a long time discouraged and oppressed, rather than assisted, by the civil magistrate; but they had acquired, and they employed within their own society, the two most efficacious instruments of government, rewards and punishments; the former derived from the pious liberality, the latter from the devout apprehensions, of the faithful.

The community of goods, which had so agreeably amused the imagination of Plato,[129] and which subsisted in some degree among the austere sect of the Essenians,[130] was adopted for a short time in the primitive church. The fervour of the first proselytes prompted them to sell those wordly possessions which they despised, to lay the price of them at the feet of the apostles, and to content themselves with receiving an equal share out of the general distribution.[131] The progress of the Christian religion relaxed, and gradually abolished, this generous institution, which, in hands less pure than those of the apostles, would too soon have been corrupted and abused by the returning selfishness of human nature;

---

[127]Concerning this dispute of the re-baptism of heretics, see the epistles of Cyprian, and the seventh book of Eusebius.

[128]For the origin of these words, see Mosheim, p. 141. Spanheim, Hist. Ecclesiast. p. 633. The distinction of *Clerus* and *Laicus* was established before the time of Tertullian.

[129]The community instituted by Plato is more perfect than that which Sir Thomas More had imagined for his Utopia. The community of women, and that of temporal goods, may be considered as inseparable parts of the same system.

[130]Joseph. Antiquitat. xviii. 2. Philo, de Vit. Contemplativ.

[131]See the Acts of the Apostles, c. ii. 4, 5, with Grotius's Commentary. Mosheim, in a particular dissertation, attacks the common opinion with very inconclusive arguments.

and the converts who embraced the new religion were permitted to retain the possession of their patrimony, to receive legacies and inheri-
tances, and to increase their separate property by all the lawful means
of trade and industry. Instead of an absolute sacrifice, a moderate proportion was accepted by the ministers of the gospel; and in their weekly or
monthly assemblies, every believer, according to the exigency of the
occasion, and the measure of his wealth and piety, presented his voluntary offering for the use of the common fund.[132] Nothing, however inconsiderable, was refused; but it was diligently inculcated that, in the article
of Tythes, the Mosaic law was still of divine obligation; and that, since
the Jews, under a less perfect discipline, had been commanded to pay a
tenth part of all that they possessed, it would become the disciples of
Christ to distinguish themselves by a superior degree of liberality,[133] and
to acquire some merit by resigning a superfluous treasure, which must
so soon be annihilated with the world itself.[134] It is almost unnecessary
to observe that the revenue of each particular church, which was of so
uncertain and fluctuating a nature, must have varied with the poverty or
the opulence of the faithful, as they were dispersed in obscure villages,
or collected in the great cities of the empire. In the time of the emperor
Decius, it was the opinion of the magistrates that the Christians of Rome
were possessed of very considerable wealth; that vessels of gold and
silver were used in their religious worship; and that many among their
proselytes had sold their lands and houses to increase the public riches
of the sect, at the expense, indeed, of their unfortunate children, who
found themselves beggars, because their parents had been saints.[135] We

---

[132]Justin. Martyr, Apolog. Major, c. 89. Tertullian, Apolog. c. 39.

[133]Irenaeus and Haeres. 1. iv. c. 27, 34. Origen in Num. Hom. ii. Cyprian de
Unitat. Eccles. Constitut. Apostol. 1. ii. c. 34, 35, with the notes of Cotelerius. The
Constitutions introduce this divine precept by declaring that priests are as much
above kings, as the soul is above the body. Among the tythable articles, they
enumerate corn, wine, oil, and wood. On this interesting subject, consult Prideaux's History of Tythes, and Fra Paolo delle Materie Beneficaire; two writers of
a very different character.

[134]The same opinion which prevailed about the year 1000 was productive of the
same effects. Most of the donations express their motive, "appropinquante mundi
fine." See Mosheim's General History of the Church, vol. i. p. 457.

[135]   Tum summa cura est fratribus,
              (Ut sermo testatur loquax)
              Offerre, fundis venditis
              Sestertiorum millia.
              Addicta avorum praedia
              Foedis sub auctionibus,
              Successor exheres gemit
              Sanctis egens parentibus.
              Haec occuluntur abditis

should listen with distrust to the suspicions of strangers and enemies: on this occasion, however, they receive a very specious and probable colour from the two following circumstances, the only ones that have reached our knowledge, which define any precise sums, or convey any distinct idea. Almost at the same period, the bishop of Carthage, from a society less opulent than that of Rome, collected a hundred thousand sesterces (above eight hundred and fifty pounds sterling), on a sudden call of charity, to redeem the brethren of Numidia, who had been carried away captives by the barbarians of the desert.[136] About an hundred years before the reign of Decius, the Roman church had received, in a single donation, the sum of two hundred thousand sesterces from a stranger of Pontus, who proposed to fix his residence in the capital.[137] These oblations, for the most part, were made in money; nor was the society of Christians either desirous or capable of acquiring, to any considerable degree, the incumbrance of landed property. It had been provided by several laws, which were enacted with the same design as our statutes of mortmain, that no real estates should be given or bequeathed to any corporate body, without either a special privilege or a particular dispensation from the emperor or from the senate;[138] who were seldom disposed to grant them in favour of a sect, at first the object of their contempt, and at last of their fears and jealousy. A transaction, however, is related under the reign of Alexander Severus, which discovers that the restraint was sometimes eluded or suspended, and that the Christians were permitted to claim and to possess lands within the limits of Rome itself.[139] The progress of Christianity and the civil confusion of the empire contributed to relax the severity of the laws; and, before the close of the third century, many considerable estates were bestowed on the opulent

---

Ecclesiarum in angulis,
Et summa pietas creditur
Nudare dulces liberos.
            Prudent. περὶ στεφάνων, Hymn 2.
The subsequent conduct of the deacon Laurence only proves how proper a use was made of the wealth of the Roman church; it was undoubtedly very considerable: but Fra Paolo (c. 3) appears to exaggerate when he supposes that the successors of Commodus were urged to persecute the Christians by their own avarice, or that of their Praetorian praefects.

[136]Cyprian. Epistol. 62.

[137]Tertullian. de Praescriptionibus, c. 30. [The stranger was the heretic Marcion.]

[138]Diocletian gave a rescript, which is only a declaration of the old law: "Collegium, si nullo speciali privilegio subnixum sit, hereditatem capere non posse, dubium non est." Fra Paolo (c. 4) thinks that these regulations had been much neglected since the reign of Valerian.

[139]Hist. August. p. 131 [xviii. 49, 6]. The ground had been public; and was now disputed between the society of Christians and that of butchers.

churches of Rome, Milan, Carthage, Antioch, Alexandria, and the other great cities of Italy and the provinces.

The bishop was the natural steward of the church; the public stock was intrusted to his care, without account or control; the presbyters were confined to their spiritual functions, and the more dependent order of deacons was solely employed in the management and distribution of the ecclesiastical revenue.[140] If we may give credit to the vehement declamations of Cyprian, there were too many among his African brethren who, in the execution of their charge, violated every precept, not only of evangelic perfection, but even of moral virtue. By some of these unfaithful stewards, the riches of the church were lavished in sensual pleasures, by others they were perverted to the purposes of private gain, of fraudulent purchases, and of rapacious usury.[141] But, as long as the contributions of the Christian people were free and unconstrained, the abuse of their confidence could not be very frequent, and the general uses to which their liberality was applied reflected honour on the religious society. A decent portion was reserved for the maintenance of the bishop and his clergy; a sufficient sum was allotted for the expenses of the public worship, of which the feasts of love, the *agapae,* as they were called, constituted a very pleasing part. The whole remainder was the sacred patrimony of the poor. According to the discretion of the bishop, it was distributed to support widows and orphans, the lame, the sick, and the aged of the community; to comfort strangers and pilgrims, and to alleviate the misfortunes of prisoners and captives, more especially when their sufferings had been occasioned by their firm attachment to the cause of religion.[142] A generous intercourse of charity united the most distant provinces, and the smaller congregations were cheerfully assisted by the alms of their more opulent brethren.[143] Such an institution, which paid less regard to the merit than to the distress of the object, very materially conduced to the progress of Christianity. The Pagans, who were actuated by a sense of humanity, while they derided the doctrines, acknowledged the benevolence, of the new sect.[144] The prospect of immediate relief and of future protection allured into its hospitable bosom many of those unhappy persons whom the neglect of the world would have abandoned to

---

[140]Constitut. Apostol. ii. 35.

[141]Cyprian. de Lapsis, p. 89, Epistol. 65. The charge is confirmed by the 19th and 20th canon of the council of Illiberis.

[142]See the apologies of Justin, Tertullian, etc.

[143]The wealth and liberality of the Romans to their most distant brethren is gratefully celebrated by Dionysius of Corinth, ap. Euseb. 1. iv. c. 23.

[144]See Lucian in Peregrin. Julian (Epist. 49) seems mortified that the Christian charity maintains not only their own, but likewise the heathen poor.

the miseries of want, of sickness, and of old age. There is some reason likewise to believe that great numbers of infants who, according to the inhuman practice of the times, had been exposed by their parents were frequently rescued from death, baptized, educated, and maintained by the piety of the Christians, and at the expense of the public treasure.[145]

It is the undoubted right of every society to exclude from its communion and benefits such among its members as reject or violate those regulations which have been established by general consent. In the exercise of this power, the censures of the Christian church were chiefly directed against scandalous sinners, and particularly those who were guilty of murder, or fraud, or of incontinence; against the authors, or the followers, of any heretical opinions which had been condemned by the judgment of the episcopal order; and against those unhappy persons who, whether from choice or from compulsion, had polluted themselves after their baptism by any act of idolatrous worship. The consequences of excommunication were of a temporal as well as a spiritual nature. The Christian against whom it was pronounced was deprived of any part in the oblations of the faithful. The ties both of religious and of private friendship were dissolved; he found himself a profane object of abhorrence to the persons whom he the most esteemed, or by whom he had been the most tenderly beloved; and, as far as an expulsion from a respectable society could imprint on his character a mark of disgrace, he was shunned or suspected by the generality of mankind. The situation of these unfortunate exiles was in itself very painful and melancholy; but, as it usually happens, their apprehensions far exceeded their sufferings. The benefits of the Christian communion were those of eternal life, nor could they erase from their minds the awful opinion, that to those ecclesiastical governors by whom they were condemned the Deity had committed the keys of Hell and of Paradise. The heretics, indeed, who might be supported by the consciousness of their intentions, and by the flattering hope that they alone had discovered the true path of salvation, endeavoured to regain, in their separate assemblies, those comforts, temporal as well as spiritual, which they no longer derived from the great society of Christians. But almost all those who had reluctantly yielded to the power of vice or idolatry were sensible of their fallen condition, and anxiously desirous of being restored to the benefits of the Christian communion.

[145]Such, at least, has been the laudable conduct of more modern missionaries, under the same circumstances. Above three thousand new-born infants are annually exposed in the streets of Pekin. See Le Comte, Mémoires sur la Chine, and the Recherches sur les Chinois et les Egyptiens, tom. i. p. 61.

With regard to the treatment of these penitents, two opposite opinions, the one of justice, the other of mercy, divided the primitive church. The more rigid and inflexible casuists refused them for ever, and without exception, the meanest place in the holy community, which they had disgraced or deserted, and, leaving them to the remorse of a guilty conscience, indulged them only with a faint ray of hope that the contrition of their life and death might possibly be accepted by the Supreme Being.[146] A milder sentiment was embraced, in practice as well as in theory, by the purest and most respectable of the Christian churches.[147] The gates of reconciliation and of Heaven were seldom shut against the returning penitent; but a severe and solemn form of discipline was instituted, which, while it served to expiate his crime, might powerfully deter the spectators from the imitation of his example. Humbled by a public confession, emaciated by fasting, and clothed in sackcloth, the penitent lay prostrate at the door of the assembly, imploring, with tears, the pardon of his offences, and soliciting the prayers of the faithful.[148] If the fault was of a very heinous nature, whole years of penance were esteemed an inadequate satisfaction to the Divine Justice; and it was always by slow and painful gradations that the sinner, the heretic, or the apostate was re-admitted into the bosom of the church. A sentence of perpetual excommunication was, however, reserved for some crimes of an extraordinary magnitude, and particularly for the inexcusable relapses of those penitents who had already experienced and abused the clemency of their ecclesiastical superiors. According to the circumstances or the number of the guilty, the exercise of the Christian discipline was varied by the discretion of the bishops. The councils of Ancyra and Illiberis were held about the same time, the one in Galatia, the other in Spain; but their respective canons, which are still extant, seem to breathe a very different spirit. The Galatian, who after his baptism had repeatedly sacrificed to idols, might obtain his pardon by a penance of seven years, and, if he had seduced others to imitate his example, only three years more were added to the term of his exile. But the unhappy Spaniard, who had committed the same offence, was deprived of the hope of reconciliation, even in the article of death; and his idolatry was placed at the head of a list of seventeen other crimes, against which a sentence, no less terrible, was pronounced. Among these we may distin-

---

[146]The Montanists and the Novatians, who adhered to this opinion with the greatest rigour and obstinacy, found *themselves* at last in the number of excommunicated heretics. See the learned and copious Mosheim, Secul. ii. and iii.

[147]Dionysius ap. Euseb. iv. 23. Cyprian, de Lapsis.

[148]Cave's Primitive Christianity, part iii. c. 5. The admirers of antiquity regret the loss of this public penance.

guish the inexplicable guilt of calumniating a bishop, a presbyter, or even a deacon.[149]

The well-tempered mixture of liberality and rigour, the judicious dispensation of rewards and punishments, according to the maxims of policy as well as justice, constituted the *human* strength of the church. The bishops, whose paternal care extended itself to the government of both worlds, were sensible of the importance of these prerogatives, and, covering their ambition with the fair pretence of the love of order, they were jealous of any rival in the exercise of a discipline so necessary to prevent the desertion of those troops which had inlisted themselves under the banner of the cross, and whose numbers every day became more considerable. From the imperious declamations of Cyprian we should naturally conclude that the doctrines of excommunication and penance formed the most essential part of religion; and that it was much less dangerous for the disciples of Christ to neglect the observance of the moral duties than to despise the censures and authority of their bishops. Sometimes we might imagine that we were listening to the voice of Moses, when he commanded the earth to open, and to swallow up, in consuming flames, the rebellious race which refused obedience to the priesthood of Aaron; and we should sometimes suppose that we heard a Roman consul asserting the majesty of the republic, and declaring his inflexible resolution to enforce the rigour of the laws. "If such irregularities are suffered with impunity (it is thus that the bishop of Carthage chides the lenity of his colleague), if such irregularities are suffered, there is an end of EPISCOPAL VIGOUR;[150] an end of the sublime and divine power of governing the church, an end of Christianity itself." Cyprian had renounced those temporal honours which it is probable he would never have obtained; but the acquisition of such absolute command over the consciences and understanding of a congregation, however obscure or despised by the world, is more truly grateful to the pride of the human heart than the possession of the most despotic power imposed by arms and conquest on a reluctant people.

In the course of this important, though perhaps tedious, inquiry, I have attempted to display the secondary causes which so efficaciously assisted the truth of the Christian religion. If among these causes we have discovered any artificial ornaments, any accidental circumstances, or any mixture of error and passion, it cannot appear surprising that mankind

---

[149]See in Dupin, Bibliothèque Ecclésiastique, tom. ii. p. 304–313, a short but rational exposition of the canons of those councils, which were assembled in the first moments of tranquillity after the persecution of Diocletian. This persecution had been much less severely felt in Spain than in Galatia; a difference which may, in some measure, account for the contrast of their regulations.

[150]Cyprian. Epist. 69 [59].

should be the most sensibly affected by such motives as were suited to their imperfect nature. It was by the aid of these causes, exclusive zeal, the immediate expectation of another world, the claim of miracles, the practice of rigid virtue, and the constitution of the primitive church, that Christianity spread itself with so much success in the Roman empire. To the first of these the Christians were indebted for their invincible valour, which disdained to capitulate with the enemy whom they were resolved to vanquish. The three succeeding causes supplied their valour with the most formidable arms. The last of these causes united their courage, directed their arms, and gave their efforts that irresistible weight which even a small band of well-trained and intrepid volunteers has so often possessed over an undisciplined multitude, ignorant of the subject, and careless of the event of the war. In the various religions of Polytheism, some wandering fanatics of Egypt and Syria, who addressed themselves to the credulous superstition of the populace, were perhaps the only order of priests[151] that derived their whole support and credit from their sacerdotal profession, and were very deeply affected by a personal concern for the safety or prosperity of their tutelar deities. The ministers of Polytheism, both in Rome and in the provinces, were, for the most part, men of a noble birth, and of an affluent fortune, who received, as an honourable distinction, the care of a celebrated temple, or of a public sacrifice, exhibited, very frequently at their own expense, the sacred games,[152] and with cold indifference performed the ancient rites, according to the laws and fashion of their country. As they were engaged in the ordinary occupations of life, their zeal and devotion were seldom animated by a sense of interest, or by the habits of an ecclesiastical character. Confined to their respective temples and cities, they remained without any connexion of discipline or government; and, whilst they acknowledged the supreme jurisdiction of the senate, of the college of pontiffs, and of the emperor, those civil magistrates contented themselves with the easy task of maintaining, in peace and dignity, the general worship of mankind. We have already seen how various, how loose, and how uncertain were the religious sentiments of Polytheists. They were abandoned, almost without control, to the natural workings of a superstitious fancy. The accidental circumstances of their life and situa-

---

[151]The arts, the manners, and the vices of the priests of the Syrian goddess are very humorously described by Apuleius, in the eighth book of his Metamorphoses.

[152]The office of Asiarch was of this nature, and it is frequently mentioned in Aristides, the Inscriptions, etc. It was annual and elective. None but the vainest citizens could desire the honour; none but the most wealthy could support the expense. See in the Patres Apostol. tom. ii. p. 200, with how much indifference Philip the Asiarch conducted himself in the martyrdom of Polycarp. There were likewise Bithyniarchs, Lyciarchs, etc.

tion determined the object, as well as the degree, of their devotion; and, as long as their adoration was successively prostituted to a thousand deities, it was scarcely possible that their hearts could be susceptible of a very sincere or lively passion for any of them.

When Christianity appeared in the world, even these faint and imperfect impressions had lost much of their original power. Human reason, which, by its unassisted strength, is incapable of perceiving the mysteries of faith, had already obtained an easy triumph over the folly of Paganism; and, when Tertullian or Lactantius employ their labours in exposing its falsehood and extravagance, they are obliged to transcribe the eloquence of Cicero or the wit of Lucian. The contagion of these sceptical writings had been diffused far beyond the number of their readers. The fashion of incredulity was communicated from the philosopher to the man of pleasure or business, from the noble to the plebeian, and from the master to the menial slave who waited at his table, and who eagerly listened to the freedom of his conversation. On public occasions the philosophic part of mankind affected to treat with respect and decency the religious institutions of their country; but their secret contempt penetrated through the thin and awkward disguise; and even the people, when they discovered that their deities were rejected and derided by those whose rank or understanding they were accustomed to reverence, were filled with doubts and apprehensions concerning the truth of those doctrines to which they had yielded the most implicit belief. The decline of ancient prejudice exposed a very numerous portion of human kind to the danger of a painful and comfortless situation. A state of scepticism and suspense may amuse a few inquisitive minds. But the practice of superstition is so congenial to the multitude that, if they are forcibly awakened, they still regret the loss of their pleasing vision. Their love of the marvellous and supernatural, their curiosity with regard to future events, and their strong propensity to extend their hopes and fears beyond the limits of the visible world, were the principal causes which favoured the establishment of Polytheism. So urgent on the vulgar is the necessity of believing that the fall of any system of mythology will most probably be succeeded by the introduction of some other mode of superstition. Some deities of a more recent and fashionable cast might soon have occupied the deserted temples of Jupiter and Apollo, if, in the decisive moment, the wisdom of Providence had not interposed a genuine revelation, fitted to inspire the most rational esteem and conviction, whilst, at the same time, it was adorned with all that could attract the curiosity, the wonder, and the veneration of the people. In their actual disposition, as many were almost disengaged from their artificial prejudices, but equally susceptible and desirous of a devout attachment; an object much less deserving would have been sufficient to fill the vacant place in their hearts, and to gratify the uncertain eagerness of their passions. Those who are inclined to pursue this reflection, instead of viewing with astonishment the rapid progress of Christianity, will perhaps be surprised that its success was not still more rapid and still more universal.

It has been observed, with truth as well as propriety, that the conquests of Rome prepared and facilitated those of Christianity. In the second chapter of this work we have attempted to explain in what manner the most civilized provinces of Europe, Asia, and Africa were united under the dominion of one sovereign, and gradually connected by the most intimate ties of laws, of manners, and of language. The Jews of Palestine, who had fondly expected a temporal deliverer, gave so cold a reception to the miracles of the divine prophet that it was found unnecessary to publish, or at least to preserve, any Hebrew gospel.[153] The authentic histories of the actions of Christ were composed in the Greek language, at a considerable distance from Jerusalem, and after the Gentile converts were grown extremely numerous.[154] As soon as those histories were translated into the Latin tongue, they were perfectly intelligible to all the subjects of Rome, excepting only to the peasants of Syria and Egypt, for whose benefit particular versions were afterwards made. The public highways, which had been constructed for the use of the legions, opened an easy passage for the Christian missionaries from Damascus to Corinth, and from Italy to the extremity of Spain or Britain; nor did those spiritual conquerors encounter any of the obstacles which usually retard or prevent the introduction of a foreign religion into a distant country. There is the strongest reason to believe that before the reigns of Diocletian and Constantine, the faith of Christ had been preached in every province, and in all the great cities of the empire; but the foundation of the several congregations, the numbers of the faithful who composed them, and their proportion to the unbelieving multitude, are now buried in obscurity, or disguised by fiction and declamation. Such imperfect circumstances, however, as have reached our knowledge concerning the increase of the Christian name in Asia and Greece, in Egypt, in Italy, and in the West, we shall now proceed to relate, without neglecting the real

---

[153]The modern critics are not disposed to believe what the fathers almost unanimously assert, that St. Matthew composed a Hebrew gospel, of which only the Greek translation is extant. It seems, however, dangerous to reject their testimony. [Ματθαῖος μὲν οὖν Ἑβραΐδι διαλέκτῳ τὰ λόγια συνεγράψατο, Papias ap. Euseb., H. E., iii., 39 and 16. Our Greek Matthew is not a translation of this, but may have been compiled from it and Mark, which is generally believed now to be the earliest of the four gospels.]

[154]Under the reigns of Nero and Domitian, and in the cities of Alexandria, Antioch, Rome, and Ephesus. See Mill, Prolegomena ad Nov. Testament, and Dr. Lardner's fair and extensive collection, vol. xv.

or imaginary acquisitions which lay beyond the frontiers of the Roman empire.

The rich provinces that extend from the Euphrates to the Ionian sea were the principal theatre on which the apostle of the Gentiles displayed his zeal and piety. The seeds of the gospel, which he had scattered in a fertile soil, were diligently cultivated by his disciples; and it should seem that, during the two first centuries, the most considerable body of Christians was contained within those limits. Among the societies which were instituted in Syria, none were more ancient or more illustrious than those of Damascus, of Beroea or Aleppo, and of Antioch. The prophetic introduction of the Apocalypse has described and immortalized the seven churches of Asia:—Ephesus, Smyrna, Pergamus, Thyatira,[155] Sardes, Laodicea, and Philadelphia; and their colonies were soon diffused over that populous country. In a very early period, the islands of Cyprus and Crete, the provinces of Thrace and Macedonia, gave a favourable reception to the new religion; and Christian republics were soon founded in the cities of Corinth, of Sparta, and of Athens.[156] The antiquity of the Greek and Asiatic churches allowed a sufficient space of time for their increase and multiplication, and even the swarms of Gnostics and other heretics serve to display the flourishing condition of the orthodox church, since the appellation of heretics has always been applied to the less numerous party. To these domestic testimonies we may add the confession, the complaints, and the apprehensions of the Gentiles themselves. From the writings of Lucian, a philosopher who had studied mankind, and who describes their manners in the most lively colours, we may learn that, under the reign of Commodus, his native country of Pontus was filled with Epicureans and *Christians*.[157] Within fourscore years after the death of Christ,[158] the humane Pliny laments the magnitude of

---

[155]The Alogians (Epiphanius de Haeres. 51) disputed the genuineness of the Apocalypse, because the church of Thyatira was not yet founded. Epiphanius, who allows the fact, extricates himself from the difficulty by ingeniously supposing that St. John wrote in the spirit of prophecy. See Abauzit, Discours sur l'Apocalypse.

[156]The epistles of Ignatius and Dionysius (ap. Euseb. iv. 23) point out many churches in Asia and Greece. That of Athens seems to have been one of the least flourishing.

[157]Lucian in Alexandro, c. 25. Christianity, however, must have been very unequally diffused over Pontus; since in the middle of the third century there were no more than seventeen believers in the extensive diocese of Neo-Caesarea. See M. de Tillemont, Mémoires Ecclésiast. tom. iv. p. 675, from Basil and Gregory of Nyssa, who were themselves natives of Cappadocia.

[158]According to the ancients, Jesus Christ suffered under the consulship of the two Gemini, in the year 29 of our present era. Pliny was sent into Bithynia (according to Pagi) in the year 110. [The evening on which the moon was first visible began the Jewish month; and by astronomical calculation of the times of conjunction we can determine that the 15th of Nisan might have fallen on Friday in the

the evil which he vainly attempted to eradicate. In his very curious epistle to the emperor Trajan, he affirms that the temples were almost deserted, that the sacred victims scarcely found any purchasers, and that the superstition had not only infected the cities, but had even spread itself into the villages and the open country of Pontus and Bithynia.[159]

Without descending into a minute scrutiny of the expressions, or of the motives of those writers who either celebrate or lament the progress of Christianity in the East, it may in general be observed that none of them have left us any grounds from whence a just estimate might be formed of the real numbers of the faithful in those provinces. One circumstance, however, has been fortunately preserved, which seems to cast a more distinct light on this obscure but interesting subject. Under the reign of Theodosius, after Christianity had enjoyed, during more than sixty years, the sunshine of Imperial favour, the ancient and illustrious church of Antioch consisted of one hundred thousand persons, three thousand of whom were supported out of the public oblations.[160] The splendour and dignity of the queen of the East, the acknowledged populousness of Caesarea, Seleucia, and Alexandria, and the destruction of two hundred and fifty thousand souls in the earthquake which afflicted Antioch under the elder Justin,[161] are so many convincing proofs that the whole number of its inhabitants was not less than half a million, and that the Christians, however multiplied by zeal and power, did not exceed a fifth part of that great city. How different a proportion must we adopt when we compare the persecuted with the triumphant church, the West with the East, remote villages with populous towns, and countries recently converted to the faith with the place where the believers first received the appellation of Christians! It must not, however, be dissembled that, in another passage, Chrysostom, to whom we are indebted for this useful information, computes the multitude of the faithful as even superior to that of the Jews and Pagans.[162] But the solution of this apparent difficulty is easy and obvious. The eloquent preacher draws a parallel between the civil and the ecclesiastical constitution of Antioch; between the list of Christians who had acquired Heaven by baptism and the list of citizens who had a right to share the public liberality. Slaves, strangers, and infants were

---

years 27, 30, 33 and 34 A.D. (29 is excluded). But the question is complicated by the uncertainty at what time the Jewish day began. See Wieseler, Synopsis, p. 407.]

[159]Plin. Epist. x. 97.

[160]Chrysostom. Opera, tom. vii. p. 658, 810.

[161]John Malala, tom. ii. p. 144 [p. 420, ed. Bonn]. He draws the same conclusion with regard to the populousness of Antioch.

[162]Chrysostom. tom. i. p. 592. I am indebted for these passages, though not for my inference to the learned Dr. Lardner. Credibility of the Gospel History, vol. xii. p. 370.

comprised in the former; they were excluded from the latter.

The extensive commerce of Alexandria, and its proximity to Palestine, gave an easy entrance to the new religion. It was at first embraced by great numbers of the Therapeutae, or Essenians of the lake Mareotis, a Jewish sect which had abated much of its reverence for the Mosaic ceremonies. The austere life of the Essenians, their fasts and excommunications, the community of goods, the love of celibacy, their zeal for martyrdom, and the warmth though not the purity of their faith, already offered a very lively image of the primitive discipline.[163] It was in the school of Alexandria that the Christian theology appears to have assumed a regular and scientifical form; and, when Hadrian visited Egypt, he found a church, composed of Jews and of Greeks, sufficiently important to attract the notice of that inquisitive prince.[164] But the progress of Christianity was for a long time confined within the limits of a single city, which was itself a foreign colony, and, till the close of the second century, the predecessors of Demetrius were the only prelates of the Egyptian church. Three bishops were consecrated by the hands of Demetrius, and the number was increased to twenty by his successor Heraclas.[165] The body of the natives, a people distinguished by a sullen inflexibility of temper,[166] entertained the new doctrine with coldness and reluctance; and even in the time of Origen it was rare to meet with an Egyptian who had surmounted his early prejudices in favour of the sacred animals of his country.[167] As soon, indeed, as Christianity ascended the throne, the zeal of those barbarians obeyed the prevailing impulsion; the cities of Egypt were filled with bishops, and the deserts of Thebais swarmed with hermits.

---

[163]Basnage, Histoire des Juifs, l. 2, c. 20, 21, 22, 23, has examined, with the most critical accuracy, the curious treatise of Philo which describes the Therapeutae. By proving that it was composed as early as the time of Augustus, Basnage has demonstrated, in spite of Eusebius (l. ii. c. 17), and a crowd of modern Catholics, that the Therapeutae were neither Christians nor monks. It still remains probable that they changed their name, preserved their manners, adopted some new articles of faith, and gradually became the fathers of the Egyptian Ascetics. [The Therapeutae were not Essenes (for whom see Grätz Gesch. der Juden. vol. 3), for they did not secede from the synagogues. P. C. Lucius (Die Therapeuten. 1879) tried to prove that they did not exist, and that Philo's treatise (to which the earliest reference is in Eusebius) is a forgery, c. 300, A.D. The genuineness is defended by Mr. Conybeare in his recent ed. and P. Wendland, die Therapeuten, 1896.]

[164]See a letter of Hadrian, in the Augustan History, p. 245 [xxix. 8, 1].

[165]For the succession of Alexandrian bishops, consult Renaudot's History, p. 24. This curious fact is preserved by the patriarch Eutychius (Annal. tom. i. p. 334, Vers. Pocock [date 10th century]), and its internal evidence would alone be a sufficient answer to all the objections which Bishop Pearnos has urged in the Vindiciae Ignatianae.

[166]Ammian. Marcellin. xxii. 16.

[167]Origen contra Celsum, l. i. p. 40 [p. 757, Migne].

A perpetual stream of strangers and provincials flowed into the capacious bosom of Rome. Whatever was strange or odious, whoever was guilty or suspected, might hope, in the obscurity of that immense capital, to elude the vigilance of the law. In such a various conflux of nations, every teacher, either of truth or of falsehood, every founder, whether of a virtuous or a criminal association, might easily multiply his disciples or accomplices. The Christians of Rome, at the time of the accidental persecution of Nero, are represented by Tacitus as already amounting to a very great multitude,[168] and the language of that great historian is almost similar to the style employed by Livy, when he relates the introduction and the suppression of the rites of Bacchus. After the Bacchanals had awakened the severity of the senate, it was likewise apprehended that a very great multitude, as it were *another people,* had been initiated into those abhorred mysteries. A more careful inquiry soon demonstrated that the offenders did not exceed seven thousand; a number, indeed, sufficiently alarming, when considered as the object of public justice.[169] It is with the same candid allowance that we should interpret the vague expressions of Tacitus, and in a former instance of Pliny, when they exaggerate the crowds of deluded fanatics who had forsaken the established worship of the gods. The church of Rome was undoubtedly the first and most populous of the empire; and we are possessed of an authentic record which attests the state of religion in that city, about the middle of the third century, and after a peace of thirty-eight years. The clergy, at that time, consisted of a bishop, forty-six presbyters, seven deacons, as many sub-deacons, forty-two acolytes, and fifty readers, exorcists, and porters. The number of widows, of the infirm, and of the poor, who were maintained by the oblations of the faithful, amounted to fifteen hundred.[170] From reason, as well as from the analogy of Antioch, we may venture to estimate the Christians of Rome at about fifty thousand. The populousness of that great capital cannot, perhaps, be exactly ascertained; but the most modest calculation will not surely reduce it lower than a million of inhabitants, of whom the Christians might constitute at the most a twentieth part.[171]

The western provincials appeared to have derived the knowledge of

---

[168]Ingens multitudo is the expression of Tacitus, xv. 44.

[169]T. Liv. xxxix. 13, 15, 16, 17. Nothing could exceed the horror and consternation of the senate on the discovery of the Bacchanalians, whose depravity is described, and perhaps exaggerated, by Livy.

[170]Eusebius, 1. vi. c. 43. The Latin translator (M. de Valois) has thought proper to reduce the number of presbyters to forty-four.

[171]This proportion of the presbyters and of the poor to the rest of the people was originally fixed by Burnet (Travels into Italy, p. 168), and is approved by Moyle (vol. ii. p. 151). They were both unacquainted with the passage of Chrysostom, which converts their conjecture almost into a fact.

Christianity from the same source which had diffused among them the language, the sentiments, and the manners of Rome. In this more important circumstance, Africa, as well as Gaul, was gradually fashioned to the imitation of the capital. Yet, notwithstanding the many favourable occasions which might invite the Roman missionaries to visit their Latin provinces, it was late before they passed either the sea or the Alps;[172] nor can we discover in those great countries any assured traces either of faith or of persecution that ascend higher than the reign of the Antonines.[173] The slow progress of the gospel in the cold climate of Gaul was extremely different from the eagerness with which it seems to have been received on the burning sands of Africa. The African Christians soon formed one of the principal members of the primitive church. The practice introduced into that province of appointing bishops to the most inconsiderable towns, and very frequently to the most obscure villages, contributed to multiply the splendour and importance of their religious societies, which during the course of the third century were animated by the zeal of Tertullian, directed by the abilities of Cyprian, and adorned by the eloquence of Lactantius. But if, on the contrary, we turn our eyes towards Gaul, we must content ourselves with discovering, in the time of Marcus Antoninus, the feeble and united congregations of Lyons and Vienna; and, even as late as the reign of Decius, we are assured that in a few cities only, Arles, Narbonne, Toulouse, Limoges, Clermont, Tours, and Paris, some scattered churches were supported by the devotion of a small number of Christians.[174] Silence is indeed very consistent with devotion, but, as it is seldom compatible with zeal, we may perceive and lament the languid state of Christianity in those provinces which had exchanged the Celtic for the Latin tongue; since they did not, during the three first centuries, give birth to a single ecclesiastical writer. From Gaul, which claimed a just pre-eminence of learning and authority over all the coun-

---

[172]Serius trans Alpes, religione Dei susceptâ. Sulpicius Severus, 1. ii. [32, 1]. There were the celebrated martyrs of Lyons. See Eusebius, v. 1. Tillemont, Mém. Ecclésiast. tom. ii. p. 316. According to the Donatists, whose assertion is confirmed by the tacit acknowledgment of Augustin, Africa was the last of the provinces which received the gospel. Tillemont, Mém. Ecclésiast. tom. i. p. 754.

[173]Tum primum intra Gallias martyria visa. Sulp. Severus, 1. ii. [*ib.*]. With regard to Africa, see Tertullian ad Scapulam, c. 3. It is imagined that the Scyllitan martyrs were the first (Acta Sincera Ruinart. p. 34). One of the adversaries of Apuleius seems to have been a Christian. Apolog. p. 496, 497, edit. Delphin.

[174]Rarae in aliquibus civitatibus ecclesiae, paucorum Christianorum devotione, resurgerent. Acta Sincera, p. 130. Gregory of Tours, 1. i. c. 28. Mosheim, p. 207, 449. There is some reason to believe that, in the beginning of the fourth century, the extensive dioceses of Liège, of Treves, and of Cologne composed a single bishopric, which had been very recently founded. See Mémoires de Tillemont, tom. vi. part i. p. 43, 411. [Duchesne, Mémoires sur l'origine des diocèses episc. dans l'ancienne Gaule, 1890.]

tries on this side of the Alps, the light of the gospel was more faintly reflected on the remote provinces of Spain and Britain; and, if we may credit the vehement assertions of Tertullian, they had already received the first rays of the faith when he addressed his apology to the magistrates of the emperor Severus.[175] But the obscure and imperfect origin of the western churches of Europe has been so negligently recorded that, if we would relate the time and manner of their foundation, we must supply the silence of antiquity by those legends which avarice or superstition long afterwards dictated to the monks in the lazy gloom of their convents.[176] Of these holy romances, that of the apostle St. James can alone, by its single extravagance, deserve to be mentioned. From a peaceful fisherman of the lake of Gennesareth, he was transformed into a valorous knight, who charged at the head of the Spanish chivalry in their battles against the Moors. The gravest historians have celebrated his exploits; the miraculous shrine of Compostella displayed his power; and the sword of a military order, assisted by the terrors of the Inquisition, was sufficient to remove every objection of profane criticism.[177]

The progress of Christianity was not confined to the Roman empire; and, according to the primitive fathers, who interpret facts by prophecy, the new religion within a century after the death of its divine author, had already visited every part of the globe. "There exists not," says Justin Martyr, "a people, whether Greek or barbarian, or any other race of men, by whatsoever appellation or manners they may be distinguished, however ignorant of arts or agriculture, whether they dwell under tents, or wander about in covered waggons, among whom prayers are not offered up in the name of a crucified Jesus to the Father and Creator of all things."[178] But this splendid exaggeration, which even at present it would be extremely difficult to reconcile with the real state of mankind, can be considered only as the rash sally of a devout but careless writer, the measure of whose belief was regulated by that of his wishes. But neither the belief nor the wishes of the fathers can alter the truth of history. It

---

[175]The date of Tertullian's Apology is fixed, in a dissertation of Mosheim, to the year 198. [197–8. His Ad Nationes, written either just before or just after, or partly before and partly after, the Apologeticum, covers the same ground briefly.]

[176]In the fifteenth century, there were few who had either inclination or courage to question, whether Joseph of Arimathea founded the monastery of Glastonbury, and whether Dionysius the Areopagite preferred the residence of Paris to that of Athens.

[177]The stupendous metamorphosis was performed in the ninth century. See Mariana (Hist. Hispan. 1. vii. ci. 13, tom. i. p. 285, edit. Hag. Com. 1733), who, in every sense, imitates Livy, and the honest detection of the legend of St. James by Dr. Geddes, Miscellanies, vol. ii. p. 221.

[178]Justin Martyr, Dialog. cum Tryphon. p. 341. Irenaeus adv. Haeres. l. i. c. 10. Tertullian adv. Jud. c. 7. See Mosheim, p. 203.

will still remain an undoubted fact, that the barbarians of Scythia and Germany who afterwards subverted the Roman monarchy were involved in the darkness of paganism; and that even the conversion of Iberia, of Armenia, or of Ethiopia, was not attempted with any degree of success till the sceptre was in the hands of an orthodox emperor.[179] Before that time the various accidents of war and commerce might indeed diffuse an imperfect knowledge of the gospel among the tribes of Caledonia,[180] and among the borderers of the Rhine, the Danube, and the Euphrates.[181] Beyond the last-mentioned river, Edessa was distinguished by a firm and early adherence to the faith.[182] From Edessa the principles of Christianity were easily introduced into the Greek and Syrian cities which obeyed the successors of Artaxerxes; but they do not appear to have made any deep impression on the minds of the Persians, whose religious system, by the labours of a well-disciplined order of priests, had been constructed with much more art and solidity than the uncertain mythology of Greece and Rome.[183]

From this impartial, though imperfect, survey of the progress of Christianity, it may, perhaps, seem probable that the number of its proselytes has been excessively magnified by fear on the one side and by devotion on the other. According to the irreproachable testimony of Origen,[184] the

---

[179]See the fourth century of Mosheim's History of the Church. Many, though very confused circumstances that relate to the conversion of Iberia and Armenia, may be found in Moses of Chorene, 1. ii. c. 78–89. [Milman notes that Gibbon "had expressed his intention of withdrawing the words 'of Armenia,' from the text of future editions" (Vindication, Works, iv. 577). Christianity spread at an early time in Armenia, but its beginnings are enveloped in obscurity, and the traditions are largely legendary. The history of the Armenian church begins with Gregory Lusavoritch (Illuminator), consecrated bishop by Leontius of Cappadocia, to which see the Armenian bishopric was at first subject. The main source for Gregory is an early Life incorporated in the history of Tiridates by Agathangelus (translated by Langlois, Fr. Hist. Graec. vol. v.).]

[180]According to Tertullian, the Christian faith had penetrated into parts of Britain inaccessible to the Roman arms. About a century afterwards, Ossian, the son of Fingal, is *said* to have disputed, in his extreme old age, with one of the foreign missionaries, and the dispute is still extant, in verse, and in the Erse language. See Mr. Macpherson's Dissertation on the Antiquity of Ossian's Poems, p. 10.

[181]The Goths, who ravaged Asia in the reign of Gallienus, carried away great numbers of captives; some of whom were Christians, and became missionaries. See Tillemont, Mémoires Ecclésiast. tom. iv. p. 44.

[182]The legend of Abgarus, fabulous as it is, affords a decisive proof that, many years before Eusebius wrote his history, the greatest part of the inhabitants of Edessa had embraced Christianity. Their rivals, the citizens of Carrhae, adhered, on the contrary, to the cause of Paganism, as late as the sixth century.

[183]According to Bardesanes (ap. Euseb. Praepar. Evangel.), there were some Christians in Persia before the end of the second century. In the time of Constantine (see his Epistle to Sapor, Vit. 1. iv. c. 13), they composed a flourishing church. Consult Beausobre, Hist. Critique du Manichéisme, tom. i. p. 180, and the Bibliotheca Orientalis of Assemani.

[184]Origen contra Celsum, 1. viii. p. 424.

proportion of the faithful was very inconsiderable when compared with the multitude of an unbelieving world; but, as we are left without any distinct information, it is impossible to determine, and it is difficult even to conjecture, the real numbers of the primitive Christians. The most favourable calculation, however, that can be deduced from the examples of Antioch and of Rome will not permit us to imagine that more than a twentieth part of the subjects of the empire had enlisted themselves under the banner of the cross before the important conversion of Constantine. But their habits of faith, of zeal, and of union seemed to multiply their numbers; and the same causes which contributed to their future increase served to render their actual strength more apparent and more formidable.

Such is the constitution of civil society that, whilst a few persons are distinguished by riches, by honours, and by knowledge, the body of the people is condemned to obscurity, ignorance, and poverty. The Christian religion, which addressed itself to the whole human race, must consequently collect a far greater number of proselytes from the lower than from the superior ranks of life. This innocent and natural circumstance has been improved into a very odious imputation, which seems to be less strenuously denied by the apologists than it is urged by the adversaries of the faith; that the new sect of Christians was almost entirely composed of the dregs of the populace, of peasants and mechanics, of boys and women, of beggars and slaves; the last of whom might sometimes introduce the missionaries into the rich and noble families to which they belonged. These obscure teachers (such was the charge of malice and infidelity) are as mute in public as they are loquacious and dogmatical in private. Whilst they cautiously avoid the dangerous encounter of philosophers, they mingle with the rude and illiterate crowd, and insinuate themselves into those minds, whom their age, their sex, or their education has the best disposed to receive the impression of superstitious terrors.[185]

This unfavourable picture, though not devoid of a faint resemblance, betrays, by its dark colouring and distorted features, the pencil of an enemy. As the humble faith of Christ diffused itself through the world, it was embraced by several persons who derived some consequence from the advantages of nature or fortune. Aristides, who presented an eloquent apology to the emperor Hadrian, was an Athenian philosopher.[186] Justin

---

[185]Minucius Felix, c. 8, with Wowerus's notes. Celsus ap. Origen., 1. iii. p. 138, 142. Julian ap. Cyril. 1. vi. p. 206. Edit. Spanheim.

[186]Euseb. Hist. Eccles. iv. 3. Hieronym. Epist. 83, [*leg.* 84. But in Migne's arrangement, ep. 70, vol. i. p. 667. Since Gibbon wrote there have been discovered, not the Apology of Aristides in its original form, but materials for reconstructing it. These consist of (1) a Syriac version or paraphrase found on Mount Sinai by Mr. J. Rendel Harris (published in Robinson's Texts and Studies, 1891), (2) a fragment of an

Martyr had sought divine knowledge in the schools of Zeno, of Aristotle, of Pythagoras, and of Plato, before he fortunately was accosted by the old man, or rather the angel, who turned his attention to the study of the Jewish prophets.[187] Clemens of Alexandria had acquired much various reading in the Greek, and Tertullian in the Latin, language. Julius Africanus and Origen possessed a very considerable share of the learning of their times; and, although the style of Cyprian is very different from that of Lactantius, we might almost discover that both those writers had been public teachers of rhetoric. Even the study of philosophy was at length introduced among the Christians, but it was not always productive of the most salutary effects; knowledge was as often the parent of heresy as of devotion, and the description which was designed for the followers of Artemon may, with equal propriety, be applied to the various sects that resisted the successors of the apostles. "They presume to alter the holy scriptures, to abandon the ancient rule of faith, and to form their opinions according to the subtile precepts of logic. The science of the church is neglected for the study of geometry, and they lose sight of Heaven while they are employed in measuring the earth. Euclid is perpetually in their hands. Aristotle and Theophrastus are the objects of their admiration; and they express an uncommon reverence for the works of Galen. Their errors are derived from the abuse of the arts and sciences of the infidels, and they corrupt the simplicity of the Gospel by the refinements of human reason."[188]

Nor can it be affirmed with truth that the advantages of birth and fortune were always separated from the profession of Christianity. Several Roman citizens were brought before the tribunal of Pliny, and he soon discovered that a great number of persons of *every order* of men in Bithynia had deserted the religion of their ancestors.[189] His unsuspected testimony may, in this instance, obtain more credit than the bold challenge of Tertullian, when he addresses himself to the fears as well as to the humanity of the proconsul of Africa, by assuring him that, if he persists in his cruel intentions, he must decimate Carthage, and that he

---

Armenian translation (published at Venice by the Mechitarists, 1878), (3) a loose Greek reproduction, incorporated in the Tale of Barlaam and Josephat (see Robinson, *loc. cit.*). In the second superscription of the Syriac version, the work is addressed to Antoninus Pius, which is inconsistent with the statement of Eusebius, who, however, had not seen the book].

[187]The story is prettily told in Justin's Dialogues. Tillemont (Mém. Ecclésiast. tom. ii. p. 334), who relates it after him, is sure that the old man was a disguised angel.

[188]Eusebius, v. 28. It may be hoped that none, except the heretics, gave occasion to the complaint of Celsus (ap. Origen., 1. ii. p. 77) that the Christians were perpetually correcting and altering their Gospels.

[189]Plin. Epist. x. 97. Fuerunt alii similis amentiae, cives Romani ... Multi enim omnis aetatis, *omnis ordinis,* utriusque sexûs, etiam vocantur in periculum et vocabuntur.

will find among the guilty many persons of his own rank, senators and matrons of noblest extraction, and the friends or relations of his most intimate friends.[190] It appears, however, that about forty years afterwards the emperor Valerian was persuaded of the truth of this assertion, since in one of his rescripts he evidently supposes that senators, Roman knights, and ladies of quality were engaged in the Christian sect.[191] The church still continued to increase its outward splendour as it lost its internal purity; and in the reign of Diocletian the palace, the courts of justice, and even the army concealed a multitude of Christians who endeavoured to reconcile the interests of the present with those of a future life.

And yet these exceptions are either too few in number, or too recent in time, entirely to remove the imputation of ignorance and obscurity which has been so arrogantly cast on the first proselytes of Christianity. Instead of employing in our defence the fictions of later ages, it will be more prudent to convert the occasion of scandal into a subject of edification. Our serious thoughts will suggest to us that the apostles themselves were chosen by providence among the fishermen of Galilee, and that, the lower we depress the temporal condition of the first Christians, the more reason we shall find to admire their merit and success. It is incumbent on us diligently to remember that the kingdom of heaven was promised to the poor in spirit, and that minds afflicted by calamity and the contempt of mankind cheerfully listen to the divine promise of future happiness; while, on the contrary, the fortunate are satisfied with the possession of this world; and the wise abuse in doubt and dispute their vain superiority of reason and knowledge.

We stand in need of such reflections to comfort us for the loss of some illustrious characters, which in our eyes might have seemed the most worthy of the heavenly present. The names of Seneca, of the elder and the younger Pliny, of Tacitus, of Plutarch, of Galen, of the slave Epictetus, and of the emperor Marcus Antoninus, adorn the age in which they flourished, and exalt the dignity of human nature. They filled with glory their respective stations, either in active or contemplative life; their excellent understandings were improved by study; Philosophy had purified their minds from the prejudices of the popular superstition; and their days were spent in the pursuit of truth and the practice of virtue. Yet all these sages (it is no less an object of surprise than of concern) overlooked or rejected the perfection of the Christian system. Their language or their silence equally discover their contempt for the growing sect, which in their time had diffused itself over the Roman empire. Those among

---

[190]Tertullian ad Scapulam. Yet even his rhetoric rises no higher than to claim a *tenth* part of Carthage.
[191]Cyprian. Epist. 79 [80].

them who condescend to mention the Christians consider them only as obstinate and perverse enthusiasts, who exacted an implicit submission to their mysterious doctrines, without being able to produce a single argument that could engage the attention of men of sense and learning.[192]

It is at least doubtful whether any of these philosophers perused the apologies which the primitive Christians repeatedly published in behalf of themselves and of their religion; but it is much to be lamented that such a cause was not defended by abler advocates. They expose with superfluous wit and eloquence the extravagance of Polytheism. They interest our compassion by displaying the innocence and sufferings of their injured brethren. But, when they would demonstrate the divine origin of Christianity, they insist much more strongly on the predictions which announced, than on the miracles which accompanied, the appearance of the Messiah. Their favourite argument might serve to edify a Christian or to convert a Jew, since both the one and the other acknowledge the authority of those prophecies, and both are obliged, with devout reverence, to search for their sense and their accomplishment. But this mode of persuasion loses much of its weight and influence, when it is addressed to those who neither understand nor respect the Mosaic dispensation and the prophetic style.[193] In the unskilful hands of Justin and of the succeeding apologists, the sublime meaning of the Hebrew oracles evaporates in distant types, affected conceits, and cold allegories; and even their authenticity was rendered suspicious to an unenlightened Gentile by the mixture of pious forgeries, which, under the names of Orpheus, Hermes, and the Sibyls,[194] were obtruded on him as of equal value with the genuine inspirations of Heaven. The adoption of fraud and sophistry in the defence of revelation too often

---

[192]Dr. Lardner, in his first and second volume of Jewish and Christian testimonies, collects and illustrates those of Pliny the younger, of Tacitus, of Galen, of Marcus Antoninus, and perhaps of Epictetus (for it is doubtful whether that philosopher means to speak of the Christians). The new sect is totally unnoticed by Senecca, the elder Pliny, and Plutarch [and Dion Chrysostom].

[193]If the famous prophecy of the Seventy Weeks had been alleged to a Roman philosopher, would he not have replied in the words of Cicero, "Quae tandem ista auguratio est, annorum potius quam aut mensium aut dierum"? De Divinatione, ii. 30. Observe with what irreverence Lucian (in Alexandro, c. 13), and his friend Celsus ap. Origen. (l. vii. p. 327, [p. 1440, Migne]), express themselves concerning the Hebrew prophets.

[194]The Philosophers, who derided the more ancient predictions of the Sibyls, would easily have detected the Jewish and Christian forgeries, which have been so triumphantly quoted by the fathers, from Justin Martyr to Lactantius. When the Sibylline verses had performed their appointed task, they, like the system of the millennium, were quietly laid aside. The Christian Sibyl had unluckily fixed the ruin of Rome for the year 195, A.U.C. 948.

reminds us of the injudicious conduct of those poets who load their *invulnerable* heroes with a useless weight of cumbersome and brittle armour.

But how shall we excuse the supine inattention of the Pagan and philosophic world to those evidences which were presented by the hand of Omnipotence, not to their reason, but to their senses? During the age of Christ, of his apostles, and of their first disciples, the doctrine which they preached was confirmed by innumerable prodigies. The lame walked, the blind saw, the sick were healed, the dead were raised, demons were expelled, and the laws of Nature were frequently suspended for the benefit of the church. But the sages of Greece and Rome turned aside from the awful spectacle, and pursuing the ordinary occupations of life and study, appeared unconscious of any alterations in the moral or physical government of the world. Under the reign of Tiberius, the whole earth,[195] or at least a celebrated province of the Roman empire,[196] was involved in a preternatural darkness of three hours. Even this miraculous event, which ought to have excited the wonder, the curiosity, and the devotion of mankind, passed without notice in an age of science and history.[197] It happened during the lifetime of Seneca and the elder Pliny, who must have experienced the immediate effects, or received the earliest intelligence, of the prodigy. Each of these philosophers, in a laborious work, has recorded all the great phenomena of Nature, earthquakes, meteors, comets, and eclipses, which his indefatigable curiosity could collect.[198] Both the one and the other have omitted to mention the greatest phenomenon to which the mortal eye has been witness since the creation of the globe. A distinct chapter of Pliny[199] is designed for eclipses of an extraordinary nature and unusual duration; but he contents himself with describing the singular defect of light which followed the murder of Caesar, when, during the greatest part of the year, the orb of the sun appeared pale and without splendour. This season of obscurity, which cannot surely be compared with the preternatural darkness of the

---

[195]The fathers, as they are drawn out in battle array by Dom Calmet (Dissertations sur la Bible, tom. iii. p. 295–308), seem to cover the whole earth with darkness, in which they are followed by most of the moderns.

[196]Origen ad Matth. c. 27, and a few modern critics, Beza, Le Clerc, Lardner, etc., are desirous of confining it to the land of Judea.

[197]The celebrated passage of Phlegon is now wisely abandoned. When Tertullian assures the Pagans that the mention of the prodigy is found in Arcanis (not Archivis) vestris (see his Apology, c. 21), he probably appeals to the Sibylline verses, which relate it exactly in the words of the gospel [*archiuis* is in all the Mss. except one, which has *arcanis,* and is certainly right. See Bindley's ed. p. 78. The official report of Pilate is said to be meant].

[198]Seneca Quaest. Natur. i. I, 15, vi. I, vii. 17. Plin. Hist. Natur. l. ii.

[199]Plin. Hist. Natur. ii. 30 [a chapter remarkable for its brevity].

Passion, had been already celebrated by most of the poets[200] and historians of that memorable age.[201]

General Observations on the Fall of the Roman Empire in the West

The Greeks, after their country had been reduced into a province, imputed the triumphs of Rome, not to the merit, but to the FORTUNE, of the republic. The inconstant goddess, who so blindly distributes and resumes her favours, had *now* consented (such was the language of envious flattery) to resign her wings, to descend from her globe, and to fix her firm and immutable throne on the banks of the Tiber.[1] A wiser Greek, who has composed, with a philosophic spirit, the memorable history of his own times, deprived his countrymen of this vain and delusive comfort by opening to their view the deep foundations of the greatness of Rome.[2] The fidelity of the citizens to each other, and to the state, was confirmed by the habits of education and the prejudices of religion. Honour, as well as virtue, was the principle of the republic; the ambitious citizens laboured to deserve the solemn glories of a triumph; and the ardour of the Roman youth was kindled into active emulation, as often as they beheld the domestic images of their ancestors.[3] The temperate struggles of the patricians and plebeians had finally established the firm and equal balance of the constitution; which united the freedom of popular assemblies with the authority and wisdom of a senate and the executive powers of a regal magistrate. When the consul displayed the standard of the republic, each citizen bound himself, by the obligation of an oath, to draw his sword in the cause of his country, till he had discharged the sacred duty by a military service of ten years. This wise institution continually poured into the field the rising generations of freemen and soldiers; and

---

[200]Virgil. Georgic. i. 466. Tibullus, l. i. [*leg.* ii.]. Eleg. v. ver. 75. Ovid. Metamorph. XV. 782. Lucan. Pharsal. i. 540. The last of these poets places this prodigy before the civil war.

[201]See a public epistle of M. Antony in Joseph. Antiquit. xiv. 12. Plutarch in Caesar. p. 471 [c. 69]. Appian. Bell. Civil. l. iv. Dion Cassius, l. xlv. p. 431 [c. 17]. Julius Obsequens, c. 128. His little treatise is an abstract of Livy's prodigies.

[1]Such are the figurative expressions of Plutarch (Opera, tom. ii. p. 318, edit. Wechel), to whom, on the faith of his son Lamprias (Fabricius, Bibliot. Graec. tom. iii. p. 341), I shall boldly impute the malicious declamation, περὶ τῆς ʹΡωμαίων τύχης. The same opinions had prevailed among the Greeks two hundred and fifty years before Plutarch; and to confute them is the professed intention of Polybius (Hist. l. i. p. 90, edit. Gronov. Amstel. 1670 [c. 63]).

[2]See the inestimable remains of the sixth book of Polybius, and many other parts of his general history, particularly a digression in the seventeenth [*leg.* eighteenth] book, in which he compares the phalanx and the legion [c. 12–15].

[3]Sallust, de Bell. Jugurthin. c. 4. Such were the generous professions of P. Scipio and Q. Maximus. The Latin historian had read, and most probably transcribes, Polybius, their contemporary and friend.

their numbers were reinforced by the warlike and populous states of Italy, who, after a brave resistance, had yielded to the valour, and embraced the alliance, of the Romans. The sage historian, who excited the virtue of the younger Scipio and beheld the ruin of Carthage,[4] has accurately described their military system; their levies, arms, exercises, subordination, marches, encampments; and the invincible legion, superior in active strength to the Macedonian phalanx of Philip and Alexander. From these institutions of peace and war, Polybius has deduced the spirit and success of a people incapable of fear and impatient of repose. The ambitious design of conquest, which might have been defeated by the seasonable conspiracy of mankind, was attempted and achieved; and the perpetual violation of justice was maintained by the political virtues of prudence and courage. The arms of the republic, sometimes vanquished in battle, always victorious in war, advanced with rapid steps to the Euphrates, the Danube, the Rhine, and the Ocean; and the images of gold, or silver, or brass, that might serve to represent the nations and their kings, were successively broken by the *iron* monarchy of Rome.[5]

The rise of a city, which swelled into an empire, may deserve, as a singular prodigy, the reflection of a philosophic mind. But the decline of Rome was the natural and inevitable effect of immoderate greatness. Prosperity ripened the principle of decay; the causes of destruction multiplied with the extent of conquest; and, as soon as time or accident had removed the artificial supports, the stupendous fabric yielded to the pressure of its own weight. The story of its ruin is simple and obvious; and, instead of inquiring why the Roman empire was destroyed, we should rather be surprised that it had subsisted so long. The victorious legions, who, in distant wars, acquired the vices of strangers and mercenaries, first oppressed the freedom of the republic, and afterwards violated the majesty of the purple. The emperors, anxious for their personal safety and the public peace, were reduced to the base expedient of corrupting the discipline which rendered them alike formidable to their sovereign

---

[4]While Carthage was in flames, Scipio repeated two lines of the Iliad, which express the destruction of Troy, acknowledging to Polybius, his friend and preceptor (Polyb. in Excerpt. de Virtut. et Vit. tom. ii. p. 1455–1465 [xxxix. 3]), that, while he recollected the vicissitudes of human affairs, he inwardly applied them to the future calamities of Rome (Appian. in Libycis, p. 136, edit. Toll.[Punica, c. 82]).

[5]See Daniel, ii. 31–40. "And the fourth kingdom shall be strong as *iron*; forasmuch as iron breaketh in pieces, and subdueth all things." The remainder of the prophecy (the mixture of iron and *clay*) was accomplished, according to St. Jerome, in his own time. Sicut enim in principio nihil Romano Imperio fortius et durius, ita in fine rerum nihil imbecillius: quum et in bellis civilibus et adversus diversas nationes aliarum gentium barbararum auxilio indigemus (Opera, tom. v. p. 572).

and to the enemy; the vigour of the military government was relaxed, and finally dissolved, by the partial institutions of Constantine; and the Roman world was overwhelmed by a deluge of Barbarians.

The decay of Rome has been frequently ascribed to the translation of the seat of empire; but this history has already shewn that the powers of government were *divided* rather than *removed*. The throne of Constantinople was erected in the East; while the West was still possessed by a series of emperors who held their residence in Italy and claimed their equal inheritance of the legions and provinces. This dangerous novelty impaired the strength, and fomented the vices, of a double reign; the instruments of an oppressive and arbitrary system were multiplied; and a vain emulation of luxury, not of merit, was introduced and supported between the degenerate successors of Theodosius. Extreme distress, which unites the virtue of a free people, embitters the factions of a declining monarchy. The hostile favourites of Arcadius and Honorius betrayed the republic to its common enemies; and the Byzantine court beheld with indifference, perhaps with pleasure, the disgrace of Rome, the misfortunes of Italy, and the loss of the West. Under the succeeding reigns, the alliance of the two empires was restored; but the aid of the Oriental Romans was tardy, doubtful, and ineffectual; and the national schism of the Greeks and Latins was enlarged by the perpetual difference of language and manners, of interest, and even of religion. Yet the salutary event approved in some measure the judgment of Constantine. During a long period of decay, his impregnable city repelled the victorious armies of Barbarians, protected the wealth of Asia, and commanded, both in peace and war, the important straits which connect the Euxine and Mediterranean seas. The foundation of Constantinople more essentially contributed to the preservation of the East than to the ruin of the West.

As the happiness of a *future* life is the great object of religion, we may hear, without surprise or scandal, that the introduction, or at least the abuse, of Christianity had some influence on the decline and fall of the Roman empire. The clergy successfully preached the doctrines of patience and pusillanimity; the active virtues of society were discouraged; and the last remains of the military spirit were buried in the cloister; a large portion of public and private wealth was consecrated to the specious demands of charity and devotion; and the soldier's pay was lavished on the useless multitudes of both sexes, who could only plead the merits of abstinence and chastity. Faith, zeal, curiosity, and the more earthly passions of malice and ambition kindled the flame of theological discord; the church, and even the state, were distracted by religious factions, whose conflicts were sometimes bloody, and always implacable; the attention of the emperors was diverted from camps to synods; the Roman world was oppressed by a new species of tyranny; and the persecuted sects became the secret enemies of their country. Yet party-spirit, however pernicious or absurd, is a principle of union as well as of dissension. The bishops, from eighteen hundred pulpits, inculcated the duty of passive obedience to a lawful and orthodox sovereign; their frequent assemblies, and perpetual correspondence, maintained the communion of distant churches: and the benevolent temper of the gospel was strengthened, though confined, by the spiritual alliance of the Catholics. The sacred indolence of the monks was devoutly embraced by a servile and effeminate age; but, if superstition had not afforded a decent retreat, the same vices would have tempted the unworthy Romans to desert, from baser motives, the standard of the republic. Religious precepts are easily obeyed, which indulge and sanctify the natural inclinations of their votaries; but the pure and genuine influence of Christianity may be traced in its beneficial, though imperfect, effects on the Barbarian proselytes of the North. If the decline of the Roman empire was hastened by the conversion of Constantine, his victorious religions broke the violence of the fall, and mollified the ferocious temper of the conquerors.

This awful revolution may be usefully applied to the instruction of the present age. It is the duty of a patriot to prefer and promote the exclusive interest and glory of his native country; but a philosopher may be permitted to enlarge his views, and to consider Europe as one great republic, whose various inhabitants have attained almost the same level of politeness and cultivation. The balance of power will continue to fluctuate, and the prosperity of our own or the neighbouring kingdoms may be alternately exalted or depressed; but these partial events cannot essentially injure our general state of happiness, the system of arts, and laws, and manners, which so advantageously distinguish, above the rest of mankind, the Europeans and their colonies. The savage nations of the globe are the common enemies of civilized society; and we may inquire with anxious curiosity, whether Europe is still threatened with a repetition of those calamities which formerly oppressed the arms and institutions of Rome. Perhaps the same reflections will illustrate the fall of that mighty empire, and explain the probable causes of our actual security.

The Romans were ignorant of the extent of their danger, and the number of their enemies. Beyond the Rhine and Danube, the northern countries of Europe and Asia were filled with innumerable tribes of hunters and shepherds, poor, voracious, and turbulent; bold in arms, and impatient to ravish the fruits of industry. The Barbarian world was agitated by the rapid impulse of war; and the peace of Gaul or Italy was shaken by the distant revolutions of China. The Huns, who fled before a victorious enemy, directed their march towards the West; and the torrent was swelled by the gradual accession of captives and allies. The flying tribes who yielded to the Huns assumed in *their* turn the spirit of conquest; the endless column of Barbarians pressed on the Roman empire with ac-

cumulated weight; and, if the foremost were destroyed, the vacant space
was instantly replenished by new assailants. Such formidable emigra-
tions can no longer issue from the North; and the long repose, which has
been imputed to the decrease of population, is the happy consequence of
the progress of arts and agriculture. Instead of some rude villages, thinly
scattered among its woods and morasses, Germany now produces a list
of two thousand three hundred walled towns; the Christian kingdoms of
Denmark, Sweden, and Poland, have been successively established; and
the Hanse merchants, with the Teutonic knights, have extended their
colonies along the coast of the Baltic, as far as the Gulf of Finland. From
the Gulf of Finland to the Eastern Ocean, Russia now assumes the form
of a powerful and civilized empire. The plough, the loom, and the forge,
are introduced on the banks of the Volga, the Oby, and the Lena; and the
fiercest of the Tartar hordes have been taught to tremble and obey. The
reign of independent Barbarism is now contracted to a narrow span; and
the remnant of Calmucks or Uzbecks, whose forces may be almost numbered, cannot seriously excite the apprehensions of the great republic of
Europe.[6] Yet this apparent security should not tempt us to forget that new
enemies, and unknown dangers, may *possibly* arise from some obscure
people, scarcely visible in the map of the world. The Arabs or Saracens,
who spread their conquests from India to Spain, had languished in poverty and contempt, till Mahomet breathed into those savage bodies the
soul of enthusiasm.

The empire of Rome was firmly established by the singular and perfect
coalition of its members. The subject nations, resigning the hope, and
even the wish, of independence, embraced the character of Roman citizens; and the provinces of the West were reluctantly torn by the Barbarian from the bosom of their mother-country.[7] But this union was
purchased by the loss of national freedom and military spirit; and the
servile provinces, destitute of life and motion, expected their safety from
the mercenary troops and governors, who were directed by the orders of
a distant court. The happiness of an hundred millions depended on the
personal merit of one or two men, perhaps children, whose minds were
corrupted by education, luxury, and despotic power. The deepest wounds

---

[6]The French and the English editors of the Genealogical History of the Tartars
have subjoined a curious, though imperfect, description of their present state. We
might question the independentce of the Calmucks, or Eluths, since they have
been recently vanquished by the Chinese, who, in the year 1759, subdued the lesser
Bucharia, and advanced into the country of Badakshan, near the sources of the
Oxus (Mémoires sur les Chinois, tom. i. p. 325–400). But these conquests are
precarious, nor will I venture to ensure the safety of the Chinese empire.

[7]The prudent reader will determine how far this general proposition is weakened by the revolt of the Isaurians, the independence of Britain and Armorica, the
Moorish tribes, or the Bagaudae of Gaul and Spain (vol. i. p. 280, vol. iii. p. 352, 402,
480).

were inflicted on the empire during the minorities of the sons and grand-sons of Theodosius; and, after those incapable princes seemed to attain the age of manhood, they abandoned the church to the bishops, the state to the eunuchs, and the provinces to the Barbarians. Europe is now divided into twelve powerful, though unequal, kingdoms, three respectable commonwealths, and a variety of smaller, though independent, states; the chances of royal and ministerial talents are multiplied, at least with the number of its rulers; and a Julian, or Semiramis, may reign in the North, while Arcadius and Honorius again slumber on the thrones of the South. The abuses of tyranny are restrained by the mutual influence of fear and shame; republics have acquired order and stability; monarchies have imbibed the principles of freedom, or, at least, of moderation; and some sense of honour and justice is introduced into the most defective constitutions by the general manners of the times. In peace, the progress of knowledge and industry is accelerated by the emulation of so many active rivals: in war, the European forces are exercised by temperate and undecisive contests. If a savage conqueror should issue from the deserts of Tartary, he must repeatedly vanquish the robust peasants of Russia, the numerous armies of Germany, the gallant nobles of France, and the intrepid freemen of Britain; who, perhaps, might confederate for their common defence. Should the victorious Barbarians carry slavery and desolation as far as the Atlantic Ocean, ten thousand vessels would transport beyond their pursuit the remains of civilized society; and Europe would revive and flourish in the American world, which is already filled with her colonies and institutions.[8]

Cold, poverty, and a life of danger and fatigue, fortify the strength and courage of Barbarians. In every age they have oppressed the polite and peaceful nations of China, India, and Persia, who neglected, and still neglect, to counterbalance these natural powers by the resources of military art. The warlike states of antiquity, Greece, Macedonia, and Rome, educated a race of soldiers; exercised their bodies, diciplined their courage, multiplied their forces by regular evolutions, and converted the iron which they possessed, into strong and serviceable weapons. But this superiority insensibly declined with their laws and manners; and the feeble policy of Constantine and his successors armed and instructed, for the ruin of the empire, the rude valour of the Barbarian mercenaries. The military art has been changed by the invention of gunpowder; which enables man to command the two most powerful agents of nature, air and

---

[8]America now contains about six millions of European blood and descent; and their numbers, at least in the North, are continually increasing. Whatever may be the changes of their political situation, they must preserve the manners of Europe; and we may reflect with some pleasure that the English language will probably be diffused over an immense and populous continent.

fire. Mathematics, chemistry, mechanics, architecture, have been applied to the service of war; and the adverse parties oppose to each other
the most elaborate modes of attack and of defence. Historians may indig-
nantly observe that the preparations of a siege would found and maintain a flourishing colony;[9] yet we cannot be displeased that the subversion of a city should be a work of cost and difficulty, or that an industrious
people should be protected by those arts, which survive and supply the
decay of military virtue. Cannon and fortifications now form an impregnable barrier against the Tartar horse; and Europe is secure from any
future irruption of Barbarians; since, before they can conquer, they must
cease to be barbarous. Their gradual advances in the science of war
would always be accompanied, as we may learn from the example of
Russia, with a proportionable improvement in the arts of peace and civil
policy; and they themselves must deserve a place among the polished
nations whom they subdue.

Should these speculations be found doubtful or fallacious, there still
remains a more humble source of comfort and hope. The discoveries of
ancient and modern navigators, and the domestic history, or tradition, of
the most enlightened nations, represent the *human savage,* naked both
in mind and body, and destitute of laws, of arts, of ideas, and almost of
language.[10] From this abject condition, perhaps the primitive and universal state of man, he has gradually arisen to command the animals, to
fertilise the earth, to traverse the ocean, and to measure the heavens. His
progress in the improvement and exercise of his mental and corporeal
faculties[11] has been irregular and various, infinitely slow in the beginning, and increasing by degrees with redoubled velocity; ages of laborious ascent have been followed by a moment of rapid downfall; and the

---

[9]On avoit fait venir (for the siege of Turin) 140 pièces de canon; et il est à
remarquer que chaque gros canon monté revient à environ 2000 écus; il y avoit
110,000 boulets; 106,000 cartouches d'une façon, et 300,000 d'une autre; 21,000
bombes; 27,700 grenades, 15,000 sacs à terre, 30,000 instrumens pour le pionnage;
1,200,000 livres de poudre. Ajoutez à ces munitions, le plomb, le fer, et le fer blanc,
les cordages, tout ce qui sert aux mineurs, le souphre, le salpêtre, les outils de toute
espèce. Il est certain que les frais de tous ces préparatifs de destruction suffiroient
pour fonder et pour faire fleurir la plus nombreuse colonie. Voltaire, Siècle de
Louis XIV. c. xx. in his Works, tom. xi. p. 391.

[10]It would be an easy though tedious task to produce the authorities of poets,
philosophers, and historians. I shall therefore content myself with appealing to
the decisive and authentic testimony of Diodorus Siculus (tom. i. l. i. p. 11, 12 [c.8],
l. iii. p. 184, &c. [c. 14, 15], edit. Wesseling). The Ichthyophagi, who in his time
wandered along the shores of the Red Sea, can only be compared to the natives
of New Holland (Damplier's Voyages, vol. i. p. 464–469). Fancy or perhaps reason
may still suppose an extreme and absolute state of nature far below the level of
these savages, who had acquired some arts and instruments.

[11]See the learned and rational work of the President Goguet, de l'Origine des
Loix, des Arts, et des Sciences. He traces from facts or conjectures (tom. i. p.
147–337, edit. 12mo) the first and most difficult steps of human invention.

several climates of the globe have felt the vicissitudes of light and darkness. Yet the experience of four thousand years should enlarge our hopes, and diminish our apprehensions; we cannot determine to what height the human species may aspire in their advances towards perfection; but it may safely be presumed that no people, unless the face of nature is changed, will relapse into their original barbarism. The improvements of society may be viewed under a threefold aspect. 1. The poet or philosopher illustrates his age and country by the efforts of a *single* mind; but these superior powers of reason or fancy are rare and spontaneous productions, and the genius of Homer, or Cicero, or Newton, would excite less admiration, if they could be created by the will of a prince or the lessons of a preceptor. 2. The benefits of law and policy, of trade and manufactures, of arts and sciences, are more solid and permanent; and *many* individuals may be qualified, by education and discipline, to promote, in their respective stations, the interest of the community. But this general order is the effect of skill and labour; and the complex machinery may be decayed by time or injured by violence. 3. Fortunately for mankind, the more useful, or at least, more necessary arts can be performed without superior talents or national subordination; without the powers of *one* or the union of *many*. Each village, each family, each individual, must always possess both ability and inclination to perpetuate the use of fire[12] and of metals; the propagation and service of domestic animals; the methods of hunting and fishing; the rudiments of navigation; the imperfect cultivation of corn or other nutritive grain; and the simple practice of the mechanic trades. Private genius and public industry may be extirpated; but these hardy plants survive the tempest, and strike an everlasting root into the most unfavourable soil. The splendid days of Augustus and Trajan were eclipsed by a cloud of ignorance; and the Barbarians subverted the laws and palaces of Rome. But the scythe, the invention or emblem of Saturn,[13] still continued annually to mow the harvests of Italy: and the human feasts of the Laestrygons[14] have never been renewed on the coast of Campania.

Since the first discovery of the arts, war, commerce, and religious zeal have diffused, among the savages of the Old and New World, those inesti-

---

[12]It is certain, however strange, that many nations have been ignorant of the use of fire. Even the ingenious natives of Otaheite, who are destitute of metals, have not invented any earthen vessels capable of sustaining the action of fire and of communicating the heat to the liquids which they contain.

[13]Plutarch. Quaest. Tom. in tom. ii. p. 275. Macrob. Saturnal. l. i. c. 8, p. 152, edit. London. The arrival of Saturn (or his religious worship) in a ship may indicate that the savage coast of Latium was first discovered and civilized by the Phoenicians.

[14]In the ninth and tenth books of the Odyssey, Homer has embellished the tales of fearful and credulous sailors, who transformed the cannibals of Italy and Sicily into monstrous giants.

mable gifts: they have been successively propagated; they can never be lost. We may therefore acquiesce in the pleasing conclusion that every age of the world has increased, and still increases, the real wealth, the happiness, the knowledge, and perhaps the virtue, of the human race.[15]

---

[15]The merit of discovery has too often been stained with avarice, cruelty, and fanaticism; and the intercourse of nations has produced the communication of disease and prejudice. A singular exception is due to the virtue of our own times and country. The five great voyages successively undertaken by the command of his present Majesty were inspired by the pure and generous love of science and of mankind. The same prince, adapting his benefactions to the different stages of society, has founded a school of painting in his capital, and has introduced into the islands of the South Sea the vegetables and animals most useful to human life.

72 73 74 75 10 9 8 7 6 5 4 3 2 1